Religious Int

MW01118246

The Ethics of War and Peace
in the Thought of Paul Tillich

MERCER
UNIVERSITY PRESS

Endowed by
TOM WATSON BROWN
and
THE WATSON-BROWN FOUNDATION, INC.

Religious Internationalism

The Ethics of War and Peace in the Thought of Paul Tillich

by
MATTHEW LON WEAVER

MERCER UNIVERSITY PRESS
Macon, Georgia USA
2010

P408

Religious Internationalism:
The Ethics of War and Peace in the Thought of Paul Tillich.

Mercer University Press is a member
of Green Press Initiative <greenpressinitiative.org>,
a nonprofit organization working to help publishers
and printers increase their use of recycled paper
and decrease their use of fiber derived from engangered forests.
This book is printed on recycled, acid-free paper
that meets the requirements of American Standard
for Information Sciences—Permanence of Paper
for Printed Library Materials.

Library of Congress Cataloging-in-Publication Data

Weaver, Matthew Lon.
    Religious internationalism : the ethics of war and peace in the thought
of Paul Tillich / by Matthew Lon Weaver. -- 1st ed.
    p.   m.
    Includes bibliographical references (p.   ) and index.
    ISBN-13: 978-0-88146-188-6 (pbk. : alk. paper)
    ISBN-10: 0-88146-188-1 (pbk. : alk. paper)
    1. Tillich, Paul, 1886–1965. 2. War—Religious aspects—Christianity.
3. Peace—Religious aspects—Christianity. 4. Christianity and international
affairs. 5. Internationalism. I. Title.
    BT736.2.W355 2010
    241'.6242--dc22

                                                              2010031057

Contents

Introduction

Tillich as Religious Internationalist

Religious internationalism seems to be a contradiction in terms. If Paul Tillich was correct that religion has to do with what concerns us ultimately, it could be argued that politics rooted in religion exalts a particular concern for purposes of power. The logical result would be the dominance of provincialism and nationalism over universalism and internationalism. This would be consistent with the picture painted by Samuel Huntington in his description of civilizational identity based in religion as the basis for conflict in the twenty-first century.[1] Such a view would give deterministic import to the Taliban of Afghanistan and the Christian fundamentalism of the United States, for example.

Yet, in the evolution of Tillich's thought one sees the opposite trend. For Tillich, the outward forms of cultic practice, doctrinal formulation, and ethical discourse were religion in a penultimate sense. They are the result of humanity's capacity for transcendence and depth, two terms which Tillich used to understand the religious dimension of human beings. However, to limit the understanding of religion to these phenomena results in a truncated transcendence, a "rising above" that has neither risen to the height of "being itself" nor plunged to the depths of the "ground of being," Tillich's phrases for the goals of true religion. His solution is a formulation of religion as one's ultimate concern that perpetually fends off penultimate truth claims, ethical norms, and political positions in their struggle to claim ultimacy. Religion in this second sense must constantly correct the idolatrous arrogance of religion in the first sense and the politics arising from it. Idolatrous, particularistic religion tends to sacralize the local and nationalistic. Transcendent and depth-penetrating religion enters into existence with unrelenting questioning: this became Tillich's *modus operandi*. It drives toward the broadest, most international, most universal perspective. It sees particularism, provincialism and nationalism as ignorant and absurd. Contrary to the instincts of twenty-first century popular religious culture, the oxymoron for Tillichian thought is religious nationalism, not religious internationalism. Although he knew that the particularistic bent was dominant,

---

[1]Samuel P. Huntington, "The Clash of Civilizations?" *Foreign Affairs* 72/3 (Summer 1993): 22-49; and Samuel P. Huntington, *The Clash of Civilizations and the Remaking of World Order* (New York: Simon & Schuster, 1996).

he came to see it as inaccurate. Therefore, it is sound to pursue his ethics of war and peace as the practice of religious internationalism.

Religion and Political Philosophy

Paul Tillich was not trained as an international theorist. He completed no treatise on the impact of religion upon the politics among nations: only a fragment remains of his one attempt to do so in the late 1930s. Throughout his career in academia, his primary concern was to probe the depths of philosophy and theology in order to interpret life's meaning as profoundly as possible. However, war and efforts to create and maintain peace defined history during the course of his life. As they defined history, they shaped Tillich as well: war brought the seeds of existentialism already present within him to full flower. Consequently, his experience and interpretation of religion and history made issues of war and peace an inescapable part of his life story and intellectual output.

As a Christian existentialist, Tillich focused upon international issues as one theme woven within the broader fabric of his approach to religion and political philosophy. Thus, the theory of religious internationalism constructed in this work draws from a political philosophy which directed Tillich's thoughts and interests to topics ranging from general political theory to ethics, from theology of culture to Marxism, economic justice and religious socialism, from World War I and nationalism to World War II projects in collaboration with the Voice of America and the Council for a Democratic Germany, and from interreligious dialogue to religion's relationship to the live issues of every period. A significant body of secondary literature gives consideration to these areas of Tillich's work.

Political Theory. With respect to Tillich's general political theory, Ronald Stone has pointed to the prophetic tradition as the unifying theme in what he has described as a (Hans) Morgenthau-(Reinhold) Niebuhr-PaulTillich school of thought on the idea of power.[2] He has also depicted

---

[2]Ronald Stone, "Ontology of Power in Niebuhr, Morgenthau, and Tillich," *Newsletter of the North American Paul Tillich Society* 28/2 (Spring 2002): 4-14. See also Ronald H. Stone, *Prophetic Realism: Beyond Militarism and Pacifism in an Age of Terror* (New York: T.&T. Clark, 2005); Guy B. Hammond, "*Prophetic Realism: Beyond Militarism and Pacifism in an Age of Terror*, by Ronald H. Stone," *Bulletin of the North American Paul Tillich* 33/1 (Winter 2007): 5-6; Jonathan Rothchild, "Review of Ronald H. Stone, *Prophetic Realism: Beyond Mili-*

the sometimes complicated relationship between Tillich and Reinhold Niebuhr at Union Theological Seminary as they took their different paths in voicing convictions on social, governmental policies.[3] Theodore Runyon has contended that Tillich was a conservative revolutionary, accepting the inevitability of revolution, but seeking positive consequences of it.[4] Guy Hammond has discussed Tillich's and Horkheimer's argument that individuals with developed consciences are required to fend off fascism.[5] And Louis C. Midgely has considered the possibility that Tillich's self-proclaimed existentialist analysis of politics is, in fact, essentialist, making it difficult to verify the norms derived from his ontological approach.[6]

Ethics. The Tillichian approach to ethics led Paul Ramsey to construe it as one in which love transforms natural justice.[7] John Carey has rendered Tillich's ethics as one of self-realization laden with moral ambiguity.[8] Konrad Glöckner understands Tillich's ethics to express the notion that the end or goal of creation—or the creative act—is the existence of personhood.[9]

Melvin Watson defined the nature of Tillich's social ethics to be based on concrete decisions in real-life contexts, rather than a series of principles.[10] Gert Hummel advanced the view that Tillich's dialectic between

---

tarism and Pacifism in an Age of Terror," *Journal of Religion* 87/3 (2007): 459-61.

[3]Ronald Stone, "Tillich and Niebuhr as Allied Public Theologians," *Bulletin of the North American Paul Tillich Society* 32/1 (Winter 2006): 3-7.

[4]Theodore Runyon, "Tillich's Understanding of Revolution," in *Theonomy and Autonomy: Studies in Paul Tillich's Engagement with Modern Culture,* ed. Carey, 267-80.

[5]Guy B. Hammond, "Why Did Westerners Become Fascists? Fromm, Tillich, and Horkheimer on Character Types," *Meeting Papers: North American Paul Tillich Society* (November 1989): 8-12.

[6]Louis C. Midgley, "Politics and Ultimate Concern: The Normative Political Philosophy of Paul Tillich" (Ph.D. thesis, Brown University, 1965).

[7]Paul Ramsey, *Nine Modern Moralists* (Englewood Cliffs NJ: Prentice-Hall, 1962).

[8]John J. Carey, "Morality and Beyond: Tillich's Ethics in Life and Death," in *Tillich Studies: 1975,* ed. Carey, 104-15.

[9]Konrad Glöckner, "Personenhaftes Sein als Telos der Schöpfung. Eine Darstellung der Theologie Tillichs aus der Perspektive seiner Ethik," *Tillich Journal: Interpretieren—Vergleichen—Kritisieren—Weiterentwickeln* 1 (1997): 74-79.

[10]Melvin Watson, "The Social Thought of Paul Tillich," *The Journal of*

Christian message and concrete situation remained a valid way to face
emerging ethical issues.[11] Jonathan Rothchild has claimed the presence of
a participation-transcendence dynamic within Tillich's thought which embodies his tension between moral imperative and concrete decision.[12]

J. Mark Thomas has rooted Tillich's theonomous social ethics in classical Greek thought.[13] David Novak has used analytical philosopher William
Frankena to consider the legitimacy of Tillich's argument for theonomy,
arguing that Tillich combines Hume's emphasis on the experiential and
Kant's emphasis on the moral in his ethical theory.[14] Terence O'Keeffe has
structured Tillich's ethics around the concepts of law and community.[15]
Joseph Fletcher saw Tillich's relativizing of tradition and the call for
courageous decision in the light of context as a negation of the law.[16] Oscar
Remick has maintained the presence of a theory of value in Tillich's
thought rooted in his idealism.[17] And Nicholas Piediscalzi has compared
and contrasted the thinking of Tillich with that of Erik Erikson on "the
origin and nature of morality and ethics."[18]

Theology of Culture. The idea of a theology of culture in Tillich's work
was the stimulus for James Luther Adams to characterize Tillich's philoso-

---

Religious Thought 10/1 (Autumn-Winter 1952–1953): 5-17.

[11]Gert Hummel, "*Morality and Beyond*: Anthropology and New Ethics in
Tomorrow's Information Society," in *Being and Doing: Paul Tillich as Ethicist*, ed.
Carey, 125-54.

[12]Jonathan Rothchild, "Global Flows, Head Scarves, and Finite Freedom:
Tillich on Globalization," *Bulletin of the North American Paul Tillich Society* 31/3
(Summer 2005): 16-21.

[13]J. Mark Thomas, "Theonomous Social Ethics: Paul Tillich's Neoclassical
Interpretation of Justice," in *Being and Doing: Paul Tillich as Ethicist*, ed. Carey,
109-23.

[14]David Novak, "Theonomous Ethics: A Defense and A Critique of Tillich,"
Soundings 49 (1986): 436-63.

[15]Terence M. O'Keeffe, "Ethics and the Realm of Praxis," in *Being and Doing:
Paul Tillich as Ethicist*, ed. Carey, 87-105.

[16]Joseph Fletcher, "Tillich and Ethics: The Negation of Law," *Pastoral
Psychology* 19 (February 1968): 33-40.

[17]Oscar E. Remick, "Value in the Thought of Paul Tillich" (Ph.D. diss., Boston
University, 1966).

[18]Nicholas Piediscalzi, "Paul Tillich and Erik H. Erikson on the Origin and
Nature of Morality and Ethics" (Ph.D. diss., Boston University, 1965).

phy as the practice of interpreting all spheres of cultural life through the lens of religion.[19] Eberhard Amelung interpreted Tillich's well-known statement that "religion is the substance of culture, culture is the form of religion" to mean that religion brings the dimension of love into culture.[20] Raymond F. Bulman has advocated the position that Tillich's theology of culture offers a humanistic theology which presents a viable alternative to secular humanism.[21] Theodore M. Greene highlighted Tillich's argument that the appropriate relationship to culture was one combining involvement with objectivity.[22] Theodor Siegfried investigated the significance of Tillich's interpretation of culture in terms of his criticism of culture as such in distinction from criticism of specific elements of cultural life.[23] Langdon Gilkey used Tillich's approach to describe the role of the theologian as a creative interpreter of culture, fully connected to the context of his or her time.[24] Peter Haigis has explicated Tillich's theology of culture as a necessary bridge over a glaring gap between philosophy and theology, calling it the Protestant interpretation of cultural realities.[25] Paul G. Wiebe has stressed the seminal importance of Tillich's 1923 book, *The System of the Sciences*, for his later work and for understanding theology's place in the academy.[26] Bulman has upheld the centrality of Tillich's notion of theonomy in Tillich's interpretation of technological society through his theology

[19]James Luther Adams, *Paul Tillich's Philosophy of Culture, Science, and Religion* (New York: Harper & Row, 1965).

[20]Eberhard Amelung, *Die Gestalt der Liebe: Paul Tillichs Theologie der Kultur* (Gerd Mohn: Gütersloher Verlagshaus, 1972).

[21]Raymond F. Bulman, *A Blueprint for Humanity: Paul Tillich's Theology of Culture* (Lewisburg PA: Bucknell University Press, 1981).

[22]Theodore M. Greene, "Paul Tillich and Our Secular Culture," in *The Theology of Paul Tillich*, ed. Kegley and Bretall, 50-66.

[23]Theodor Siegfried, "The Significance of Paul Tillich's Theology for the German Situation," in *The Theology of Paul Tillich*, ed. Kegley and Bretall, 68-83.

[24]Langdon Gilkey, "The Role of the Theologian in Contemporary Society," in *The Thought of Paul Tillich*, ed. Adams, Pauck, and Shinn, 330-50.

[25]Peter Haigis, "Tillich's Early Writings in Social Philosophy and Social Ethics within the Context of His Theology of Culture," *North American Paul Tillich Society Newsletter* 26/1 (Winter 2000): 21-30.

[26]Paul G. Wiebe, "The Significance of *The System of the Sciences* within Tillich's Thought," in *Tillich Studies: 1975*, ed. Carey, 76-87.

of culture.[27] A. Arnold Wettstein has affirmed the usefulness of Tillich's theology of culture in interpreting what he terms the supercultural context of modern technological civilization.[28] Jari Ristiniemi has declared that Tillich's message to the technological age is to reject objectification and to embrace community with all of life: people, animals, and things.[29]

Ronald Stone has posited Tillich's method of correlation as the appropriate way to relate politics to culture.[30] Russell Manning has noted the fruitfulness of Tillich's theology of culture in the postcolonial era because of its simultaneous openness to new cultural formulations and refusal to be equated with any formulations.[31] Kelton Cobb has submitted that Tillich's theology of culture defers to cultural elitism to the neglect of the substance present in popular culture.[32] And Victor Nuovo has rejected Tillich's theology of culture as a contradictory and, therefore, self-defeating project.[33]

Religious Socialism. Tillich's engagement with Marx, his struggle for economic justice, and his perspectives on religious socialism prompted John Carey to relate Tillich's interest in Marx to Tillich's interest in the

---

[27]Raymond F. Bulman, "Theonomy and Technology: A Study in Tillich's Theology of Culture," in *Kairos and Logos: Studies in the Roots and Implications of Tillich's Theology*, ed. Carey, 213-33.

[28]A. Arnold Wettstein, "Re-Viewing Tillich in a Technological Culture," in *Theonomy and Autonomy: Studies in Paul Tillich's Engagement with Modern Culture*, ed. Carey, 113-33.

[29]Jari Ristiniemi, "Politics of Soul in a Changing Society: Tillich's Political Pathos of the 1920's in Light of Nietzsche's Moral Philosophy," *Bulletin of the North American Paul Tillich Society* 31/3 (Summer 2005): 9-15.

[30]Ronald H. Stone, "The Correlation of Politics and Culture in Paul Tillich's Thought" *Soundings* 49 (1986): 499-511.

[31]Russell Manning, "Tillich's Theology of Culture after Postcolonialism," *Newsletter of the North American Paul Tillich Society* 28/2 (Spring 2002): 25-32.

[32]Kelton Cobb, "Expanding the Stock of Sources in Tillich's Theology of Culture," *Meeting Papers: North American Paul Tillich Society* (November 1992): 13-23. Cf. Kelton Cobb, "Reconsidering the Status of Popular Culture in Tillich's Theology of Culture," *Journal of the American Academy of Religion* 43/1 (Spring 1995): 53-85.

[33]Victor Nuovo, *Visionary Science: A Translation of Tillich's "On the Idea of a Theology of Culture" with an Interpretive Essay* (Detroit: Wayne State University Press, 1987).

interpretation of history.[34] John R. Stumme has outlined the interaction between theology and the practice of religious socialism during the blossoming of Tillich's social thought in the Weimar period of German history.[35] James V. Fisher has inquired into the beginnings of Tillich's political writing arising within the turmoil of church-state debates following World War I.[36] He has endorsed the perspective that socialism was an example of Tillich's general rejection of separating the sacred from the secular.[37] Dennis P. McCann has asserted that Tillich's religious socialism was a creative synthesis based in an existential understanding of religion, expressed in his unique religious language.[38] Roger Shinn has focused on the commitment to interpret and to change civilization within Tillich's religious socialism as a response to Marx's counsel that philosophers persistently do the former to the neglect of the latter.[39] Ronald Stone has spoken of the broad range of social and political issues to which Tillich applied his religious socialism in both his German and American periods.[40] Stone has clarified Tillich's dialectical relation to socialism as an "essential"—rather than an ephemeral—part of his thought.[41] Marion Enzmann has held that the Weimar period manifests Tillich's legitimization of politics as a theological theme.[42] Anna L. Peterson has read Tillich's

---

[34]John J. Carey, "Tillich, Marx and the Interpretation of History: A Prototype of a Marxist-Christian Dialogue," *The St. Luke's Journal of Theology* 14/1 (January 1971): 3-15.

[35]John R. Stumme, *Socialism in Theological Perspective: A Study of Paul Tillich, 1918–1933* (Missoula MT: Scholars Press, 1978).

[36]James V. Fisher, "The Politicizing of Paul Tillich: The First Phase," in *Tillich Studies: 1975*, ed. Carey, 27-38.

[37]James V. Fisher, "Review Essay: The Socialist Decision," *Newsletter of the North American Paul Tillich* 3/1 (December 1977): 21-27.

[38]Dennis P. McCann, "Tillich's Religious Socialism: 'Creative Synthesis' or Personal Statement?" in *The Thought of Paul Tillich*, ed. Adams, Pauck, and Shinn, 81-101.

[39]Roger L. Shinn, "Tillich as Interpreter and Disturber of Contemporary Civilization," in *The Thought of Paul Tillich*, ed. Adams, Pauck, and Shinn, 44-62.

[40]Ronald H. Stone, *Paul Tillich's Radical Social Thought* (Lanham MD: University Press of America, 1986).

[41]Ronald H. Stone, "Christian Ethics and the Socialist Vision of Paul Tillich," in *Tillich Studies: 1975*, ed. Carey, 51-62.

[42]Marion Enzmann, "Die politischen Ideen Paul Tillichs in der Weimarer

political thought as a general defense of socialism.[43] Walter Weisskopf has portrayed Tillich's *The Socialist Decision* as a dialectical project with a double tripartite structure: it involves the historical, psychological and ontological dimensions through which it assembles the interplay of the romantic, bourgeois and socialist principles.[44]

Walter F. Bense has described the tensions between Tillich and his former friend and colleague, Emanuel Hirsch, specifically over Hirsch's distortion of Tillich's kairos doctrine into a tool for endorsing racist nationalism.[45] Eberhard Amelung has argued that the Kairos Circle took the distortive, ideological moves of making the economy the Unconditional for modern industrial society, separating the understanding of society from its legal system, and masking the reality that modern industrial society has created an ambiguous mixture of greater freedom and greater dehumanization.[46] Stone has appraised the Kairos Circle to be a group not dominated by Tillich (following Stumme and contra Amelung), but one in which theistic and atheistic voices contributed to discussions about the direction of the

---

Republik," *Tillich Journal: Interpretieren—Vergleichen—Kritisieren—Weiterent-wickeln* 1 (1997): 68-71.

[43]Peterson, Anna L., "Paul Tillich's Political Ethics: In Defense of Socialism," *Meeting Papers: North American Paul Tillich Society* (November 1992): 38-49.

[44]Walter A. Weisskopf, "Tillich and the Crisis of the West," in *The Thought of Paul Tillich*, ed. Adams, Pauck, and Shinn, 63-80.

[45]Walter F. Bense, "Tillich's *Kairos* and Hitler's Seizure of Power: The Tillich-Hirsch Exchange of 1934–1935," in *Tillich Studies: 1975*, ed. Carey, 39-50. See two books by A. James Reimer on the Tillich-Hirsch relationship: *The Emanuel Hirsch and Paul Tillich Debate: A Study in the Political Ramifications of Theology*, Toronto Studies in Theology 42 (Lewiston/Queenston/Lampeter: Edwin Mellen Press, 1989); and *Paul Tillich: Theologian of Nature, Culture, and Politics* (Münster: Lit Verlag, 2004). See also the comment on Reimer's work in Jack Forstman, *Christian Faith in Dark Times: Theological Conflicts in the Shadow of Hitler* (Louisville: Westminster/John Knox Press, 1992) 214-15, and the review of Reimer's later book, Guy B. Hammond, "Review: A. James Reimer, *Paul Tillich: Theologian of Nature, Culture, and Politics*," *Bulletin of the North American Paul Tillich Society* 33/4 (Fall 2007): 5-6.

[46]Eberhard A. Amelung, "Religious Socialism as Ideology: A Study of the Kairos Circle in Germany between 1919 and 1933" (Th.D. thesis, Harvard University, 1962).

new German (Weimar) republic.[47] Langdon Gilkey emphasized the
centrality of the doctrine of kairos in Tillich's writings of the 1920s and
1930s, which was never surrendered but which gradually receded as
Tillich's optimism for the post-World War II world declined.[48] Stone has
reasoned that Tillich's approaches to such topics as utopianism, anti-
Semitism, and economics were influenced by his relationship to the
Frankfurt School and its critical-theoretical treatments of society and
psychology.[49] Terence O'Keeffe has said that while Tillich had friendships
and associations with members of the Frankfurt School, there seems to have
been no mutual influence on one another's thinking.[50]

Eduard Heimann believed that Tillich underestimated the dehumanizing
end of the dialectic in Marxist theory.[51] Clark A. Kucheman has analyzed
whether Tillich adequately argued the case for socialism as the preferable
embodiment of justice and has questioned whether the economic divisions
present in the twentieth century were necessary consequences of capitalism.[52] Charles C. West has suggested that Tillich's religious socialism was
unrealistic about the capacity of the church to shape communism, failing to
see the impossibility of a dialogue with communism that could have
integrity.[53]

James W. Champion has explored the connections between Tillich's
German and American periods, noting the often missed presence of political
and social concerns in his later works.[54] Brian Donnelly has posed the

[47]Ronald H. Stone, "Kairos Circle," *Meeting Papers: North American Paul
Tillich Society* (November 1989): 23-27.

[48]Langdon Gilkey, "Tillich's Early Political Writings," in *Gilkey on Tillich*
(New York: Crossroad, 1990) 3-22.

[49]Ronald Stone, "Tillich's Critical Use of Marx and Freud in the Social Context
of the Frankfort School," *Union Seminary Quarterly Review* 33/1 (Fall 1977): 3-9.

[50]Terence O'Keeffe, "Tillich and the Frankfurt School," in *Theonomy and
Autonomy: Studies in Paul Tillich's Engagement with Modern Culture*, ed. Carey,
67-87.

[51]Eduard Heimann, "Tillich's Doctrine of Religious Socialism," in *The
Theology of Paul Tillich*, ed. Kegley and Bretall, 312-25.

[52]Clark A. Kucheman, "Professor Tillich: Justice and the Economic Order,"
The Journal of Religion 46/1, part 2 (January 1966): 165-83.

[53]Charles C. West, *Communism and the Theologians* (New York: Macmillan,
1958).

[54]James W. Champion, "Tillich and the Frankfurt School: Parallels and

explicit and implicit presence of Marx in the thought of the later Tillich.[55] And George H. Williams wrote of Tillich's call for socialists and Christians to seek that which united them as World War II arose.[56]

War and Nationalism. The chaplaincy in which Tillich served during World War I gave rise to Donald Arther's depiction of life at the front which served as the context of Tillich's thinking, writing, and pastoring during World War I.[57] Erdmann Sturm has discussed Tillich's first decade of preaching as a combination of pastoral care and apologetics toward working class congregations, military units, and gatherings of the cultured class.[58] Sturm has also voiced the sentiment that Tillich's World War I chaplaincy sermons amounted to a nationalistic war theology out of touch with the brutal realities of the war.[59] Ronald MacLennan has explained the

---

Differences in Prophetic Criticism," *Soundings* 49 (1986): 512-30.

[55]Brian Donnelly, *The Socialist Emigre: Marxism and the Later Tillich* (Macon GA: Mercer University Press, 2003). John Carey has also written of the continuing interest of Tillich in Marx and Marxism until the end of his life. John J. Carey, "Tillich, Marx, and the Interpretation of History," *Meeting Papers: North American Paul Tillich Society* (November 1989): 1-7.

[56]George H. Williams, "Priest, Prophet, and Proletariat: A Study in the Theology of Paul Tillich," *The Journal of Liberal Religion* 1 (Chicago; Winter 1940): 25-37.

[57]Donald Arther, "Paul Tillich as a Military Chaplain," *North American Paul Tillich Society Newsletter* 26/3 (Summer 2000): 4-12.

[58]Erdmann Sturm, "Zwischen Apologetik und Seelsorge: Paul Tillichs frühe Predigten (1908–1918)," in *Spurensuche: Lebens- und Denkwege Paul Tillichs, Tillich-Studien, Band 5*, ed. Nord and Spiegel, 85-104. This first appeared as "Between Apologetics and Pastoral Care: Paul Tillich's Early Sermons (1908–1918)," *North American Paul Tillich Society Newsletter* 26/1 (Winter 2000): 7-20. Cf. Peter Haigis, "Erdmann Sturm (Hg): Ergänzung- und Nachlaßbäde zu den Gesammelten Werken Paul Tillichs, Bd. 7 Frühe Predigten (1909–1918), Berlin, New York, 1994," *Tillich Journal: Interpretieren—Vergleichen—Kritisieren—Weiterentwickeln* 1 (1997): 17-19.

[59]Erdmann Sturm, " 'Holy Love Claims Life and Limb': Paul Tillich's War Theology (1914–1918)," *Zeitschrift für neuere Theologiegeschichte* 2 (1994): 60-84. Cf. Peter Haigis, "Erdmann Sturm (Hg): ,Holy Love Claims Life and Limb. Paul Tillich's War Theology (1914–1918),' *Zeitschrift für neuere Theologiegeschichte*, 1994, 60-84," *Tillich Journal: Interpretieren—Vergleichen—Kritisieren—Weiterentwickeln* 1 (1997): 52-56.

complexity of Tillich's thinking in the context of World War I, maintaining that an inner turmoil and reflection was occurring which was deeper than that revealed in his public work.[60]

The phenomenon of nationalism as a destructive reality for Europe and a grave concern to Tillich brought about Richard Gutteridge's treatment of the tragic and disappointing response of German Protestants to anti-Semitism from the end of the nineteenth century through the mid-twentieth century, descending to its lowest point during the Hitler years.[61] Jack Forstman has elucidated the theological and political tensions among the dominant theologians during the time of Nazi rule, among them tensions between Tillich and Karl Barth as well as Tillich and Emanuel Hirsch.[62] A. James Reimer has questioned whether Tillich's theonomous-cultural approach is as effective as Barth's dogmatic-confessional approach in stimulating ethical behavior.[63] Jean Richard has defended a national consciousness corrected by a democratic spirit—versus bald nationalism—rooted in the thought of Tillich.[64]

Tillich's World War II presidency of the Council for a Democratic Germany occasioned a book by Petra Liebner.[65] And Tillich's speeches for the Voice of America were the basis of earlier parts of my own work—in which I called the speeches expressionistic propaganda—and became the source of a debate-in-print with Matthias Wolbold.[66]

---

[60]Ronald MacLennan, "World War I and Paul Tillich: The Deconstruction and Reconstruction of Theology," Unpublished paper delivered before the "Nineteenth-Century Theology Group" (A90), American Academy of Religion, San Francisco (23 November 1997). See chap. 1 for a deeper discussion of Sturm's and MacLennan's contrasting perspectives.

[61]Richard Gutteridge, *Open Thy Mouth for the Dumb! The German Evangelical Church and the Jews, 1879–1950* (Oxford UK: Basil Blackwell, 1976).

[62]Forstman, *Christian Faith in Dark Times*.

[63]A. James Reimer, "Tillich, Hirsch, and the Confessing Church: On Issues Related to War and Peace," Unpublished paper delivered before the "Issues in the Thought of Paul Tillich Group" (A220), American Academy of Religion, San Francisco (24 November 1997).

[64]Jean Richard, "The Question of Nationalism," in *Religion in the New Millennium: Theology in the Spirit of Paul Tillich*, ed. Bulman and Parrella, 35-43.

[65]Petra Liebner, *Paul Tillich und der Council for a Democratic Germany: 1933 bis 1945* (Frankfurt am Main: Peter Lang, 2001).

[66]Matthias Wolbold, ,,Meine Deutschen Freunde! Die politischen Rundfunk-

Interreligious Dialogue. The interreligious interests of Tillich moved Terence Thomas to support the notion that Tillich's return to an encounter with other world religions was an unstated kairos, an implied new boundary situation for his thinking, which had occurred too late in his life to reach full maturity.[67] Jörg Eickoff has claimed that Tillich's universal concept of revelation results in a conditional exclusivism that enables interreligious dialogue which avoids self-exaltation and opens the way to a more universal understanding of God.[68] Claude Geffré has contended that Tillich's idea of faith as "ultimate concern" is the path for the effective encounter of other religions.[69] Ruwan Palapathwala has argued for an understanding of Tillich's *Systematic Theology* that sees it as a springboard for constructing spirituality unbound to particularism, yet relevant to one's time.[70] Marc Boss has considered the work of Tillich and Lindbeck to advocate an understanding of interreligious relationships that are informed by context,

---

reden Tillichs während des Zweiten Weltkriegs," in *Spurensuche: Lebens- und Denkwege Paul Tillichs, Tillich-Studien*, Band 5, ed. Nord and Spiegel, 183-98. Cf. "Rundfunkarbeit deutscher Exilanten in den USA. Hintergründe und Wirkung," in *Tillich Journal: Interpretieren—Vergleichen—Kritisieren—Weiterentwickeln* 4 (2000): 131-36, and Matthias Wolbold, "Tillich als expressionistischer Propagandist? Eine Antwort auf die Vorwürfe Matthew Lon Weaver," *Tillich Journal: Interpretieren—Vergleichen—Kritisieren—Weiterentwickeln* 3 (1999): 84-87. Cf. Matthew Lon Weaver, "Paul Tillich and the Voice of America," *North American Paul Tillich Society Newsletter* 24/3 (Summer 1998): 19-29. See chap. 4 for details of our debate.

[67]Terence Thomas, "On Another Boundary: Tillich's Encounter with World Religions," in *Theonomy and Autonomy: Studies in Paul Tillich's Engagement with Modern Culture*, ed. Carey, 193-211. See also Terence Thomas, *Paul Tillich and World Religions* (Cardiff, Wales: Cardiff Academic Press, 1999).

[68]Jörg Eickoff, "The New Being in Christ: Tillich's Universal Concept of Revelation as a Contribution to Interreligious Encounter in the Pluralistic Situation of Postmodernity," *Newsletter of the North American Paul Tillich Society* 28/3 (Summer 2002): 18-23.

[69]Claude Geffré, "Paul Tillich and the Future of Interreligious Ecumenism," in *Paul Tillich: A New Catholic Assessment*, ed. Bulman and Parrella, 268-88.

[70]Ruwan Palapathwala, "Beyond Christ and *System*: Paul Tillich and Spirituality in the Twenty-First Century," in *Religion in the New Millennium: Theology in the Spirit of Paul Tillich*, ed. Bulman and Parrella, 205-19.

respectful of particularities, but open to mutual transformation.[71] Robison James has declared that Tillich's approach to other religions was one of reciprocal inclusivism.[72] Joseph Kitigawa has compared the contrasting methods of Tillich and Hendrik Kraemer for interreligious understanding: Tillich did so by means of a theological history of religions, Kraemer through a theological approach to comparative religions.[73]

David H. Nikkel has examined the tension between Tillich's Christo-centrism and his acceptance of the inbreaking of revelation within other religions.[74] Masao Abe has affirmed Tillich's dynamic typology of interreligious interpretation, but has rejected Tillich's embrace of Christ's crucifixion as the criterion for the legitimacy of all religions as contradictory to his dynamic typology.[75] Robert M. Price has advanced the idea that Tillich's apparent Christocentrism can be overcome through his method of correlation, replacing the notion of the fragmentary nature of particular non-Christian revelations with the idea of localized revelations, one of which was Jesus as the Christ.[76] M. Thomas Thangaraj has stated that Tillich's later thought moved from Christian apologetic theology to a tripodic dialogic theology using faith, religion and culture as a more sound basis for

---

[71]Marc Boss, "Religious Diversity: From Tillich to Lindbeck and Back," in *Religion in the New Millennium : Theology in the Spirit of Paul Tillich*, ed. Bulman and Parrella, 177-95.

[72]Robison B. James, *Tillich and World Religions: Encountering Other Faiths Today* (Macon GA: Mercer University Press, 2003).

[73]Joseph Kitigawa, "Tillich, Kraemer, and the Encounter of Religions," in *The Thought of Paul Tillich*, ed. Adams, Pauck, and Shinn, 197-217.

[74]David H. Nikkel, "Polarities in Tillich's Thought on Revelation in the World Religions," *Newsletter of the North American Paul Tillich Society* 26/4 (Fall 2000): 2-6.

[75]Masao Abe, "A Buddhist View of 'The Significance of the History of Religions for the Systematic Theologian,'" *Meeting Papers: North American Paul Tillich Society* (November 1988): 1-8. Cf. Terence Thomas, "Response to Masao Abe's 'A Buddhist View of "The Significance of the History of Religions for the Systematic Theologian," ' " *Meeting Papers: North American Paul Tillich Society* (November 1988): 9-13.

[76]Robert M. Price, "Tillich on Christian Faith and the Plurality of World Religions," *Bulletin of the North American Paul Tillich Society* 30/4 (Fall 2004): 19-25.

interreligious dialogue.[77]

David Novak has asserted that Martin Buber taught Tillich about divine relationality, but that modern Judaism can be taught by Tillich about divine being.[78] Franklin Sherman has posited the presence of a relationship between Tillich's correlational method and the existential situation of Jewish life and thought in modern times.[79] Glenn David Earley held that a more vigorous application of the Protestant principle by Tillich to Christianity itself, a more accurate understanding of Judaism, and an attentiveness to Judaism's own questions are necessary correctives to Tillich's understanding of Judaism.[80]

Langdon Gilkey inquired into the relationship of Tillich's openness to nonbeing within God to Buddhist notions of Nothingness.[81] Eiko Hanaoka

---

[77]M. Thomas Thangaraj, "Faith, Religion, and Culture: A Tripod for Interreligious Dialogue," *Meeting Papers: North American Paul Tillich Society* (November 1991): 43-47.

[78]Novak, David, "Tillich and Buber," *Meeting Papers: North American Paul Tillich Society* (November 1990): 9-16. Cf. Marc Krell, "Constructing a Public Theology: Tillich's and Buber's Movement Beyond Protestant and Jewish Boundaries in Weimar Germany," unpublished paper delivered before the "Tillich: Issues in Theology, Religion, and Culture Group" (A19-124), American Academy of Religion, Philadelphia (19 November 2005); and Richard A. Falk, *Martin Buber and Paul Tillich's Radical Politics and Religion* (New York: National Council of Protestant Episcopal Churches, 1961).

[79]Franklin Sherman, "Tillich's Method of Correlation: Some Resonances in Jewish Thought," *Meeting Papers: North American Paul Tillich Society* (November 1990): 17-20. Cf. Albert H. Friedlander, "Tillich and Jewish Thought," in *The Thought of Paul Tillich*, ed. Adams, Pauck, and Shinn, 175-96. Guy Hammond has used the thought Martin Buber as a mediating vehicle for a discussion of the nature of human relationships in the thought of Tillich and Emmanuel Levinas. Guy B. Hammond, "The Primacy of Ethics: Relationality in Buber, Tillich, and Levinas," *Bulletin of the North American Paul Tillich Society* 30/3 (Summer 2004): 24-30.

[80]Glenn David Earley, "An 'Everlasting Conversation': Judaism in the Life and Thought of Paul Tillich" (Ph.D. diss., Temple University 1983). Cf. Glenn D. Earley, "Tillich and Judaism: An Analysis of the 'Jewish Question,'" in *Theonomy and Autonomy: Studies in Paul Tillich's Engagement with Modern Culture*, ed. Carey, 267-80.

[81]Langdon Gilkey, "Tillich and the Kyoto School," *Meeting Papers: North American Paul Tillich Society* (December 1987): 1-10.

has drawn a connection between Zen Buddhism (God as absolute nothing-ness) and Christianity (God as ground of being) in Tillich's idea of the "God above the God of theism."[82] Yoshinori Takeuchi stressed that Tillich's comments on being, nonbeing, and being-itself were the basis for useful conversations with Buddhism.[83] Taitetsu Unno has argued that Tillich's understanding of Buddhism was largely restricted to Zen Buddhism, leading Tillich to neglect the understanding of compassion in Shin Buddhism that is analogous to that taught within Christianity.[84]

Jawad Ashr has used Tillich's thought in efforts to begin the con-struction of a theologically rooted Islamic anthropology.[85] And Basit Koshul has found that Tillich's thought resonates with the idea of the am-biguity of the divine found in Islamic teaching.[86]

Specific Social Issues. Tillich's existentialist makeup led to his engage-ment with his times. Bernard Martin has submitted that the existentialist characteristic of Tillich's theological approach derives from his commit-ment to "conversing" with the philosophical and cultural currents of his time rather than the exposition of traditional Christian theological dogma.[87] Lubomir Mirejovsky has endorsed the viewpoint that from the end of World War I to the end of his life, Tillich worked as a philosopher of peace.[88] Ronald Stone has said that while Tillich was no pacifist, his contributions to the cause of peace involved actions and policies that confronted the root

---

[82]Eiko Hanaoka, "Paul Tillich in Japan," trans. Thomas F. O'Meara, *Bulletin of the North American Paul Tillich Society* 32/3 (Summer 2006): 6-9.

[83]Yoshinori Takeuchi, "Buddhism and Existentialism: The Dialogue between Oriental and Occidental Thought," in *Religion and Culture: Essays in Honor of Paul Tillich*, ed. Leibrecht, 291-318.

[84]Taitetsu Unno, "Compassion in Buddhist Spirituality," in *Religion in the New Millennium: Theology in the Spirit of Paul Tillich*, ed. Bulman and Parrella, 165-76.

[85]Jawad Ashr, "Paul Tillich and the Reconstruction of Sin and Salvation in Islamic Theological Anthropology," *Newsletter of the North American Paul Tillich Society* 29/1 (Winter 2003): 27-42.

[86]Basit Koshul, "The Divine, the Demonic, and the Ninety-Nine Names of Allah: Tillich's Idea of the 'Holy' and the Qur'anic Narrative," *Newsletter of the North American Paul Tillich Society* 29/1 (Winter 2003): 42-48.

[87]Bernard Martin, *The Existentialist Theology of Paul Tillich* (New York: Bookman Associates, 1963).

[88]Lubomir Mirejovsky, "Peace Issues in the Work of Paul Tillich," *North American Paul Tillich Society Newsletter* 14/2 (April 1988): 5-10.

causes of war and, therefore, laid the groundwork for peace.[89]

John B. Lounibos has looked at Tillich's understanding of freedom, rooted in his debt to Schelling, as one of hope pursuing liberation.[90] Jean Richard has upheld the position that Tillich's religious socialist thought and his life-experience in the early decades of the twentieth century possess helpful support to theologies of liberation.[91] Luis G. Pedraja has maintained that Tillich's doctrine of the inbreaking of the divine into culture and his serious consideration of the cultural location of any given theology make him a fertile partner in discussions of liberation theology.[92] H. Frederick Reisz has contended that Tillich's thought can provide the basis for a theology of "liberating" which transcends the apparent impasse between Tillich's ontological approach and liberation theology's commitment to praxis.[93] José Míguez Bonino has seen in Tillich a helpful source for Latin American liberation thought, specifically with regard to posing socialism as an option, reflecting critically on the types of socialist options, and giving consideration to the relationship of religion to socialism.[94] Stone has established a parallel between the religious socialism of Tillich and the liberation theology of Gustavo Gutierrez in their use of Marx as a basis for indigenous, existential social thought.[95] Anthony A. Akinwale suggests that Tillich's method of correlation cultivates a pluralism that makes him a

[89]Stone, Ronald H., "Paul Tillich on Peace," *Meeting Papers: North American Paul Tillich Society* (November 1989): 17-22.

[90]John B. Lounibos, "Paul Tillich's Structures of Liberation," in *Tillich Studies: 1975*, ed. Carey, 63-74.

[91]Jean Richard, "The Socialist Tillich and Liberation Theology," in *Paul Tillich: A New Catholic Assessment*, ed. Bulman and Parrella, 148-73.

[92]Luis G. Pedraja, "Tillich's Theology of Culture and Hispanic Theology," *Newsletter of the North American Paul Tillich Society* 25/3 (Summer 1999): 2-10.

[93]H. Frederick Reisz, Jr., "Liberation Theology of Culture: A Tillichian Perspective," in *Kairos and Logos: Studies in the Roots and Implications of Tillich's Theology*, ed. Carey, 271-82.

[94]José Míguez Bonino, "Rereading Tillich in Latin America: From Religious Socialism to the Exile," in *Religion in the New Millennium: Theology in the Spirit of Paul Tillich*, ed. Bulman and Parrella, 19-33.

[95]Stone, Ronald H., "Paulus und Gustavo: Religious Socialism and Liberation Theology," *Meeting Papers: North American Paul Tillich Society* (December 1987): 17-26.

helpful partner in addressing the concerns of African theologians.[96]

Mary Ann Stenger has reasoned that Tillich's movement beyond traditional theological language, his ontological approach to theology, the
dynamics between being and nonbeing, and his stand against idolatry can
serve as supports for feminist thought.[97] Sharon Burch has posed a parallel
between the feminist understanding of identity as the creative negotiation
of life's experiences and Tillich's theology of culture as the perspective
from which theology negotiates the broad range of cultural experiences.[98]
Linda Moody points to Tillich's sense of openness to new symbolic expressions for theological truths as his chief contribution to feminist liberation
theology.[99] Peter Slater has voiced the conviction that the power of forgiveness in Tillich's concept of creative justice has been manifested in everything from the South African Truth and Reconciliation Commission, to the
cancellation of third world debt, to the willingness of a woman of color to
forgive her white attackers.[100] However, Tabea Rösler has stated that
Tillich's anthropology risks falling into a self-centeredness that can be
corrected by feminist thinkers offering a more fully multidimensional
understanding of existence.[101] And Judith Plaskow has claimed that there is

---

[96]Anthony A. Akinwale, "Tillich's Method of Correlation and the Concerns of
African Theologians," in *Paul Tillich: A New Catholic Assessment*, ed. Bulman and
Parrella, 189-217. See also Sylvester I. Ihuoma, *Paul Tillich's Theology of Culture
in Dialogue with African Theology*, Tillich Studies 11 (New Brunswick NJ:
Transaction Press, 2005).

[97]Mary Ann Stenger and Ronald H. Stone, *Dialogues of Paul Tillich* (Macon
GA: Mercer University Press, 2002). Cf. Mary Ann Stenger, "Paul Tillich and the
Feminist Critique of Roman Catholic Theology," in *Paul Tillich: A New Catholic
Assessment*, ed. Bulman and Parrella, 174-88.

[98]Sharon Burch, "Women and Religion and the New Millennium," in *Religion
in the New Millennium: Theology in the Spirit of Paul Tillich*, ed. Bulman and
Parrella, 109-20.

[99]Linda A. Moody, "Paul Tillich and Feminist Theology: Echoes from the
Boundary," *Meeting Papers: North American Paul Tillich Society* (November
1993): 18-24.

[100]Peter Slater, "The Relevance of Tillich's Concept of Creative Justice in the
New Millennium," in *Religion in the New Millennium: Theology in the Spirit of
Paul Tillich*, ed. Bulman and Parrella, 45-53.

[101]Tabea Rösler, "Anthropological Perspectives in Tillich's Systematic
Theology: A Constructive Framework in Dialogue with Feminist Process

a conflict between Tillich's understanding of personhood in terms of self-actualization and his understanding of union with the ground of being as requiring the surrender of self.[102]

Anne Marie Reijnen has formulated a Tillich-inspired criterion of just punishment as a basis for analyzing the state's use of power in practicing capital punishment.[103] Ronald Stone has seen points in Tillich's life in which he advocated resistance, leading Stone to advocate contemporary resistance to patterns of fundamentalism, greed, violence and domination.[104] And Guy Hammond has used Tillich's theology of history to confront President George W. Bush's self-understanding as a providentially placed instrument for the promulgation of freedom.[105]

Thus, it can be said that dozens of scholars have been provoked to explore the implications of Tillich's political philosophy for a wide range of social and cultural issues

Religious Internationalism

Given the larger context of Tillich's existentialist political philosophy, it is not surprising to discover that one can paint a portrait of Tillich's approach to the ethics of war and peace. This book considers the rich and varied hues of Tillich's thought in order to paint such a picture. It tells the story of his intellectual development into a religious internationalist.

Theologies," *Bulletin of the North American Paul Tillich Society* 31/3 (Summer 2005): 33-41. Cf. Tabea Rösler, " 'You Never See with the Eyes Only': Reconfiguring Paul Tillich's Concept of Personhood," *Bulletin of the North American Paul Tillich Society* 32/2 (Spring 2006): 27-33. See also Rachel Baard, "Original Grace, Not Destructive Grace: A Feminist Appropriation of Paul Tillich's Notion of Acceptance," *Journal of Religion* 87/3 (July 2007): 411-34.

[102]Judith Plaskow, *Sex, Sin and Grace: Women's Experience and the Theologies of Reinhold Niebuhr and Paul Tillich* (Lanham MD: University Press of America, 1980).

[103]Anne Marie Reijnen, "Paul Tillich and Capital Punishment: The Meaning of Power," *Bulletin of the North American Paul Tillich Society* 31/4 (Fall 2005): 6-10.

[104]Ronald Stone, "The Religious Situation and Resistance in 2001," in *Religion in the New Millennium: Theology in the Spirit of Paul Tillich*, ed. Bulman and Parrella, 55-62.

[105]Guy B. Hammond, "Does the 'Road of Providence' Lead to Freedom? George Bush, Paul Tillich, and the Theology of History," *Bulletin of the North American Paul Tillich Society* 32/2 (Spring 2006): 8-14.

In chapter 1 I begin the story by describing Tillich's intellectual heritage, pointing to his nationalistic roots in imperial Germany, and examining the sermons he penned as a chaplain in the German army during World War I. While Tillich was intellectually aware of both the centrality of power dynamics and of the necessity to transcend the particular, I will show that Tillich remained, at least publicly, loyal to the nationalism of Wilhelmine Germany during these years.

In chapter 2 I will proceed with a description of Tillich's awakening to the thought of Karl Marx soon after war's end. Marx's early thought influenced Tillich's thinking to the end of his life, but it was during the interwar years that he first came under its influence. Economics became a significant factor in his interpretation of the politics among nations and remained central from this point forward. Tillich came to see economic structures as either liberating or oppressive forces in the lives of people. His sensitivity to trends in history—envisioned through the dialectical structure of history which Marx gleaned from Hegel—was another fruit of his engagement with Marxian thought: the notions of kairos (ripened or fulfilled time) and the demonic (form-destroying force) became important to him in this period. Tillich was affiliated with the religious socialist movement fermenting in Europe during this time. Consequently, the Weimar period became one of deep reflection upon German culture, the patterns of history, and—implicitly—the impact this can have on a nation's engagement with other nations. *The Religious Situation* and *The Socialist Decision* were works of primary importance during this stage.

In chapter 3 I will focus on Tillich's thinking during his years as an exile in the United States. With the rise of Nazism, Tillich was relieved of his chair of the philosophy department at the University of Frankfurt. After a brief period of assessing his future in Germany, he made his way to the United States, thanks to the offer of a position at New York's Union Theological Seminary. Biographically, what was most significant for Tillich's interwar period in the United States was the seriousness with which he took his unchosen circumstance of being a thinker "on the boundary." This sensitized him to provincial and nationalistic tendencies. During this period, Tillich produced the one work—and this, a fragment—in which he gave special attention to religion and international thought, *Religion und Weltpolitik*. On March 4, 1940, he became a U.S. citizen. In September of the same year, he became professor of Philosophical Theology at Union.

With chapter 4 I will turn to the period when Hitler's murderous tyranny had spread beyond the borders of Germany and the Second World War had begun. Tillich's thoughts weighed the meaning and aims of the war, its meaning being a constant theme until the war's conclusion. The documents which recorded Tillich's thoughts on the war most comprehensively were his Voice of America speeches, more than five hundred pages of material he wrote for broadcast over short-wave to the European continent, to the German people. Tillich was one of many prominent Europeans invited by the Office of War Information to participate in this effort. Because it is unknown how many or how few heard the broadcasts, the most conservative way to interpret them is as Tillich's journal on the many forces influencing the behavior of nations—particularly Germany—during the course of the war.

Chapter 5 will cover the same period as chapter four, but the audience this time will be the English-speaking world. From his perspective on the boundary, he both exhorted Germans to resist (chapter four) and Americans and Britons to pursue policies with just, creative, transformative outcomes. As the war moved toward its conclusion, Tillich agreed to head the Council for a Democratic Germany. However, it soon became clear that Germany's postwar prospects would be dictated by forces that made the Council's work moot. Tillich became much less optimistic about the prospects of a truly changed, reintegrated world as the Cold War descended: the optimism and fullness of kairos became the pessimism and emptiness of vacuum.

Yet, this was quite consistent with Tillich's philosophy of history. History provides moments and periods that are more or less opportune for change. While the time under the Weimar Republic had been a fertile period, Tillich saw post-World War II Europe and the post-World War II era as presenting a different situation. In chapter six I will describe Tillich's interpretation of this period of time. For him their prospects were inopportune, unappealing, and depressing.

However, religion could continue to do its work in such periods. The pattern of transcendence and engagement was appropriate in periods of vacuum as well, probing for moments in history when fate permitted free acts of reconciliation by individuals and nations. Tillich's *Systematic Theology* was his effort to formulate the complete story of the relation of religion to existence, including the political dimension. Its three volumes were published between 1951 and 1963. Though they were his central Cold War project, other shorter works—among them, *Love, Power, and Justice*; *The Courage to Be*; *Dynamics of Faith*; and *Christianity and the Encounter of the World Religions*—were produced during the same period. In these three works, Tillich gave attention to the ontological elements of social and personal existence and—true to his dialectical/correlational method and mission—showed his growing edge (in his late 70s) in pondering the encounter (versus Huntington's "clash") of the world religions. Vacuum did not result in passive inactivity for Tillich, but called for venturing courage.

One sees resonances throughout this story with elements of realism, liberalism, and radical thought.[106] Tillich began as a realist and never fully left realism behind: the primal and ontological significance of power and the inescapability of ambiguity and sin in human existence remained throughout. However, Tillich fully engaged classical liberalism and its vision of the harmonious development of freely thinking and acting human beings. He cherished creative freedom, in particular. Though World War I removed the illusion of human development toward harmonious existence for Tillich, he never lost hope. The fragments of reconciliation that repeatedly crop up within history testified to the importance of an utopian vision despite the impossibility of harmony actualized within existence. And, as cited before, radical or socialist thought became prominent following World War I and remained present—explicitly and implicitly— until the end of Tillich's life.

In the final chapter of the book, I will combine construction, critique and conclusion. I will argue that elements of an ethic on war and peace can be gleaned from Tillich's thought. I will use Tillich's own thinking on ethics and morality to frame these elements, weighing Tillich's construction to determine its strengths, identify its weaknesses, and suggest some reformulations. In the end, I will attempt to show that the thought of Paul Tillich provides ample and provocative material for assembling an ethic of war and peace rooted in religion that can generate constructive discussion regarding the path toward a united world, rooted in social and economic justice, while respecting the diversities of religion and culture, in short, an ethic of religious internationalism.

---

[106]This is not to say that Tillich explicitly seeks to "place" himself with respect to realism, liberalism, and socialism. It is simply to observe that all three themes arise within his thinking.

Chapter 1

Prewar and World War I—
Pious Nationalist

Introduction

Following Gymnasium, Paul Tillich began theological studies at the University of Berlin in the winter of 1904. Beginning in the winter of 1905, he studied at the University of Halle.[1] His most important teacher at Halle was Martin Kähler. In Tillich's words, Kähler "combined traditions of Renaissance humanism and German classicism with a profound understanding of the Reformation and with strong elements of the religious awakening of the middle of the nineteenth century."[2] From Kähler, Tillich learned of the fullness of the Pauline doctrine of justification by faith,[3] "gain[ing] the insight that man is justified by grace through faith, not only as a sinner but even as a doubter."[4] Tillich's second most important teacher at Halle was Fritz Medicus, a young lecturer in philosophy and a specialist in Fichte and German classical philosophy.[5] Medicus led a revival in German idealism, functioning as one of the inspirations for Tillich's interest in Schelling.[6] With his understanding of Schelling cultivated by Medicus and his knowledge of Luther deepened by Kähler, Tillich began a path towards a "theonomous philosophy" shorn of utopianism regarding the human condition.[7]

Tillich's membership in the Wingolf Fellowship led him into lifelong friendships. In 1908, it led to his friendship with Emanuel Hirsch.[8] In the Fellowship, he experienced "friendship, spiritual exchange on a very high

---

[1]Wilhelm and Marion Pauck, *Paul Tillich: His Life and Thought* (San Francisco: Harper & Row, 1976) 17-19.

[2]Paul Tillich, Author's introduction to *The Protestant Era* (Chicago: University of Chicago Press, 1948) xiii.

[3]Paul Tillich, *On the Boundary: An Autobiographical Sketch* (New York: Scribner's, 1936/1964/1966) 48.

[4]Pauck, *Paul Tillich*, 19.

[5]Pauck, *Paul Tillich*, 19-20.

[6]Tillich, *On the Boundary*, 47.

[7]Tillich, *On the Boundary*, 52, 76.

[8]Pauck, *Paul Tillich*, 30.

level, intentional and unintentional education, joy of living, seriousness about the problems of communal life generally, and Christian fellowship especially."[9]

In October 1907, Tillich returned to studies at the University of Berlin. In 1910, the University of Breslau awarded him a Ph.D. in philosophy for which he prepared *The Construction of the History of Religion in Schelling's Positive Philosophy: Its Presuppositions and Principles.*[10] In 1912, the University of Halle awarded him a Licentiate in Theology for which he submitted *Mysticism and Guilt-Consciousness in Schelling's Philosophical Development.*[11] In 1913, he made an initial foray into the assembly of a systematic theology which, understandably, has significant resonance with the foundations laid in the dissertations.[12] And in 1915, while serving in the war, Tillich completed his Habilitation thesis.[13]

The early writings of Tillich seem to be irrelevant to a discussion of his political thought. Tillich gave little overt attention to the political implications of his theology within them. They are significant because they offer something of the theological framework through which Tillich interpreted the world over the subsequent half-century.

The central documents that reflect Tillich's political perspective during the war are his chaplaincy sermons. These have the air of a conventional religious endorsement of a governing regime's war-cause by an official of that regime. At a certain level, their function in the present context is to illustrate the politically uncritical Tillich of the early years. However, to end the discussion at this level would result in a superficial characterization of this stage in Tillich's thought.

In this chapter I will begin with a brief summary of Tillich's first

———————————

[9]Paul Tillich, "Autobiographical Reflections," in *The Theology of Paul Tillich*, ed. Kegley and Bretall, 11-12.

[10]Paul Tillich, *The Construction of the History of Religion in Schelling's Positive Philosophy: Its Presuppositions and Principles*, thesis at Breslau (1910), trans. Victor Nuovo (Lewisburg PA: Bucknell University Press, 1974).

[11]Paul Tillich, *Mysticism and Guilt-Consciousness in Schelling's Philosophical Development*, thesis at Halle (1912), trans. Victor Nuovo (Lewisburg PA: Bucknell University Press, 1974).

[12]Paul Tillich, *Systematische Theologie* (1913), trans. Uwe Carsten Scharf (Berlin/New York: Walter de Gruyter, 1999).

[13]Sturm, "Between Apologetics and Pastoral Care," 7.

dissertation, *The Construction of the History of Religion in Schelling's Positive Philosophy: Its Presuppositions and Principles*, to bring to light elements of his thought that will be key to his later political theory. For that reason, Following this, I will turn to a much fuller description of the war sermons to establish what Tillich saw religion to say that was of use to warriors. Then I will present a theological-political framework for contextualizing the entire period.

Schelling and the Construction of the History of Religions

F. W. J. von Schelling labored during the time of Hegel, Fichte, and Goethe. Tillich savored the memory of discovering and purchasing Schelling's collected works from a book store in Berlin.[14] In *The Construction of the History of Religion*, Tillich sought "to present the construction of the history of religion as the focal point of Schelling's positive philosophy."[15] Schelling understood God, humanity, and the world at large in a dialectical manner. He saw the metaphysical structure of all three as centered around three principles he termed "potencies."[16] The first potency is that of expansion and is characterized by subjectivity, by untrammeled and irrational (or, perhaps, nonrational) power. It is the principle of self-assertion and naked desire.[17] It is the potency of freedom and potential being. It involves "infinite possibility" and is "the subject of everything that is."[18] In Schelling's understanding of God, this is the first person of the Christian Trinity, God the Father.[19]

The second potency is that of contraction in which the formative impact of objectivity and reason lifts its head against the force of the first potency. Love and selflessness dominate here. It is the potency of necessity and actual being.[20] This is the potency of Christ in the Trinity.[21]

---

[14]Paul Tillich, *Perspectives on 19th and 20th Century Protestant Theology* (New York: Harper & Row, 1967) 142; Tillich, *On the Boundary*, 47.

[15]Tillich, *The Construction of the History of Religion*, 41.

[16]Tillich, *The Construction of the History of Religion*, 43-46.

[17]Tillich, *The Construction of the History of Religion*, 45-49.

[18]Tillich, *The Construction of the History of Religion*, 50, 51.

[19]Tillich, *The Construction of the History of Religion*, 55.

[20]Tillich, *The Construction of the History of Religion*, 50.

[21]Tillich, *The Construction of the History of Religion*, 55.

Finally, there is the third potency which transcends the subject-object positions of the first and second principles, mediating and unifying them. It is the potency of "what ought to be or what shall be."[22] Here, the third person of the Trinity, the Holy Spirit, has its place.[23]

Tillich devoted significant space to interpreting the relationship among the potencies developed in Schelling's thought. First, he described Schelling's definition of the nature of God, humanity and world according to this triad of powers.[24] He then presented Schelling's outline of the story of religion. For Schelling, the history of religion began with the dominance of the first potency in prehistoric polytheism.[25] From here it evolved through the periods of humanity's mythological interpretation of world history, what Schelling termed natural religion. In this period, God allowed for the separation of the potencies, giving in to necessity.[26] During this period, the second potency evolved further and operated to return estranged existence to unity with God—the period of the second potency's natural efficacy—crowned by God's self-revelation in Judaism and Christianity, that is, the period of revealed religion.[27] At this stage, the potencies were spiritually reunited: "God, as the supernatural, as freedom and personality and spirit, is the principle of revelation."[28] It is not the realm of reason. Speaking of the "supra-rationality of revelation," Tillich interprets Schelling to say that revelation "lies not within the intellectual sphere, but within the moral sphere," one in which humanity "'must broaden the smallness of his thought to the greatness of the divine.'"[29] It is by God's act—by God's assertion of the divine will—that humanity experiences "the moment of the absolutely wonderful."[30] In Schelling's reading of Christianity, the selflessness of the second principle conquered the selfishness of the first—the period of the second potency's supernatural efficacy—and set the

[22]Tillich, *The Construction of the History of Religion*, 50.
[23]Tillich, *The Construction of the History of Religion*, 55.
[24]Tillich, *The Construction of the History of Religion*, 59-64, 66-70, 71-76.
[25]Tillich, *The Construction of the History of Religion*, 77-80.
[26]Tillich, *The Construction of the History of Religion*, 80ff., 132-34.
[27]Tillich, *The Construction of the History of Religion*, 102ff.
[28]Tillich, *The Construction of the History of Religion*, 137.
[29]Tillich, *The Construction of the History of Religion*, 138.
[30]Tillich, *The Construction of the History of Religion*, 139.

stage for the third potency in philosophical religion.[31]

Once again, the interplay of these potencies—or powers or forces or principles—forms the structure of God, humanity, world, and history for Schelling. Further, while God is able to keep these potencies in balance within the Godhead, and while humanity is the one being able to apprehend such a structure in life, human history shows that humanity is incapable of keeping them in balance. Everything from the inner reality of individuals to the relations among nations is rooted in this dynamic structure of the powers at the foundation of existence.[32]

Tillich never abandoned the structure he saw in Schelling's work. For the discussion of Tillich's religious internationalism, the relevance of Schelling is the doctrine of the potencies, understood by him as woven into reality and rumbling through history. He embraced the notion that power—the interplay of the dynamics expressed by the Schellingian potencies—is at the heart of reality. In the end, the presence or absence of peace is governed by the state of relations among the competing powers of being at work within international life.[33] More, Tillich would consistently call for ethical and just behavior by linking it to humanity's ability to transcend its provincialism, to "broaden the smallness of his thought to the greatness of the divine."

A final point to note is this: already in this work from 1910 Tillich took seriously the meaning of non-Christian religions.[34] His interpretation of these religions is open to some question.[35] However, as we consider his thought in light of our own period, in which world conflict and religion are closely associated, it is vital to understand that Christianity's relationship to other religions was a topic of works by Tillich that framed his career (his

---

[31]Tillich, *The Construction of the History of Religion*, 135-37.

[32]Tillich, *The Construction of the History of Religion*, 125.

[33]Victor Nuovo notes in his introduction to his translation, "The abiding deep structure of Tillich's thought is the system of the potencies. Wherever one looks in Tillich's works he will encounter them, from pure theology to political and cultural interpretation." Victor Nuovo, Translator's itroduction to *The Construction of the History of Religion in Schelling's Positive Philosophy*, by Paul Tillich (Lewisburg PA: Bucknell University Press, 1974) 23-25.

[34]Tillich, *The Construction of the History of Religion*, 80ff., 93ff.

[35]Nuovo, Translator's introduction to *The Construction of the History of Religion*, 29ff.

1910 dissertation and his 1963 book, *Christianity and the Encounter of World Religions*[36]) and that Tillich looked with growing sympathy upon the corrective impact of other religions upon Christianity's truth claims.

With this general sense of the dialectical framework of Tillichian thought as expressed in this very early work, we now turn to Tillich's first effort to see war through the eyes of his religious perspective, his World War I chaplaincy sermons.

World War I Chaplaincy Sermons

Tillich entered the service of the German Imperial Army with an enthusiasm shared by soldiers on both sides of the conflict. He was a passionate German nationalist at this time. In 1898 his father had traveled with Kaiser Wilhelm II to Jerusalem. With the outbreak of World War I, Paulus was in a position to serve Kaiser and Fatherland. He entered that service with full existential force.[37]

The sermons Paul Tillich preached as a chaplain in the German army during the war covered a full range of issues. In addition to the ninety-three published sermons that are the basis of this discussion, there are texts of thirteen funeral sermons and unpublished outlines and fragments of fifty further sermons.[38] Erdmann Sturm, the editor of the volume of published sermons, regretted that he was able to date only one-third of them. However, even with this limitation, there is enough documentary evidence to show that in Tillich's public capacity as chaplain, he never swayed from support of the German war effort. As his later reflections confirmed, Tillich submitted to the chain of command in his duties. War broke Tillich emotionally: he attested to two breakdowns during the war.[39] However, his sermons give little evidence of any progressive disenchantment with the war. Carl Ratschow has described them as, first, "strictly theological and exegetical sermons" and, second, as pieces intended "to make it easier for the

---

[36]Paul Tillich, *Christianity and the Encounter of World Religions* (New York: Columbia University Press, 1963). The lectures in this book were originally delivered at Columbia University in 1961 as the fourteenth in the series known in America as the Bampton Lectures.

[37]Pauck, *Paul Tillich*, 9, 40-41.

[38]Sturm, " 'Holy Love Claims Life and Limb,' " 61.

[39]Pauck, *Paul Tillich*, 49, 54.

oppressed to endure."[40]

In the face of the breadth of the material, the content of the sermons will be summarized under five general areas: (1) Christian piety: matters of doctrine and practice; (2) soldierly qualities; (3) the Fatherland and sacrifice; (4) war, peace, and reconciliation; and (5) power and weakness.

Christian Piety: Matters of Doctrine and Practice. Much of Tillich's preaching was traditional Christian orthodoxy. He called his military congregants to see God as the source and basis of all things, as the director and ruler of the world and of world events, and as the goal of all things: all things are from, through, and to God.[41] Life is from God.[42] God is our goal in all things.[43] Tillich described God's message to us as this: "I have torn open heaven in order to come into your night, in order to illuminate the night of your future as well."[44] God's goals and purposes are behind the things of life.[45] Tillich spoke of Christ's direction and rule of the world[46] and of Christ's victory over four powers on earth: fate, pain, sin, and death.[47] Because "the Lord giveth [and] the Lord taketh away," humanity

---

[40]Carl Heinz Ratschow, *Paul Tillich*, trans. Robert P. Scharlemann (Iowa City IA: North American Paul Tillich Society, 1980) 17.

[41]Paul Tillich, "Feldpredigt 111 (1916)," and "Feldpredigt 147 (1917)," in "Feldpredigten 1914–1918," *Frühe Predigten (1909–1918), Ergänzungs- und Nachlassbände zu den Gesammelten Werken von Paul Tillich*, Band VII (Berlin/New York: Walter de Gruyter, 1994) 483, 599. The ninety-three chaplaincy sermons are found on pp. 357-645 of the seventh volume of Tillich's unpublished and/or posthumous works in the German version of his collected works: they are sermons 68 through 160 of the volume. Henceforth, they will be cited by sermon number, year, and page number (from the German volume): e.g., using the very first two citations, F.P. 111 (1916) 483 and F.P. 147 (1917) 599. All translations of German documents in this book are mine. After their initial citation, each volume of the *Gesammelten Werken von Paul Tillich* will be abbreviated as *GW* followed by the volume number, and each volume of the *Ergänzungs- und Nachlassbände zu den Gesammelten Werken von Paul Tillich* will be abbreviated as *GW-E/N* followed by the volume number.

[42]Tillich, F.P. 84 (1915) 401-402.

[43]Tillich, F.P. 75 (1915) 377.

[44]Tillich, F.P. 74 (1914) 375.

[45]Tillich, F.P. 111 (1916) 485.

[46]Tillich, F.P. 139 (1917) 571.

[47]Tillich, F.P. 109 (1916) 478-79.

was in no position to demand anything from God.[48] God is the source of power and grace, participating with us in the brokenness of war.[49] At a point at which the army was experiencing difficult weeks on the Somme, Tillich preached that even amidst war's horrors, we must thank God for life as a gift.[50]

Tillich described God as a companion, as the source and giver of strength, as One who loves. He described Christ as the one inexhaustible source of power that arises out of our souls' depths.[51] He saw eternal love as the one force stronger than death.[52] As God's friends, we are sought by God and need never be lonely.[53] God makes demands of us, but God does not demand without giving infinitely much in return.[54] God bears our cares, worries, and concerns.[55] God's "nevertheless" (*dennoch*)—a powerful image for Tillich of the God's grace in forgiving our sin—enables us to say *dennoch* to the brokenness and sufferings of life.[56] Expressed in another way, God's patience toward us is basic to God and should evoke our own patience.[57]

A sense of blessedness, of the nearness of eternity, of God's imminence and its fruit of inner peace were a significant focus for Tillich's war sermons. He spoke of the yearning for God's imminence within human beings.[58] He invited his hearers to immerse themselves in God: "Sink yourself into the depth of the divine, sink your own 'I' into the eternal sea of God's love, the waves of which surge in your heart day by day."[59] He cited the image of Shepherd as a powerful symbol of God's deep, personal care for each person: "You can believe that you're without God. He is not without you. You can deny God. He is with you as the true shepherd, and

---

[48]Tillich, F.P. 147 (1917) 597, 599.
[49]Tillich, F.P. 97 (1916) 441.
[50]Tillich, F.P. 117 (1916) 500.
[51]Tillich, F.P. 96 (1916) 437.
[52]Tillich, F.P. 153 (1917) 619.
[53]Tillich, F.P. 158 (1918) 637.
[54]Tillich, F.P. 129 (1917) 540.
[55]Tillich, F.P. 71 (1914) 365.
[56]Tillich, F.P. 108 (1916) 474, 476.
[57]Tillich, F.P. 88 (1915) 413.
[58]Tillich, F.P. 74 (1914) 374.
[59]Tillich, F.P. 69 (1914) 361.

the best which you have—your power, your heroism, and your pride he has given you."[60]

Tillich pointed to Paul's doctrine of justification by faith as the root of Luther's understanding of humanity's path to God.[61] He preached that God wants us to sense that we're blessed to the deepest extent.[62] He believed that religion had wrongly placed a heavy burden on people. Instead, "Religion is joy. . . . "[63] Tillich pointed to the sources of power for inner life: joy, culture, love.[64] He proclaimed the Spirit as the basis for life, the unifying force of all community.[65]

Tillich related divine love to the love that connects soldiers with loved ones back home: "Divine love has bridged worlds; what are a few hundred leagues for it?"[66] He argued that God comes to replace that which is broken within our hearts in order to become our confidante and friend.[67] He pointed to the Lord's Prayer as teaching God's knowledge of us, and as providing a basis for the unity of the human race.[68] He called for an understanding of prayer as drawing near to God versus making requests to God.[69] Prayer cannot change God, nor is it a business contract with God: through prayer we should seek conformity of our will with God's, following the example of Jesus.[70] The Eucharist—or Lord's Supper—is a path to unity with God's Spirit.[71] It is the symbol of God's desire to be one with us, just as wine and bread become one with our bodies.[72] Tillich wrote, "The actual, living perceptible presence of God is what Luther did not want to miss and which for him formed the real mystery of the Last Supper."[73]

---

[60]Tillich, F.P. 146 (1917) 596.
[61]Tillich, F.P. 152 (1917) 613-14.
[62]Tillich, F.P. 154 (1917) 624.
[63]Tillich, F.P. 131 (1917) 546.
[64]Tillich, F.P. 133 (1917) 551-53.
[65]Tillich, F.P. 160 (1918) 643.
[66]Tillich, F.P. 155 (1917) 627.
[67]Tillich, F.P. 140 (1917) 575.
[68]Tillich, F.P. 107 (1916) 472.
[69]Tillich, F.P. 79 (1915) 387.
[70]Tillich, F.P. 134 (1917) 555.
[71]Tillich, F.P. 103 (1916) 459.
[72]Tillich, F.P. 119 (1916) 509.
[73]Tillich, F.P. 138 (1917) 568.

Despite war, Tillich saw inner "peace on earth" as perpetually present by means of Christ's peace-giving presence.[74] As a result, "new courage, new will-to-love and will-for-victory pours out of God's nearness. What you did [in recent battles] was perfect love. That remains your honor for all time. What was given to you is God's friendship. It is your best unto eternity."[75] We can believe that eternal goals are attainable, beyond the horrific loss of human lives and dreams[76] and that the Invisible can be our focus, not the visible horrors of war.[77]

The condition and care of the soul occupied significant attention in Tillich's preaching. He exhorted soldiers to remember that they have a soul,[78] or, more poetically, "Remember you have wings."[79] Tillich spoke of the soul as the "organ" of religion:

> God and the soul, God and my soul, that is the heartbeat of religion, that is the source-point of the Reformation, that is the deepest, most fragile thing and most living thing in your life as well. . . . When the divine is within you, is with you, and a strength from above fills you at all times, then you have the religion of the soul. Then your heart is God's house, then every day is Sunday for you, and every day is a day of celebration, then you are pastor, teacher, priest, and church for yourself.[80]

Having a soul "means, ultimately, to have an organ for things which are not of this world, for duty and love, truth and beauty, God and eternity."[81] The Spirit is "the inner essence, the peculiar quality, the character, the personal life of a person."[82] He declared, "the soul is indeed the most powerful thing and more powerful than all the earth's power."[83] Our immortal souls are the closest and most precious things within us.[84] Thus,

---

[74]Tillich, F.P. 124 (1916) 523.
[75]Tillich, F.P. 158 (1918) 638.
[76]Tillich, F.P. 104 (1916) 462.
[77]Tillich, F.P. 87 (1915) 410.
[78]Tillich, F.P. 129 (1917) 538.
[79]Tillich, F.P. 94 (1916) 430.
[80]Tillich, F.P. 150 (1917) 606, 607.
[81]Tillich, F.P. 129 (1917) 538.
[82]Tillich, F.P. 141 (1917) 577.
[83]Tillich, F.P. 139 (1917) 572.
[84]Tillich, F.P. 93 (1916) 427.

human beings are more than dust, they possess divinity, a royal dignity.[85] Care for one's soul is an appropriate concern.[86] Tillich preached that the deepest truths of scripture speak to our very souls.[87] He cited Augustine's comment that souls are restless "until they rest in God."[88] They thirst for God.[89] Their sanctification is the deepest basis for being "divine fighters."[90] He distinguished Sunday souls from everyday souls: "[E]veryday souls never come out beyond the dusty country road of daily life. The Sunday soul has wings and rises again and again into light, clear heights."[91] Finally, there is a relative simplicity to acknowledging the soul, doing so at day's beginning and end, in letters, and among comrades.[92]

Tillich preached of the nearness and distance of God's kingdom in life and the fact of that kingdom beyond death. He believed human beings were strangers on earth, possessing "a holy foreignness to the world,"[93] existing as "orphans on earth."[94] We are moved to seek the Spirit when we recognize the limits of creation.[95] There is a thirst for life that is basic to all creatures, but it is really a deeper thirst, unquenchable by life or death.[96] Further, the mutual tearing apart of Christendom in a world war testified to the fact that Christ's kingdom was not "of this world."[97]

In Tillich's view, the opening statement of the Lord's Prayer teaches about the distance of God's Kingdom, that is, God's transcendence of the brokenness of the world.[98] He preached that God allows this world to pass away to reveal his "majesty and grace."[99] The Easter message is that "the

---

[85]Tillich, F.P. 102 (1916) 455.
[86]Tillich, F.P. 143 (1917) 586.
[87]Tillich, F.P. 149 (1917) 605.
[88]Tillich, F.P. 93 (1916) 428.
[89]Tillich, F.P. 82 (1915) 396.
[90]Tillich, F.P. 104 (1916) 462.
[91]Tillich, F.P. 127 (1917) 533.
[92]Tillich, F.P. 129 (1917) 539.
[93]Tillich, F.P. 120 (1916) 513.
[94]Tillich, F.P. 121 (1916) 516.
[95]Tillich, F.P. 141 (1917) 578.
[96]Tillich, F.P. 82 (1915) 396.
[97]Tillich, F.P. 81 (1915) 393.
[98]Tillich, F.P. 107 (1916) 472-73.
[99]Tillich, F.P. 116 (1916) 499.

best lies above us" in the hope of resurrection.[100] For him, even more profoundly than the death-life pattern of nature, the law of resurrection is that eternal life is stronger than death.[101] The kingdom is present in lives lived sacrificially and transcendently.[102]

Our response to God is to be gratitude, according to Tillich.[103] We should surrender our self-chosen paths to God's path for us.[104] We should live our lives by Luther's teaching that Christians are free from and free for things, people, and self, "lord of all things . . . subject to no one . . . subservient slave to all things . . . subject to everyone."[105] We are to be messengers of God as individuals, soldiers, and as nation.[106] We become rulers over fear, because of our unassailable relationship with God: "We would be slaves of fear . . . if that which humanity could take from us were our best. But now we are rulers of fear, because there is something within that is unassailable, impregnable, hidden, our eternal worth, our life in God."[107]

However, our response is repeatedly the opposite of gratitude and faithfulness. Sin, doubt, rejection of God, and a distancing of God is often the state of affairs. The cross is the symbol for that situation. God's judgment is a logical response. Tillich believed the world to have entered a time in which sin and untruth lay spread upon the earth and over the nations: "has the lie, the ancient serpent, become more powerful than God, has God had to abandon the earth before the power of sin?"[108] A Spirit of darkness had descended upon Christendom.[109] It was the sin of blindness rather than evil, something that Jesus had expressed from the cross.[110] The question was whether God's love was compatible with the brutality of war, in the case of an early sermon amidst the Battle of Soissons.[111] The horror of war

---

[100]Tillich, F.P. 101 (1916) 454.
[101]Tillich, F.P. 137 (1917) 565.
[102]Tillich, F.P. 130 (1917) 543.
[103]Tillich, F.P. 68 (1914) 357-58.
[104]Tillich, F.P. 105 (1916) 464.
[105]Tillich, F.P. 118 (1916) 504; see also Tillich, F.P. 151 (1917) 610-12.
[106]Tillich, F.P. 112 (1916) 488.
[107]Tillich, F.P. 159 (1918) 640.
[108]Tillich, F.P. 106 (1916) 467.
[109]Tillich, F.P. 72 (1914) 367.
[110]Tillich, F.P. 135 (1917) 557.
[111]Tillich, F.P. 77 (1915) 382.

provoked doubt in God.[112] Tillich saw it to be a period conspiring to make humanity senseless to God's light.[113]

Given the state of reality (the "hatred, misery, and injustice without equal of this war"), it was a period which shattered optimism over the possibility of bringing into being God's kingdom.[114] The crucifixion symbolized the myriad of ways the entire human race fights against God's will.[115] The cross is the sign of God's discontentment with the ways of the world, of individuals, and of communities.[116] Grave-crosses illustrate the struggle between light and darkness in every human heart.[117] The cross is God's judgment on the world borne by those God loves (that is, Germany).[118] Germany bore the sword of Christ's righteous judgment on Europe.[119] Tillich pointed out that self-judgment was required by those bearing the sword of judgment.[120] Humility must characterize our truth claims regarding God.[121] But, the feeling of distance from God should not lead to hopelessness: at times, the apostles and prophets experienced that same distance.[122]

The seasons of Advent and Christmas were an entry point of Tillich's into the nature of God's love and into matters of peace, joy and hope. He believed that we could not bear God's coming with the sword of justice, power or spirit.[123] Thus, God came in the form of the infant, Jesus. Tillich called his listeners to sense the streams of hope in the light of Christ's birth which continue to stretch forth to humanity.[124] God can take us back to Bethlehem even amidst war.[125] In fact, there is no peace like that in the

---

[112]Tillich, F.P. 146 (1917) 595.
[113]Tillich, F.P. 106 (1916) 466.
[114]Tillich, F.P. 130 (1917) 541.
[115]Tillich, F.P. 99 (1916) 445-47.
[116]Tillich, F.P. 119 (1916) 508.
[117]Tillich, F.P. 100 (1916) 450.
[118]Tillich, F.P. 114 (1916) 494.
[119]Tillich, F.P. 86 (1915) 406.
[120]Tillich, F.P. 86 (1915) 407.
[121]Tillich, F.P. 142 (1917) 580.
[122]Tillich, F.P. 93 (1916) 429.
[123]Tillich, F.P. 155 (1917) 627.
[124]Tillich, F.P. 91 (1915) 423.
[125]Tillich, F.P. 72 (1914) 369.

stable of Bethlehem.[126] There was the hidden blessedness and fragile power of God.[127] The story of the infant Christ—weakness and helpless—teaches that we must become weak to become strong, to become victors in life and death.[128] In the face of this, in the third war-Christmas of 1916, in an enemy land, Tillich called the soldiers to rejoice.[129]

Soldierly Qualities. When speaking of soldierly qualities, Tillich spent much time on personal character and behavior. He admonished his listeners to see that God seeks out the faithful in the land.[130] God breaks willful selves.[131] Banality and sin rob us of our human dignity.[132] Bad language is demeaning (to self and others).[133] He spoke of our repeated choice either to pursue or flee God's light.[134] A good or bad conscience is a consequence of whether or not we surrender to God.[135] Even care and concern can become sinfully debilitating: enslaving, humiliating, and weakening types of care are wrong.[136]

Tillich reminded his military congregants that each person is a unique, irreplaceable being, "an eternal thought of God."[137] God takes particular, unique pleasure in each of us that we should share with each other.[138] The Spirit perpetually functions as the humanizing, transcendent force in human life.[139] The work of eternal goodness is to purify, inspire, and energize the inner person.[140] God's *dennoch* to us (God's gracious and forgiving act of acknowledging, yet saying "nevertheless" to, our sinfulness) enables us to

---

[126]Tillich, F.P. 124 (1916) 523.
[127]Tillich, F.P. 125 (1916) 526.
[128]Tillich, F.P. 92 (1915) 426.
[129]Tillich, F.P. 125 (1916) 527.
[130]Tillich, F.P. 113 (1916) 488-91.
[131]Tillich, F.P. 148 (1917) 601.
[132]Tillich, F.P. 102 (1916) 456.
[133]Tillich, F.P. 73 (1914) 371.
[134]Tillich, F.P. 106 (1916) 466-69.
[135]Tillich, F.P. 105 (1916) 465.
[136]Tillich, F.P. 143 (1917) 585.
[137]Tillich, F.P. 120 (1916) 514.
[138]Tillich, F.P. 124 (1916) 523.
[139]Tillich, F.P. 160 (1918) 643.
[140]Tillich, F.P. 117 (1916) 502.

say *dennoch* to life—no to passions, yes to love.[141]

This is why mistreatment of one another is onerous. The will of the flesh is hostility to others, self and God.[142] Tillich counseled, "Think about it, when you dishonor your brother, you dishonor the one living in him; when you hurt your brother, you hurt the one who suffers with him; when you are hateful to your brother, you have hatred for the one who is his friend, the eternal God!"[143]

We are to be responsible people. Responsibility is what distinguishes human beings from other creatures. It is our burden, and there is no clear distinction in this: "Surely we are all—through our responsibility for ourselves and humanity—equally princes and rulers, and in the seriousness and holiness of responsibility there is no difference between king and beggar."[144]

Tillich exhorted his listeners to be satisfied with what they had, but to be dissatisfied with what they were in terms of the fruits of the Spirit described in Galatians 5.[145] He presented Christ's suffering and weakness as God's way of awakening good and bad conscience, leading to forgiveness.[146] He called them to unite their wills with God's will[147] remembering that a believer is one who is "Free from every law, independent of the judgment of the world, humble before the eternal God, trusting not in our work, but in his power."[148] He counseled them that the future of both nation and self is determined by their personal conduct.[149] He led them to ponder the potentially profound impact of the Spirit-filled person who knows that the "entire secret of the Spirit is that God is near, perceptible, perceivable, living and powerful."[150]

Interwoven with these general comments on character and behavior, Tillich spoke of matters peculiar to soldiers in wartime. He called them to

---

[141]Tillich, F.P. 108 (1916) 474, 475.
[142]Tillich, F.P. 103 (1916) 458.
[143]Tillich, F.P. 119 (1916) 511.
[144]Tillich, F.P. 157 (1918) 634.
[145]Tillich, F.P. 110 (1916) 480ff.
[146]Tillich, F.P. 136 (1917) 562.
[147]Tillich, F.P. 148 (1917) 601.
[148]Tillich, F.P. 152 (1917) 617.
[149]Tillich, F.P. 157 (1918) 635.
[150]Tillich, F.P. 160 (1918) 644.

cultivate manly courage[151] to develop the capacity to look death in the face.[152] He described the joy associated with discipline[153] and the fact that lack of discipline was a primary enemy of the solider.[154] He affirmed the call to love enemies, reminding them that it is not hate for individuals in war but hate for the will of enemy nations that drives armed conflict.[155]

Tillich distinguished heroism from cowardice: "A coward fears humanity, a hero fears God."[156] God raises up heroes to benefit nations: just as God blessed Israel with David's line, so God blessed Germany with the house of Hohenzollern.[157] Sacrifice and heroism in war are acts of love.[158] Heroic actions bear the light of the world Christ called us to shine.[159] Heroic action gives each day an eternal significance that cannot be measured according to empirical time: they are profound moments in history. This explains the significance of youthful heroes whose life-meaning is far deeper than the decades of shallowness of some lives, though the events of heroism last but days or hours.[160]

Speaking of the meaning of camaraderie, Tillich grounded it deeply within the Eucharist event. The Eucharist unites the spirits of participants with one another.[161] The Eucharist should transform a participant's perspective on his brother.[162] Tillich's particular communion request was that the soldiers become more than comrades.[163] He called them to be a light to their comrades.[164]

The Fatherland and Sacrifice. The relationship of soldier to Fatherland was a deep and significant one to Tillich. In the opening months of the war,

---

[151]Tillich, F.P. 83 (1915) 399.
[152]Tillich, F.P. 102 (1916) 457.
[153]Tillich, F.P. 68 (1914) 358.
[154]Tillich, F.P. 69 (1914) 360.
[155]Tillich, F.P. 77 (1915) 382.
[156]Tillich, F.P. 69 (1914) 361.
[157]Tillich, F.P. 89 (1915) 416.
[158]Tillich, F.P. 158 (1918) 636-38.
[159]Tillich, F.P. 144 (1917) 587.
[160]Tillich, F.P. 126 (1916) 530.
[161]Tillich, F.P. 103 (1916) 459.
[162]Tillich, F.P. 119 (1916) 510.
[163]Tillich, F.P. 138 (1917) 569.
[164]Tillich, F.P. 144 (1917) 589.

he called the Fatherland their single concern.[165] He spoke of love of Fatherland and also described their homeland as a beloved Mother.[166] A year into the war, Tillich preached of service to country as service to an invisible force:

> For the sake of holy love, for the land of my home, for the sake of pride in being a German and the bonds of community which link me with the spirit of my people, for the sake of the majesty and honor and the German Empire: all of that is invisible and yet true and actual and a thousand times more worthwhile than clothing and food, work and success, rest and comfort, because the visible is passing, but the invisible is eternal.[167]

Another place where one perceives his sense of the Fatherland's deep spiritual significance is in a sermon from 1917 based on Jesus' declaration to Satan that humanity does not live by bread alone:

> [It is t]he Fatherland, for which we live and die, which lets our hearts beat more deeply, which is our home soil, which gave first imprint on our souls, which is the mother language in which we think and speak, which is the German essence which goes through us out of which we speak and behave, which is the spirit of the greatness of our people, which is the wonderful, hidden and yet living soul of our people, in which we all take part, which is God among us and with us. We live not by bread alone, and for that reason we are prepared to live and to die for God and Fatherland.[168]

Elsewhere, Tillich applied his doctrine of God's forgiving *dennoch* to Germany's response to the hostility of the world. Like a "hammer which proves its invincibility day by day," it enabled Germany to stand against the world's powerful nations.[169] Further, God's self-revelation in the heroic Christ was paralleled by God's self-revelation in German history.[170] Tillich hailed the impact of Prussian culture and discipline as a source of inner power.[171] He argued that when soul, honor, conscience and Fatherland are

---

[165]Tillich, F.P. 74 (1914) 373.
[166]Tillich, F.P. 77 (1915) 381.
[167]Tillich, F.P. 87 (1915) 410.
[168]Tillich, F.P. 145 (1917) 593.
[169]Tillich, F.P. 108 (1916) 474.
[170]Tillich, F.P. 89 (1915) 418.
[171]Tillich, F.P. 133 (1917) 552.

more important than bread and life, a person lives at a deeper dimension.[172]

The Kaiser symbolized the relationship of Germans to Germany. On the Kaiser's birthday of each of the first three years of the war, Tillich made the qualities or policies of the nation's leader the core of his sermons. In 1915, he argued that the nation owed the Kaiser thanks for the goodness of life bestowed on the Fatherland, for war preparations prior to war's outbreak, for arousing united enthusiasm for war.[173] In 1916, Tillich lifted up the Kaiser as the personal expression of the state and, therefore, the object of love for his subjects, pointing to him as a vehicle of transcendence.[174] In 1917, Tillich saw the Kaiser as worthy of thanks more than ever, for seeking peace, both domestically and internationally. The word, peace, "rings on in the hearts of our hate-filled enemies as a thorn and as a secret fruit. It rings on in the thoughts of the deceived and misled nations as doubt in, and anger toward, their rulers. It rings above all in the soul of the German people and has awakened there a wonderful, overpowering reverence."[175]

The final "Kaiser" sermon—there is none listed for 1918—became the basis for Tillich's call for further sacrifice as an expression of love to family and homeland: "Holy love demands new sacrifices from you, holy love demands life and limb! The highest love becomes the highest force."[176] Earlier on, Tillich had equated serving God with serving the Fatherland: "We should never serve to exalt ourselves, but in humility and obedience surrender to God, each for himself and our entire nation. With that, he will neither depart from us nor reject us. Give to God what is God's! First, complete and unsurpassable service to Fatherland."[177] Sacrifice for country proved that soldier and homeland belonged to each other.[178] Therefore, be sanctified, just fighters for the Fatherland.[179] Realize that death on battlefield produces victory and greatness for the Fatherland.[180] The faithful

---

[172]Tillich, F.P. 145 (1917) 592.
[173]Tillich, F.P. 78 (1915) 383-84.
[174]Tillich, F.P. 95 (1916) 434.
[175]Tillich, F.P. 128 (1917) 535.
[176]Tillich, F.P. 128 (1917) 537.
[177]Tillich, F.P. 78 (1915) 385.
[178]Tillich, F.P. 95 (1916) 436.
[179]Tillich, F.P. 104 (1916) 463.
[180]Tillich, F.P. 90 (1915) 420.

serve as an iron wall around their nation and people.[181] Keep being the light for the sake of (among other things) the Fatherland.[182] Ultimately, love of Fatherland means working that Germany may become an eternal part of God's kingdom.[183]

As alluded to in passing, Tillich saw sacrifice for something greater than oneself as a crucial element in one's relationship to the Fatherland. Tillich told his audience that sacrifice was basic to life.[184] He spoke of the great holy law of sacrifice.[185] Once again, he argued that the kingdom is present in lives lived sacrificially and transcendently.[186] God's salvation of the guilty through the suffering of the innocent was an operable theme in his thoughts on Germany's role in the war. Parallel to the experience of ancient Israel, he pointed to what he saw as the necessity of Germany's innocent suffering on behalf of guilty nations.[187] He equated the majesty of courageous sacrifice on the cross with the sacrifice of soldiers in war.[188] He saw Christ's sacrificial spirit as alive in heroism and in self-sacrifice for

----

[181]Tillich, F.P. 113 (1916) 491.

[182]Tillich, F.P. 144 (1917) 588.

[183]Tillich, F.P. 95 (1916) 436.

[184]Tillich, F.P. 68 (1914) 359.

[185]Tillich, F.P. 85 (1915) 404. Sturm cites an unpublished sermon outline in which Tillich wrote, "'Christendom and almost the whole world has become a great sacrificial altar, where the blood of hundreds of thousands of young and strong human lives is shed on the altar of the homeland (Sturm, "Holy Love . . . ," 71).'" In the 1916 piece, "Der Begriff des christlichen Volkes (1. und 2. Version)," Tillich distinguished between an individual's sacrifice over against a nation's will-to-power: "The will of the nation is the will to power. Not sacrifice but victory. Not religious [practice], but the practice of power. Here lies the decision: the surrender to the others occurs through power, the surrender to God through sacrifice. . . . Our conversion is our will to war. Our surrender is our will to victory. Our obedience is our will to sacrifice." Paul Tillich, "Der Begriff des christlichen Volkes, 1. und 2. Version (1916)," in *Religion, Kultur, Gesellschaft—Unveröffentlichte Texte aus der Deutschen Zeit (1908–1933), Erster Teil: Ergänzungs- und Nachlassbände zu den Gesammelten Werken von Paul Tillich*, Band X, ed. Erdmann Sturm (Berlin/New York: de Gruyter, 1999) 116.

[186]Tillich, F.P. 130 (1917) 543.

[187]Tillich, F.P. 114 (1916) 492.

[188]Tillich, F.P. 83 (1915) 399.

others.[189] The words of the Eucharist—blood poured out and body broken—had taken on new meaning for him.[190] Soldiers were called to die in order to produce fruit for others[191] and as a faithful denial of self.[192]

Tillich believed that gratitude to God was the appropriate response to the eternal goodness embodied in the wounded and the dead[193] whose actions were acts of love.[194] He preached that suffering was always to be "on behalf of."[195] He repeatedly called for sacrifice for Fatherland.[196] He called for a self-sacrificial enthusiasm: "Come out of yourself, so calls the Fatherland, so calls this time to everyone of you. Sacrifice yourself for that which is greater than you, for your Fatherland, for all times to come, for your God who needs you for his work on earth."[197] Tillich spoke of Germany's victimization by, and innocence before, the world.[198] In one instance, he disparaged a labor strike in the German munitions industry as self-interest undercutting the war effort in direct contradiction to the duty to sacrifice.[199]

War, Peace, and Reconciliation. Tillich would come to speak of the war as as inhuman and murderous.[200] He noted the losses caused by the war.[201] He observed that estimates and hopes for the war's end were wrong, illustrating that God's ways are not ours.[202]

Yet, Tillich preached that God draws near to us in war and peace.[203] He spoke of the peace God can give despite—and even amidst—the war.[204]

---

[189]Tillich, F.P. 139 (1917) 572.
[190]Tillich, F.P. 70 (1914) 363.
[191]Tillich, F.P. 90 (1915) 420.
[192]Tillich, F.P. 80 (1915) 390.
[193]Tillich, F.P. 117 (1916) 501, 503.
[194]Tillich, F.P. 158 (1918) 636-38.
[195]Tillich, F.P. 98 (1916) 444.
[196]Tillich, F.P. 70 (1914) 363; F.P. 85 (1915) 404.
[197]Tillich, F.P. 84 (1915) 401.
[198]Tillich, F.P. 111 (1916) 484.
[199]Tillich, F.P. 133 (1917) 553.
[200]Tillich, F.P. 116 (1916) 498.
[201]Tillich, F.P. 72 (1914) 368.
[202]Tillich, F.P. 92 (1915) 425.
[203]Tillich, F.P. 79 (1915) 386.
[204]Tillich, F.P. 115 (1916) 496; Tillich, F.P. 122 (1916) 521.

War, for Tillich, was a time to learn to pray to God and to turn to God.[205] He declared God to be standing beyond war in holy rest and that faithful service participates in this rest: "When even the nations rage and the globe is burning and we stand in the midst of the fire, God stands beyond, beyond all times and nations, in holy rest, and whoever serves God faithfully has a part in this rest of God."[206] God was at work among the nations in the war;[207] in wartime, "Eternity has appeared in time. . . . "[208] He wrote, "Every earthly fighter is a divine fighter, because God's battles are fought out in the roaring wars of nations. Beloved friends, that is what turns every battle into a work of, and service to, God."[209] Even more stridently he continued, "There is no conflict between Christianity and war. The battle sword and the sword of justice are both of God. . . . "[210] At the same time, war and suffering indicated humanity's hostility to God.[211] War manifested the struggle between good and evil in the human heart.[212] Surprise at war's horror symbolized humanity's idolatrous clinging to the world.[213]

Tillich preached of the perpetual restlessness of souls in earthly existence.[214] He warned that the lack of inner peace was the basis for weakness in war.[215] The message of Advent resonated with the cry and hope for peace.[216] He declared that the child of Bethlehem was the source of true, deeper peace.[217] In one place he put it, "Eternal, divine, saving love descends on Christmas. . . . And with him peace which no war can

---

[205]Tillich, F.P. 71 (1914) 365.

[206]Tillich, F.P. 71 (1914) 365.

[207]Tillich, F.P. 85 (1915) 405; Tillich, F.P. 112 (1916) 486. Erdmann Sturm makes reference to an unpublished sermon outline in which Tillich draws a parallel between the call of Abram to leave his homeland for a new place of God's choosing and the call of Germany to go to war (Sturm, "Holy Love," 66-67).

[208]Tillich, F.P. 125 (1916) 525.

[209]Tillich, F.P. 104 (1916) 462.

[210]Tillich, F.P. 128 (1917) 536.

[211]Tillich, F.P. 115 (1916) 495.

[212]Tillich, F.P. 100 (1916) 448.

[213]Tillich, F.P. 116 (1916) 499.

[214]Tillich, F.P. 93 (1916) 428.

[215]Tillich, F.P. 76 (1915) 378.

[216]Tillich, F.P. 154 (1917) 622.

[217]Tillich, F.P. 72 (1914) 369.

disturb."[218] One of the fruits of "this bloodiest of wars . . . [was] humanity's longing for peace without end."[219] Tillich admonished that only forgiveness could save humanity, even the nations of world, even between victor and defeated.[220] More profoundly, "Where hatred or hostility, envy or bitterness toward one another dwells in a human heart, God cannot enter in."[221]

Reconciliation with enemies was a priority before participating in the eucharist in Tillich's messages.[222] He described the deep basis for reconciliation in the image of God in Christ, possessing both the seriousness with which God uncovers and repairs sin and the gracious goodness with which God bears and forgives our guilt.[223] He believed that God had come to bring humanity closer by means of the destructive storms of world war.[224] As already noted, he wrote of the Spirit as the basis for life, as a unifying force of all community.[225] At the fourth war Christmas, he exptressed the yearning that enemies, as well, be "embraced by the band of eternal love in the spirit of Christmas, in the richness of the Spirit."[226] On one Holy Week of the war, he rued the prospect of the flight of forgiveness: "Woe to humanity and to future generations, if the hatred and the passion for vengeance and if the lies which make this war so unchivalrous and awful are not overcome by forgiveness! Only if defeated and victor extend their hands and forget what was and make a new beginning can the nations of Europe be saved. Only forgiveness can save us."[227]

Power and Weakness. The fall from power of the Russian czar spoke to Tillich of Isaiah's teaching, "mountains give way and the hills fall."[228] In contrast to this, he preached of the ordinary sources of power: the support of others; one's consciousness of duty; iron discipline and order; holy

---

[218]Tillich, F.P. 123 (1916) 522.
[219]Tillich, F.P. 139 (1917) 572.
[220]Tillich, F.P. 135 (1917) 559-60.
[221]Tillich, F.P. 138 (1917) 569.
[222]Tillich, F.P. 71 (1914) 364.
[223]Tillich, F.P. 153 (1917) 618.
[224]Tillich, F.P. 140 (1917) 576.
[225]Tillich, F.P. 160 (1918) 643.
[226]Tillich, F.P. 155 (1917) 627.
[227]Tillich, F.P. 135 (1917) 560.
[228]Tillich, F.P. 156 (1917) 629. See Isaiah 54:10.

enthusiasm; tough will; and joyful humor.[229] He described how it was displayed in the fates of individuals and the destinies of nations.[230] Tillich spoke of sources of power for inner life.[231] He called purity, sacrifice, and the acknowledgement God the source of life as the roots of strength.[232]

As noted before, Tillich preached that Christ was the one inexhaustible source of power.[233] He pointed to Christ's capacity to overcome the powers of earth and history.[234] He spoke of the basic law of nature—the strong rule over the weak—and of Jesus' respect for this. However, Tillich leaned on Luther to remind his listeners that Jesus gave the law of love to guide the exercise of all power at all levels of society.[235] He even spoke of Christ as a Lord of holy, sword-bearing rage: "Our Lord and Master was not a man with a soft, effeminate heart, easily moved by every feeling, constantly only kind and meek in dignity, but he was a man with a sword in his hand, full of holy rage and merciless seriousness."[236] Tillich declared, "Christianity is sword-religion. The sword of Christ is over us, the sword of Christ is in our hand to judge and save our hearts, our nation and all nations of the earth. He shall precede us, our armies, our souls, the one who has come not to bring peace, but the sword, and whose name is Savior of the world."[237]

Complementing his comments on power and strength, Tillich preached of weakness as both vice and virtue. On the one hand, he condemned weakness as an undermining force for a soldier and a nation fighting a war. He supported Germany's rejection of a peace rooted in weakness. When tempted by such weakness, Tillich exhorted his listeners to envision "the entire Fatherland and your wives and the questioning eyes of your children, whose future peace must be built upon your strength . . . the houses and fields of your homeland with everything in them and upon them in richness and beauty. All of these yearn for peace, for your peace, for the peace that

---

[229]Tillich, F.P. 96 (1916) 437.
[230]Tillich, F.P. 156 (1917) 629-30.
[231]Tillich, F.P. 133 (1917) 551-53.
[232]Tillich, F.P. 84 (1915) 400-402.
[233]Tillich, F.P. 96 (1916) 437.
[234]Tillich, F.P. 109 (1916) 478-79.
[235]Tillich, F.P. 132 (1917) 549.
[236]Tillich, F.P. 86 (1915) 406.
[237]Tillich, F.P. 86 (1915) 408.

arises out of your strength."[238] Further, Tillich was concerned that soldiers deal with sinfulness in their lives, for guilt makes us weak.[239] He warned that denial of God leads to betrayal and that weakness leads to hostility toward God.[240]

At the same time, Tillich preached of the great theological significance of the notion of weakness. He reminded the soldiers that "God's love is fragile and still like the child in Mary's lap . . . hidden and invisible like the Christmas story, and yet it is more powerful than all the powers of earth and more blessed than life's fortune and more expansive than the sun and the stars."[241] The poor, fragile Christ child's entry at Christmas shows that God's ways are not ours.[242] Confounding expectations of strength, God "has chosen the poorest, the weakest, the most broken . . . he wants to dwell in your heart."[243] In fact, Christ's weakness "was world-overcoming force."[244] The infant Christ—the epitome of weakness and helpless—says we must become weak to become strong, to become victors in life and death.[245] Turning from the infant Christ to the crucified Christ, Tillich described the suffering and weakness of the crucified Christ as reassuring amidst the brokenness of war.[246] More deeply, Christ's suffering and weakness were for the sake of humanity.[247] While they are to maintain overt strength in battle, Tillich called the soldiers to understand that we are to "become weak before God so that we become strong . . . ,"[248] that God desires our prayers in times of deepest weakness, in our own Gardens of Gethsemane.[249] God knows that all people, of all classes, are burdened with weakness: "The King with the golden crown, he goes along next to the beggar on crutches and the old man next to the child, and the soldier next to the mother, and the

---

[238]Tillich, F.P. 128 (1917) 537.
[239]Tillich, F.P. 84 (1915) 400.
[240]Tillich, F.P. 80 (1915) 391.
[241]Tillich, F.P. 125 (1916) 526.
[242]Tillich, F.P. 155 (1917) 626.
[243]Tillich, F.P. 125 (1916) 525.
[244]Tillich, F.P. 96 (1916) 438.
[245]Tillich, F.P. 92 (1915) 426.
[246]Tillich, F.P. 81 (1915) 393.
[247]Tillich, F.P. 136 (1917) 561.
[248]Tillich, F.P. 96 (1916) 438.
[249]Tillich, F.P. 98 (1916) 443.

judge next to the condemned: wretched and heavy-laden are they all!"[250]

With this summary of Tillich's four years of chaplaincy, we turn to the analysis of Erdmann Sturm and Ronald MacLennan to begin to interpret them.

Sturm and MacLennan. Erdmann Sturm writes that despite Tillich's later reflections on the war as a period of profound and catastrophic change, "These sermons hardly let us visualize anything of the abysmal experience of the war."[251] Further, Sturm believes that Tillich's war sermonizing illustrates that his thought "fits into the broad stream of the war theology of the national-conservative Protestantism of that time."[252] Sturm argues that the writing of Jacob Böhme, Schelling and Goethe was the basis for "a religious patriotism or nationalism . . . that profoundly defined German Protestantism, especially during the First World War."[253]

For Sturm, Tillich's sermons reveal a disconnect between his theology and the reality soldiers were facing, citing the testimony of such soldiers. A student penned these words in 1914, "'Masses of human beings are butchering one other without knowing, hating, loving one another. A curse to the few giving rise to war without having to go into the terrors of war!'"[254] A theological student asked in 1915, "What on earth have we all done . . . that we are hounded around like animals, that we are freezing and running around in loused and torn up clothes . . . and finally are killed like vermin? Why, at last, do they not make peace?'"[255] Sturm argues that it was Tillich's "war theology" that blinded him to the reality of these soldiers.[256] Sturm concludes that, up until the end of the summer 1918 war offensive, Tillich's blinding "war theology" ends in concealing "the brutal reality of war and the necessity to understand this war as the work of human beings and as sin and to take responsibility *for* this war, *in* this war, and *beyond* it, for future problems in society and state."[257] Rather than judging

---

[250]Tillich, F.P. 131 (1917) 546.
[251]Sturm, "Holy Love," 61.
[252]Sturm, "Holy Love," 62.
[253]Sturm, "Holy Love," 65.
[254]Sturm, "Holy Love," 67.
[255]Sturm, "Holy Love," 67.
[256]Sturm, "Holy Love," 68.
[257]Sturm, "Holy Love," 84.

nationalism's demonic character, Tillich's war theology legitimized it.[258] With Germany's failures in the summer campaign of 1918, Tillich renounced his war theology.[259]

Ronald B. MacLennan is critical of Sturm's conclusion that the war sermons were merely about a nationalistic war theology to the exclusion of prophetic critique of the war as sin. In a way, MacLennan is concerned that Sturm takes the sermons out of several contexts: the role of an army chaplain in building morale for the cause and in sensitively responding to the immediate needs of listeners; the fact that Tillich was occasionally accused of not being nationalistic enough; the reality of Sturm's disagreement with Tillich's notion (shared by MacLennan) that God participates in our suffering; and the documentary evidence that Tillich's thought was changing during the war (which Sturm recognizes but also minimizes).[260] Even though Tillich was silent in his chaplaincy sermons regarding political change, he wrote of a radical change in his thought in correspondence with his family. He wrote to his sister Johanna:

> Yesterday as I sat under the (Christmas) tree I suddenly had the thought that is not at all a new one with overwhelming clarity that everything living, struggling, progressing, spirit-filled, profound, attractive is outside of what we call parish and church. . . . Where are the great progressing motives of ethics? They are with the Russian Revolution and the German Social Democrats, on the one hand, with Nietzsche and the more profound artists, on the other. . . .[261]

In a letter to his father the same week, Tillich said:

> The development in the East is certainly most gratifying. The spirit of the Russian revolutionaries is the most original that the war has brought forth: Childlike, simple, profound, humane! Trotsky's telegrams and the armistice agreement are according to my perception more imbued with the original Christian spirit than the whole lot of battlefield sermons in all the lands west of the Vistula. Should it be that here on the soil of the ancient Greek mysticism a new era of church history might crawl forth from the diapers of

[258]Sturm, "Holy Love," 84.
[259]Sturm, "Holy Love," 84.
[260]Ronald MacLennan, "World War I and Paul Tillich: The Deconstruction and Reconstruction of Theology," Unpublished paper delivered before the "Nineteenth Century Theology Group" (A90), American Academy of Religion, San Francisco (23 November 1997) 4-5.
[261]Sturm, "Holy Love," 81-82.

unrecognizable beginnings through the mystical-simple character of the
Russian people? The West has created the social idea; should the East enact it?
These are my Christmas ideas 1917![262]

Sturm opines, "Here for the first time the connection between the war
experience and the idea of religious socialism becomes visible in Tillich's
thinking."[263]

The core of MacLennan's argument is that much more was happening
in Tillich's thinking than revealed in the sermons: "Against the surface
ordinariness of the preaching of a military chaplain a contrasting darkness
does rather regularly appear," manifested in mental breakdowns, in the need
for restorative leisure activities and in the content of correspondence with
family and friends at home.[264] Using a metaphor based on "sappers"—those
soldiers who undertook the risky task of tunneling beneath enemy lines to
plant explosives beneath those lines—MacLennan writes, "In similar
fashion, the surface of Tillich's thought generally remains relatively
unchanged through most of the war. But beneath the surface, huge voids are
being carved out, of which only occasional evidence appears on the
surface."[265]

The Sturm-MacLennan discussion is very useful for interpreting the
sermons. Sturm is justifiably unrelenting in preventing us from too quickly
pardoning Tillich's short-comings in preaching as a chaplain. Tillich's
ideology at the time was an undeniable German nationalism, particularly
revealed in the spiritual connection of Germans to Kaiser and Fatherland,
in self-righteousness with respect to Germany and its international behavior,
particularly seen in his repeated reference to the theologically laden notion
of innocent Germany's vicarious suffering on behalf of the other guilty
nations, and, finally, in a "war theology" repeatedly attributing
Christological and eschatological significance to the war.

At the same time, MacLennan rightfully hesitates to accept Sturm's
over generalizations. The evidence simply does not support the argument
that Tillich was out of touch with the existential experience of the soldiers
or the significance of the war as profound human sin. A significant

---

[262]Sturm, "Holy Love," 82n.44.
[263]Sturm, "Holy Love," 82n.44.
[264]MacLennan, "World War I," 5, 6.
[265]MacLennan, "World War I," 7.

proportion of the material in the sermons is devoted to communicating the driving imminence of a God who seeks to accompany the soldiers and be united with them to the degree that the wine and bread of Eucharist is united with their bodies, combined with the elevating transcendence of a God drawing the soldiers to embrace the divine in the face of the horrors of war. It is logical to assume that the realities of war, the experience of battlefields from which Tillich himself helped carry the wounded and the dead,[266] were a direct motivation for Tillich's effort to connect his military congregation with God. As for the sinfulness of the war, Tillich repeatedly lifts up the cross and Christ's crucifixion as symbols for the descent of sin upon Christendom, pointing as well to the inhumanity and murderousness of the war, the vengeful hatreds and passions of the war, the weaknesses that weigh down people of all ranks, while lifting up forgiveness as the only hope for the human race: that is a pretty comprehensive catalog of sin, even if Tillich enunciated it from an occasionally self-righteous perspective.

Political-Theological Framework: Luther

To establish a theological and political framework for understanding Tillich's preaching during the war years, the discussion now turns to Martin Luther, the founding thinker of Tillich's own church and the proponent of the political viewpoint that had remained dominant in Lutheranism at least up until the time of World War I. The point is not that Tillich made particular reference to Luther or Schelling in the sermons. Rather, this section argues that Luther's interpretation of the scriptural mandates and Schelling's interpretation of the ontological structure of reality as the interplay of powers or potencies is the structure upon which Tillich could base his participation in the war, submitting to the will of the German Empire.

Luther's comments on the role and authority of government can be seen in his 1515 *Commentary on Romans* and his 1523 treatise, "Temporal Authority: To What Extent It Should Be Obeyed." In his words on chapter 13 of the Apostle Paul's Letter to the Roman church, Luther seemed more concerned with the overreach of church authority than with abuse of power by secular government: "Christians should honor the power of governments and not use their liberty of grace as a cloak for their maliciousness."[267] In

---

[266]Pauck, *Paul Tillich*, 51.

[267]Martin Luther, *Commentary on Romans (1515)*, trans. J. Theodore Mueller

another place, he argued, "There is nothing that angers the clerics, these widely opened mouths avariciously coveting temporal things, more than when the freedom of the churches, with their rights, their possessions and their powers is attacked."[268]

Luther affirmed the basic necessity of secular government: "In the preceding chapter the Apostle taught that Christians must not throw into disorder the institution of the Church. Here he teaches that they must not violate the temporal government; for both these institutions are of God."[269] He had no illusion about the perfection of earthly rulers: "Governments (at times) are only usurped and managed in ways not ordained (by God). So also other blessings (of God) are misused, and yet do not lose their value (by such misuse). . . . Wherever there is governmental power, there it is instituted by God. That is, wherever governments exist, they are ordained solely by God."[270]

Luther's 1523 tract on temporal authority was based on a series of sermons on the topic. In this three-part work, Luther defended the legitimacy of temporal government, explicating his doctrine of two governments or realms (part one), established the limits of temporal government (part two), and described how legitimate power was to be executed (part three).

Luther defended the legitimacy of temporal authority with a full range of biblical texts: from Romans 13's direction to be subject to the ruling authorities, to the implicit presence of an ordering institution following Cain's slaying of Abel and following the Flood in the command to avenge murder; from the proportionate, reciprocal punishment commands of Exodus 21, to Christ's adherence to that guidance in his counsel to Peter against violence in the Matthean version of the scene in the Garden of Gethsemane.[271] Luther interpreted texts that appeared to speak against temporal government (the admonishments against resisting enemies) in a purely individualistic way: they concerned the Christian's response to

(Grand Rapids MI: Kregel Publications, 1954) 180.

[268]Luther, *Commentary on Romans (1515)*, 182.

[269]Luther, *Commentary on Romans (1515)*, 180.

[270]Luther, *Commentary on Romans (1515)*, 181.

[271]Martin Luther, "Temporal Authority," trans., J. J. Schindel, in Luther's *Works 45: The Christian in Society II*, ed. Walther I. Brandt (Philadelphia: Muhlenberg Press, 1962-71) 85-87.

attacks directed specifically against them, not attacks threatening others.[272] He argued for the necessity of temporal government because of the predominance of the unrighteous in the world, citing 1 Timothy, "'The law is not laid down for the just but for the lawless.'"[273] In this, the basis for the two governments is laid: the spiritual government exists to produce Christian and righteous people; the temporal government exists to restrain unchristian and unrighteous people.[274] Christians abide by this temporal authority, not because it is necessary for their own happiness, but for the benefit of the rest of the world.[275] This is the same reason that Christians can participate in secular government, even serving as soldiers or executioners, not for personal benefit, but "to restrain wickedness and to defend godliness" for the benefit of others.[276]

In describing the limits of temporal government, Luther established the boundaries of earthly authority on Romans 13's limit on government, on 1 Peter 2's teaching on the limits of human ordinances, on Christ's distinction between that which is rendered to Caesar and that which is rendered to God (in Matthew 22), and the distinctions between the divine and human spheres offered in Genesis 1:26 and Psalm 115:16.[277] He directed his comments to both secular authorities and what he judged to be unbiblical church authorities:

> [W]here the temporal authority presumes to prescribe laws for the soul, it en-
> croaches upon God's government and only misleads souls and destroys them.
> We want to make this so clear that everyone will grasp it, and that our fine
> gentlemen, the princes and bishops, will see what fools they are when they
> seek to coerce the people with their laws and commandments into believing
> this or that."[278]

Instead, with regard to matters of the soul—an inward matter dealing with one's relationship to God—the sole authority is the Bible.[279] In a specific instance of temporal government's overreaching its authority at the

---

[272]Luther, "Temporal Authority," 87-88.
[273]Luther, "Temporal Authority," 89.
[274]Luther, "Temporal Authority," 91ff.
[275]Luther, "Temporal Authority," 94-95.
[276]Luther, "Temporal Authority," 101-103.
[277]Luther, "Temporal Authority," 110-11.
[278]Luther, "Temporal Authority," 105, 107.
[279]Luther, "Temporal Authority," 106, 108.

time (the command to turn in all copies of the New Testament to state officials), Luther wrote, "This should be the response of their subjects: they should not turn in a single page, not even a letter, on pain of losing their salvation."[280] Reminding bishops and princes that their rule is to be Christian service, he warned them of the inability of subjects to continue to endure their tyranny.[281]

Finally, turning to the right enactment of this biblically limited temporal authority, Luther's counsel is rooted in one sentence: "[C]ursed and condemned is every sort of life lived and sought for the benefit and good of self; cursed are all works not done in love."[282] He taught that temporal authorities must be devoted to their subjects, must not simply defer to the powerful, must render justice to the wicked, and—most importantly—must be subject to God.[283] Noteworthy in this context are Luther's teachings that princes are never to resist their superiors with force of arms and that if a prince is known to be wrong in conducting war, the people are not required to follow him: "No, for it is no one's duty to do wrong; we must obey God (who desires the right) rather than men [Acts 5:29]."[284]

All of this can be applied to Tillich's thinking during the World War I years and even placed within the general framework of his pre-Schellingian roots. Tillich believed—as do many nationalistic patriots in all periods—his nation was functioning, in Schelling's terms, as part of the second potency, as a force of selfless love and justice, against the irrationally expansive and selfish forces of the first potency attacking it from east and west. It is reasonable to assume that he did so, at least partially, as a result of Luther's doctrine of a government's presumption of legitimacy, even that of bad government.

Tillich's description—more, proclamation—of a deep spiritual connection between soldier and Fatherland seems to support Sturm's argument that German idealism fed a mystical patriotism among Germans. This would have exacerbated the consequences of Luther's presumption of government legitimacy, taking it to the point of an uncritical assumption that such a government—such a "Mother/Father"—would be predisposed

---

[280]Luther, "Temporal Authority," 112.
[281]Luther, "Temporal Authority," 116, 117.
[282]Luther, "Temporal Authority," 118.
[283]Luther, "Temporal Authority," 120-26.
[284]Luther, "Temporal Authority," 124, 125.

to act lovingly on behalf of His or Her mystical children. As MacLennan noted in his paper, this is hardly extraordinary: for example, a similar spirit fed the animus for the entry of the United States into World War I.[285]

The problem arises when the presumption of governmental legitimacy is stripped of the third element of Luther's doctrine of temporal authority: the rule of love. When a government is not measured against the canon of love with openness and integrity and self-criticism, it finds itself on the slippery slope destined for cynical Machiavellianism.[286] Put another way,

---

[285]MacLennan, "World War I," 2.

[286]It is tempting to bring Machiavelli into the discussion at this point. In his most famous work, *The Prince*, Machiavelli wrote of policies for the conqueror. Machiavelli, Niccolo. *The Prince and the Discourses on the First Ten Books of Titus Livius* (New York: Modern Library, 1950).

Written in 1513 to please the rulers (the Florentine house of Medici), *The Prince* is an example of uncritical deferral to authority (Max Lerner, introduction, *The Prince*, xxxv). Machiavelli pointed to the dynamics of alliances with—and hostilities within—conquered territories. He offered several lines of counsel both on controlling newly acquired territory and on negotiating power relationships with neighboring governments. He thought that wise leaders understood the importance of a preoccupation with war (6-10, 15-16, 18-19, 21-23, 53-55). He argued that you must please whoever holds your political fate in their hands: "you must follow its humor and satisfy it, and in that case, good works will be inimical to you" (36-39, 66-72). Machiavelli advised: "[I]t is necessary that [a prince] should be prudent enough to avoid the scandal of those vices which would lose him the state . . . [but] if one considers well, it will be found that some things which seem virtues would, if followed, lead to one's ruin, and some others which appear vices result in one's greater security and well-being" (57). He wrote that liberality can be perceived as imprudent and that limited cruelty can on occasion prevent even crueler disorder and chaos. He thought it necessary to honor commitments only when it is in your interest to do so, and that appearance is everything. Therefore, while appearing to have all positive virtues, do what is necessary to conquer and to maintain power, for (using that line that resounds through the centuries to the present) "the end justifies the means" (57-60, 63-66). Finally, survival required a competent flexibility in governance in the face of circumstances that fortune puts forth (85-88, 91-94). Its relevance here is that it sketches the danger of uncritical deferral to authority.

Of course, *The Prince* must be distinguished from the more extensive and more deeply considered and influential work by Machiavelli—written 1513–1517, published posthumously in 1531—*Discourses on the First Decade [or the First Ten*

when governments are permitted to function under the mere appearance of righteousness, justice and love, they have descended to the Machiavellian.

Perhaps a salient element of Schelling's teaching in the discussion here is that power must be met with power. Of course, this assumes one is in a position to assert—or to foment the assertion of—such power. For instance, one wonders how Sturm imagines Tillich should have asserted—or have gained permission from the chain of command to assert—such power, such resistance, as an imperial chaplain. Tillich was already engaging in an inner battle. As noted above, he experienced at least two mental breakdowns at the front. He sought out life-affirming solace in Nietzsche's *Thus Spake Zarathustra*. Tillich's wife even bore two children by his friend, Carl Richard Wegener, while Tillich was away at war.[287] To then expect Tillich to resist the chain of command stretches credulity.

This points to the deepest weakness of Luther's doctrine of temporal authority and the subjection to rulers: subjection equals the surrender of the right to criticize. When combined with Luther's judgment that temporal rulers tend to be dolts—and even more of them tend towards corruption[288]— the avenue of effective criticism, particularly criticism of monarchical government, would have been all but closed to a military chaplain on the battlefield.

Conclusion

The apparently nonpolitical thought of Tillich's pre-1918 period is a surprising source of material with which to begin the construction of his religious internationalism. From Schelling's thought, one sees Tillich's perceptions of the transcendental impact of revelation and the centrality of power dynamics. In his personal participation in the war, one witnesses the dangers of idolatry and ideology. As a consequence, this period presents these elements for beginning to construct his ethics of war and peace:

1. The inherent provincialism of human thought must be broadened to something closer to "the greatness of the divine";
2. The voice of religion is to be that of the ultimate concern which holds up all human claims to relentless scrutiny;

Books] of Titus Livius [Livy], with its sympathetic views on republican government.
    [287]Pauck, *Paul Tillich*, 80.
    [288]Luther, "Temporal Authority," 113.

3. Power is of central importance;
4. The power position of an entity is significant;
5. Political idolatry is a perpetual risk for the bearers and institutions of power; and
6. The ideological distortion of the institutions and doctrines of religion is an ever present danger.

Chapter 2

The Religious-Socialist
Theologian of Culture

Introduction

The Germany to which Tillich and his compatriots returned was forced to face life after defeat. Democracy came to Germany in the war's aftermath by way of revolution. A. J. P. Taylor characterized the Weimar Republic that arose as a six-year experience of democracy framed by two shorter nondemocratic periods: the preceding period, four years of "political and economic confusion"; the succeeding period, three years of "temporary dictatorship, half-cloaked in legality, which reduced the republic to a sham long before it was openly overthrown."[1] Though it was a culturally rich period, it was weighed down by political antagonisms, economic instability, and ongoing tensions with the victors in the war created by Germany's shifting capacity to meet its obligations under the Treaty of Versailles.[2]

Tillich's political self-consciousness was awakened by the war. He came home to a broken nation and a broken marriage. According to the Paucks, the experience left him "utterly transformed. The traditional monarchist had become a religious socialist, the Christian believer a cultural pessimist, the repressed puritanical boy a 'wild man.'"[3] There was a live revolutionary spirit fueled by Marxist thought operating in several countries in these years following World War I, that is, at the time of Tillich's own newly enlivened political interest. For decades, the Social Democratic Party (SDP) had been a strong presence in Germany, the birthplace of Marxism. With war's end and the Kaiser's abdication, it rose to even greater prominence. However, the German socialist movement was divided among other parties more radical than the SDP, among them the Independent Social Democratic Party of Germany (USPD) and the German Communist Party (KPD). Mutinous movements in the military fueled revolutionary

---

[1]A. K. P. Taylor, "The Immediate Circumstances," in *The Nazi Revolution*, ed. John L. Snell and Allan Mitchell (Lexington MA: D.C. Heath, 1973) 3.

[2]A. J. Nicholls, *Weimar and the Rise of Hitler* (New York: St. Martin's Press, 1991) 1-12, 20-25, 29, 32, 61, 65.

[3]Pauck, *Paul Tillich*, 41, 55.

dynamics beginning in Kiel and spreading throughout Germany in October and November 1918. A Soviet Republic was established in Bavaria for a time in 1919.[4]

However, beyond Germany much was happening. Most prominent was the Russian Revolution of 1917, leading to the beginning of Soviet republics in various regions, culminating in the Union of Soviet Socialist Republics in 1922.[5] Beyond the Soviet Union were revolutionary movements establishing a Finnish Socialist Workers' Republic (early 1918), an Alsace Socialist Republic (late 1918), a Slovak Soviet Republic (1918–1919), a Hungarian Socialist Republic (1919), a Galician Soviet Socialist Republic (bordering Poland and the Soviet Union, mid–1920), and a Persian Soviet Socialist Republic (1920-21).[6] In Austria and Sweden, socialism was a significant presence from the time of the Second International of 1889. An Austro-Marxist brand of socialism influenced the Social Democrats there to be less collaborative with rightist powers than was the case in Germany in the post-World War I years. In the case of Sweden, socialism found its entry into political life to be less volatile there than elsewhere in Europe, perhaps based on Sweden's more homogenous culture. Further, there was a lesser degree of class tension and a less sharp urban/rural divide.[7]

Tillich makes specific reference to the Russian Revolution, as subsequent pages will show. However, when he thought of concrete socialism, he tended to focus on the German situation. His primary concern was with

---

[4]Nicholls, *Weimar*, 6-7, 12-20, 34-35.

[5]Richard Pipes, *Russia Under the Bolshevik Regime* (New York: Vintage, 1995).

[6]Eino Jutikkala and Kauko Pirinen, *A History of Finland* (New York: Dorset Press 1988); Jean Eschbach, *Au Coeur de la Resistance Alsacienne. Le Combat de Paul Dingler*, Fondateur De La 7eme Colonne D'Alsace, Chef Du Reseau Martial (Colmar: Do Bentzinger, 2003); Stanislav Kirschbaum, *A History of Slovakia : The Struggle for Survival* (Griffin NY: St. Martin's, 1996); Bela Menczer, "Bela Kun and the Hungarian Revolution of 1919," *History Today* (London) 9/5 (May 1969): 299-309; Norman Davies, *White Eagle, Red Star: the Polish-Soviet War, 1919–1920* (United Kingdom: Pimlico, 2003); and Kayhan Barzegar, "Socialist Republic of Gilan: The First Offensive of the October Revolution," *Discourse Quarterly Magazine* 3/4 (Spring 2002): 89-104.

[7]Albert S. Lindemann, *A History of European Socialism* (New Haven CT: Yale University Press, 1983) 247-55.

socialist theory and its relationship to Christian thought. Therefore, one finds no real attention to the broader picture of the consequences of Marxist thought on the non-German, non-Russian situation.

While he was never a party activist, during the Weimar period Tillich became an active cultural theologian and—as one part of that—an active political theorist. His political analysis was part of the broader religious socialism movement, associated with Leonhard Ragaz and Karl Barth among others.[8] The more particular context for his early religious socialism was a group which became known as the Kairos Circle, characterized by some members as a naïve group gathered to address the problems of the world "which they regarded as now open to new creative possibilities."[9] While group members were not attached to a party, their socialism kept them in tension with the conservatism dominating the German church.[10]

During this period, Tillich's teaching career took him from the University of Berlin (1919–1924) to the University of Marburg (1924–1925), to the Universities of Dresden (1925–1929) and Leipzig (1927–1929), and finally to the University of Frankfurt (1929–1933) where he occupied the chair of the philosophy department from which he was subsequently fired with the rise of Nazism.[11] While in Frankfurt, he had ongoing professional and social contact with members of the Frankfurt School at the Institute for Social Research.[12]

The thought driving the material from this period is in marked contrast to his chaplaincy sermons. Tillich was convinced that the world was experiencing the collapse of Western capitalist civilization: the war had

---

[8]Pauck, *Paul Tillich*, 69. In his thought, Tillich distinguished between legalistic, romantic, practical-political, and dialectical types of religious socialism, putting himself in the last category. Paul Tillich, "Religious Socialism (1930)," in *Political Expectation*, ed. James Luther Adams (New York: Harper & Row, 1971; repr.: Macon GA: Mercer University Press, 1981) 40-42.

[9]Pauck, *Paul Tillich*, 68, 70.

[10]Pauck, *Paul Tillich*, 72-74.

[11]Pauck, *Paul Tillich*, 288.

[12]For the impact of the Frankfurt School as a context for significant discussion and as a stimulation of analysis for Tillich, see O'Keeffe, "Tillich and the Frankfurt School," 67ff.; Champion, "Tillich and the Frankfurt School," 512ff.; Stone, "Tillich's Critical Use of Marx and Freud": 3-9; Stone, *Paul Tillich's Radical Social Thought*, 63ff.; and Stumme, 39ff.

been the natural outcome of that collapse. Therefore, the thinking of the early Marx became important for him, and Tillich brought the sociological-economic question to play with full force in his analysis.[13] His political works during the Weimar era attack capitalism and argue for a particular kind of socialism—religious socialism—as the alternative for a culture wounded by the ravages of capitalism. He shared the view that a nation's culture affected its behavior in the politics among nations. He unrelentingly delved into the economic and political issues of the period, driving them to a level of existential and ontological significance.[14] Thus, Tillich interpreted German reality as one who looked at all elements of the culture through his own theological framework, rooted in the belief that all of existence has infinite significance and is founded in the divine: he viewed all of culture theonomously. Here, I will consider Tillich's thinking under three headings: (1) religious socialist theologian of culture; (2) the religious situation; and (3) culture in general—politics in particular.

Religious-Socialist Theologian of Culture

It was not long after his discharge from the army in January 1919 that Tillich gave two public lectures that expressed the spirit of the political-cultural work to come. The first, entitled "On the Idea of a Theology of Culture," was delivered before the Kant Society in Berlin on April 16, 1919.[15] Because he was convinced that World War I had arisen as the death knell of capitalism and its ideology of bourgeois liberalism, Tillich was moved to consider what went wrong in Western civilization. After World War I there was a clear gap between traditional religion and the cultural revolution in central and eastern Europe. Religious socialism was an attempt to bridge that gap. Tillich's labors in this area were the efforts of a theologian of culture.[16] The thoughts presented in the 1919 lecture are but

---

[13]Stumme, *Socialism in Theological Perspective*, 104, 108.

[14]Weisskopf, "Tillich and the Crisis of the West," 75.

[15]Pauck, *Paul Tillich*, 64. Tillich gives a comprehensive description of theology's place within the analysis of reality in his 1923, *The System of the Sciences*, trans. Paul Wiebe (Lewisburg PA: Bucknell University Press, 1981) in which theology is considered one of the sciences of spirit (human or normative sciences) in the academy.

[16]Theodore M. Greene thought that his work in this area attested to his being "the most enlightening and therapeutic theologian of our time." Greene, "Paul

a beginning: the entire Weimar period saw Tillich offering occasional pieces—articles, lectures and books—that are the products of a theologian of culture practicing his craft.

"On the Idea on a Theology of Culture." Put succinctly, Tillich believed that Western civilization had become superficial. To a civilization that had ignored the divine, he sought to show the presence of God—the Unconditioned—at the depths of all of reality. In the lecture, "On the Idea of a Theology of Culture," Tillich stated, "[T]hroughout everything, the reality forces itself upon us that is simultaneously a No and a Yes to things. It is not a being, it is not substance, it is not the totality of beings. It is, to use a mystical formulation, what is beyond being . . . an actuality of meaning, indeed, the ultimate and most profound actuality of meaning that convulses everything and builds everything anew."[17]

In this understanding, religion does not censor or dictate culture, functioning heteronomously.[18] All cultural forms and sciences possess their own rules, "the laws that govern their employment," their autonomous quality.[19] The goal of a theology of culture is theonomy, an analysis that reveals the deepest—sometimes form-exploding—substance within those forms.[20] Culture as a whole is the realm of religious cultural analysis by the theologian of culture. Such a thinker classifies culture's elements "from the point of view of religious substance realized in them."[21] Such a theologian

---

Tillich and Our Secular Culture," 50.

[17]Paul Tillich, "On the Idea of a Theology of Culture," 1919, trans. Victor Nuovo, *Visionary Science: A Translation of Tillich's "On the Idea of a Theology of Culture" with an Interpretive Essay* (Detroit: Wayne State University Press, 1987) 24-25.

[18]*Visionary Science*, 25.

[19]*Visionary Science*, 26. See also Paul Tillich, "Basic Principles of Religious Socialism (1923)," in *Political Expectation*.

[20]Tillich, "On the Idea," 26. See also Tillich, "Basic Principles," 73, 74, 75.

[21]Tillich, "On the Idea," 27. On the nature of the cultural crisis, the theological and cultural divide, see Tillich, "Kirche und Kultur (1919)," in *GW-E/N X*, 233-36 and Tillich, "Die Krisis von Kultur und Religion (1920)," *GW-E/N X*, 293-302. In another place, Tillich wrote of the comprehensiveness of the religious claim: "It is unbearable to conceive it as a separate domain. Religion is everything, or it is nothing." (Tillich, "The Spiritual World in the Year 1926," PTAH 420:004, 8.) This is the first of many unpublished articles and speeches that will be sources for this and future chapters which are found at the Paul Tillich Archive of the Harvard-

is culturally placed himself or herself, but from that position "fashions the ideal design for a culture religiously fulfilled."[22] Further, such a person must have a basic quality of openness. Though committed to reform versus revolution, the theologian of culture "stands freely within the living cultural movement, open not only to every other form but also to every new spirit. Of course, he also lives off the soul of a definite [and necessary] concreteness . . . but he is always prepared to expand this concreteness, to change it."[23] The specific task of the church in this process is that of "removing the vital religious elements within the cultural community from chance by creating a specifically religious sphere for them, to gather them and concentrate them, theoretically and practically, and thereby to make them into a powerful, indeed, into the most powerful factor of culture, one that bears all the rest."[24]

The form-exploding potency of spiritual substance was breaking into a postwar world and was the basis of Tillich's view that civilization was coming apart at its seams. Tillich described the way such a process operated:

> The revelation of an overwhelming substance occurs in this way: form becomes more and more inadequate for the reality that is supposed to be contained by it, so that this reality in overwhelming abundance shatters it. And yet, this overwhelming and this shattering are themselves still form. The task of a theology of culture, then, is to trace this process in every sphere and

Andover Library at Harvard Divinity School. Please note that in citing these sources, I will use the notation created by Erdmann Sturm: the acronym PTAH designating the Paul Tillich Archive at Harvard; the first number designating the box number; and the number following the colon designating the file number within the box.

[22]Tillich, "On the Idea," 27. On the nature of the cultural crisis, the theological and cultural divide, see Tillich, "Kirche und Kultur (1919)," in *GW-E/N X*, 233-36 and Tillich, "Die Krisis von Kultur und Religion (1920)," *GW-E/N X*, 293-302. In another place, Tillich wrote of the comprehensiveness of the religious claim: "It is unbearable to conceive it as a separate domain. Religion is everything, or it is nothing." (Tillich, "The Spiritual World in the Year 1926," PTAH 420:004, 8.) See also Tillich, "Religion und Kultur (1920)," *GW-E/N X*, 275ff.

[23]Tillich, "On the Idea of a Theology of Culture," 37.

[24]Tillich, "On the Idea of a Theology of Culture," 38.

creation of culture and to bring it to expression.[25]

This framework has relevance for understanding art, science, individual and social ethics, and the state.[26] The goal is a theonomous perspective that would call forth a cultural community, "a universal human community . . . whose teachers are the great creative philosophers, whose priests are artists, whose prophets are visionaries of a new ethics of person and community, whose bishops are those who lead the community to new goals, whose deacons and almoners are those who guide anew economic processes."[27]

Christianity and Socialism Lecture. Tillich delivered his second lecture, "Christianity and Socialism," on May 14, 1919 at a meeting of the Independent Socialist Party, a group more radical than the ruling Social Democrats but less so than the communists. Friends of his were party members, though Tillich was not. It was an appearance that caught the attention and drew the admonishment of his church overseers.[28] The lecture was published later that year in a pamphlet entitled, "Socialism as a Church Question," and its content is also found in a report to the Protestant Consistory of Brandenburg, "Christianity and Socialism."[29]

---

[25]Tillich, "On the Idea of a Theology of Culture," 26.

[26]Tillich, "On the Idea of a Theology of Culture," 30.

[27]Tillich, "On the Idea of a Theology of Culture," 33-34. See also Paul Tillich, "Die religiöse Erneuerung des Sozialismus (1922)," in *GW-E/N X*, 311-27. See Reisz, "Liberation Theology of Culture" and John W. Murphy, "Paul Tillich and Western Marxism," *American Journal of Theology & Philosophy* 5/1 (January 1984): 20ff. on Tillich's religious socialism as a bridge between praxis and theological ontology in cultural analysis. For a less optimistic view on the empowering impact of socialism, see Reinhold Niebuhr, "Biblical Faith and Socialism: A Critical Appraisal," in *Religion and Culture: Essays in Honor of Paul Tillich,* ed. Walter Leibrecht (New York: Harper & Brothers, 1959) 51ff.

[28]Pauck, *Paul Tillich,* 68-69.

[29]Paul Tillich and Carl Richard Wegener, "Der Sozialismus als Kirchenfrage (1919)," in Paul Tillich, *Christentum und Soziale Gestaltung. Frühe Schriften zum Religiösen Sozialismus, Gesammelte Werke, Band II* (Stuttgart: Evangelisches Verlagswerk, 1962) 13-20, and Paul Tillich, "Christentum und Sozialismus. Bericht an das Konsistorium der Mark Brandenburg (1919)," in Paul Tillich, *Impressionen und Reflexionen. Ein Lebensbild in Aufsätzen, Reden und Stellungnahmen, Gesammelte Werke, Band XIII* (Stuttgart: Evangelisches Verlagswerk, 1972) 154-60. See Tillich, "Religious Socialism," 42-44, for a discussion of the relationship between socialism and religion later in the Weimar period.

The piece is divided into three sections: "the relationship of Christianity to the social order generally and to the socialist order in particular"; "the perspective of socialism and social democracy toward Christianity and the church"; and "the tasks of the church over against socialism and its parties."[30] Among the fifteen points under section one are these ideas: the love ethic of Jesus is a norm for human and social life, making some social orders acceptable and others unacceptable; capitalism's cultivation of a dog-eat-dog system of competition which creates conditions that dull the spirits of workers makes it an unacceptable economic order; and Christian love is consistent with the socialist economic order.[31] Among the eight points under section two, the following is found: socialism must be held to account for lack of subtlety in its treatment of religion; a distinction must be made between socialism's attitude toward Christianity as a whole and socialism's perspective on a state church that fails to see socialist economics as closer to the love ethic than the bourgeois-capitalist order which it supports; and, as distinct from Luther's basic doctrine prohibiting revolution, Reformed (Calvinist) Christianity defends a limited right to revolution, Thomistic thought speaks of a specific duty to revolt, and even Luther provided for exceptions to his basic doctrine.[32] Finally, among the seven points of the

---

[30]Tillich, "Der Sozialismus als Kirchenfrage," 13, 16, 18.

[31]Tillich, "Der Sozialismus als Kirchenfrage," 13-16; Tillich, "Christentum und Sozialismus," *GW XIII*, 155-57. On the absence of a basis for rooting socialist structure (directly) in the life and teachings of Jesus, see Tillich, "Die prinzipiellen Grundlagen und die nächsten Aufgaben unserer Bewegung I (1919)," *GW-E/N X*, 238 and Tillich, "Christentum und Sozialismus II (1920)," *GW II*, 30. Tillich wrote that comparing the Kingdom of God ethic with the ethic of struggle in Marxism was as inaccurate as comparing the ethic of struggle in Christianity with the classless society of Marxism. Rather, the struggle against heretics in John's letters and Christ as bearer of the sword corresponded to the Marxist class struggle, and the unavoidability of struggling against heresy corresponded with the unavoidability of class struggle within capitalism. Paul Tillich, "Book Review: Alexeiev's *Die marxistische Anthropolgie und die christliche Menschenauffassung* (1920s)," PTAH 209:045, pp. 2-3.

[32]Tillich, "Der Sozialismus als Kirchenfrage," 16-18; Tillich, "Christentum und Sozialismus," 157-59. On the necessity that socialism confront its position toward the Christian principle, see Tillich, "Christentum, Sozialismus und Nationalismus (1924)," *GW XIII*, 163. On socialism as risk, see Tillich, "Sozialismus aus dem Glauben (1928)," PTAH 209:038, 2-3.

third section, Tillich offered these thoughts: Christianity's perspective on socialism should be basically positive; reform is not enough and, therefore, Christian love should become embodied through "destroying the basis of economic misery," "stopping the possibility of economic egoism," and "destroying the roots of war through supra-national organization"; church representatives should be permitted to participate in the socialist movement; church leadership must endorse socialism; and short term conflicts over this question in the church will be inevitable.[33]

Additional Core Concepts. I will now address additional concepts which Tillich used in his cultural interpretation in the ensuing years. Heterononomy, autonomy, theonomy, and the mutual understanding of Christianity and socialism are central themes for understanding the theology of culture, rooted in religious socialism, which Tillich had begun to assemble. Three more themes became central for it as Tillich more fully developed this line of his thought in the years that followed: kairos; the demonic; and power.

Tillich wrote the article, "Kairos," for the journal *Die Tat* in 1922. The word, kairos, is the Greek term (καιρός) for "opportune or seasonable time,"[34] or "a welcome time," or "the right, proper, favorable time."[35] It is a word that became significant for Tillich's thought from this time forward. He actively participated in the circle by the same name. Tillich's stated purpose for writing this article was a summons to "a consciousness of

---

[33]Tillich, "Der Sozialismus als Kirchenfrage," 18-20; Tillich, "Christentum und Sozialismus," 159-60. Tillich criticized a book by friend and colleague Emanuel Hirsch for both a distortive amalgamating of different forms of socialism and for an inadequate treatment of Luther's social conservatism: "Book Review: Hirsch's *The Kingdom of God* (1922)," PTAH 209:017. Tillich called for socialism and Christianity to "become one in a new world and economic order, whose foundation is an economic order formed by justice, whose ethic is an affirmation of every person because he [or she] is a person, and whose religious substance is an experience of the divine in every human thing and of the eternal in everything temporal." Tillich, "Christentum und Sozialismus II (1920)," 33.

[34]Joseph Henry Thayer, trans. and ed., *The New Thayer's Greek-English Lexicon of the New Testament* (Peabody MA: Hendrickson, 1981) 318.

[35]William F. Arndt and F. Wilbur Gingrich, eds., *A Greek-English Lexicon of the New Testament and Other Early Christian Literature* (Chicago: University of Chicago Press, 1979) 394-95.

history whose roots reach down into the depth of the unconditional . . . on the basis of the conception of kairos, a demand for a consciousness of the present and for action in the present in the spirit of kairos."[36] Tillich wrote of "the invisible community of those who believe in the kairos . . . [a community] which bears all and in which the significance of all work is introduced into culture and religion, proletariat and church."[37]

Tillich rejected both escapism based on religion as well as mechanistic cyclicality built upon technology: to him, both were unaware of history.[38] He also rejected the revolutionary and conservative versions of absolute philosophies of history as dangerously devoid of respect for the past and, consequently, surprised by the outcomes of the future, yet idolatrously absolutizing their particular visions of that future. He saw the indifference of crisis theology to history—with its perpetual negation of meaning in history—as a failure to see the negation of the old as the simultaneous kairotic in-breaking of the new.[39] While more sympathetic to relativistic interpretations of history—particularly dialectical relativism—the progressive ideas within some forms of it struck Tillich as utopian.[40]

The theonomous philosophy of history which Tillich advocated takes seriously the notion of kairos: any "turning-point in history in which the eternal judges and transforms the temporal."[41] It draws from both absolute and relative philosophies of history, including "the demand that everything

---

[36]Paul Tillich, "Kairos (1922)," in *The Protestant Era* (Chicago: University of Chicago Press, 1948) 32.

[37]Paul Tillich, "Die religiöse und philosophische Weiterbildung des Sozialismus (1924)," *GW II*, 131.

[38]Tillich, "Kairos," 33, 34.

[39]Tillich, "Kairos," 36, 37, 38. Crisis theology was the movement largely spawned by Swiss theologian Karl Barth. Tillich raised a warning against confessional idolatry in "Die prinzipiellen Grundlage . . . I (1919)," 248. Tillich saw the antireligious Marx and Nietzsche functioning as pioneering forces of prophecy, Marx rooted in Jewish prophetism for the sake of justice, Nietzsche rooted in Luther for the sake of the creative, and both standing against the "god" bourgeois society. Tillich, "Kairos II: Ideen zur Geisteslage der Gegenwart (1926)," in *Der Widerstreit von Raum und Zeit, Gesammelte Werke Band VI* (Stuttgart: Evangelisches Verlagswerk, 1963) 31.

[40]Tillich, "Kairos," 39-41.

[41]Tillich, "Kairos," 47.

relative become the vehicle of the absolute and the insight that nothing relative can ever become absolute itself."[42] He described the condition necessary for discerning a kairos:

> the consciousness of the kairos is dependent on one's being inwardly grasped by the fate and destiny of the time. It can be found in the passionate longing of the masses; it can become clarified and take form in small circles of conscious intellectual and spiritual concern; it can gain power in the prophetic word; but it cannot be demonstrated and forced; it is deed and freedom, as it is also fate and grace.[43]

He saw socialism as the movement most prophetically sensitive to the kairos of that time.[44]

During his Dresden period, Tillich wrote an essay on the demonic as it enters into history. Influenced by the thought of Augustine, Tillich defined it as "the unity of form-creating and form-destroying strength."[45] Satanic power is the form-destroying principle absent form-creative power. The power of genius is form-creating power devoid of the destructive.[46] From the inexhaustible, abysmal dimension of the divine comes the demonic: "Form of being and inexhaustibility of being belong together. Their unity in the depth of essential nature is the divine, their separation in existence, the relatively independent eruption of the 'abyss' in things, is the demonic."[47] As John Wilson puts it, Tillich saw the demonic [as] the first principle or potency manifesting itself as a fallen principle in all human life.

---

[42]Tillich, "Kairos," 47.

[43]Tillich, "Kairos," 48.

[44]See also Tillich, "Basic Principles," 58-61.

[45]Paul Tillich, "The Demonic: A Contribution to the Interpretation of History (1926)," in *The Interpretation of History* (New York: Scribner's, 1936) 81. For Augustine's thoughts on the divine/demonic tension behind history, the mixture of both in actual existence, the basis for engaging history and for transcending indifference to the state (founding it in the Unconditioned), see Paul Tillich, "Die Staatslehre Augustins nach de civitate dei (1925)," in *Begegnungen: Paul Tillich über sich selbst und andere, Gesammelte Werke Band XII* (Stuttgart: Evangelisches Verlagswerk, 1971) 88, 91, 93, 94, 96. In the same piece, Tillich noted Augustine's contrast of the city of God and the city of humanity and Augustine's avoidance of designating the latter as the city of the devil. "Die Staatslehre," 85.

[46]Tillich, "The Demonic," 80, 81-82.

[47]Tillich, "The Demonic," 84.

As the root of evil it controls or tries to control the form principle.[48] In short, "Demonry is the form-destroying eruption of the creative basis of things."[49] It arises within personality, overwhelming its unity, in "the possessed state." It exists in correlation with the state of grace: "The difference is only that in the state of grace the same forces are united with the highest form which contradict the highest form in the possessed state."[50]

Tillich saw this same structure ruling in society. There, "The object of demonic destruction is the personality standing in social connection and the social structure itself, which is built up by the former. . . . The breaking of personality becomes demonic at the moment when Will to Power and Eros abuse the social form and its just claim to sacrifice [by individual personalities] for their destructive aim."[51]

Attempts by religion to free consciousness from the demonic have ranged from mysticism (ecstatic unity with the divine), exclusivism (exclusive devotion to a specific "perfect ethical-social idea"), and sacramentalism (the bearing and overcoming of demonic destruction by the divine).[52] Tillich believed that attempts by the profane world to overcome the demonic through the tools of rationality lose the abysmal depth of the divine in the process.[53] All attempts to overcome the demonic find that it is inescapable.[54]

Tillich identified intellectualism, estheticism, capitalism, and nationalism as the demonries powerfully operative at the time of his writing.[55] He

---

[48]John Wilson, Comment to Matthew Lon Weaver, 13 March 2006.

[49]Tillich, "The Demonic," 85. This understanding is strongly connected to Tillich's (and Schelling's) interpretation of the first two potencies. For a legitimate monotheism, no ontological power independent of God is possible. Therefore, both the creative and the destructive arise from the divine.

[50]Tillich, "The Demonic," 87-88.

[51]Tillich, "The Demonic," 92.

[52]Tillich, "The Demonic," 102-105.

[53]Tillich, "The Demonic," 108.

[54]Tillich, "The Demonic," 106-107, 109, 111.

[55]Tillich, "The Demonic," 117ff. In another place, Tillich referred to the heteronomous threat to autonomous rationalism, citing specifically to "the demonic subjectivity of pragmatism" ("Basic Principles," 71). He referred to "The catastrophe of rationalism and pragmatism as practical unspirituality in theory" ("Die gegenwärtige Krisis von Kultur und Religion [1922]" GW-E/N X, 310). Tillich called capitalism the dominant demonization springing from Christian humanism

wrote, "There is only one certainty, that the demonic is overcome in eternity, that in eternity the demonic is depth of the divine and in unity with divine clarity."[56] The struggle of religious socialism was against the demonic in the religious and natural realms, using elements of autonomy— rationalism, liberalism, democracy—to open up reality "to the theonomous elements of past and present spiritual situations."[57]

In 1931, having arrived at the University of Frankfurt two years before, Tillich published an article which gave special attention to a phenomenon that had been a problem for socialism during the entire course of its prominence in the 1920s: power.

According to Tillich, to assert might against might is the nature of all encounters: "Everything living, in an encounter, appears as a union of remaining within itself and advancing beyond itself. . . . "[58] The strength of one's might is measured by the extent to which one can advance beyond self without losing self. Being is "a constantly changing balance of mights in encounter."[59] The power of the group is defined by the degree to which it successfully asserts its will—its might—in encounters with other groups.[60] "[P]ower is might on the level of social existence."[61]

_____

("Religious Socialism," 50). See also Tillich, "The Class Struggle and Religious Socialism (1929)" in *Paul Tillich on Creativity*, by Jacqueline Ann K. Kegley (Lanham MD: University Press of America, 1989) 104-105.

[56]Tillich, "The Demonic," 122.

[57]Tillich, "Basic Principles," 69. It can work within "every party, confession, movement, so far as the latter make room for their work and allow for the struggle against the demonic elements within themselves" ("Basic Principles," 88). "It touches upon all areas of economic, social, and spiritual life and attempts to influence them, on the one hand, in terms of the religious principle and, on the other, with regard to the present social reality" ("Religious Socialism," 56). In a 1930 review of Tillich's collection of essays published as *Religiöse Verwicklichung*, E. Seeberg asks whether Tillich is correct in posing the comprehensive presence of the demonic within reality, while the divine is present as a "hidden power." See E. Seeberg, "Review of *Religiöse Verwicklichung*," *Deutsche Literaturzeitung* 1/17 (26 April 1930): 773.

[58]Paul Tillich, "The Problem of Power: Attempt at a Philosophical Interpretation (1931)," in *The Interpretation of History* (New York: Scribner's, 1936) 182.

[59]Paul Tillich, "The Problem of Power."

[60]Tillich, "The Problem of Power," 183.

[61]Tillich, "The Problem of Power," 183.

Tillich argued that power is neither held by an individual to the exclusion of a group, nor by a group to the exclusion of individuals. Dictatorships depend on a supporting group, and ruling groups have individuals who function overtly or covertly in a guiding way.[62] The group which rules does so because it seems to represent the will of the society as a whole.[63] The society's support of this power combines implicit consent with the demand that their leaders' power "express[es] the meaning of life and might of existence of the total group."[64]

Power, interest, and culture coexist with the law, in Tillich's view: "the law and politics of a state are always the expression as well of the interest of the groups in power. . . . Only through being the expression of an existence, therefore of a power, is culture concrete, real culture and not an abstraction, an impotent Utopia."[65] The play of power within societies is always dynamic: might against might is the continuing state of affairs. Tillich challenged Marx's belief that the proletarian revolution would bring about societal homogeneity, saying that such homogeneity would be "a static-vegetative final stage" and "the end of history."[66]

For Tillich, spiritual power exists—spirit has life—only when it "is the expression of a vital tendency," when it is supported "by a social interest."[67] Truth exerts power "only as concrete truth, that is, as the truth of a life-tendency . . . as the truth of a society . . . as the truth within society, which is inwardly powerful."[68]

By establishing power positions through which laws can be made and political action occur, societal unity occurs. Tillich saw the confrontation of trends undermining unity as the task of power, using "conviction and compulsion," that is, implicit consent and force.[69] Instability arises when power holders maintain the tools of compulsion without society's consent. Revolution occurs when a group having society's implicit consent defeats

---

[62]Tillich, "The Problem of Power," 184-85.
[63]Tillich, "The Problem of Power," 185.
[64]Tillich, "The Problem of Power," 187.
[65]Tillich, "The Problem of Power," 189.
[66]Tillich, "The Problem of Power," 188.
[67]Tillich, "The Problem of Power," 191.
[68]Tillich, "The Problem of Power," 192.
[69]Tillich, "The Problem of Power," 192.

those possessing only "the apparatus of power."[70] Revolutions succeed only when they structure their power in a way convincing to society.[71]

,Nations are the largest societal entities in which power operates effectively, according to Tillich.[72] He saw universal human society to be possible only with the creation of a nation-transcending power "in which the sovereignty of the national groups is broken by an all-inclusive power."[73]

Tillich asserted that if might defines existence and power social existence, the surrender of might and power means the disintegration of existence.[74] As a consequence, any ideas promoting the renunciation of power either oppose existence or require a different basis.[75] For example, from a position of might or power, one can choose one's relationship to them within existence, choosing to "advance beyond the sphere" structured by might and power to one more transcendent: Christianity and Buddhism are examples of religions embracing such a perspective.[76] More than this, because meaning involves transcendence, all meaningful understandings of might and power require some understanding of transcendence and imply, therefore, some degree of renunciation.[77]

National Socialism understood the importance of power, according to Tillich, but it did not see that "power without consent" and power that does not fulfill society's demand to embody society's sense of meaning "is not power but only robbery and violation."[78] Tillich called socialism to take power more seriously, not renounce power from a position of powerlessness (which ends its existence), yet to maintain its utopian vision in a way that energized its power struggle, with the hope that it would persuade society to see socialism as the embodiment of society's vision of existence.[79]

The social ethics of religious socialism took power seriously, according to Tillich. He wrote, "The development of a meaningful society, in which

---

[70]Tillich, "The Problem of Power," 194.
[71]Tillich, "The Problem of Power," 194.
[72]Tillich, "The Problem of Power," 194-95.
[73]Tillich, "The Problem of Power," 196.
[74]Tillich, "The Problem of Power," 197.
[75]Tillich, "The Problem of Power," 197.
[76]Tillich, "The Problem of Power," 197.
[77]Tillich, "The Problem of Power," 198.
[78]Tillich, "The Problem of Power," 200-201.
[79]Tillich, "The Problem of Power," 200-202.

the possibility exists to recognize the meaningful power of being of another, or, what amounts to the same thing, the formation of a community as the unity of power and love, is the socioethical ideal of religious socialism."[80]

Bridging the Sacred and the Secular

Tillich's theology of culture makes the argument that religion has something to say to all spheres of reality. I will now turn to examples of his practice of the sacred/secular dialectic: (1) faith and realism; (2) the holy and the profane; (3) Christianity and social structure; and (4) critical and creative Protestantism.

Faith and Realism. Tillich argued for the primacy of the viewpoint expressed by the designation, "self-transcending realism." It is a perspective that he applied to all realms of existence. It is universal.[81] It unites two concepts which seem incompatible: realism and faith. It challenges a realism lacking spiritual depth and an idealism that is incapable of making contact with the divine.[82]

Tillich contextualized self-transcending realism among the classic schools of realism. He was aware of three schools: technological realism; mystical realism; and historical realism. In technological realism, reason and power of being unite in order to control the world. Its presence in the modern world makes it practically futile to struggle against it.[83] Mystical realism—in direct opposition to technological realism—"seek[s] for the

---

[80]Tillich, "The Problem of Power," 53. For further comments on the philosophy of power, see Paul Tillich, "Philosophie der Macht (mid-1920s)," PTAH 112:007 and Paul Tillich, "Philosophie der Macht (1929)," in *Religion, Kultur, Gesellschaft: Unveröffentlichte Text aus der deutschen Zeit (1908–1933) Zweiter Teil, Ergänzungs- und Nachlassbände zu den Gesammelten Werken von Paul Tillich,* Band XI (Berlin/New York: de Gruyter/Evangelisches Verlagswerk GMBH, 1999) 226-32. For comments on the inapplicability of a Jesus' love ethic in a simplistic way, on the importance of law, and on the undeniable misuse of law, see Tillich, "Religiöser Sozialismus und Pazifismus (1923/1924)," in *GW-E/N X,* 371-74.

[81]Paul Tillich, "Realism and Faith," in *The Protestant Era* (Chicago: University of Chicago Press, 1948) 67. See also "Gläubiger Realismus I (1927)," in *Philosophie und Schicksal: Schriften zur Erkenntnislehre und Existenzphilosophie, Gesammelte Werke Band IV* (Stuttgart: Evangelisches Verlagswerk, 1961) 77ff.

[82]Tillich, "Realism and Faith," 67-68.

[83]Tillich, "Realism and Faith," 69-70.

inner power of things beyond (or below) the level at which they are calculable or dominable."[84] Yet, neither one is rooted in concrete existence. They practice abstraction: technological realism for utilitarian reasons; mystical realism "for the sake of essence and intuition."[85] For historical realism, "The really real is asked for in time and space, in our historical existence."[86] It is contemporaneity which historical realism brings to the table. Historical realism is committed to digging into the depths of personal and social existence.[87] Self-transcending realism affirms historical realism's contemporaneity, but takes the further step of penetrating to its depth of meaning, to its "religious depth . . . [where] the ground of our being . . . breaks into our existence and . . . judges us and heals us."[88]

The Holy and the Profane. According to Tillich, the history of Western civilization displays a cycle with regard to religion and culture: religion attempts to impinge on the cultural dimension in a way that heteronomously crushes the legitimate functions of culture (in embodying human autonomy); and culture rejects the absolute meaning of its creations (autonomy devoid of theonomy).[89]

Tillich described two levels of meaning: concrete meaning and absolute or ultimate meaning. The latter is "the basis and the abyss of meaning."[90] He wrote, "[W]e call [the] object of the silent belief in the ultimate meaningfulness, this basis and abyss of all meaning which surpasses all that is conceivable, *God*. And we call the direction of the spirit which turns toward Him, *religion*."[91] The abysmal quality of God, of the Unconditional, is its inexhaustibility.[92] The distinction between holy and profane occurs at the existential level, not at the essential level: "One cannot be essentially profane, but one can be consciously profane. One cannot be essentially

---

[84]Tillich, "Realism and Faith," 71.

[85]Tillich, "Realism and Faith," 71.

[86]Tillich, "Realism and Faith," 71.

[87]Tillich, "Realism and Faith," 75.

[88]Tillich, "Realism and Faith," 77, 78.

[89]Paul Tillich, "Church and Culture (1924)," in *The Interpretation of History* (New York: Scribner's, 1936) 231-33.

[90]Tillich, "Church and Culture," 222.

[91]Tillich, "Church and Culture," 222.

[92]Tillich, "Church and Culture," 223.

holy, but one can be so consciously."[93] Within existence, the profane lacks
deeper meaning, and the holy lacks adequate form.[94]

Applied to community, society is human community devoid of meaning
and church is community devoid of adequate form.[95] The fact that church
and society exist separately speaks against both. As Tillich put it, "the
Church is the perpetual guilty conscience of society and society the
perpetual guilty conscience of the Church."[96] True holiness is accomplished
by God through revelation to redeem church and society, religion and
culture.[97] Holiness understood in this way "means to be situated in this
tension, in religion over religion and in culture over culture and through this
superposition to lead both sides toward redemption, to fill the profane forms
with the content of the holy and to express the contents of the holy in the
profane forms."[98] By acknowledging the essential oneness of church and
culture, the truth is recognized that "the substance of culture is religion and
the form of religion is culture."[99] Yet, their existential tension and
separation remains. Humanity's responsibility is one of preparation, with
the church subjecting its forms to judgment and with culture filling its
forms with meaning. He expressed his hope in this way: "There are many
in society and many in the Church who can prepare the way. When there are
enough, and when their waiting and their action have become profound
enough, the a new 'Kairos,' a new fullness of time will have arrived."[100]

---

[93]Tillich, "Church and Culture," 223.

[94]Tillich, "Church and Culture," 225.

[95]Tillich, "Church and Culture," 226.

[96]Tillich, "Church and Culture," 227.

[97]Tillich, "Church and Culture," 227, 229, 233-34. On the communal as an
indispensable element in constituting personhood and the holy as the founding
element of every community, see Paul Tillich, "Die Umstellung der Debatte
(1922)," in *GW-E/N X*, 333-34.

[98]Tillich, "Church and Culture," 227.

[99]Tillich, "Church and Culture," 235.

[100]Tillich, "Church and Culture," 240. For other comments on the philosophical
bases of religious socialism, see "Die religionsphilosophischen Grundlagen des
‚religiösen Sozialismus (1924/1925),'" *GW-E/N X*, 454-66.

Christianity and Social Structure. Tillich saw Christianity and modern Western society to be interwoven.[101] The impact of Christianity's doctrine of creation is seen in the belief that "the divine essence . . . is present everywhere" and that existence has "a unitary meaning, a unitary origin and goal."[102] Protestantism brought attention to the importance of individual personality and conscience and the meaningful quality of daily life.[103]

But the "this-worldly" quality of existence eventually lost much of its soul, becoming secularized, being reduced to "self-sufficient finitude."[104] Citing Weber's recognition of the "psychic rewards" in Calvin's notion of work, Tillich wrote, "In Calvinism alone is there the holiness of rigorous work" as the confirmation of predestination: "Earning a living in itself, work as such, is set above the person, all inactivity is declared godless and profit viewed as divine blessing. With that, Calvinist ethics has come completely into the bourgeois-capitalist channel."[105]

Luther's doctrine of civil authority maintained the continuing passivity toward earthly authority, making Christianity's influence on contemporary society quite weak.[106] Christianity was largely assimilated to the world, "transformed into the economic and technical mastery of the world, into humanitarianism and the worldly development of personality."[107] Tillich observed this at a 1928 exhibition at the Dresden Technical Institute, "The Technical City." In response to that event, he wrote an essay interpreting the city as a symbol both of humanity's attempt to escape the strangeness of existence—its uncanniness (*Umheimlichkeit*, "homelessness")—and of humanity's search for fulfillment through technological control.[108] Yet, he

---

[101]Paul Tillich, "Christianity and Modern Society (1928)," in *Political Expectation*, ed. James Luther Adams (New York: Harper & Row, 171; repr.: Macon GA: Mercer University Press, 1981) 1-2.

[102]Tillich, "Christianity and Modern Society," 2-3. See also Tillich, "Religious Socialism," 44.

[103]Tillich, "Christianity and Modern Society," 3.

[104]Tillich, "Christianity and Modern Society," 4.

[105]Paul Tillich, "Wirtschaftspolitik unter kulturtheologischem Gesichtspunkt (1919)," in *GW-E/N XII*, 239-40.

[106]Tillich, "Christianity and Modern Society," 7-8.

[107]Tillich, "Christianity and Modern Society," 5-6.

[108]Paul Tillich, "The Technical City as Symbol (1928)," in *The Spiritual Situation in Our Technological Society*, ed. J. Mark Thomas (Macon GA: Mercer

pointed to the inability of technical creations to respond to us, that they "cannot speak as life speaks to life."[109] This creates a new uncanniness, this time toward the irreconcilably strange and lifeless technological world. It also has a life-dissipating impact upon human life which is "deadened by our being in the service of that which we ourselves have brought to lifelessness . . . condemned to be servants of the servant of humankind."[110]

Thus, Tillich sought to awaken Western existence to the depth of life beneath the veneer of technological existence. His friend, colleague, and fellow religious socialist, Eduard Heimann, wrote that their use of the word "religious" was not "designed to pull the teeth of socialism and make it respectable."[111] Rather, Tillich called religious socialism "the exceedingly difficult attempt, on both the intellectual and the social level, to work toward a new form of future society in which the autonomous life of that society will be filled with the meaning-giving essence of Christianity,"[112] attacking the problem at the point of greatest social tension: the conflict between the middle class and the proletariat."[113] With this description of

---

University Press, 1988) 182. In another place, Tillich wrote of the ambiguity of the large city, as expressive of Protestant dynamism over against Catholic being, on the one hand, and the demonic meaninglessness of pure dynamism on the other hand. See Paul Tillich, "Religion und Großstadt (1928)," *GW-E/N XI*, 195. On the ambiguity of technology in general, see Tillich's notes for "Religion und Technik (1929/1930)," *GW-E/N XI*, 248-49, and Paul Tillich, "Der natürlich-schöpfungsmächtige und geschichtlich-eschatologische Sinn der Technik (1929/1930)," *GW-E/N XI*, 250-51.

[109]Tillich, "The Technical City," 183. See Wettstein, "Re-Viewing Tillich," 128ff.

[110]Tillich, "The Technical City," 183. See also Tillich, "Basic Principles," 74, 75, 76, 77-78, 81-83; Tillich, "Religious Socialism," 50.

[111]Heimann, "Tillich's Doctrine," 315.

[112]Tillich, "Christianity and Modern Society," 8. See also Paul Tillich, "Socialism (1930)," PTAH 421:023 and Tillich, "Basic Principles," 78.

[113]Tillich, "Christianity and Modern Society," 8. See also Tillich, "Religious Socialism," 48-50. Tillich notes there that agreement with Marx's sociology did not mean agreement with his economics. The only requirement of an acceptable economics was its capacity to defeat capitalism and give meaning. This explains his careful references to relying on the philosophical views of the early Marx in *The Socialist Decision*, e.g. See Stumme, *Socialism in Theological Perspective*, 106. Tillich pointed to the religious impact of movements outside of the institutional

Tillich's general understanding of the sacred/secular relationship, I will turn
to the relationship of Tillich's Protestantism to this theme.

Critical and Creative Protestantism. Tillich understood religious socialism theologically as embodying the radicalized dialectic of the Protestant-
prophetic principle. This principle carries with it the "No" and the "Yes" of
the boundary situation, the "No" in the experience of the presence of the
Unconditioned, the "Yes" of the experience of justification, and an
openness to the new embodied in culture and community.[114] Thus, it is
important to see Protestantism's role in his religious socialist interpretation
of culture. In 1929, Tillich examined Protestantism's relation to culture in
three articles: "The Protestant Message and the Man of Today";
"Protestantism as a Critical and Creative Principle"; and "The Formative
Power of Protestantism."[115]

To a German culture insecure within the autonomous spirit with which
he characterized intellectual and theological thought of the late 1920s,
Tillich presented a Protestantism that went beyond the mysticism and
sacramentalism of Catholicism in facing the "human boundary-situation."[116]
Human beings are created to live in freedom, accepting "the unconditional
demand to realize the true and to actualize the good."[117] When one
experiences the inevitable failure to do so "in its unconditional and
inescapable character, the human border-situation is encountered. The point
at which not-being in the ultimate sense threatens us is the boundary line of

---

church in his "Nichtkirchliche Religionen (1928)," in *Die Frage nach dem
Unbedingten: Schriften zur Religionsphilosophie, Gesammelte Werke Band V*
(Stuttgart: Evangelisches Verlagswerk, 1964) 13ff.

[114]Paul Tillich, "Die evangelische Kirche und der Mensch der Gegenwart (mid-
1920s)," PTAH 112:002; and Paul Tillich, "Die prinzipiellen Grundlagen und die
nächsten Aufgaben unserer Bewegung II (1919)," *GW-E/N X*, 250-55. Tillich
contrasted the forceful "No" of Calvinist predestinarian position to the dialectic of
"Yes" and "No" of Lutheran justification- position in Tillich, "Die prinzipiellen
Grundlagen . . . (II)," 239-40.

[115]On Tillich's dialectical embrace of Protestantism and socialism, see Stumme,
Socialism in Theological Perspective, 32-50.

[116]Paul Tillich, "The Protestant Message and the Man of Today (1928)," in *The
Protestant Era* (Chicago: University of Chicago Press, 1948) 194-97.

[117]Tillich, *The Protestant Era*, 198.

all human possibility, the human border-situation."[118] In Tillich's interpretation, Protestantism brings people to face the boundary situation.[119] In facing the cultural disintegration and abysmal meaningless of the period, humanity was experiencing the boundary-situation which Protestantism announced.[120]

The Protestant principle delineated by Tillich is both critical and creative.[121] Its prophetic criticism works from beyond form: it facilitates "the shattering of life and spirit by that which is beyond both of them."[122] In Protestant criticism, prophetic and rational criticism work together to give it an understanding of truth rooted in that which is beyond being, borne by rational thought deepened by the Unconditioned, and tempered by grace.[123]

Tillich took seriously the radically prophetic "No" raised by Karl Barth's theology of crisis.[124] At the same time, he criticized Barth's group for not being self-critical, for "not pass[ing] through the fire of its own criticism."[125] Tillich sought a way for "criticism and creation" to be united to further the formative impact of Protestantism,[126] to hold all of life under the "judgment and promise" of justification:

---

[118]Tillich, *The Protestant Era*, 198.

[119]Tillich, *The Protestant Era*, 199.

[120]Tillich, *The Protestant Era*, 202.

[121]Paul Tillich, "Protestantism as a Critical and Creative Principle (1929)," in *Political Expectation*, ed. James Luther Adams (New York: Harpr & Row, 1971; repr.: Macon GA: Mercer University Press, 1981) 10, 12. In 1928, Tillich saw the religious situation to require a message to German society of "threatened" but "sustained." (Paul Tillich, "Die religiöse Lage der Gegenwart [1928]," *GW-E/N XI*, 220-24.)

[122]Tillich, "Protestantism as a Critical and Creative Principle," 10, 12.

[123]Tillich, "Protestantism as a Critical and Creative Principle," 15-18.

[124]Paul Tillich, "The Formative Power of Protestantism (1929)," in *The Protestant Era* (Chicago: University of Chicago Press, 1948) 207.

[125]Tillich, *The Protestant Era*, 208. See Tillich's 1923 article, "Critical and Positive Paradox: A Discussion with Karl Barth and Friedrich Gogarten," in *The Beginnings of Dialectical Theology*, ed. James M. Robinson (Richmond VA: John Knox Press, 1968) 133-41, and Tillich, "The Problem of a Protestant Social Ethic (1926)," PTAH 209:033, p. 3.

[126]"The Formative Power of Protestantism," 208.

Luther, the young monk, stood in the depth of this boundary-situation and
dared to reject all safeguards that piety and the church wished to extend to him.
He remained in it and learned in it that just this and only this is the situation in
which the divine 'Yes' over the whole of human existence can be received; for
this 'Yes' is not founded on any human achievement, it is an unconditional and
free sovereign judgment from above human possibilities.[127]

Rather than fighting humanism, Tillich called Protestantism to insist on
being the substance filling guardian of the material of reality (*Sachlich-
keit*),[128] deepening humanism with a sense of the Unconditional,[129] possessing a dialectical relationship with humanism.[130]

Tillich saw prophetic criticism bringing about forms of grace: "The
form of grace is the form of that which lies beyond being and freedom. . . .
It is actual in objects not as an object but as the transcendent meaning of an
object."[131] The form of grace "is realized only in rational forms . . . in such
a way that, on the one hand, it gives to them a meaning that transcends
them, while, on the other hand, it unites with the particular meaning
inherent in the rational forms . . . the form of grace is a fulfillment of the
rational form."[132] In all living forms there is "a hidden form of grace that is
identical with its power to be," not predisposing that it "become a form of
grace," but serving as the basis through which prophetic criticism can shape
it into a realization of grace.[133]

Protestantism declares, "The form of grace cuts across the secular."[134]
Tillich called the sacred-profane distinction invalid for Protestantism.
Church congregations are simply "an explicit expression of the transcendent
significance of all sociological forms."[135] Protestantism has a three-part

---

[127]Tillich, "The Protestant Message and the Man of Today," 201.
[128]Paul Tillich, "Gegenwart und Religion (1929)," PTAH 206:025, 17.
[129]Tillich, "Die religiöse Lage der Gegenwart," 224.
[130]Paul Tillich, "The Church and Humanistic Society (1930)," PTAH 420:005.
[131]Tillich, "Protestantism as a Critical and Creative Principle," 24-25.
[132]Tillich, "Protestantism as a Critical and Creative Principle," 26-27.
[133]Tillich, "Protestantism as a Critical and Creative Principle," 28, 29.
[134]Tillich, "Protestantism as a Critical and Creative Principle," 35.
[135]Tillich, "Protestantism as a Critical and Creative Principle," 36. While
affirming concrete religion, the Protestant principle "forbids a confessionalism that
considers itself absolute." Further, rather than abandoning nonreligious forms,
religious socialism penetrates to their depth to find their deepest meaning. (Tillich,

message to proclaim: first, the boundary-situation must be radically experienced; second, when a person faces the boundary situation with utter seriousness, that person simultaneously experiences the divine "Yes" of assurance, wholeness, affirmation, and meaning in the face of disintegration within existence; and, thirdly, the "New Being" enables us to experience theonomous existence "directly and intentionally" in religious institutions, "indirectly and unintentionally" in cultural forms.[136] In this way, Protestantism is released for "form-creation," creating forms which are open to secular criticism to undermine traces of idolatry, are related to the present, concrete situation, daringly express grace, and manifest belief-ful realism.[137] It does so by enabling "autonomous forms [to] become bearers of ultimate meaning."[138] To the degree that such nonreligious entities do this more effectively than the church, "they and not the churches represent Protestantism for the man of today."[139] Yet, the chief task of Protestantism is preparation for the operation of grace.[140]

The Protestant principle informed Tillich's understanding of the state: "The state is the power of a community that realizes itself in the positing of justice."[141] Tillich described three possible relationships between the state and its "spiritual values": the state as the oppressive Hobbesian Leviathan which subjects all values to itself; the Hegelian "state as God on earth" which is the "bearer of all spiritual values"; and the watchman state of liberalism, which assumes just enough power to enable peaceful existence and ensure justice.[142] The Protestant understanding of the state's relationship to the church is that the state "tacitly transfers" responsibility for spiritual matters to the church: as the depth dimension of all reality, a religious element remains with the state; however, it is not the direct

---

"Religious Socialism," 54.)

[136]Tillich, "The Protestant Message and the Man of Today," 203-205.

[137]Tillich, "The Formative Power of Protestantism," 214-16.

[138]Tillich, "The Formative Power of Protestantism," 220-21.

[139]Tillich, "The Protestant Message and the Man of Today," 205.

[140]Tillich, "Protestantism as a Critical and Creative Principle," 39. See also Tillich, "Basic Principles of Religious Socialism," 58-61.

[141]Paul Tillich, "The State as Expectation and Demand (1928)," in *Political Expectation* (New York: Harper & Row, 1971; repr.: Macon GA: Mercer University Press, 1981) 99.

[142]Tillich, "The State as Expectation and Demand," 100-101.

caretaker of spiritual matters (thus, the transfer); and the tacitness leaves the boundary between state and church murky and penetrable.[143]

Tillich saw a parallel situation in economics. Mercantilist economics corresponds to the Leviathan model. Free trade economics corresponds to the state as watchman. The state as God on earth perceives economics as "the lowest grade of holiness."[144] The state's "tacit transfer" of economics to the powers of economic production—rooted in the Protestant principle—defines the relationship in ways "that express the fundamental candor of the relationship [between the state and economic power-holders], . . . the participation of the state in the meaning of the economy, in its goal and its social structure, and the state's renunciation of its own productivity."[145]

States need the "real and concrete concentration of power" to exist.[146] The structure of this power may be overt or hidden. Tillich argued for unmasking the powers of "the great capitalists" behind democracy: "Concealed by democracy, they utilize it and undermine it, they bear it and at the same time destroy it."[147] Instead, a polarity between the power of being of the true power-holders and the ideal of democracy as corrective must be made manifest.[148]

When Tillich turned to the relationship among states, he stated, "The polarity of criticism and formative power, of what ought to be and what is, is valid for the inner structure of the state as well as for the relationship of states to one another."[149]

To Tillich, an expanding community required a deeper source of meaning, and he found this in the church, but only in a way consistent with the Protestant principle of self-criticism, "when the church always stands dialectically towards its own forms and existence."[150] Nonetheless, given the inescapability of this meaning-giving basis, "political unity can extend only as far as church unity."[151]

---

[143]Tillich, "The State as Expectation and Demand," 105.

[144]Tillich, "The State as Expectation and Demand," 106-107.

[145]Tillich, "The State as Expectation and Demand," 108.

[146]Tillich, "The State as Expectation and Demand," 108.

[147]Tillich, "The State as Expectation and Demand," 110.

[148]Tillich, "The State as Expectation and Demand," 111.

[149]Tillich, "The State as Expectation and Demand," 113.

[150]Tillich, "The State as Expectation and Demand," 113.

[151]Tillich, "The State as Expectation and Demand," 113.

Tillich saw the proletariat as the embodiment of the experience of the threat of the boundary situation enunciated by the "No" of the Protestant dialectic.[152] In three 1922 writings (published in the Gesammelte Werke as a group under the title "Masse und Geist"), Tillich addressed the impact of capitalism on the life of the masses, having been moved my "its misery, its formlessness, and its creative force."[153] The texts are "Masse und Persön-lichkeit," (addressing the ethical-social dimension), "Masse und Bildung," (focusing on the spiritual/intellectual/pedagogical dimension), and "Masse und Religion" (dealing with the philosophical-religious dimension). In the first, Tillich declared that "out of the depth of a new substance, a new humanity must be born in which the contrast between mass and personality is overcome."[154] In the second, he advocated for a pattern of enculturation to develop in which a "mechanized masses" are replaced by the organic and dynamic masses.[155] In the third, he called for religion in the sense of an inner transcendence—a connection of the meaning of all things with the Unconditioned—combined with an immanence in which the masses see "the actuality of the holy not in the soul and not in the church, but in the world."[156]

Tillich was convinced that Protestantism had failed the proletariat in a basic way: it called the masses to religious decision, while being silent about the religious significance of the social and political life. In this, Protestantism was untrue to its unrelenting principle of holding everything conditional accountable to the unconditioned depth of the prophetic spirit.[157] The failure of Protestantism with respect to the proletariat was its failure to embody its principle.[158]

---

[152]Tillich, "The Class Struggle and Religious Socialism," 102ff.

[153]Paul Tillich, "Masse und Geist (1922)", *GW II*, 35.

[154]Tillich, "Masse und Geist (1922)", *GW II*, 35.

[155]Tillich, "Masse und Geist (1922)", *GW II*, 35.

[156]Tillich, "Masse und Geist (1922)", *GW II*, 35.

[157]Paul Tillich, "The Protestant Principle and the Proletarian Situation" (1931) in *The Protestant Era* (Chicago: University of Chicago Press, 1948) 161-62.

[158]Tillich, "The Protestant Principle and the Proletarian Situation," 163. In "Die gegenwärtige Krisis von Kultur und Religion," Tillich wrote of a twofold cultural crisis: (1) "the creation of the mechanized masses and the individualistically formed individual persons"; (2) "the impossibility of rationally creating and overlapping spiritual substance." Tillich, "Die gegenwärtige Krisis von Kultur und Religion,"

Consistent with the religious socialism rooted in it, the Protestant principle understands humanity as the unity of body and spirit, rather than dualistically. Tillich believed that institutional Protestantism had failed to do this in social ethics.[159] Again, the primary victims of this failure were the masses of the proletariat. As previously noted, the primary demonic force perpetrating this victimization was capitalism, an ideology, given its concealment of the truth regarding its impact upon existence.[160]

Tillich called it one of the Protestant principle's most significant tasks to expose such "concrete ideologies" within itself and culture at large.[161]

310.

[159]Tillich, "The Protestant Principle and the Proletarian Situation," 167.

[160]Tillich, "The Protestant Principle and the Proletarian Situation," 168-69. See "Sozialismus und Christentum (1919)," GW-E/N X, 231-32, on the class struggle and international capitalism. See Tillich's inquiry into capitalism as innately sinful in the outline notes "Ist der Kapitalismus an sich Sünde? (1920s)" PTAH 112:001. On the objectification brought about by capitalism, see Tillich, "Christentum, Sozialismus, und Nationalismus (mid-1920s)," 163. For Tillich's condemnation of the Von Papen government for the ideological use of Christianity as a justification for continuing to provoke class struggle, at the cost of the proletariat, see "Christentum als Ideologie (1932)," GW XIII, 179, 180. On the issue of dehumanization by the capitalist structure, see Shinn, "Tillich as Interpreter," 44-50; and Richard, "The Socialist Tillich," 162ff. For the resonance of Tillich's thought on the masses with liberation's thought on the poor, see Richard, "The Socialist Tillich," 168; and Bonino, "Rereading Tillich," 19-33. Bonino wrote of socialism as a consequence of the life experience of both Tillich and the liberation theology school: it was the result "of a life experience—war in the case of Tillich and the 'encounter of the poor' in our case." Bonino, "Rereading Tillich," 27. Bonino overstated a distinction when he commented on liberation thought: "Here, we were not challenged by the 'revolutionary worker' but by the 'nonperson,' those whom Marx would discard as revolutionary agents—the *lumpen*." Bonino, "Rereading Tillich," 28. Dehumanization, depersonalization, "thingification" is the issue with both the *lumpen* and the worker. On Tillich's correction of Lukacs and orthodox Marxism in objectifying the masses through "a hidden attempt to master nature," see Champion, "Tillich and the Frankfurt School," 520.

[161]Tillich, "The Protestant Principle and the Proletarian Situation (1931)," 170. On Tillich's appropriation of Marx's concept of ideology, see Terence M. O'Keeffe, "Ideology and the Protestant Principle," *Journal of the American Academy of Religion* 51/2 (June 1983): 288ff.

Historical Protestantism had failed the proletariat on at least five fronts, according to Tillich: reducing all truth to "the letters of a sacred book"; excluding worldly activity from its concern; emphasizing the conscious and the rational while ignoring the impact of the subconscious on human life; replacing Catholic hierarchy with the worldly hierarchies of political absolutism and capitalism which stand against the proletariat; and endorsing nationalism and the powers behind it.[162]

For Tillich, anticipation, "calling," and the bridging of the sacred and secular divide are central to giving hope to the proletarian situation. Anticipation is rooted in the tension between an awful present and a hoped for future. The Protestant principle works to maintain this, while keeping it from falling into utopianism.[163] Religious socialism saw the proletariat to possess the call and impulse to engage in the class struggle against capitalism.[164] That the Protestant principle would be embodied in the proletarian movement displays the limitlessness of the unconditional: it "permeates every moment of daily life and makes it holy,"[165] it bridges the sacred/secular divide. Tillich suspected that socialism itself, "under the disguise of a secular theory and practice," represented "a special religious type, namely the type that originates in Jewish prophetism and transcends the given world in the expectation of a 'new earth'."[166]

Culture in General—Politics in Particular

Perhaps the two most important examples of cultural analysis by Tillich during Weimar were his books, *The Religious Situation* and *The Socialist Decision*. The first is a general analysis of German culture, midway through the 1920s. The second is a concentrated political analysis of Germany as it was about to fall to Hitler.

---

[162]Tillich, "The Protestant Principle and the Proletarian Situation," 176-80.

[163]Tillich, "The Protestant Principle and the Proletarian Situation," 171-72.

[164]lTillich, "The Protestant Principle and the Proletarian Situation," 174. See also Tillich, "Religious Socialism," 47. On class stratification and the class struggle, see Paul Tillich, "Klassenschichtung und Geisteslage (1926)," *GW-E/N XI*, 18ff, and Tillich, "The Class Struggle and Religious Socialism," 95ff.

[165]Tillich, "The Protestant Principle and the Proletarian Situation," 174-75.

[166]Tillich, "The Protestant Principle and the Proletarian Situation," 175.

The Religious Situation. Wilhelm and Marion Pauck called Tillich's
The Religious Situation his first successful book. Tillich's concern in it was
to give a comprehensive analysis of the impact of capitalism upon it.[167] The
year of its German publication (1926) was one Tillich characterized by
political disillusionment, an economically weaker socialism, and—
spiritually—"pacification . . . tiredness . . . resignation."[168] To him, capitalism had separated the temporal from its roots in the eternal, ending in meaninglessness: "If any present has meaning it has eternity."[169] Tillich saw
capitalism as blinding humanity to God's glory in creation, as failing to free
humanity from the demonic in nature, and ignoring "the sacredness of
human personality."[170]

---

[167]The full title of the work is *Die religiöse Lage der Gegenwart*. The inclusion
of *der Gegenwart* ("of the present") communicates Tillich's concern for meaning
in a particular historical context. Tillich's existential sensitivity was embodied in
his regular analysis of the "situation" or *Lage*. Among the situational reflections he
offered during the Weimar years were these: "Kairos. Ideen zur Geisteslage der
Gegenwart (1926)"; "Klassenschichtung und Geisteslages (1926)"; "Die Bedeutung
der Gesellschaftslage für das Geistesleben (1927)," *GW II*, 133-38; "Die
gegenwärtige Lage des Protestantismus (mid-1920s)" PTAH 110:010; "Die geistige
Lage des Sozialismus (late 1920s)," PTAH 201:001; "Die religiöse Lage der
Gegenwart (1928)"; "Die Geisteslage der Gegenwart: Ruckblick und Ausblick
(1930)," *GW X*, 108-120; "Die Protestantismus und die proletarische Situation
(1930)," *GW-E/N XI*, 287-290; "The Protestant Principle and the Proletarian
Situation (1931)"; "Die geistige Lage des Sozialismus (1931)"; "Der Sozialismus
und die geistige Lage der Gegenwart (1932)," *Neue Blätter für den Sozialismus*
(Potsdam) 3/1 (January 1932): 14-16. (Discussion with Henrik de Man of a
broadcast talk by Gustav Radbruch.)
[168]Tillich, "The Spiritual World in the Year 1926," 3, 9. At about the same
time, Tillich weighed whether it was necessary to either consolidate the gains of the
Protestant dialectic or radicalize it, leaning himself in the radical direction. See
Tillich, "Die gegenwärtige Lage des Protestantismus (mid-1920s)."
[169]Paul Tillich, *The Religious Situation*, 1926, trans. H. Richard Niebuhr (New
York: Meridian Books, 1932) 35.
[170]Tillich, *The Religious Situation*, 48, 49. On the influence of Max Weber's
thoughts regarding the impact of capitalism upon Tillich's thesis in *The Religious
Situation*, see Ronald H. Stone, "Paul Tillich: On the Boundary between
Protestantism and Marxism," *Laval théologique et philosophique* 45/3 (October
1989). Stone writes: "Max Weber haunts the socialist writing of Paul Tillich" (395).

As a consequence, Tillich called science to stop focusing on the particular to the neglect of the totality, on parts versus structure, on explaining
rather than understanding, on existence to the exclusion of essence and
meaning.[171] Tillich was concerned about a scientific methodology—from
the physical to the social sciences—which failed to connect specific
elements with a larger context of meaning. He called for a "belief-ful
realism" open to the Unconditional, the eternal.[172] He praised expressionism
for challenging the self-sufficiency of either the artist or the object,
expressing instead "the transcendental reference in things to that which lies
beyond them is expressed."[173]

Tillich attacked the politics of capitalism in which "the attitude toward
material things comes to be dominating, loveless, without the sense of
community with them,"[174] and where workers "are [so] impoverished
spiritually for the sake of their service to the machine, that the mechanical
production of the human mass takes place . . . soldering together atomized
individuals which have lost all individual quality."[175] Tillich spoke for a
religious socialism that raised "the demand for that which we have
designated *belief-ful realism*, that is an unconditional acceptance of the
serious importance of our concrete situation in time and of the situation of
time in general in the presence of eternity," which supports unromantic,
antiutopian, yet hopeful transcendence beyond the capitalist illusion of

---

[171] *The Religious Situation*, 59-78. In this, Tillich was arguing for the deepening
of scientific inquiry, not the restriction thereof. See his piece, "The Freedom of
Science (1932)," in *The Spiritual Situation in Our Technological Society* ed.
J. Mark Thomas (Macon GA: Mercer University Press, 1988) 61-64.

[172] Tillich, *The Religious Situation*, 81-83. In a 1927 article, Tillich called
belief-ful realism "a comprehensive attitude . . . not a theoretical worldview, but
also not a life-praxis, but rather [it] lies at a level of life beneath the split between
theory and praxis." Paul Tillich, "Über gläubigen Realismus (1927)," in *Main
Works/Hauptwerke*, vol. 4 of *Writings in the Philosophy of Religion* (Berlin/New
York: De Gruyter, 1987) 194. On the "belief-ful" element in belief-ful realism,
Tillich elsewhere wrote that it has to do with espousing that "points beyond itself
to its unconditional, eternal meaning." Tillich, "Sozialismus aus dem Glauben," 3.
See also Tillich, "Basic Principles," 70.

[173] Tillich, *The Religious Situation*, 88. See also Tillich, "Basic Principles," 70.

[174] Tillich, *The Religious Situation*, 106.

[175] Tillich, *The Religious Situation*, 111. See also "Basic Principles," 74, 75, 76,
77-78.

"self-sufficient finitude."[176]

In the realm of ethics, Tillich believed that capitalism was hypocritical in its morality and proposed a communal life resting "on the foundation of the eternal."[177] It would understand sexuality as realizing "eternal meanings present in the relation of the sexes," medicine as reviving "the central mind-body, doctor-patient relationship,"[178] education as "rest[ing] upon a common relationship of both teacher and taught to something ultimate,"[179] and "an ideal of community and personality which has transcendent references and which every one, quite apart from his cultural background and education, is able to realize."[180]

Lastly, Tillich turned to religion itself. He wrote of "act[ing] and wait[ing] in the sense of *Kairos* [which] means to wait upon the invasion of the eternal and to act accordingly."[181] He criticized Catholicism and Protestantism for cultivating a culture of "self-sufficient finitude."[182] Beyond the autonomy of capitalism and the heteronomy of church institutions, Tillich pointed to theonomy and its goal of "the free devotion

---

[176]Tillich, *The Religious Situation*, 116. Tillich covers the religious socialist alternative to the economics and materialism of capitalism in "Die ökonomische Gesichtsauffassung, ihre geistigen Zusammenhänge und ihre gegenwärtige Umbildung," (1923/1924) in *GW-E/N X*, 404-25. On Tillich's concept of "the unconditional demand" as a corrective to the objectification of the prophetic in Reinhold Niebuhr and Juan Luis Segundo, see McCann, "Tillich's Religious Socialism," 88ff.

[177]Tillich, *The Religious Situation*, 144-45. See also "Religious Socialism," where Tillich described a religious socialistic ethics as dynamic, seeking out the demand present within being itself, as "devotion to the dynamic meaning and its demands that are inherent in things and situations." Tillich, "Religious Socialism," 51.

[178]Tillich, *The Religious Situation*, 141.

[179]Tillich, *The Religious Situation*, 146-47. See also Tillich, "Basic Principles," 85-86.

[180]Tillich, *The Religious Situation*, 152-53. Elsewhere, Tillich wrote of Protestant ethics as a communal reality, as a matter that goes beyond abstract universals: "every real ethic is concrete, it stands in the kairos . . . [as a] law of dynamic truth." See Tillich, "The Problem of a Protestant Social Ethic," 7, 9.

[181]Tillich, *The Religious Situation*, 176.

[182]Tillich, *The Religious Situation*, 186.

of finite forms to the eternal."[183] The church could contribute to this through "a union of the priestly spirit of [Catholicism] and the prophetic spirit of [Protestantism]."[184]

The Socialist Decision. As Nazism's rise to power seemed to be drawing near, two of Tillich's responses to that prospect caught the attention of National Socialists. Tillich prepared the document, "The Church and the Third Reich: Ten Theses," for a 1932 book sent to Hitler entitled, *Die Kirche und das Dritte Reich: Fragen und Forderungen deutscher Theologen.*[185] In it, he warned the Protestant Church against passively surrendering to Nazi demonism through an escapist and otherworldly understanding of the Kingdom of God and the abandonment of its prophetic role of advocating for social and political justice.[186]

The book, *The Socialist Decision,* was the culmination of Tillich's political analysis during Weimar. It is a work which capped the dialectical struggle Tillich undertook throughout his post-World War I period in Germany. The interplay between religion and national identity that one sees in Tillich was manifested in broader cultural tensions which arose from this period into the early years of Hitler's rule.[187] Before discussing the book, I will attempt to describe the nature of that tension.

Tillich did not embrace socialism to the complete exclusion of political romanticism. His treatment of romanticism showed a commitment to bringing socialism critically and creatively to bear on the cultural issues of the day. Tillich knew the cultural fabric of Germany to be one characterized by this same tension: socialism ran up against a nation that had evolved an organic sense of its identity. Anthony Smith has written of the roots of this "German 'organic version' of nationalism."[188] It was informed by Johann

---

[183]Tillich, *The Religious Situation,* 216.

[184]Tillich, *The Religious Situation,* 218.

[185]Mark Kline Taylor, "Introductory Comment" to "The Church and the Third Reich: Ten Theses," by Paul Tillich, in *Paul Tillich: Theologian of the Boundaries,* ed. Mark Kline Taylor (London: Collins, 1987) 116.

[186]Paul Tillich, "The Church and the Third Reich: Ten Theses," in *Paul Tillich: Theologian of the Boundaries,* ed. Mark Kline Taylor (London: Collins, 1987) 117-18.

[187]I will comment on those tensions briefly in the following chapter, specifically with regard to the rupture in German theological circles.

[188]Anthony D. Smith, *Theories of Nationalism* (New York: Harper & Row,

Gottfried von Herder's view that the world is composed of a number of distinct cultures, "unique organic 'nations' or language groups."[189] Under the influence of Johann Gottlieb Fichte, it asserted that national identity arises by means of struggle and requires the absorption of individual identity into national identity. Thus, education became the primary tool for accomplishing this, enculturating the individual into the collective national will.[190]

For Tillich this was an existential struggle. He freely expressed his roots in romanticism: "Romanticism means not only a special relation to nature; it means also a special relation to history. To grow up in towns in which every stone is a witness of a period many centuries past produces a feeling for history, not as a matter of knowledge, but as a living reality in which the past participates in the present."[191] He wrote of the paternalistic culture of his youth, a Prussian society which was "authoritarian without being totalitarian," Lutheran patriarchy manifested in family, school, and empire, and a highly developed, hierarchical bureaucracy, expressed most impressively (to Tillich) in the military. Tillich's enthusiasm for military display dissipated only with the beginning of his experiences on the front line of the First World War.[192] The conservative Lutheran culture from which he came distorted and judged democracy and socialism to be both wrongly disruptive and criminal.[193]

The romanticism of Schelling expressed Tillich's appreciation of nature. The sea was a source of thinking for him on matters ranging from the infinite to the "dynamic mass."[194] Reading Nietzsche during the war reaffirmed the Schellingian influence in his thinking. According to Ratschow, Nietzschean thought was a path for Tillich toward a vitalism rooted in Schelling.[195] Tillich's membership in the Prussian civil service bureaucracy informed his sense of the duty of individuals to "the 'organic

---

1971) 17.

[189]Smith, *Theories of Nationalism*, 17.

[190]Smith, *Theories of Nationalism*, 17. See also K. R. Minogue, *Nationalism* (New York: Basic Books, 1967) 57-69.

[191]Tillich, "Autobiographical Reflections," 5.

[192]Tillich, "Autobiographical Reflections," 7.

[193]Tillich, "Autobiographical Reflections," 9.

[194]Tillich, *On the Boundary*, 17, 18.

[195]Ratschow, *Paul Tillich*, 18. See Tillich, *On the Boundary*, 18.

whole'" and his willingness to submit to authority.[196] The religious milieu of his youth—maturing within a pastor's home in a small German town—provided the early context for a sense of the mysteries of religious thought and tradition.[197]

However, for Tillich, these were all matters of the givenness of the past, not the predisposition for the future. He wrote,

> My attachment to my native land in terms of landscape, language, tradition and mutuality of historical destiny has always been so instinctive that I could never understand why it should have to be made an object of special attention. The overemphasis of cultural nationalism in national education and intellectual productivity is an expression of insecurity about national ties. . . . I have always felt so thoroughly German by nature that I could not dwell on the fact at length. Conditions of birth and destiny cannot really be questioned. We should instead ask: What shall we do with this which is given in our lives? What should be our criterion for evaluating society and politics, intellectual and moral training, cultural and social life?[198]

Tillich referred to roots of a more revolutionary spirit in his past and in his religious tradition: "Perhaps it was a drop of the blood which induced my grandmother to build barricades in the Revolution of 1848, perhaps it was the deep impression of the words of the prophets against injustice and the words of Jesus against the rich; all these were words which I learned by heart in my early years."[199] While World War I still raged, he discovered the depth of the class division in Germany and the association of the church with the ruling class from the perspective of the working class.[200] The war served as a crucible for past presuppositions and as a basis for learning regarding politics and war, as well as economics, imperialism and classism.[201] Tillich wrote of his entry into the religious socialist movement as "the definitive break with philosophical idealism and theological transcendentalism," bringing about an awakening "to the religious significance of political Calvinism and social sectarianism, over against the

---

[196]Tillich, *On the Boundary*, 21-22.
[197]Tillich, *On the Boundary*, 59.
[198]Tillich, *On the Boundary*, 93-94.
[199]Tillich, "Autobiographical Reflections," 12.
[200]Tillich, "Autobiographical Reflections," 12.
[201]Tillich, *On the Boundary*, 32-33.

predominantly sacramental character of my own Lutheran tradition."[202]

These tensions within Tillich presaged his later self-positioning on the boundary. Tillich was conscious of social guilt from early on for being part of the privileged class. His attraction to the city saved him from undue romanticism and affirmed the city as central to "the critical side of intellectual and artistic life."[203] A sense of duty was present in every conscious act of Tillich's life: in basic decisions; in decisions against tradition especially; in insecurity in the face of the new; and in a desire for systematic order.[204] Tillich later saw his boundary position as the reason for not completely rejecting feudalism with his choice in favor of socialism.[205] In the early 1950s, Tillich summarized this tension: "The balance of [the romantic and revolutionary motives] has remained the basic problem of my thought and life ever since [the decision in favor of religious socialism]."[206] With these thoughts in mind, I turn to the most important product of Tillich's navigation of the stormy political waters raging as Nazism loomed threateningly on the horizon, *The Socialist Decision*.

The Socialist Decision is an extensive examination of the weaknesses of German socialism, published in the twilight of the Weimar Republic. Max Horkheimer later noted, "'after reading some sections of his writings, it was I who told him that, in my opinion, if he did not leave the country, he would pay with his life.'"[207] The book examines the interplay of socialism, bourgeois liberalism, and political romanticism, seeking a path to the future with seriousness and hope.[208]

---

[202]Tillich, "Author's Introduction," xviii.

[203]Tillich, *On the Boundary*, 19-20, 17.

[204]Tillich, *On the Boundary*, 22.

[205]Tillich, *On the Boundary*, 20.

[206]Tillich, "Autobiographical Reflections," 9. Mark Lewis Taylor has written of the tension between the prophetic and romantic spirits as it applies to the political milieu of the United States in the early twenty-first century. See Taylor, "Prophetic Spirit and Political Romanticism in the U.S. Today." Unpublished paper delivered before the "Tillich: Issues in Theology, Religion and Culture Group" (A18-125), American Academy of Religion, San Diego (18 November 2007).

[207]Bonino, "Rereading Tillich," 19-33.

[208]Paul Tillich, *The Socialist Decision* (1933), trans. Franklin Sherman (New York: Harper & Row, 1977) xxxvi-xxxvii. Comments helpful for understanding the context of *The Socialist Decision* are found in the writings of Ronald Stone: "Tillich: Radical Political Theologian," *Religion in Life* 46 (Spring 1977): 44-53;

In *The Socialist Decision*, Tillich described a double basis for political behavior: the myths of origin and the unconditional demand of the new. The first grows out of the "being" side of humanity. The second arises out of humanity's self-consciousness. Tillich pointed out, "The demand that human beings experience is unconditional, but it is not alien to human nature,"[209] leading humanity to true fulfillment, leading to justice.[210] Tillich saw these two roots at the heart of the primary political movements of his day: "The consciousness oriented to the myth of origin is the root of all conservative and romantic thought in politics. . . . The breaking of the myth of origin by the unconditional demand is the root of liberal, democratic, and socialist in politics."[211]

The primary characteristics of the myths of origin are cyclicality, the sacrality of space, and the holiness of being: space dominates time.[212] The sacralization of space is expansive and permits a single ethic: "Might makes right."[213] Tillich simultaneously affirmed the powers of origin in the principle of political romanticism, while strongly opposing its destructive irrationality.[214]

The shattering of the myth of origin is what Tillich called "the world-historical mission of Jewish prophetism."[215] Prophetism and rationalism

<hr>

"Tillich's Critical Use of Marx and Freud": 3-9; and *Paul Tillich's Radical Social Thought*. Franklin Sherman has advocated the fruitfulness of Tillich's thought in *The Socialist Decision* for the construction of modern socialism in "Tillich's Social Thought: New Perspectives," *The Christian Century* 93/6 (25 February 1976). Jean Richard has applied thoughts from *The Socialist Decision* on the national identity/democracy dialectic to the Quebec-Canada issue in "The Question of Nationalism," 35-43.

[209]Tillich, *The Socialist Decision*, 5.
[210]Tillich, *The Socialist Decision*, 5-6.
[211]Tillich, *The Socialist Decision*, 4, 5.
[212]Tillich, *The Socialist Decision*, 13-17. Tillich spoke elsewhere of a sacramentalism in which relationships "to the soil, possessions, the family, the tribe, the class, the nation, and the politicocultic hierarchy" have sacred significance. Tillich, "Basic Principles," 73.
[213]Tillich, *The Socialist Decision*, 19.
[214]Tillich, *The Socialist Decision*, 40.
[215]Tillich, *The Socialist Decision*, 20. On Tillich's connection of the prophetic to Marx, see John Carey, "Tillich, Marx, and the Interpretation of History," 9-12.

threaten political romanticism.[216] Reason sees reality as a source of tools for rationality and empirical analysis, dissipating the power of the myths of origin.[217] While prophetism maintains its tie to mythic origins—that is, it seeks a return to their deepest meaning—autonomy severs its connection to origins.[218] Prophetism primarily seeks reform. Autonomy seeks revolution. Political romanticism responds to both, using the very tools it criticizes within these movements: it claims to possess a higher justice than prophetism, and it uses the Enlightenment's tools of rational analysis to justify its irrational assumptions.[219]

Tillich believed the socialist principle had to redefine its relationship to the bourgeoisie. He defined the bourgeois principle as "the radical dissolution of all conditions, bonds, and forms related to the origin into elements that are to be rationally mastered, and the rational assemblage of these elements into structures serving the aims of thought and action."[220] In principle, the "free play of productive forces" (as in liberalism) or the subjection of nature by the decisive action of individuals (as in democracy) are to result in progressive harmony.[221] In practice, trust in laissez faire economics overshadows the democratic corrective. Harmony does not follow from the rational mastery of resources, and the corrective function of the democratic, prophetic demand for justice that is able to keep the expansive forces of the origin in check is lost.[222]

The beneficiaries of free market economics turn to alliances with prebourgeois forces to cope with disharmony while practicing "freedom"

---

[216]Tillich, *The Socialist Decision*, 24.

[217]Tillich, *The Socialist Decision*, 24.

[218]Tillich, *The Socialist Decision*, 24.

[219]Tillich, *The Socialist Decision*, 25-26.

[220]Tillich, *The Socialist Decision*, 48. In a review of Heinrich Eildermann's *Urkommunismus und Urreligion*, Tillich castigates the author for supporting a socialism rooted in a materialistic understanding of history that perpetuates the image of humanity as "the spiritless, soulless, community-less machine of instinct and industry" which capitalism created and which socialism is intended to overthrow. Paul Tillich, "Book Review: Eildermann's *Urkommunismus und Urreligion* (1921)," PTAH 209:009, 2.

[221]Tillich, *The Socialist Decision*, 50-51.

[222]Tillich, *The Socialist Decision*, 51-52.

as freedom from restraint.[223] The dehumanized victims of the free market (the proletariat) appeal to the bourgeoisie to live by its principle, seeing democracy (with its rational critique) as the path to a just distribution of resources, even if it requires the temporary period of a dictatorship by the proletariat.[224] In Tillich's view, by failing in this, the bourgeois principle turns out to be "a corrective, not a normative principle."[225]

The groups refusing any alliance with prebourgeois forces—socialism among them—radicalize the bourgeois principle.[226] Socialism sees disharmony as inevitable in the laissez faire approach. Therefore, it seeks market control on behalf of justice. Democratic critique seems to prevail here. Yet, socialism does not possess the persuasive power to defeat the bourgeois and prebourgeois forces at the ballot box. Consequently, alliances with the forces of the origin are required of socialism as well.[227] Tillich asked, "Can socialism be the fulfillment of the bourgeois principle when at the same time it is the expression of its destruction? Must not the struggle against bourgeois society question the bourgeois principle itself?"[228]

Tillich believed that a relevant socialism had to have a self-understanding that considered both its particularity (bound to the proletariat) as well as its universality (including all of society).[229] Cut off from the proletariat, socialist theory stays in the conceptual realm. Cut off from its transcendent dimension, the proletariat is imprisoned in the class struggle.[230]

According to Tillich, it was important for socialism to confront its own inner conflicts manifested in these areas: its vision of a utopian future; human nature; society; culture; community; and economics. The socialist belief in a utopian future of harmony was unhistorical, yet borne by a school entrenched in history.[231] Thus, Tillich believed socialism must turn

---

[223]Tillich, *The Socialist Decision*, 52-53.
[224]Tillich, *The Socialist Decision*, 53-54.
[225]Tillich, *The Socialist Decision*, 54.
[226]Tillich, *The Socialist Decision*, 58.
[227]Tillich, *The Socialist Decision*, 58-61.
[228]Tillich, *The Socialist Decision*, 58. On his characterization of socialism's relationship to bourgeois capitalism as "antinomic," see Tillich, "Die geistige Lage des Sozialismus," an essay from the Frankfurt period.
[229]Tillich, *The Socialist Decision*, 58.
[230]Tillich, *The Socialist Decision*, 61-64.
[231]Tillich, *The Socialist Decision*, 69.

to an expectation looking to a justice consistent with present circumstances and fulfilling its true origin.[232] While socialism advocated a rationalistic critique bringing about human transformation, it was mute on how to do so and misunderstood humanity's nonrational side.[233] Therefore, Tillich said that it should embrace life as a "complex of vital, erotic, aesthetic, and religious impulses . . . [allowing for] an ascendancy of so-called 'spiritual' impulses over the life-preserving tendencies."[234] Societal and universal harmony, with the proletariat as the tool thereto, conflicted with reality as an arena of power struggle.[235] As a consequence, Tillich declared that socialism must understand power in a positive way, as the means for fulfilling the primal claim of the true origin for justice in the concrete situation,[236] and democracy should be corrective rather than constitutive, since even democratic governmental processes can be used for domination.[237] In culture, socialism's approach to science ignored the prerational basis for human fulfillment, its pursuit of universal education faced insuperable barriers, and its exaltation of the proletariat ignored the proletariat's dissipated cultural and intellectual capacities.[238] In the face of this, Tillich asserted that socialism must reconnect with its cultural roots, returning to its prophetic, "religious" dimension, supported by the powers of origin, "by revealing to reason the inner infinity of being, and at the same time, by offering it support and structure."[239] Socialism failed to see community as "the expression of a unity that also exists apart from a common struggle and a common enemy . . . rest[ing] on some form of

---

[232]Tillich, *The Socialist Decision*, 132. On Tillich's nonutopian synthesis over against Marx and Hegel, see James Luther Adams, "Tillich's Interpretation of History," in *The Theology of Paul Tillich*, ed. Charles W. Kegley and Robert W. Bretall (New York: Macmillan, 1952) 308.

[233]Tillich, *The Socialist Decision*, 74.

[234]Tillich, *The Socialist Decision*, 136, 137.

[235]Tillich, *The Socialist Decision*, 75-78.

[236]Tillich, *The Socialist Decision*, 140, 141.

[237]Tillich, *The Socialist Decision*, 142.

[238]Tillich, *The Socialist Decision*, 82-85. Tillich commented on the riddle of the masses as "bearers of the future" in "Die soziale Zukunft in der Seele der Masse," PTAH 110:003.

[239]Tillich, *The Socialist Decision*, 146, 147, 150.

origin, on *eros* and destiny, and not . . . grounded in reason."[240] To remedy this, Tillich called it to affirm national community while resisting national-ism's exaltation of a particular nation, measuring all nations against the standard of the prophetic standard of justice.[241] Finally, the proletariat discovered conflicting economic interests within itself and the need for alliances with its antagonists to reach its goals.[242] Tillich's response to these dynamics was a call for steps rooted in an understanding of concrete economic realities: a "standardization of needs" through equal income, and the development of a need tradition that would avoid economic disruption; technological progress possessing controls that mediate its impact upon the labor force and its, consequent, capacity to consume;[243] a new "meaning of work . . . so constituted that work serves people and does not destroy them";[244] and the subjection of national and international economic behavior to the claim of justice.[245]

Tillich sought legitimate foundations for socialism to overcome its multi-layered, inner conflict. The socialist principle's primary concept of expectation stood against objectification and dehumanization as it threatened from both directions: "Expectation . . . overcomes an objectified bond of origin ('Everything remains the same') as well as an objectified expectation ('Someday everything will become new'). It is nonobjectified expectation ('The new breaks into the old')."[246] Tillich understood expectation's transcendence in terms of the perpetual prophetic demand and its imminence through its rational comprehensibility.[247]

Finally, the socialist principle had to confront the Marxism of the 1930s along three lines: its materialism; its dialectics; and its dogmatism. For Marx, "Materialism is economism."[248] Socialism had to cease maintaining the bourgeois ideology of harmony, revealing the disharmony within

---

[240]Tillich, *The Socialist Decision*, 146, 147, 150.

[241]Tillich, *The Socialist Decision*, 152. On socialism and the norm of justice, see Tillich, "Christentum und Sozialismus (II)," 31.

[242]Tillich, *The Socialist Decision*, 89-91.

[243]Tillich, *The Socialist Decision*, 153-57.

[244]Tillich, *The Socialist Decision*, 157.

[245]Tillich, *The Socialist Decision*, 153-60.

[246]Tillich, *The Socialist Decision*, 104.

[247]Tillich, *The Socialist Decision*, 109-12.

[248]Tillich, *The Socialist Decision*, 115.

society.[249] He called into question a history as ruled either by necessity (Hegel, Marx, and prophetism) or by freedom ("ethical socialism"), seeking a true dialectic: "Socialist action proceeds from the inner conviction that it corresponds to the meaning and impulse of history,"[250] seen most vividly in the proletariat in its almost instinctive response to the injustices of capitalism.[251] Finally, socialism had to reject a dogmatism that had undermined its impact.[252]

Ultimately, Tillich was convinced that socialism's success depended on its "reliance on its own principle, in which powers of origin and prophetic expectation are combined," with expectation as the primary factor.[253]

Conclusion

If his labors during the First World War were Tillich's first attempts to see war from a theological perspective, the post-World War I and Weimar years were ones in which Tillich began to see the culture of a nation in a theological way, revealing dynamics therein that are implicitly related to the decision for or against war: war led Tillich to look at culture, because unjust cultures foment reckless wars. Religiously rooted cultural analysis led Tillich to take seriously the questions of economics and society. The critical and creative capacity of Tillich's construct, the Protestant principle, led him to question some economic assumptions and to endorse other ones that he believed would lead to a more just society. The failure to embody that just society sowed seeds for discontent that made Germany ripe for collapse before forces able to amass the streams of discontent.

John Stumme has described the religious socialism of Paul Tillich as concrete, critical, comprehensive, and constructive.[254] Yet, it was also impotent in the face of the political anemia of social democracy and the dynamically irrational nationalism of Hitler. Tillich's severe criticism of capitalism understandably came under attack by a Western world dominated

---

[249]Tillich, *The Socialist Decision*, 118. See also Tillich, "Die religiöse und philosophische Weiterbildung des Sozialismus," 121-22.

[250]Tillich, *The Socialist Decision*, 121, 122.

[251]Tillich, *The Socialist Decision*, 123.

[252]Tillich, *The Socialist Decision*, 124-26.

[253]Tillich, *The Socialist Decision*, 162.

[254]Stumme, *Socialism*, 244-50.

by capitalism.[255] However, its primary weakness may not have been weakness at all: it may have been bad timing, a failure to discern whether a kairos had arrived, a time which was ready to give consideration to the value of Tillichian religious socialism.

The elements for an ethic of war and peace from Tillich's thought during this period include the following:

1. A nation's cultural health is of significant importance to its bellicosity;
2. Religion—as the source of meaning for all of existence—must inform one's understanding of culture: theonomy as the depth of autonomy and the autonomous rejection of heteronomy;
3. Religion is critical and creative and is embodied in the Protestant principle;
4. The Protestant principle measures all truth claims—including those involving culture and politics (as a subset of culture)—by the standards of love and justice;
5. Economics is a central factor in a nation's cultural health—this includes the socialist critique of capitalism;
6. Views asserting religious significance that are penultimate—that make claims alleging ultimacy, but that contradict the norms of love and justice—are either idolatrous or irreligious;
7. History is of central importance, with these particularly significant phenomena: power as the primal force which enables being (historical existence); *kairoi* as those periods ripe for creative

---

[255]Robert Fitch was a sharp critic of Tillich's social ethics, wondering why he embraced the idea of "religious socialism" while discounting the possibility of a "religious capitalism," and perplexed that Tillich saw the modern era to be experiencing the collapse of capitalism rather than the collapse of feudalism. Robert E. Fitch, "The Social Philosophy of Paul Tillich," *Religion in Life* 27/2 (Spring 1958): 253, 254. Clark A. Kucheman believed that Tillich did not adequately prove a causative connection between capitalism and conditions in the modern era. Kucheman, "Professor Tillich," 165ff. Eberhard A. Amelung interpreted Tillich's religious socialism as ideology ("analysis of the existing conditions exhibit[ing] a high degree of selectivity or of distortion of the facts"), giving undue centrality to economics, neglecting the role of law, and overdrawing the "thingification" of the masses. Amelung, "Religious Socialism as Ideology," v, vii.

action; and the demonic as power destructively divorced from the creatively ordering dynamics of history; and

8. Ethical action is consistent with a *kairos*, embodies self-transcending realism ("believing realism"), and rises above a sacred-secular or holy-profane distinction by seeing all realms of existence as potentially ripe for creative, theonomous activity.

Chapter 3

Forced Intellectual Émigré—
American Interwar Period

Introduction

The descent of Germany into Nazi rule shattered Tillich's personal and professional life. It was a time combining pride with horror. He was proud to join his Jewish colleagues on the first list of faculty members fired from their positions at the University of Frankfurt in April 1933 as the only Protestant on that list. However, his political views put him at significant risk. In August 1933, Reinhold Niebuhr cabled an offer of a post at New York City's Union Theological Seminary. On November 3, Tillich and his wife and daughter arrived in New York.[1] Colleagues Theodor Adorno, Max Horkheimer, and Max Wertheimer found positions at Columbia University. Adolf Löwe went to work for the New School for Social Research.[2]

In addition to his teaching responsibilities at Union, Tillich helped other émigrés cope with the crisis of their changed circumstances through his presidency of Self-Help for German Émigrés, Inc.[3] Tillich continued to produce writings that reflected or informed his views on politics among nations. He enunciated these views from his preferred spiritual and intellectual position "on the boundary." From there, Tillich's differences with other German Christian and religious scholars with respect to Nazi rule became clear. Tillich tried to interpret the German and European situation to his American audience. He presented his views on the Christian interpretation of history and the importance of Christian action within history to this same audience. Finally, he produced the piece that most directly addresses the theme of the present work, his fragment on religion and world politics.

---

[1]Pauck, *Paul Tillich*, 130-38, 308n.1.
[2]Pauck, *Paul Tillich*, 155.
[3]See PTAH 201 for materials on Self-Help for German Émigrés, Inc. As noted previously, in citing sources from the Paul Tillich Archive at Harvard, I will use the notation created by Erdmann Sturm: the acronym PTAH designating the Paul Tillich Archive at Harvard; the first number designating the box number; and the number following the colon designating the file number within the box.

The Boundary Position

At the beginning of this short autobiography, *On the Boundary*, Tillich
wrote, " 'The boundary is the best place for acquiring knowledge.' . . . Since
thinking presupposes receptiveness to new possibilities, this position is
fruitful for thought; but it is difficult and dangerous in life, which again and
again demands decisions and thus the exclusiveness of alternatives. This
disposition and its tension have determined both my destiny and my work."[4]
The rise of Nazism brought the existing divisions—the boundaries—
between German theological circles into sharp relief.[5] Understandably, it
continued the intellectual struggles over national and religious identity, over
church and culture, and over faith and war which had brewed since World
War I. Jack Forstman and Robert Ericksen have written extensively on these
matters. Ericksen has described New Testament scholar Gerhard Kittel's
justification for anti-Semitism, theologian Paul Althaus's doctrines of
revelation and church/state relations which encouraged church endorsement
of state power, and Emanuel Hirsch's interpretation of the Kingdom of God
as most adequately manifested in Nazi Germany.[6] Forstman has addressed
a full range of tensions, largely placing representatives of the "dialectical"
school (primarily Karl Barth and Friedrich Gogarten) against a range of
opponents. One set of tensions was between Barth and Hirsch. It
represented a generational shift from the old debate between positivists
(who wanted to preserve traditional expressions of Christian truth against
reason) and liberals (who were willing to embrace modern research
techniques). In the face of these former paths of doctrinalism and relativism,
Barth charted one placing all human formulations and directions in question
in light of God's word. Hirsch endorsed the capacity of humanity to
embody God's will.[7]

　　According to Tillich, Hirsch had provided theological justification for

---

[4]Tillich, *On the Boundary*, 13.

[5]Two sources of information for understanding these divisions are Robert P.
Ericksen, *Theologians under Hitler: Gerhard Kittel, Paul Althaus, and Emanuel
Hirsch* (New Haven CT: Yale University Press, 1985) and Forstman, *Christian
Faith in Dark Times*. For the general relationship between Tillich's thought and the
German situation, see Siegfried, "The Significance of Paul Tillich's Theology."

[6]Ericksen, *Theologians under Hitler*.

[7]Forstman, *Christian Faith in Dark Times*, 22-71.

National Socialism: in terms of dialectics, he affirmed the "Yes" of God, God's affirmation of Nazi Germany.[8] Tillich asserted that Hirsch had "perverted the prophetic, eschatologically conceived Kairos doctrine into a sacerdotal-sacramental consecration of a current event."[9] Hirsch had surrendered the critical "No" of God.[10] Barth, to Tillich's thinking, provided theological justification to apolitical theological transcendentalism: he emphasized the "No" of God, diminishing the priority and import of human activity.[11] Tillich's primary criticism of Barth's thought was first that it was wrongly termed dialectical and, second, that its failure to be dialectical demeaned the significance of human existence.[12] Dialectics involves a synthesis of two opposing ideas. However with Barth, in the divine-human

---

[8]Paul Tillich, "Open Letter to Emanuel Hirsch (1 October 1934)," trans. Victor Nuovo and Robert Scharlemann, in *The Thought of Paul Tillich* (San Francisco: Harper & Row, 1985) 357-62. See Reimer, *The Emanuel Hirsch and Paul Tillich Debate*. Reimer should be read in light of Forstman's commentary, *Christian Faith in Dark Times*, 210-21.

[9]Tillich, "Open Letter to Emanuel Hirsch," 363.

[10]"Um was es geht. Antwort an Emanuel Hirsch." *Theologische Blätter* (Leipzig) 14/5 (May 1935): 117-20.

[11]Paul Tillich, "What Is Wrong with the 'Dialectic' Theology?" *The Journal of Religion* 15/2 (April 1935): 129-30. Tillich blamed Barth both for disconnecting the transcendent faith from immanent faithfulness, in the process "destroy[ing] the effects of religious socialism," leading to "the defeat of the German proletarian movement in general." Paul Tillich, "The Religious Situation in Germany Today," *Religion in Life* 3/2 (Spring 1934): 170-71. He also interpreted the dominance of "rigid fanatical orthodoxy" in the Confessing Church as the fruit of Barth's work. Paul Tillich, *My Travel Diary: 1936—Between Two Worlds* (New York: Harper & Row, 1970) 83. Of Barth, Berdyaev wrote, " 'The doctrine of Karl Barth and the dialectical theology mean a dehumanization of Christianity.' " Paul Tillich, "Nicholas Berdyaev," *Religion in Life* 7/3 (Summer 1938): 414-15. The Eranos Circle (a group surrounding Carl Jung of which Rudolf Otto was a founding member), had similar escapist tendencies. When he spoke before the group during his 1936 trip, the politicism of Tillich's lectures there divided the group: the young for him, the elders feeling his attitude to be out of place. Tillich said the latter were correct, "For what they practice there is unpolitical mysticism." Tillich, *My Travel Diary*, 157.

[12]For an interpretation of Tillich's dialectics, see Adams, "Tillich's Interpretation of History."

relationship paradoxical separation continues: "Between God and man there is a hollow space which man is unable of himself to penetrate."[13] Barth had surrendered the "Yes" of God. Tillich believed religious socialism was a middle way of self-critical, but responsible political action.[14]

With his fellow émigrés, Tillich lived the boundary situation. During a five-and-a-half month trip to Europe in 1936, he occasionally recorded his perspective on the land of his birth. On a lunch stop in Holland, Tillich told of being able to see Germany "without any feeling of homesickness. Dead, destroyed; barbed wire and Gestapo."[15] While in Basel, Switzerland, Tillich went to a part of the city "surrounded on three sides by Germany. Uncanny feeling, like being pushed into a sack. The nearest lights are German, the streetcars cross the border."[16] The status of being between his native land and a new land gave him much to ponder. The result was that boundary and migration became even more important symbols for him.

On the Boundary was published the same year Tillich traveled to Europe. Tillich framed his thoughts around a series of dialectical tensions significant in his life. He attributed his dialectical sense of history to the contrasting temperaments of an East German father and a West German mother.[17] He appreciated both the electricity of the city as well as the earthiness of the country (including the sea as symbolic of the "abyss of dynamic truth").[18] He felt himself liberated from "the narrowness of the petit bourgeoisie" in negotiating the gap between the bourgeoisie and the

---

[13]Tillich, "What Is Wrong with the 'Dialectic' Theology?" 133. By 1939, Tillich argued that Barth had turned from an apolitical transcendentalism. Barth prohibited neutrality when the political arena "makes a religious claim," for when it does so, "It is—as [Barth] calls it later—a new Islam. And as the Church in the Reformation was not neutral to the attack of the Turks on Christian Europe so the Church today must support the enemies of the new Islam, that is of National Socialism." Paul Tillich, "Book Review: Karl Barth's *The Church and the Political Problem of Our Day*" (1939), typewritten manuscript, PTAH 522:026, 2. Tillich noted that Barth called anti-Semitism "sin against the Holy Ghost." Tillich, "Book Review: Karl Barth's *The Church*," 3.

[14]Stone, *Paul Tillich's Radical Social Thought*, 89-90.

[15]Tillich, *My Travel Diary*, 72.

[16]Tillich, *My Travel Diary*, 116.

[17]Tillich, *On the Boundary*, 14.

[18]Tillich, *On the Boundary*, 15, 18.

working classes. He identified with Shakespeare's Hamlet and found therapy in Botticelli's angels.[19] He experienced the theory-practice tension vividly amidst the postwar German revolution.[20] He struggled to assert himself autonomously specifically in relation to the heteronomy of his father: this marked his entire life.[21] He found Schelling helpful in unifying theology and philosophy. He saw Heidegger's philosophy to be a helpful expression of humanity as finite freedom.[22] He synthesized the religion and society tension into religious socialism.[23] He called into question a strict separation between the sacred and the secular.[24] He believed that Lutheranism taught socialism about sin and that socialism taught Lutheranism about the demonic.[25] He drew on the essentialism of idealism and the existentialism of Marxism to embrace ambiguity and reject the masking of ambiguity which Marx called ideology.[26] He appreciated the United States—where "representatives of all nations and races can live as citizens"—as one forced from his native land to an alien land.[27] And he acknowledged God's ultimate limitation upon us, in whose presence "even the very center of our being is only a boundary and our highest level of accomplishment is fragmentary."[28]

In other places, Tillich reflected on the theological meaning of emigra-

---

[19]Tillich, *On the Boundary*, 27, 28.

[20]Tillich, *On the Boundary*, 32.

[21]Tillich, *On the Boundary*, 36-38.

[22]Tillich, *On the Boundary*, 51, 52, 57.

[23]Tillich, *On the Boundary*, 62.

[24]Tillich, *On the Boundary*, 66ff.

[25]Tillich, *On the Boundary*, 76, 80. Reflecting on the two primary perspectives that informed the preparatory discussions on the Oxford Conference (which he took part in during his 1936 trip), Tillich saw himself "on the boundary" between the Lutheran-German and the Anglo-Saxon. Tillich, *My Travel Diary*, 38.

[26]Tillich, *On the Boundary*, 81ff.

[27]Tillich, *On the Boundary*, 96. Jerald Brauer's introduction to *My Travel Diary* cites Tillich: "Emigration at the age of forty-seven means that one belongs to two worlds: to the Old as well as to the New into which one has been fully received." Brauer notes that Tillich thought emigration was both an inner and an outer reality: "To part from ways of thinking, of believing, from traditions, from political commitments." Jerald Brauer, introduction to Tillich, *My Travel Diary: 1936— Between Two Worlds* (New York: Harper & Row, 1970) 11-12.

[28]Tillich, *On the Boundary*, 98.

tion and the boundary situation. He wrote that from Abraham onward, God's absolute claim challenged all human relationships and ways of living and thinking.[29] Emigration was "a protest against the nationalistic distortion of Christianity and defamation of humanity."[30] He emphasized the creative potential of emigration: "Periods of transformation always are periods of separation and emigration. Father- and mother-lands have to be left. Children-lands have to be found."[31]

In a 1937 article, Tillich argued for "an essential relationship between mind and migration," declaring that migration was

> natural for the creative mind. And . . . it is the mind's power and dynamic nature to transcend any given actuality, to strive toward universal concepts, to create tools, machines and institutions independent of immediate needs, to find norms, laws and categories which constitute the world in which it lives, to which it belongs and from which it is at the same time separated as an individual self.[32]

This led Tillich to consider the adequacy of technology, religion, and mental creativity as media of cultural cross-fertilization. Intellectual migration was the most effective means of cross-fertilization, according to Tillich. It requires community, and it involves creative transformation of

---

[29]Paul Tillich, "Christianity and Emigration," *Presbyterian Tribune* (New York) 52/3 (29 October 1936): 13.

[30]Tillich, "Christianity and Emigration," 16. At the end of the quoted section, the text of the article has "distortion of Christianity and deformation of humanity." However, the manuscript at the Paul Tillich Archive at Harvard has "defamation of humanity" (PTAH 416:005).

[31]Tillich, "Christianity and Emigration," 16.

[32]Paul Tillich, "Mind and Migration," *Social Research* 4/3 (September 1937): 295, 296. Tillich related a London conversation during his 1936 journey in which he stressed the importance of immigrants' "feel[ing] at home in the New World without regard for what is going on back in Germany." On the same trip, while speaking to a person who was reflecting on Swiss narrowness, Tillich emphasized the importance of seeing "his role of immigrant in a more positive light." Tillich, *My Travel Diary*, 63, 118. Tillich believed emigration was key to the success of the great migrating cultures: the Greeks, the Jewish exile in Babylon, the Arab and Christian encounter in the crusades, and the experience he shared with his fellow exiles. But, he also noted that the transcending capacity of mind and migration is not predetermined to be creative. Tillich, "Mind and Migration," 298-99.

that which is received.[33]

Intensive, intellectual, interdisciplinary group discussion was another practice of the boundary situation for Tillich. The collapse of the harmony of autonomous rationalism meant "the end of the Protestant-humanist era,"[34] but it did not mean the end of the Protestant principle. Having benefited from such a practice in the Kairos Circle and elsewhere, Tillich advocated the formation of "an order or fellowship" willing to bring about the renovation of Protestantism outside of existing churches and distinct from movements resisting involvement in the world.[35] He called for a "post-Protestantism" or a "new Catholicism" borne "by a group which relatively withdraws itself from the ecclesiastical realization of Protestantism and, in the sociological form of a closed movement, an alliance or an order, prepares politically and spiritually the structure of that which is to come."[36] These religious orders would be a context in which "leading intellectuals and men of affairs . . . would meet regularly to analyze key issues confronting mankind," to approach the boundary of their respective fields to engage in cross-disciplinarian discussion.[37]

Interpreter of the German and European Situation

Europe and the United States. From the boundary position, Tillich interpreted the European situation to the United States. He compared the social functions of the sacramental, socially conservative Mother church predominant in Europe with the theocratic, socially and political active, "ruling and commanding father" church of the United States.[38] He stated the

---

[33]Tillich, "Mind and Migration," 300-302. Luther's translation of Paul's writings and the Renaissance's use of Greek culture exemplified this transformative process: "the foreign has to become our own in order to be creative." Tillich, "Mind and Migration," 303-304.

[34]Tillich, "Mind and Migration," 53.

[35]Paul Tillich, "The End of the Protestant Era," *The Student World* 30/1 (First Quarter 1937): 52.

[36]Tillich, "The End of the Protestant Era," 57.

[37]Jerald Brauer, endnotes to Paul Tillich's *My Travel Diary: 1936—Between Two Worlds* (New York: Harper & Row, 1970) 187-88.

[38]Paul Tillich, "The Social Functions of the Churches in Europe and America," *Social Research: An International Quarterly of Political and Social Science* 3/1 (February 1936): 93-95.

basic contrast in this way: "Sacramentalism is independent of individual and social activities. 'The Holy' is given before human activity begins"; in contrast, "theocracy deals with the problem of realizing the will of God . . . us[ing] political power in order to change social institutions and individual morality in obedience to the divine commandments."[39] Sacramentalism leans toward authoritarian power and theocracy toward democracy.

Tillich perceived the United States to be dominated by a technologically fueled capitalism concerned with the two dimensional, horizontal ("horizon to horizon") realm.[40] Pragmatism was the dominant philosophy: "knowledge as a means of subjection, facts and relations, but not meanings; finally dependent on tool-making; philosophy [as] instrumentalistic, making the refined tools of logic; but little contemplative interest in natural or historical lives; the pragmatic point of view; progress through science."[41] The religious endorsement of technology and capitalism as tools of God's providential plan for the United States was consistent with the world-transforming motivation of theocracy.[42] Empirical activism becomes everlasting activism in an afterlife.[43] The consequences of the two-dimensional perspective is that it must face limits in the finite sphere. This is "the horizontal infinity which always remains finite."[44] Anxiety in the face of failure in the two-dimensional drives humanity to the third, vertical dimension. This existential anxiety provokes the question of where to find the courage to face existence.[45]

In contrast to this, the European church was, at the least, noncommittal on capitalism and technology and, to a degree, distrustful of it: "Generally speaking, capitalism in Europe has been without a religious sanction."[46] Religious socialism was a church movement, after all, though this was a middle position in the face of Marxism's inability to find a functional social

[39]Tillich, "The Social Functions of the Churches in Europe and America," 93, 94.
[40]Paul Tillich, "The Relation of Religion to American Culture (mid to late 1930s)," PTAH 409:007, 3-4.
[41]Tillich, "The Relation of Religion to American Culture," 6.
[42]Tillich, "The Social Functions," 95-98.
[43]Tillich, "The Relation of Religion to American Culture," 8.
[44]Tillich, "The Relation of Religion to American Culture," 3.
[45]Tillich, "The Relation of Religion to American Culture," 9-10.
[46]Tillich, "The Social Functions," 100-101.

ethic within the church and the church's hostility to Marx.[47] Given the European church's social passivity and the American church's ties to capitalism, Tillich doubted that either could contribute constructively to postcapitalist reconstruction.[48]

Downfall of Church and Country. Tillich explained the German situation to his audience, first in articles, then in speeches. He wrote about the downfall of Germany and the German church. He wrote on matters of strategy. He characterized the church conflict in Germany between the official German Christian Church (led by Reichsbishop Ludwig Müller) and the Confessing Church (led by Martin Niemöller) as a response to government encroachment on the church. It was not the church engaging in political discussion about general issues in German life. A good number of the preachers were Nazis. The majority were apolitical conservatives. Even the Confessing Church was led by a World War I submarine commander (Niemöller).[49] The relative conservatism of both sides was related to Luther's two-kingdom doctrine described in chapter one, which gave secular government the room to exert significant power and brought about a political culture respectful of strong political power holders. Challenging this line of thought, Tillich admonished the German church to see that its "religious resistance to attacks made upon religion . . . must result in religious resistance to the fundamental political idea behind the present form of government."[50]

Fundamentally, Enlightenment rationalism had failed to produce the harmony it had promised, and, in this, it had failed church and culture. God became a philosophical idea unconnected to the nonrational. This created a vacuum into which other nonrational forces could enter: the labor/proletarian/religious socialist movement and the new paganism at the heart of Nazism.[51] While Christian humanism maintains the high notion of human dignity in the face of both demonic attack and secularist determination, it also asserts the fundamental presence of the divine within humanity.[52] Tillich's form of religious socialism attempted unsuccessfully

---

[47]Tillich, "The Social Functions," 101-102.
[48]Tillich, "The Social Functions," 104.
[49]Tillich, "The Religious Situation in Germany Today," 163.
[50]Tillich, "The Religious Situation in Germany Today," 166.
[51]Tillich, "The Religious Situation in Germany Today," 166-69.
[52]Tillich, "The Religious Situation in Germany Today," 168-69.

to reconnect Marxism to its prophetic roots, to bridge the separation within Lutheranism between the private and the public, the religious and the political, and to activate a socially passive Christianity.[53]

The new paganism was founded on "the sacredness of blood and soil and power and race and national values which are minimized by Christian ethics."[54] There was a vigorous nationalistic mythology outside the church. However, efforts to "paganize" the church itself seemed to have failed.[55] Tillich pointed to the limited but exciting impact of the struggle of orthodox Protestantism and Roman Catholicism against the new paganism.[56]

In Tillich's view, Nazism's goal was a "dechristianized state church," with nationalism "elevated to religious power against prophetic and Christian universalism,"[57] that is, "a post-Christian pagan tribal religion."[58]

---

[53]Tillich, "The Religious Situation in Germany Today," 169-70. Tillich wrote, "What can the lower middle class man demand if he accepts religious socialism? He can't keep any kind of sectarianism, but he is right in distinguishing the proletarian movement and the church of Christ. He can't keep moralism, but he is right in stressing the importance of every individual soul and therefore of individual moral demands and religious hopes. He can't keep utopianism, but he is right in showing that an irrational fate is deciding over the most rationalized society and that the real power of life is belief and not reason. These three points are . . . what religious tried to teach the workers." Paul Tillich, "Middle Class Problems in Germany" (late 1930s?) PTAH 404:006, 9.

[54]Tillich, "The Religious Situation in Germany Today," 171.

[55]Tillich, "The Religious Situation in Germany Today," 171-72.

[56]Tillich, "The Religious Situation in Germany Today," 172. Tillich warned of the potential for the rise of the same pagan spirit within the United States and in "all Christian countries." Tillich, "The Religious Situation," 173. Tillich reported Fedor Stepun's description of the decrepitness of the various classes of pre-Revolutionary Russia. He wrote, The "religious substance of Russia is distorted into a demonic attitude in all those groups: the defenders of monarchy, through the reactionary abuse of Christianity as a means for power; in the intelligentsia, through the exaggerated interpretation of a political ideal as a doctrine of redemption; in the peasantry, through the destructive outbreak of a blind life." Paul Tillich, "The Soul of a Revolution: Review of Fedor Stepun's *The Russian Soul and Revolution*," *Christendom* 1/2 (Winter 1936): 366.

[57]Paul Tillich, "The Religious Struggle in Germany" (1939 or 1940) PTAH 404:001, 2.

[58]Paul Tillich, "The Religious Situation in Germany" (1939/1940?) PTAH

With the Reformation, the nation rose up as "the boundary of Christianity" (against Catholicism), and with the onset of liberal democracy over against absolutism, nation became "the boundary of pure reason."[59] With the disintegration of the nation built on reason, nation became a concept "breaking through the boundary of reason and Christianity."[60] The nation gained new ultimacy as "the ultimate principle of reintegration which gives meaning to life, subordinating all other meanings and raising an infinite or totalitarian claim . . . the national claim, the unconditional, untouchable and ultimate claim."[61]

National Socialism frustrated the church's basic operations, severing it from public activities, blocking its communications, imprisoning its representatives, and threatening its finances. National Socialism exerted its power by means of indoctrination, public defamation of officials without opportunity for a just defense, condemning Roman Catholic internationalism, and seducing Protestantism to its purposes.[62] The spirit of its attack was anti-Semitic, antihumanistic, and tribal.[63] Tillich saw the question to be "whether true Christianity again has to go into the catacombs."[64]

He offered this conclusion at the time: "Europe has missed her providential moment, her kairos (the right moment from the point of view of eternity) and tries in vain to escape the destructive consequences of this failure."[65] In a message perhaps aimed at Barth's group, Tillich wrote,

---

404:002, 2.

[59]Tillich, "The Religious Struggle in Germany," 3.

[60]Tillich, "The Religious Struggle in Germany," 4.

[61]Tillich, "The Religious Struggle in Germany," 5.

[62]Tillich, "The Religious Struggle in Germany," 8.

[63]Tillich, "The Religious Struggle in Germany," 9.

[64]Tillich, "The Religious Struggle in Germany," 11.

[65]Paul Tillich, "A Historical Diagnosis (Impressions of an European Trip)," *Radical Religion* 2/1 (Winter 1936): 11. The presuppositions of this situation were these: the nineteenth century proved the idea of progress to be invalid; foreign policy was dictated by the ruling classes; the political Left was impotent; fascism's potency was rooted in its ability to consolidate the masses under authoritarianism and to nurture nationalism; and international organization was necessary in the face of a "multitude of nations on a narrow space in a narrow world." Paul Tillich, "The Political Situation in Europe Since the Munich Conference" (1939?) PTAH 406A:002, 1-4.

"Nobody can escape the threat against his historical existence. Man has a realm of religious and humanistic reservation; but it cannot be separated—at least not in the present European situation —from the realm of religious and humanistic obligation."[66] The "therapy" Tillich heard discussed on his 1936 Europe trip was either to "save what can be saved" or "prepare for tomorrow."[67]

The Future Relationship with the Jewish People. Tillich had close personal and professional relationships in the Jewish community, from the early days of the Kairos Circle to his professorship in Frankfurt. He defended Jewish students and confronted Brown Shirts on the University of Frankfurt campus.[68] The meaning he found in Marx was strongly related to what he took to be Marx's resonance with the Jewish prophetic tradition: it was Jewish prophetism that he bluntly placed over against political romanticism in *The Socialist Decision*.[69] Tillich's position placed him in direct opposition to much of German Christianity.[70] He did not comment on Marx's own expressed hostility to Judaism and the Jewish spirit.[71]

In his first public speech in English, Tillich addressed a protest meeting at Madison Square Garden on the meaning of anti-Semitism. He admonished Germans in the audience to understand "the destruction of the German mind and soul which is involved in the destruction of Jewish lives and homes."[72] To Christians in the audience, he claimed that the Nazis were

---

[66]Tillich, "A Historical Diagnosis," 16.

[67]Tillich, "A Historical Diagnosis," 16-17.

[68]Pauck, *Paul Tillich*, 70-72, 127-28.

[69]For the relationship of Tillichian thought to Jewish thought, see Earley, "Tillich and Judaism: An Analysis of 'The Jewish Question,' "; Earley, "An 'Everlasting Conversation' "; and Friedlander, "Tillich and Jewish Thought."

[70]See Richard Gutteridge, *Open Thy Mouth for the Dumb! The German Evangelical Church and the Jews, 1879–1950* (Oxford: Basil Blackwell, 1976); Guenter Lewy, *The Catholic Church and Nazi Germany* (New York: Da Capo Press, 1964/2000) 268ff.; and Uriel Tal, *Christians and Jews in Germany: Religion, Politics, and Ideology in the Second Reich, 1870–1914* (Ithaca/London: Cornell University Press, 1975).

[71]Karl Marx, "On the Jewish Question," 1843, in *The Marx-Engels Reader*, ed. Robert C. Tucker (New York: W. W. Norton, 1978) 26-52.

[72]Paul Tillich, "The Meaning of Anti-Semitism," *Radical Religion* 4/1 (Winter 1938): 34.

engaged in "a demonic struggle against the God of Abraham and the prophets, who is also the God of Jesus and of St. Paul, of Augustine and of Luther, the God whose name is Jehovah, the Lord of Hosts."[73] Among the Jewish members of the audience, Tillich sought to inspire "a new and powerful community of peoples, races and creeds, transcending their differences" rather than the "poisoned fruits" of vengeance."[74]

Tillich appealed for his audience to decide for the true Germany held captive by the Nazi impostors. He described the levels of complicity that led to the rise of Hitler. He spoke of the roots of German culture which would be squandered if Nazism were not conquered.[75] He called for a decision against those persecuting Jews and the true Germans and in favor of both the true Germany and the Jewish people.[76]

Religious-Socialist Interpreter of History

Hitler's ascent to power forced Tillich to apply religious socialism to the rise of tyranny. Here that project is considered under three headings: history and the Kingdom of God; church and state; and biblical tradition and Marxism.

History and the Kingdom of God. Tillich constructed his argument on the meaning of history by combining the transcendent idea of the Kingdom of God with the imminent ideas of socialism, Nietzschean life philosophy, and modern "world"-consciousness.[77] Among other places, he outlined this to a great extent in his presentation to the 1937 Oxford Conference on Life and Work.[78]

Tillich saw history to be composed of the subjective element of memory and the objective element of event. It is a combination of nature and the free activity of human beings. It is comprised of those human activities related to the group, entities with both the power to exist and values for which they

---

[73]Tillich, "The Meaning of Anti-Semitism," 34.

[74]Tillich, "The Meaning of Anti-Semitism," 36.

[75]Paul Tillich, "Germany Is Still Alive," *Protestant Digest* 1 (February 1939): 45-46.

[76]Tillich, "Germany Is Still Alive," 46.

[77]Paul Tillich, "History as *the* Problem of Our Period," *The Review of Religion* 3/3 (March 1939):

[78]Ronald H. Stone, Introduction to *Theology of Peace,* by Paul Tillich (Louisville: Westminster/John Knox Press, 1990) 12.

are responsible.[79] Arguing that freedom, humanity and history are intertwined, Tillich understood their relationship in this way: "Man is that being who is able to determine his being in freedom through history. . . . Freedom is that faculty of man by which he is able to determine his being through history. . . . History is that happening through which man determines his own being, including his freedom."[80] History involves "directed time," time understood meaningfully. In the biblical figure of Abraham, Tillich saw "that essentially historical nation in which the national gods were negated on principle; time conquered space, justice replaced power, the future overruled the present, hope conquered tragic heroism."[81] History has a beginning, a center, and an end. Its center dictates its meaning. In Christianity, history is given meaning with Christ as the center, the onset of the expectation of the Kingdom of God as the beginning, and the complete realization of Christ's Kingdom as the end.[82]

Progress is both a legitimate and illegitimate concept for understanding history: technology, political unification, and increasingly humanized relationships bear a quality of progress; artistic and moral behavior cannot be understood in such a way. The ultimate meaning of history is beyond history, but meaning is experienced in fragmented and ambiguous ways within history.[83]

The Kingdom of God symbolically captures history's meaning, including transcendence and imminence, dynamically at work in history while not equated with history. In opposition to the Kingdom of God are the "kingdoms" of the world, functioning demonically as a combination of form-breaking force and creative drive. The Kingdom of God as a symbol implies its own ultimate victory, accomplished dynamically within history as the "fulfillment of the ultimate meaning of existence against the

[79]Paul Tillich, "The Kingdom of God and History (1938)," in *Theology of Peace*, by Paul Tillich, ed. Ronald H. Stone (Louisville: Westminster/John Knox Press, 1990) 27-29.

[80]Paul Tillich, "Freedom in the Period of Transformation," in *Freedom: Its Meaning*, ed. Ruth Nanda Anshen (New York: Harcourt, Brace, 1940) 124.

[81]Tillich, "History as *the* Problem of Our Period," 260-61.

[82]Tillich, "The Kingdom of God and History," 29-30.

[83]Tillich, "The Kingdom of God and History," 31-33. Berdyaev called the rationalist belief in progress " 'idolatry to coming generations.' " Tillich, "Nicholas Berdyaev," 415.

contradictions of existence."[84]

With its understanding of Christ as the bearer of salvation and the center of history, Christianity sees human history as salvation history. The term, kairos—fulfilled or opportune or right time —expresses the idea of Christ's coming as the fulfillment of a period of expectation and "the beginning of the period of reception or actualization."[85] Kairos stands "between socialist utopianism and Christian transcendentalism," a matter of "acting with full responsibility for a limited purpose."[86] Salvation is a comprehensive reality, "related to individuals as well as groups, to mankind as well as to nature, to personalities as well as to institutions."[87]

Tillich saw the church—understood as far broader than Christian churches—as "the community of those partly visible and partly invisible, who live in the light of the ultimate meaning of existence, whether in expectation or reception . . . [rooted in] the power which gives meaning to historical life as a whole."[88] Individual destiny is related to the larger social context. History finds "its meaning and frame of reference" in the church, and the church's goal is to turn "latent church history into manifest church history."[89] The prototypical pattern of the Christ event—preparation/kairos/reception—is the pattern for smaller subdivisions of history "as the rhythm of 'critical' and 'organic' periods."[90]

In history, essence and existence are generally in contradiction, according to Tillich. Salvation is the overcoming of that contradiction. Salvation both judges and supports history. History manifests salvation partially: "Salvation is actual within world history to the extent in which the

---

[84]Tillich, "The Kingdom of God and History," 33-36. The Kingdom of God is the symbol of "the transcendental meaning of existence." Tillich, "History as *the* Problem of Our Period," 262. The crucial question to be answered in the affirmative for history to have meaning is this: "Has historical action any ultimate importance, has the Kingdom of God any realization in history or only beyond history?" Tillich, "History as *the* Problem," 263.

[85]Tillich, "The Kingdom of God and History," 37.

[86]Paul Tillich, "The Religious Socialist Movement in Germany between the World Wars" (1939 at earliest) PTAH 408:030, 4.

[87]Tillich, "The Kingdom of God and History," 38.

[88]Tillich, "The Kingdom of God and History," 39.

[89]Tillich, "History as *the* Problem of Our Period," 262.

[90]Tillich, "The Kingdom of God and History," 40.

destructive forces are overcome, the power of the demonic is broken, and the final fulfillment of meaning appears."[91]

Historical interpretation is done by one active in history, reflecting on "the meaning, the purpose, and the presuppositions of his historical action."[92] Christian interpretation is done by the church in order to shape the church itself and to shape one's time. Kairos is the basis for action: both "the unique kairos" of Christ as the center of history, as well as the particular kairotic turning points. In the first case, the demonic hold was broken "in principle"; in the second, present day manifestations of the demonic are confronted. Within the situations of history, the demonic (as threat) and the kairotic (as promise) are both present.[93]

Two contradictory trends operate in history with respect to freedom, in Tillich's thought. First, he saw a trend towards expanding political freedom. Second, he saw a trend reserving outward freedom for those to whom fate had given power, and limiting the freedom of all others to merely internal freedom.[94]

Tillich saw meaningful freedom as historical freedom or creative freedom, "Freedom for *meaningful* creativity, freedom for *autonomous* creativity, freedom for *self-fulfilling* creativity."[95] Political freedom is to ensure historical freedom, requiring the existence of powerful governments "checked by democratic correctives."[96] However, his observation was that such circumstances occur rarely. In periods of transformation—of self-destructive capitalism, dehumanizing nationalism and technological civilization—historical freedom must find ways to be embodied "in spite of" the oppressive circumstances of such periods. This means that meaningful creativity is limited to "the revolutionary attitude." Autonomous creativity occurs under a myriad of protective, esoteric cloaks. Self-fulfilling creativity occurs in a present experience of eternal life (not escape to an afterlife) and in an attitude of anticipation.[97] Tillich used the dialectic of demand and expectation to express the reality that a time of kairos is a

---

[91]Tillich, "The Kingdom of God and History," 41-43.
[92]Tillich, "The Kingdom of God and History," 44.
[93]Tillich, "The Kingdom of God and History," 45-46.
[94]Tillich, "Freedom in the period of Transformation," 128-29.
[95]Tillich, "Freedom in the period of Transformation," 131.
[96]Tillich, "Freedom in the period of Transformation," 135.
[97]Tillich, "Freedom in the period of Transformation," 135-43.

combination of responsible human action and divine promise.[98]

In Tillich's view, the demonic forces in operation at the time were capitalism, nationalism, and dictatorship. Capitalism's autonomy created the class struggle and subjected all spheres to its processes, creating societal disintegration.[99] Religious socialism responded to this with a combination of biblical-prophetic and Marxist sociological criticism. Nationalism exalted nation to the level of highest good. The prophetic viewpoint lifts up the Kingdom of God as the standard, diminishing the import of national space and lifting up the priority of time over space. Christianity is called to point to the demonisms of particularism—spatial-ism, racism, and nationalism—which, in their abandonment of the primacy of time, reject history.[100] Dictatorial power demonically challenges the authority of God and the values of the Kingdom of God, that is, "formal justice, truthfulness, and freedom."[101]

In the face of these manifestations of the demonic, the church is called to a twofold task of resistance: disengage from the forces of disintegration; and active preparation for the new. The first task is relatively self-evident. The second requires a rethinking of the ultimate meaning of history from the perspective of history's center (the Christ) and an application of the results of this rethinking to reality in and outside the church. Further, active preparation calls the church to activity outside its formal bounds that confront the noted demonisms: using socialism's "material justice" against capitalism; drawing on pacifism's vision of the unity of humanity against nationalism; and defending human dignity as expressed through the rights

---

[98]Tillich, "The Kingdom of God and History," 55-56.

[99]One way Tillich defined the demonic was "Structure against individual will. The 'good' capitalist and the 'good' nationalist. The demonic self-destruction of the peace policy." Tillich, "The Religious Socialist Movement," 4. In his address to the Fall 1940 conference of the Fellowship of Socialist Christians, "The Meaning of the Triumph of Nazism," Tillich spoke of Nazism as the consequence of the disintegration of German and European culture. Charles Stinnette, Jr., "Fellowship Conference," *Christianity and Society* 5/4 (1940): 45-46. Berdyaev echoed Tillich's (and socialism's) view that the meaning of World War I was the catastrophe of capitalism, a catastrophe affecting all of culture. Tillich, "Nicholas Berdyaev," 414-15.

[100]Tillich, "The Kingdom of God and History," 47-50.

[101]Tillich, "The Kingdom of God and History," 50, 51.

of man against dictatorship.[102]

Church and State. Tillich wrote that the Gospel is transcendent in its source and fulfillment and imminent in its application and significance: "the kingdom of God is not only of another world; it is also *in* this world . . . the detachment in principle must be followed by a concern in actuality."[103] Tillich was mindful of the range of ways Christianity worked out the transcendence-imminence dialectic within the church-state relationship. Roman Catholicism equates the Kingdom of God with the church, therefore asserting its authority over all realms of life. Calvinism asserts God's sovereignty over all realms of life. Eastern Orthodoxy, specifically in Russia, had united church and state in the czar, but then asserted church authority over religious rites and state authority over politics. And Lutheranism, dominant within Germany, rejects the identification of the Kingdom of God with the church and distinguishes private and public morality.[104]

The state is the organized embodiment of power.[105] A state uses its power to establish a social order by means of laws. As an extension of its traditional law-giving role, the modern state became an autonomous bureaucratic entity.[106] Equal justice seems to be a part of the concept of state. However, the question becomes whether power or justice will take priority, whether the "law concept of state" or the "power concept of state" will govern the situation.[107]

---

[102]Tillich, "The Kingdom of God and History," 54-55.

[103]Paul Tillich, "The Gospel and the State," *Crozer Quarterly* 15/4 (October 1938): 251-52.

[104]Paul Tillich, "The Totalitarian State and the Claims of the Church," *Social Research: An International Quarterly on Political and Social Science* 1/4 (November 1934): 420-23.

[105]Paul Tillich, "Church and State: Lecture Two from Three Lectures at Union Seminary" 1938 (PTAH 408:009), 2.

[106]Tillich, "Church and State: Lecture Two . . . ," 3-4.

[107]Tillich, "Church and State: Lecture Two . . . ," 4. Plato took seriously power theory in his discussion of the state. Tillich associated Machiavelli with "the invention of state reason" as a promoter of the power concept. Tillich noted that Machiavelli "prefers republic, but writes in order to advise a tyrant to use any immoral means in order to maintain the state," a fact understandable in the Italian situation. Tillich, "Church and State," 5. Tillich gave as examples of raison d'etat over against political rights the absolute monarchy of prerevolutionary France, Ivan

The dialectical tension between power and law in the state expresses
that power is necessary to tame demonic chaos, but that law is required to

---

IV of Russia, and Frederic Wilhelm I of Germany, and he noted the analogous
religious examples of the Russian czar as God on earth ("God's power on earth is
the power of state and church in identity") and the secular political claims of
Roman Catholic popes, spawning the response of Machiavelli noted before. Tillich,
"Church and State," 5-7. (Tillich crossed out comments regarding Hobbes's
Leviathan in his list of secular examples at this point, perhaps to stay with examples
of rulers embodying this power model versus a theorist thereof.) He pointed to
Lutheranism as the exemplar of "spiritualism with respect to the church and power
theory with respect to the state." Tillich, "Church and State," 8. Finally, the thought
of Marx and Nietzsche were the basis for two unrestricted power theories of state,
according to Tillich: Russian communism and German fascism. (Tillich, "Church
and State," 9-12.) Turning to the law theory of state, Tillich cited Plato, Aristotle,
and Plotinus for the comment, "the state is essentially an organization of justice."
Tillich, "Church and State," 12. With Platonic idealism, Stoic rationalism, and
Epicurean atomism, "the concept of state is fulfilled if justice and consequently the
happiness of all is realized." Tillich, "Church and State," 13. Roman Catholicism
uses natural law (through social contract theory) as the basis for criticizing the state,
but also for asserting its own secular power aims. Bourgeois state theory was also
rooted in natural law, standing against feudalism, religious fanaticism, and absolute
princes: "Its powerful state was supposed to serve the realization of the natural laws
of justice, freedom, equality, the rights of man." Tillich, "Church and State," 14.
However, the examples of Prussia, revolutionary France, and England illustrate that
the law-theory of state requires power. Tillich, "Church and State," 14-15.
Religious perspectives possessing a strong sociological concern are consistent with
the law-theory of state. The right to criticize the state and the expectation of
tolerance by the state is present in Roman Catholicism, Calvinism and American
denominationalism. However, tolerance is not necessarily connected with the law
theory. The level of tolerance plays out variously in both the law-theory and power-
theory of state. The tolerance of religion may indicate that a state views religion as
being little or no threat. Both theories of state can use tolerance—or the absence
thereof—based on need. Tillich, "Church and State," 16-17. Tillich believed that
Christianity acknowledged the need for both theories. The difficult question is the
tension and imbalance between a prospective international system based on the law-
theory over against nation states founded on the power-theory. The church needed
to be wary of being "paganized" by the power state and marginalized by the law
state. Tillich, "Church and State," 18.

give order to the state and prevent it from becoming demonic.[108] Tillich argued that totalitarianism seemed to represent the victory of the power pole. The economic insecurity of bourgeois capitalism had led to "the concentration of the national state," the prerequisite of totalitarianism.[109] The antidemocratic culture of eastern and central Europe was another basis of the totalitarian state.[110] Russian totalitarianism stood against capitalism and for the spread of "communist enlightenment" on behalf of "the individual and the full development of his collectivistic activities," the success of which would mean the downfall of authoritarianism and totalitarianism.[111]

Under German totalitarianism, the state was raised to mythic, unconditional significance, subordinating all other cultural spheres to its power.[112] Tillich broadly criticized Christianity's response to state power: Roman Catholicism for its equation of God and church; the Anglicans for functioning as a tool of both the state and the ruling class; German Lutheranism for its history of requiring strong state rule, with the ultimately destructive affects of Nazism; and the American church for its blind idealism.[113] Caving in to Nazi totalitarianism continued Germany's cultural disintegration rather than furthering reintegration.[114] Christianity under Hitler had submitted to human power and defied God's sovereignty.[115] Applying the relationship of law and power to the discussion of international politics, Tillich wrote, "[A]s long as there are sovereign nations which act according to their natural will to power, it is idealistic utopianism to assume that those States could be subjected to law without an

---

[108]Tillich, "The Gospel and the State," 253-54.

[109]Tillich, "The Totalitarian State," 408-10.

[110]Tillich, "The Totalitarian State," 410-11.

[111]Tillich, "The Totalitarian State," 413.

[112]Tillich, "The Totalitarian State," 413-15. Emanuel Hirsch described the state as the "mysterious sovereign" who was "not God . . . but an immediate revelation of God." "The Totalitarian State," 415-17.

[113]Paul Tillich, "The European War and the Christian Churches," *Direction* (Darien CT) 2/8 (December 1939): 11. Tillich and Carl Mennicke were of common mind that the place where social pedagogy was most needed was the United States. Tillich, *My Travel Diary*, 65.

[114]Tillich, *My Travel Diary*, 50.

[115]Tillich, "The Totalitarian State," 419-20.

embracing power strong enough to enforce the law."[116]

The second dialectical tension in the Gospel-State question is whether individuals are the priority for the state or the state is the goal of individuals belonging to it. Liberal democracy is based on the former. Authoritarian models lean on the latter.[117] Christianity never completely surrenders the significance of individual dignity, "the infinite value of each individual personality as a potential image and child of God."[118] But, Tillich believed "Christianity never has and never should neglect" the pole of authority.[119] Tillich favored a doctrine "in which community is the first and individuality is the second, but in which not the State as such and not the individual as such are the ultimate goal of history but the honor and glory of the Kingdom of God."[120]

The third and final dialectical tension described by Tillich is that between form and content. States driving towards form are simply the protective institution of other life forms independent of it. States driving towards content have a meaningful, creative purpose or spiritual substance.[121] This dialectic played itself in history: from the primal, tribal identity of "state" and religion to the transcendent Roman "abstract state" in the pre-Christian period; the prophetic protest against equating state and religion and in denying immediate access to God, epitomized by Jewish prophecy; the evolution from Constantine's Christian state to a Christian government without "direct religious functions"; and the twentieth century secularization of the state, creating a vacuum filled by a regressive tribalism.[122] Tillich wrote, "the Gospel is the fundamental and everlasting protest against tribal religion, religious nationalism and State adoration."[123]

Biblical Tradition and Marxism. Tillich argued that the conditions of mass disintegration—"the social and intellectual situation of late capitalism"—required mass reintegration.[124] His religious socialism was a

[116]Tillich, "The Gospel and the State," 255.
[117]Tillich, "The Gospel and the State," 255-56.
[118]Tillich, "The Gospel and the State," 256.
[119]Tillich, "The Gospel and the State," 257.
[120]Tillich, "The Gospel and the State," 258.
[121]Tillich, "The Gospel and the State," 258.
[122]Tillich, "The Gospel and the State," 259-60.
[123]Tillich, "The Gospel and the State," 260.
[124]Paul Tillich, "The End of the Protestant Era (1937)?" in *The Protestant Era*

Christian-Marxist hybrid. This was possible because he believed that Marxism and Christianity shared some common concerns: the understanding of human nature in a larger context (related to God in Christianity, related to society in Marxism); the belief in an original perfect state of humanity; the perception of actual human nature as a contradiction to that original harmony; a concern for the perilous state created by this contradiction; a sense of existence as the partial, fragmentary overcoming of this state of contradiction; and a vision of a final overcoming of the contradiction.[125]

In Tillich's construction, the divergence between Marxism and Christianity relates to Christianity's transcendence and Marxism's immanence, the differences in their diagnosis and resolution of the contradiction between original and actual human nature,[126] and Protestantism's individualism versus Marxism's socialism. While communism, fascism, and Roman Catholicism were mass movements able to respond to the need for mass reintegration, Protestantism had to change to survive.[127]

Tillich called the church as a whole to a theoretical and a practical strategy. The church lacked a precise knowledge of communist history and theory.[128] Thus, Tillich explained communism as the secularized prophetic: a natural mass response to mass disintegration rooted in the demonisms of capitalism and nationalism.[129] Communism attested to the absence of a

---

(Chicago: University of Chicago Press, 1948) 223, 225. This is a different piece from "The End of the Protestant Era," *The Student World* 30/1 (First Quarter 1937).

[125]Paul Tillich, "The Christian and the Marxist View of Man" (Universal Christian Council for Life and Work, December 1935) PTAH 402:017, 9-13.

[126]Tillich, "The Christian and the Marxist View of Man," 14-17.

[127]"The End of the Protestant Era?" 226, 229.

[128]Paul Tillich, "The Church and Communism," *Religion and Life* 6/3 (Summer 1937): 347-49.

[129]Tillich, "The Church and Communism," 350-51. Tillich wrote of the analogies he believed existed between Marxist doctrine and biblical prophecy. First is the third stage of history represented by the 1,000-year reign of Christ in Revelation and the third stage (the human stage of history) in Marxist thought. Tillich, "Marx and the Prophetic Tradition," *Radical Religion* 1/4 (Autumn 1935): 21-22. Second is a philosophy of life that is "historical," that is, linear rather than circular (as in Greek mythology and philosophy). History is not about pursuing the true or the false, but is a struggle between good and evil from which we cannot escape into a history-transcending one-ness with God. Tillich, "Marx and the

prophetic spirit within the church. At the same time, Tillich summoned the churches to challenge communism's secularism, utopianism, lies, and tyranny.[130]

Further, Tillich believed church leaders should be taught about communism. The church should publicly echo "the communistic criticism of the present social demonries," but not endorse any political party or movement, sliding into idolatry.[131] The laity should work to combine communist and Christian principles in their lives. Finally, the church as a whole needed both to work to become an embodiment of the Kingdom of God and to consider communism in the same light as every other historical movement, with a combination of "religious reservation" and "religious obligation."[132]

Prophetic," 22-23. In contrast to the general transcendence of Zoroastrianism and the general immanence of Egyptian religion, the prophetic position mixes the two: the prophetic—with all if its immanent concerns—never loses the transcendent. Tillich argued that further parallels with the prophetic tradition manifested a "latent transcendence" within Marxism. The pronouncement of God's willingness to sacrifice the nation dominated by a repressive ruling class parallels Marx's description of the necessity of toppling an ideologically driven oppressor. The type of conflict they describe is the same: the struggle for justice. A dualism between the perpetrators and victims of justice exists in both. The election of a specifically defined group to bring about this liberation to justice is present in both. Finally, freedom and necessity are combined within each of them: for the prophets, humanity is "under divine decree," yet that decree "is accomplished through human actions"; for Marx, a structural necessity towards revolution may exist, but the proletariat must act. Tillich, "Marx and the Prophetic," 23-28. Tillich succinctly stated the relationship between necessity and human freedom: "Whoever destroys this union between dialectic necessity and human freedom misses the import of our historical existence. He is Utopian, if he expects everything of human freedom; he is fatalist, if he rests inactive upon necessity, and depends upon the automatic fulfillment of structural laws." Tillich, "Marx and the Prophetic," 28.

[130]Tillich, "The Church and Communism," 351-53.

[131]Tillich, "The Church and Communism," 354-55.

[132]Tillich, "The Church and Communism," 356-57. Such a view was confirmed by discussions and news regarding the Russian situation which Tillich had during his 1936 European trip.: on 26 April 1936, his friend Adolf Löwe expressed very positive feelings toward Russia (Tillich, *My Travel Diary*, 47); on June 8, 1936, Tillich recorded Hendrik de Man's desire to see Russia taking "the lead position" if war broke out (Tillich, *My Travel Diary*, 93); and on 26 August 1936, Tillich recorded the "shattering revelation" that "Stalin [had] had his former comrades-in-

All of this would put Christianity into the position to understand the attacks of dialectical materialism (Marx's analysis of capitalism) upon Christianity: the "lack of prophetic protest" in past church-state alliances;[133] liberal bourgeois humanism's use of ideology to conceal capitalist economic exploitation;[134] Christian idealism and transcendentalism that diminishes the importance of social justice and politics; and individualism and escapism that neglects social heroism.[135] Christianity could then push dialectical materialism to see that the import of history, social justice, and politics is one of unconditional depth.[136] More than this, in all its forms, rites, and practices, Christianity must speak to those yearning for reintegration. In its openness to the secular world, Christianity must point to the holy within all spheres of life. It should bear the prophetic protest against ultimate claims by penultimate powers.[137] Christianity must affirm transcendence (not escapism) as way to survive "situations of complete social despair" and love as the life-giving, creative root of social justice.[138] Taken together, this would protect social heroism from utopianism and resignation.[139]

Religion and World Politics

In addition to analyses of Christianity's relationship to the state and to political ideology, Tillich addressed the role of religion within international affairs. The place where he expressed his views most directly, systematically, and extensively was in an unfinished work from 1939, "Religion und Weltpolitik."[140]

---

arms shot" (Tillich, *My Travel Diary*, 167).

[133]Paul Tillich, "The Attack of Dialectical Materialism on Christianity," *The Student World* 31/2 (Second Quarter 1938): 118.

[134]Tillich, "The Attack of Dialectical Materialism on Christianity," 119-21. Tillich argued that Christianity should see ideology more deeply as idolatry and false prophecy, sharpen its anti-ideological weapon—the suspicion of ideology—and direct it particularly against itself.

[135]Tillich, "The Attack of Dialectical Materialism on Christianity," 123-24.

[136]Tillich, "The Attack of Dialectical Materialism on Christianity," 121-23.

[137]Tillich, "The End of the Protestant Era?" 229-30.

[138]Tillich, "The Attack of Dialectical Materialism on Christianity," 123-24.

[139]Tillich, "The Attack of Dialectical Materialism on Christianity," 124-25.

[140]While the *Gesammelte Werke, Band IX* gives 1938 as the date for the work,

Introduction. Tillich centered "the theme of the whole book and the leading idea for all solutions which are put forward in it" around religion's claim upon world politics: "the demand placed by religion on world politics is that it be *world*-politics."[141] The dynamics of world history from 1914 to the time of his writing seemed to convince Tillich that all parochial movements—such as nationalism—destructively, oppressively and unjustly exalted the smaller perspective over the larger one. Therefore, *world* became his metaphor for transcending the limited viewpoint of the local. He declared that "national politics should turn itself into the instrument for world politics, because the political goal is not 'nation', but rather 'world.' "[142] In short, "Religion demands that 'world' become political reality."[143]

Tillich believed history showed a pattern of collective de-politicization against which a later individualistic, economically motivated, international middle class arose, but which was incapable of bringing internationalism into reality. The roots of de-politicizing life were planted by the Roman Empire. Its victory over city and national-states, and its policy of centralization led to "the de-politicization of general consciousness, the separation of culture and political life, and the identification of political behavior with governmental behavior."[144] Epicurus' notion of private life gave "classic expression to the alienation of politics from the rest of life." The admonition of Paul and early Christianity to be subject to governing authorities set the basis for "debasing political citizenship in favor of citizenship in the kingdom of heaven."[145] By Luther's time, political conduct was limited to negative police power, possessing no positive, creative mandate.[146]

Theocratic internationalism proceeded simultaneously with Roman de-politicization. The church took on ever more political functions: "politics

---

documents in the Paul Tillich Archive at Harvard record 1939 in Tillich's own handwriting as the date of composition (PTAH 205A:001 and 205A:002).

[141] Paul Tillich, "Religion und Weltpolitik, Ein Fragment (1939)," in *Die Religiöse Substanz der Kultur: Schriften zur Theologie der Kultur, Gesammelte Werke, Band IX:* (Stuttgart: Evangelisches Verlagswerk, 1967) 139.

[142] Tillich, "Religion und Weltpolitik, Ein Fragment," 139; Tillich's emphasis.

[143] Tillich, "Religion und Weltpolitik, Ein Fragment," 139.

[144] Tillich, "Religion und Weltpolitik, Ein Fragment," 140-41.

[145] Tillich, "Religion und Weltpolitik, Ein Fragment," 141.

[146] Tillich, "Religion und Weltpolitik, Ein Fragment," 141.

was born again as church politics."[147] Popes Gregory VII and Innocence III combined ideas derived from Roman imperialism with Stoic ideas and with Platonic thoughts on the Greek city-state. They saw "the Christian church as representing the universal kingdom of God in history": political will and the prophetic interpretation of history were combined in their thought.[148] National empires were "forerunners of completed theocracies" and "opposing principalities . . . [were] antigodly, with their end foretold."[149] This was later seen in the Byzantium emperor-papacy and in the power over the church of German emperors.[150]

However, the impracticality of these claims ultimately allowed nationalistic movements to become victorious. The conflicting claims of Rome and the German emperors planted seeds for antagonism toward theocracy and internationalism. It was natural for Machiavelli to focus on the realities of the city-state polity amidst the turmoil caused in Italy by a politicized papacy.[151] Consequently, the spirit of the Hobbesian Leviathan—"expansion and defense"—dominated late-Renaissance Europe.[152]

Nationalism was eventually challenged by capitalism's expansion of markets by means of colonies. The bourgeoisie's exclusively economic interests led Tillich to interpret Kant's vision of "eternal peace" for the sake of the individual as too abstract to chart how to establish political peace in such a world. Worse, the void in political theory led to the nationalistic exploitation of economics.[153]

Despite all of this, Tillich declared that "international political thought [had] not disappeared."[154] He saw it in the anticapitalist-proletarian movements, in church and humanist pacifist groups, and in the League of Nations. The fact that contemporary dictatorships were aggressively challenging the idea of a just world order put the international idea at center

---

[147]Tillich, "Religion und Weltpolitik, Ein Fragment," 141.

[148]Tillich, "Religion und Weltpolitik, Ein Fragment," 141-42.

[149]Tillich, "Religion und Weltpolitik, Ein Fragment," 142.

[150]Tillich, "Religion und Weltpolitik, Ein Fragment," 142.

[151]Tillich wrote that Machiavelli "gives classic expression to the new meaning of politics." "Religion und Weltpolitik," 143.

[152]"Religion und Weltpolitik," 143.

[153]"Religion und Weltpolitik," 144.

[154]"Religion und Weltpolitik," 144.

stage.[155] From this historical introduction, Tillich moved to the first and more extensively developed part of his two-part discussion, the concept of world.

The Concept of World. Tillich's discussion of the conception of world in this document follows the following outline: world-"having"; the technological world-concept and the idea of progress; the theoretical world-concept and the problem of ideology; the moral world-concept and the problem of justice; and the political world-concept and the problem of power.

The "having" of world is a concept Tillich credited largely to Martin Heidegger's existentialism. To have a world means three things. First, it means "to belong to an all-encompassing oneness/unity." The completeness of the self depends on "the universality of that which is ever against the self."[156] We are who we are in relationship to a larger universal entity, a relationship which Tillich called the world-self-correlation. Without this, we are less than human.[157] Second, having world means "to belong to a structure which constitutes the unifying relationship of world (and self)." The mathematically meaningful cosmos of Pythagoras and the logos of Parmenides indicate that world-having requires a structure without which world and consciousness would crumble into chaos.[158] Third, to have world means the possession of "eternity for the free self."[159] Tillich wrote, "The eternity of the world is the possibility of endless transcendence beyond every world-having/worldly [*welthaft*] given."[160] Politically, the denial of the "world-political/ internationalist idea turns the political into a captive, in principle, a ready-made function of a limited, vegetative or brutish group existence and cuts it off from the eternal, world-having possibility."[161]

By *technische* and *Technik* Tillich meant science and technology. For him, to conceptualize and, subsequently, to produce anything—whether primitive or sophisticated—testifies to the capacity for eternal transcendence within human beings. This distinguishes human beings from

[155]"Religion und Weltpolitik," 144-45.
[156]"Religion und Weltpolitik," 146.
[157]"Religion und Weltpolitik," 145-46.
[158]"Religion und Weltpolitik," 146-47.
[159]"Religion und Weltpolitik," 145, 146, 147, 148.
[160]"Religion und Weltpolitik," 147.
[161]"Religion und Weltpolitik," 148.

animals.[162]

Within this capacity for technological invention, Tillich placed his discussion of the idea of progress. Tillich made seven assertions regarding progress: First, because it is an essential part of the technological world-concept, it is incorrect to reject completely the notion of progress. Second, while progress participates in the process of capturing the eternal (through theoretical conceptualizations) on behalf of the finite (concrete tools/products), it does not question "why" or "for what" in the world-having sense of an eternal goal. Third, the eternal goal or meaning is not amenable to the idea of progress, given that meaning manifests itself to a self and given that there is no meaning against which to measure progress. Fourth, progress is inappropriate for such areas as philosophy and art, creative forms based on a "free grasp of meaning in the interplay of world and self."[163] A phenomenon may be better or worse representation of a style, but one period is not better than another period. Fifth, in ethics, progress is limited by freedom: decision-making patterns which surrender freedom surrender humanity, personality, and character as well. Sixth, there is no biological basis for the idea of progress. Plants, animals, and humanity each have an eternal significance untouched by the relative quality of their organs of adaptation. And, seventh, both religion and politics are realms of "grasping and actualizing eternal meaning and not that of [the] means-end-relationship" of technological progress.[164]

Given that technological development requires a knowledge of the peculiar qualities of the material being shaped, theoretical knowledge is as ancient as technological knowledge. It too is rooted in the self-world-correlation. It includes the pluralistic and the particular:

Without an element of identity of differences, pluralism comes to as little as monism without an element of difference in the identity. For the world political problem, that means that the world-unity which is given with the constitution of the world does not exclude a multiplicity of relatively independent political powers, but that the 'sovereignty' of those or the denial of the elements of identity among them abolishes 'world.'[165]

[162]"Religion und Weltpolitik," 149.
[163]"Religion und Weltpolitik," 152.
[164]"Religion und Weltpolitik," 153, 154.
[165]"Religion und Weltpolitik," 154.

Thus, pluralism and monism are both legitimate, and the denial of either denies the truth.

The theoretical approach arises from the double effort to establish the nature of structure: ontologically and scientifically. For Tillich, the late 1930s was characterized by the denial and denigration of the ontological and the exaltation of the scientific. However, science without ontological critique became vulnerable to being overwhelmed (and being made subject to) the pseudoscientific and the nontheoretical, as in Nazism.[166]

Tillich declared that "the theoretical inexhaustibility of the world is the sharpest expression for the infinitude of world-having."[167] The self's search for answers—its process of questioning the world—is unending. Further, the self-world-correlation which is at play—while requiring an infinite distance between self and world—requires a certain identity between the structures of self and world in order for theory to be possible. Ideology arises out of "the double character of theory": humanity as "knowing self" both stands over against the world and belongs to the world. This creates the perpetual tension within political theory, "the extent to which a theoretical world view expresses the world's structure and the extent to which it expresses the structure of being of a particular self (or a particular group)."[168] This describes the subjective and objective dimensions of knowledge. Tillich argued that if either is excluded, distorted knowledge results: pure objectivity (logical positivism) deprives it of "any connection to the knowing self"; pure subjectivity (National Socialist philosophy) deprives it of its "theoretical character, distance and objectivity."[169] Tillich argued that the particular and the pluralistic are united in "the knowing self, reflecting on itself, continuously maintaining the suspicion of ideology against itself, and making the decision in relationship to an analysis of the concrete situation, in which a spiritual creation should arise."[170]

Tillich discounted the capacity of the technical and the theoretical (now conflated) to maintain world: "Neither the infinite transcendence of technological activity nor the inner inexhaustibility of theoretical objectivity are

---

[166]"Religion und Weltpolitik," 155.
[167]"Religion und Weltpolitik," 155.
[168]"Religion und Weltpolitik," 156.
[169]"Religion und Weltpolitik," 157.
[170]"Religion und Weltpolitik," 158.

capable of serving as the foundation for the self-world-correlation or world-having. Neither possesses the strength to prevent the intermixture of self and world and, with that, the destruction of the correlation."[171] One sees the world as technologically conquerable. The other feels the self dominated and determined by the world. They are simultaneous, noncontradictory, and mutually strengthening tendencies. The self cannot escape its infinite side, but attempts to carry out an "infinite" struggle in the finite realm (the world), in contradiction to the nature of the world. The self's aspiration to dominate the world requires adaptation to the peculiar structure of the world: "The mass person—having turned into a machine through its service to the machine—is the symbol for this turn of the technological will-to-rule into its opposite."[172] The moral conception of the world prevents the collapse of the self-world-correlation.

The moral is "primarily an expression of the boundary on which each individual self experiences other individual selves," a boundary on which each self offers the unconditional and often unspoken claim "to be acknowledged . . . as the bearer of a self-world-correlation," that is, "the acknowledgement of the encountered self as self," creating an I-you (*ich-du*) relationship, a claim (taken as a whole) bearing the name, "justice."[173] Tillich declared that the unconditional claims of the moral world precede the technological-theoretical world: "When Heraclitus says, 'Those who are awake share a common world, while asleep each person has their own world,' we must add that those who promote a common theory are not yet awake, but only those who are aroused by the claim of the other."[174]

Justice protects the self's capacity for decision, equality, freedom, and happiness. The capacity for decision requires that each self be seen as an individual whose claim to be acknowledged as a self is fulfilled. Justice requires each self to be seen equally as selves "in the sense of world-having."[175] The self is free when it "has" world rather than simply being a part of it and when it "represents" or "exhibits" the world's structure: unlimited economic exploitation lacks the infinite structure commensurate

---

[171]"Religion und Weltpolitik," 159.
[172]"Religion und Weltpolitik," 160.
[173]"Religion und Weltpolitik," 160, 162.
[174]"Religion und Weltpolitik," 162.
[175]"Religion und Weltpolitik," 163.

with that freedom.[176] Happiness is found by an infinite, unconditioned self which is "completely at one with itself as part of the world."[177] This happiness is lost either through escapism (rejecting the world) or through the objectifying dehumanization: unhappiness comes from debasing either world or self. Justice is crucial, but always vulnerable: "A just order cannot forcibly bring about happiness. The moral world is constantly threatened by its own presupposition: freedom."[178]

For Tillich, the existence of an ethical world was dependent upon the interplay of mutually acknowledging, decision-making selves who make up political communities which bring together the other, aforementioned conceptions of world. Totalitarianism seeks to deny this, spelling its own destruction, given the political realm's dependence on "the practicality of technological activity, the purity of theory, the concrete ethical decision within the individual self."[179] The political world-concept is the basis for all others and requires power and justice. Their effective existence requires tradition, law and ethos: "Tradition gives the other two substantial form, law forms tradition into statute and gives it effective force, ethos (using tradition, law and education) forms the individual self in the sense of the ethical substance of the whole."[180] All of this requires power, "power to be in the relationship of being in general . . . and power to make one's way in the interplay of individual encounters, to preserve tradition, to enforce the law, and to carry out education."[181] The image used by prophetic religion for a complete world was a political one: the kingdom of God.[182]

The self exists to the degree it offers resistance in the encounter with other selves. The self has the capacity both to form itself and to form the world: this is its infinitude and exhaustibility. The meaning of infinitude and inexhaustibility is captured by the myth of life-after-death, philosophy's notion of the soul's immortality, and Christianity's doctrine of the resurrection.[183]

---

[176]"Religion und Weltpolitik," 163-64.
[177]"Religion und Weltpolitik," 164, 165.
[178]"Religion und Weltpolitik," 165, 166.
[179]"Religion und Weltpolitik," 166-67.
[180]"Religion und Weltpolitik," 167.
[181]"Religion und Weltpolitik," 167-68.
[182]"Religion und Weltpolitik," 168.
[183]"Religion und Weltpolitik," 169.

Tillich saw the state as the necessary entity through which the ethical (justice) and the natural (power) are manifested. It embodies the just limitation placed on the self by other selves. Justice is the saving factor, voicing the rights and the claims of the self.[184]

Both the execution of justice and the exercise of power in history are carried out by individuals. They speak (and/or possess the power to speak) for a small or large group or for themselves, no matter the form of government. Through them, the unconditional, universal claims of justice are actualized in history. Democracies—theoretically the guarantors of justice—can be ruled by majorities resistant to the universal claim of justice. Dictators occasionally can fulfill those claims. The benefit of democracy is its amenability to ordered change intended to bring about greater justice, over against the need for revolutionary action to accomplish change in nondemocratic systems: "the more claims of individuals it is capable of perceiving and translating into reality, the more just a power is."[185]

Tillich understood states as necessary, but he also saw them to be potential barriers to the existence of "world." He declared, "The teaching of the sovereignty of the nation-state is the clearest and sharpest form in which world as political reality is denied."[186] States tend to give unconditional force to their power, rather than limiting their power.[187] The existence of world required some other notion than the unchallengeable, sovereignty of particular nations.

Two basic patterns of world-creation had been imperialism (the Roman and British Empires) and international organization (League of Nations) to which some sovereignty was sacrificed. Rome crushed national identity. Britain cultivated balance-of-power schemes. The League either failed to overcome national sovereignty or acted imperialistically.[188]

Tillich supported a third alternative that erodes away state sovereignty through "the formation of overlapping communities as future bearers of a unified world-power."[189] Tillich called this "the horizontal solution in

---

[184]"Religion und Weltpolitik," 169-71.
[185]"Religion und Weltpolitik," 171-72.
[186]"Religion und Weltpolitik," 173.
[187]"Religion und Weltpolitik," 173-74.
[188]"Religion und Weltpolitik," 174-75.
[189]"Religion und Weltpolitik," 175.

contrast to the vertical one of imperialism and the unworkable mixed solution of the League."[190] Tillich wrote that this part of his framework would be developed in the second and third parts of his book: he only began part two; and part three was, evidently, never begun. However, he did offer five fundamentals which he had intended to build upon more extensively later. First, the previously developed notion of justice as the mutual acknowledgement of each encountered self as free, world-having beings possessing equal dignity is rooted in the biblical idea of the "neighbor." Second, the community of neighbors is built on direct interaction. Third, upon these direct encounters, the nature of indirect encounters are to be understood. Fourth, upon both of these, justice is abstractly codified. And, fifth, the abstract becomes concrete through actual encounters.[191] Tillich believed that justice defined intra-nationally was incapable of leading to world.

Tillich asserted that "the political" is part of what it means to be human. The lower limit of the political is "naked power" without cognizance of "the power and dignity of the individual," and the upper limit of the political is that in which justice is executed without power (which Tillich characterized as an "angelic-world") out of which pacifism and world-renunciation can arise.[192]

Religion and the Concept of World. Following the above discussion of the world-concept, Tillich's fragment gives the beginning of his thoughts on religion and the world-concept: the relation of religion to world-having and religion's relationship to the technological and theoretical conceptions of world.

Tillich sought to look behind the self-world-correlation to the root from which it arises and in which self and world are unified: the correlation's religious dimension. This involves three questions: #1—whether and why one must look beyond the self-world-correlation, a correlation which he called, "the human"; #2—what comes into view when one transcends the human; and #3—how that which is visible only through transcending the human relates to the human.[193]

Transcendence implies and assumes the religious. Tillich probed

---

[190]"Religion und Weltpolitik," 175.
[191]"Religion und Weltpolitik," 175-76.
[192]"Religion und Weltpolitik," 177.
[193]"Religion und Weltpolitik," 177-78.

beneath religion as "a particular religious form" to a religious philosophy concerned with "the point at which the religious breaks into the human, the limits of the self-world-correlation."[194] He specified the relationship of the self to world more particularly: each determines the other without establishing the other; and the integrity of each is maintained without denying the impact each has on the other. This position rejects Fichte's self-exalting idealism and Nietzsche's world-exalting naturalism in favor of a "bearing-ground" beneath each, beholden to neither, a ground symbolically designated, "beyond self and world."[195] Religious philosophy "disclose[s] this structure of religious consciousness," using symbols derived from religion, but unhindered by religion in analyzing their structure.[196]

The "beyond self and world" lies at the foundation of self and world, or being and freedom, and is beyond the theoretical and the ethical: "it cuts through all world views and gives them their peculiar quality. . . . The religious qualifies the other world-concepts, but adds nothing to them."[197] It is captured in the symbol of creation, as well as its separation from that which is beyond, captured in the symbol of the Fall. While the self-world-correlation is not determined or conditioned by existence, its created-ness confirms the correlation. It offers a "yes, but" to that correlation, going beyond humanistic formulations.[198] The creation myth displays a primordial wisdom concerning world, long before the theoretical world-concept is conceived. And the religious myth shows "a primordial wisdom concerning the threat of world long before political reflection held out the prospect for world catastrophes . . . the Fall is an act, thus it has the element of freedom within itself which belongs to an act; and it is simultaneously event, thus it has the element of necessity within itself which belongs to an occurrence."[199]

To the symbols of creation and fall as central to world-having, Tillich added the kingdom of God. The kingdom of God both confirms the

---

[194]"Religion und Weltpolitik," 177-78.
[195]"Religion und Weltpolitik," 178-79.
[196]"Religion und Weltpolitik," 179.
[197]"Religion und Weltpolitik," 179-80.
[198]"Religion und Weltpolitik," 180. Tillich said that the creation notion is foundational for the world-concept "in the double sense of moving beyond and moving toward it" (180-81).
[199]"Religion und Weltpolitik," 180-81, 182.

construction of a politically based moral order while holding out the symbol of an ultimate community rooted in love which qualifies fragmented, penultimate historical communities. Prophetic religion is the bearer of this symbol.[200]

After considering the relationship of religion to world-having, the fragment concludes with two sections that begin to draw the relationship of religion to the different concepts of world: Tillich addresses religion's relationship to the technological world-concept and to the theoretical world-concept.

The Old Testament creation story and the Prometheus story from Greek mythology informed Tillich's treatment of religion and technology. On the one hand, the creation story affirms humanity's role as co-creator. However, humanity is continuously tempted to supersede the limits established for humanity: see the Prometheus myth and the story of Adam and Eve in the Garden of Eden. By transgressing its limits, humanity robs God. Technology leads to progress and to *hubris*,[201] but points to supra-historical fulfillment.[202]

Turning to religion and the theoretical, Tillich suggested that theory's antagonism toward religion exalts the objective over the subjective. Yet, to treat the realm of "the unconditioned," theory must use the matter of being which it seeks to transcend. And the Kantian construction of the ethical based purely on the ethical claim could not avoid rooting it theoretically. Though Hegel's formulation led to state-idolatry, it mustered both religion and theory, subjectivity and objectivity, to establish their primordial unity, endeavoring "to draw the beyond self-and-world into the self and, through it, into the world."[203]

The world-transcending qualification is an important corrective for the purely theoretical, because it ultimately corrects ideology.[204] It provides a corrective limited by neither objective reason nor subjective knowledge, yet grasped by the historical individual as the locus of truth, in the manner

---

[200]"Religion und Weltpolitik," 182-83. Tillich declared extreme, world-escaping religious mysticisms as essentially irrelevant to the discussion of world politics and religion.

[201]"Religion und Weltpolitik," 183-84.

[202]"Religion und Weltpolitik," 185.

[203]"Religion und Weltpolitik," 189.

[204]"Religion und Weltpolitik," 189.

understood by Kierkegaard: "The truth is historical, that is the prophetic insight."[205] False prophecy turns historically bound truth into ideology. Thus, true prophets maintain a self-critical suspicion of ideology, directed even at themselves, as noted before: "the truth which [the prophetic spirit] grasps—or by which it is grasped—is never only 'theoretical' in the sense of objectifying distance, but also 'practical' in the sense of unconditioned demand."[206] Limited to neither political theory nor ecclesiastical institutions, "The prophetic spirit blows where it wills, within churches and parties, and against churches and parties."[207] At this point, the fragment concludes.

Conclusion

Tillich experienced Union Theological Seminary to be a shelter and refuge. It was an important help in coping with the loss of a way of life in his homeland and in rebuilding life and career in a new place. From his position of exile, he observed, "If New York is the bridge between the continents, Union Seminary is the lane of that bridge, on which the churches of the world move."[208] Tillich found "that a too quick adaptation is not what the New World expects from the immigrant, but rather preservation of the old values and their translation into the terminology of the new culture."[209]

Tillich had landed in a place where his boundary perspective could thrive, where he could put into practice "the mind's power and dynamic nature to transcend any given actuality."[210] In this new situation, he could inform people ignorant about the German church and larger culture. He could translate elements of the political-theological framework he had developed within the fertile spirit of Weimar into a new historical period as well as a new geographic place, tracing the meaning of the collapse to which his philosophy of history had attested. On the boundary between retrospect and prospect, he could begin to sketch an outline of the relation of self and world in the broader world. Thus, the elements of a religious internationalism that are affirmed in a special way during this period of

---

[205]"Religion und Weltpolitik," 190.
[206]"Religion und Weltpolitik," 190.
[207]"Religion und Weltpolitik," 191. See John 3:8.
[208]Tillich, "Autobiographical Reflections," 16-17.
[209]Tillich, "Autobiographical Reflections," 19.
[210]Tillich, "Mind and Migration," 296.

Tillich's thought are these:

1. The perspective most conducive to a truthful interpretation of history is the dynamic boundary;

2. The *kairoi* are opportune periods for just and loving action within history to which participants in history can develop a sense of timing;

3. Religion bears the "suspicion of ideology" as a critical principle against all holders and institutions of power;

4. Religious orders of leading people of letters willing to approach the boundaries of their disciplines can function as fruitful, intellectual and spiritual centers for cultivating creative, cultural patterns;

5. Ethical behavior embraces "world," affirms human dignity, advocates active participation in history, is rooted in "the beyond self and world," stands for justice and love, and stands against injustice and hatred, including the unjust, space-bound, and dehumanizing provincialisms of nationalism, racism, and capitalism;

6. Cultures have vulnerabilities to idolatry which must be unveiled;

7. Cultures have groups vulnerable to injustice at the hands of the powerful;

8. Love and justice require that the self-world correlation be kept in balance, rejecting both arrogant imposition of self as well as the crushing domination by "world";

9. Prophetic, sacred texts can be central, primal sources for religious internationalism; and

10. Religion affirms international organization and looks on national sovereignty with deep suspicion.

Chapter 4

World War II—Tillich's Message to His Audience in Germany: The Voice of America Speeches

Introduction

From March 1942 through May 1944, Tillich wrote speeches for the Voice of America (VOA). The VOA invited Tillich, along with other celebrated personalities from lands conquered by Nazi Germany, to speak to his former compatriots based on his knowledge and experience of his former homeland and his new homeland. He was asked to speak the truth as he knew it.[1] The extent to which family, friends, and colleagues knew of his activity is unclear.[2] During the period Tillich wrote the speeches, he alluded to his radio broadcasts elsewhere on at least three occasions in print.[3]

The Voice of America was headed by Robert Sherwood. It was a section of the Office of War Information. Its goal was to use truth as an element of persuasion in the Allied forces' psychological warfare against the Axis powers. Its overseers saw its work to be the production of what they termed "white" propaganda. "White" propaganda used truth as the means of persuasion. Sherwood was unwilling to allow the VOA to be a propagator of "black" propaganda, communications which combined truth

---

[1]Karin Schäfer-Kretzler, "Einleitung," Paul Tillich's *An meine deutschen Freunde, Ergänzungs- und Nachlass-bände zu den Gesammelten Werken von Paul Tillich, Band III* (Stuttgart: Evangelisches Verlagswerk, 1973) 14.

[2]Tillich's biographers, Wilhelm and Marion Pauck, describe his VOA work as "an activity so wrapped in secrecy that not even his closest friends knew of it." Pauck, *Paul Tillich*, 198. This may reflect that Tillich did not make the speeches a frequent topic of conversation with his colleagues. Tillich's daughter, Erdmuthe Tillich Farris, seemed surprised to learn that her father had written the speeches. (Conversation with MLW in San Francisco, November 1997.)

[3]Paul Tillich, "Was soll mit Deutschland geschehen?" (Summer 1942) *GW XIII*, 281; Paul Tillich, "Comment on 'The Report of the Commission on a Just and Durable Peace'" *The Witness* 26 (8 April 1943): 4; and Paul Tillich, "The God of History" *Christianity and Crisis* 4/7 (1 May 1944): 5-6.

with falsehood.[4] Thus, Tillich's speeches were a part of a particular project within the Office of War Information.[5]

---

[4]Lawrence C. Soley, *Radio Warfare: OSS and CIA Subversive Propaganda* (New York: Praeger Publishers, 1989) 69, 71; Holly Cowan Shulman, *The Voice of America: Propaganda and Democracy, 1941–1945* (Madison: University of Wisconsin Press, 1990) 9, 25; and Clayton D. Laurie, *The Propaganda Warriors: America's Crusade Against Nazi Germany* (Lawrence: University of Kansas, 1996) 7, 119, 123.

[5]In three separate articles, Matthias Wolbold disputes my treatment of Tillich's work as propaganda. (Matthias Wolbold, "Meine Deutschen Freunde!"; "Against the Third Reich. Zur amerikanischen Erst-veröffentlichung der politischen Rundfunkreden Paul Tillichs," *Tillich Journal* 3 [1999]: 26-29; and "Tillich als expressionistischer Propagandist?") The less important criticisms of Wolbold arise from his wish that I had written an article on rhetoric rather than one on the content of the speeches within the general framework of rhetoric, purely subjective matters. The core of Wolbold's criticism arises in his review of my 1998 article on the VOA speeches (Weaver, "Paul Tillich and the Voice of America"). His review is the article "Tillich als expressionistischer Propagandist? Ein Antwort. . . . " Mr. Wolbold is critical of my use of propaganda theory as the beginning basis for understanding Tillich's VOA speeches. Yet, the VOA's administrators called what they produced "propaganda." Tillich's participation in the VOA's mission makes it impossible to exclude the issue of propaganda as a central element for understanding the speeches. The ambiguity of this is entirely consistent with Tillich's philosophical/theological understanding of what it means to be human: finite freedom or freedom combined with fate. We exercise our freedom, but we do so within limits often beyond our control. Tillich exercised his freedom in the production of the speeches, but he did so within the limits of the VOA's structure and goals. (This makes Wolbold's claim that the VOA speech-writers produced their work without "conscious propagandistic intent" irrelevant: whatever their intent, it was shaped by the institution using the speeches for its propagandistic purposes. See Wolbold, "Meine Deutschen Freunde! Die politischen Rundfunkreden Tillichs," 184-85.) Mr. Wolbold thinks I give inadequate attention to the 1943 change in the leadership of the VOA and its consequences for the content of the broadcasts (Wolbold, "Tillich als expressionistischer Propagandist?" 86). In fact, I give a quite literal characterization of the impact of this change in leadership and explain the intergovernmental agency disputes occurring at the time, implying the direction to which a leadership change might lead. My sources indicate that the truth content of speeches produced by authors for the VOA was not affected by the events of 1943 (Weaver, "Paul Tillich and the Voice of America,"

The impact of the VOA broadcasts was difficult to determine. The laws of atmospheric physics made the success of their short-wave broadcasts

---

24). Content was a concern to those critical of the VOA at the time only to the degree that VOA broadcasts risked making promises that the military could not effectively keep and that did not adequately reflect the ambiguousness of the relationship between the United States and its various international partners: that is, the timing of the liberation of the occupied territories and the prospects for Allied victory. Mr. Wolbold argues that I fail to connect my general account of Tillich's larger intellectual output—specifically religious socialism and the Protestant Principle—to the speeches (Wolbold, "Tillich als expressionistischer Propagandist?": 86). In point of fact, I did that in the article. (Weaver, "Paul Tillich and the Voice of America," 19-21, 26.) Further, I wrote of the political impact of World War I upon Tillich: "his passive conservatism turned into a more activist socialism." (Weaver, "Paul Tillich and the Voice of America," 24.) Wolbold disputes this by misquoting me: he leaves out the crucial word, "more." This permits him to say that I am wrong to see Tillich as a socialist activist following the war. In so doing, he denigrates Tillich's largely theoretical output on the necessary relationship of religious socialism to the future of Germany. Tillich changed from the political conservative of the German Lutheranism within which he was nurtured to the religious socialist theorist of the Weimar period. Tillich was silent on politics prior to the war. In comparison with his nonpolitical (conservative) position prior to the war, any rhetoric that was socialist was a "more activist socialism." Further, church authorities admonished him for a radical political speech he gave following the war (Pauck, *Paul Tillich*, 68). Wolbold falsely concludes that I reduce Tillich's VOA speeches to "merely/purely propagandistic activity" understood in the negative sense (Wolbold, "Meine Deutschen Freunde! Die politischen Rundfunkreden Tillichs," 185). Wolbold sets up that misstatement by a discussion of the distinction between white and black propaganda, a distinction that I included in my own article three years before. The groundwork I laid by distinguishing white and black propaganda was an effort to see the speeches as an exercise in persuasive truth telling (with which Wolbold agrees) and both my "expressionist propaganda" formulation and my passages on the speeches as the embodiment of Tillich's Protestant Principle were considered efforts to establish Tillich's work as weighty pieces of significant value, utterly distinguishable from the nonsense of Goebbels and his ilk. While Wolbold is uncomfortable with my formulation, "expressionist propaganda," Ristiniemi asserted the notion of Tillich's ethics as expressionism nine years later. See Jari Ristiniemi, "Ethics and Expressionism: Things, Individuals, and Common Concerns," *Bulletin of the North American Paul Tillich Society* 33/3 (Summer 2007): 23-28.

unpredictable. On occasion, VOA staffers wondered whether there was an audience at the other end any greater than the number of people in the broadcast facility at a given time. When VOA broadcasts could be sent over the more dependable medium- and long-waves of the BBC, they were subject to potential censor by British authorities.[6] The project embodied Tillich's notion of humanity as the combination of freedom and fate, as life functioning within the context of structured necessity.[7]

Tillich wrote a total of one hundred twelve complete speeches. In addition, there are two speech fragments. These one hundred fourteen extant documents were, at the least, Tillich's journal of theological and philosophical reflections on the Nazi regime and the war.[8] They served as a means for Tillich to reflect weekly, over the course of twenty-six months, on the causes of the war, the dynamics of world politics, the operative forces within German culture, and the mutual perception of the people of the Allied and Axis nations: in short, they give us his interpretation of the meaning of world events in the heat of the moment in which they occurred.

----

[6]Shulman, *The Voice of America*, 26-27.

[7]There are many places where Tillich wrote in such terms. One place was in the speech he gave in May 1942, "Storms of Our Times," *Anglican Theological Review* 25/1 (January 1943): 16.

[8]The third posthumous volume of the *Gesammelten Werke* contains eighty-seven of the speeches (Paul Tillich, *An meine deutschen Freunde: Die politischen Reden Paul Tillichs während des Zweiten Weltkriegs über die "Stimme Amerikas" [1942–1944]. Ergänzungs- und Nachlassbände zu den Gesammelten Werken von Paul Tillich III.* Stuttgart: Evangelisches Verlagswerk, 1973); Paul Tillich, *Against the Third Reich*, ed. Ronald H. Stone and Matthew Lon Weaver, trans. Matthew Lon Weaver (Louisville: Westminster/John Knox Press, 1998) contains translations of fifty-five of the speeches; the Paul Tillich Archive at Harvard University's Andover-Harvard Library has the written and typed manuscripts of all 114 documents (boxes 602A, 602B, 603A, 603B, and 604). In the matter of dating, the archival material and the material cited from *Against the Third Reich* will use the American practice of placing the month first, day second, and year third. The material cited from *An meine deutschen Freunde* will use the European practice of placing the day first, month second, and year third. As noted previously, in citing sources from the Paul Tillich Archive at Harvard, I will use the notation created by Erdmann Sturm: the acronym PTAH designating the Paul Tillich Archive at Harvard; the first number designating the box number; and the number following the colon designating the file number within the box.

Radio broadcasts between the nation that had saved him from the ascent
of Hitler and the nation of his birth provided another medium for Tillich's
boundary perspective. Here, their content—more than five hundred pages
of material—are summarized under five headings: Cultural Renewal; Guilt;
Freedom, Politics, and Resistance; Justice and Economics; and Nationalism
and Internationalism.

Cultural Renewal

The German Cultural Inheritance. In a number of speeches, Tillich spoke
about the German culture. He commented on its profound inheritance. He
castigated Nazism for destroying that inheritance. He called for its post-
Nazi reconstruction.Tillich saw three primary legacies from Germany's
past: the Christian; the human and the Germanic.[9]

The primary fruits of Germany's Christian legacy were the "Old
Testament belief in justice and the New Testament belief in truth and love
[which] lived within the hearts of the masses who did not know much of
Christianity."[10] German history, philosophy, and literature testified to the
centrality of justice in Germany's past.[11] Tillich's very first speech faced
head-on the horror of German oppression of Jews. He directed his remarks
specifically to German Protestants. The call to oppose Nazism and to stand
with Jews on this question had a clear and substantial basis in biblical
theology: Christianity is rooted in Judaism; the prophetic tradition of
scripture (while wanting to defend the nation of Israel) specifically opposes
nationalist idolatry; and National Socialist idolatry and nationalism directly
contradict this.[12] From the Christian scriptures, Tillich drew vivid analogies
for the impact of Nazism upon Germany and the world. He described the
mutual opposition of figures of Hitler and Christ: will-to-power opposed to
powerlessness.[13] Mixing his sense of the power of art with his own poetic

[9]Paul Tillich, "The Germanic Legacy (3/2/1943)," *Against the Third Reich*
(Louisville: Westminster/John Knox Press, 1998) 121.

[10]Paul Tillich, "The Christian Legacy (3/8/1943)," *Against the Third Reich*
(Louisville: Westminster/John Knox Press, 1998) 126.

[11]Paul Tillich, "Justice and Humanity (5/11/1942)," *Against the Third Reich*
(Louisville: Westminster/John Knox Press, 1998) 26-27.

[12]Paul Tillich, "The Question of the Jewish People (3/31/1942)," *Against the
Third Reich* (Louisville: Westminster/John Knox Press, 1998) 13-16.

[13]Paul Tillich, "Die fünfte Kriegs-Weihnacht (14/12/1943)," *An meine*

sensibility, Tillich offered this poignant interpretation of Germany's fifth
war-Christmas:

> On the pictures of German painters of old, a ruin is often found as the place
> where the Christmas story took place. Under a half-crumbled roof, Mary seeks
> shelter from rain and snow. Between crumbling pillars the sheep graze, while
> shepherds adore the marvel of the holy night, through empty window holes.
> Such pictures did not tell us much in previous years in which we understood
> what ruins were only from pictures. Today, a portion of the German people live
> among the ruins, and with almost every day, the ruins multiply. Perhaps you
> again, like your fathers, are seeking the Savior among the ruins and are
> discovering the child of Christmas through the cracked walls of your houses.
> Certainly he is more likely to be found there than behind the glittering shop
> windows of past Christmas markets or in the new, magnificent structures of the
> National Socialist Herods, or in the palaces of defeated kings! As long as we
> are seeking the Christ child in markets and palaces, we will not find him. Much
> more likely, he is in the bomb-torn foxholes of the British and the Russians, in
> the quarters of the German working-class or in the loaded stock-cars in which
> mothers with their infants are driven into the death-camps of the east; or in the
> dark nights in which innocent hostages look forward to their deaths in the
> coming morning; or in the cold rooms in which badly fed, freezing women and
> children mourn the deaths of their father and husband and son. There, above
> all, can we find the Savior, the child in the manger, the child among the ruins.[14]

Further, Tillich saw the experience of Nazism as the experience of
Christ's passion.[15] The greatness of the suffering of Christ is the fact of
innocent suffering which explains its saving, healing import:

> [P]recisely because it is the picture of innocent one, it points beyond itself. It
> has a helping, saving force for everyone who is grasped by it. It displays, to
> perfection, the radiating, reconciling power that innocent suffering has, when
> it is borne with inner greatness. It gives us the feeling that we do not have to
> despair, that within all the guilt and self-destruction of people, something has
> remained in which life can come to a reconciliation with itself.[16]

---

deutschen Freunde (Stuttgart: Evangelisches Verlagswerk, 1973) 284-85.
    [14]Tillich, "Die fünfte Kriegs-Weihnacht (14/12/1943)," 286-87.
    [15]Paul Tillich, "The Passion Story of Nazism (Palm Sunday 1943)," Against the
Third Reich (Louisville: Westminster/John Knox Press, 1998) 141-44.
    [16]Paul Tillich, "A German Good Friday (3/28/1944)," Against the Third Reich
(Louisville: Westminster/John Knox Press, 1998) 238.

He observed the world movement toward unity within the Christian ecumenical movement over against the divisiveness of Nazism.[17] Nationalism divided the world; Christianity sought to unify it.[18] The churches of the world offered the message that revenge brings not peace but new evil. Tillich declared, "[T]he churches do not let up in their demands: justice, not revenge; construction, even of the defeated, not destruction; a new beginning for all, even Germany! This is a hope, a genuine hope."[19]

Tillich described the fruits of the humanistic legacy of Germany as reason, respect for human dignity, and the acknowledgement that each person is a member of the human race.[20] Intellectuals were important custodians of this legacy. Tillich described the breadth responsibility of intellectuals:

> In a deep sense, every thought and writing and utterance and form must be revolutionary. It must attempt to give expression to the everlasting discontent with everything that is—a discontent that distinguishes the human being from the beast—it must attempt to change human life, the personal and the social. It must be a bit prophetic, it must condemn and demand, it must give hope. If it does not do that, it is a beautiful sport, but without seriousness.[21]

From Goethe, Tillich drew the teaching of reverence for other human beings. Goethe's insight was that life and relationships are destroyed by disdain and cynicism. Instead, reverence should be the basis for all thought and action, "reverence for those who are superior to [us], reverence for those who are equal to [us], and reverence for those who are beneath [us]."[22] In another place he put it, "Speak of that which human-being means—that

---

[17]Paul Tillich, Voice of America Speech 39b (1/1943), PTAH 602:001 (39b).

[18]Paul Tillich, "Welteinheit der Christenheit: Grund zur Hoffnung (12.10.1943)," *An meine deutschen Freunde* (Stuttgart: Evangelisches Verlagswerk, 1973) 269.

[19]Tillich, "Welteinheit der Christenheit: Grund zur Hoffnung (12/10/1943)," 272.

[20]Paul Tillich, "The Human Legacy (3/16/1943)," *Against the Third Reich* (Louisville: Westminster/John Knox Press, 1998) 130-31.

[21]Paul Tillich, "The Intelligentsia and Germany's Conquest (9/4/1942)," *Against the Third Reich* (Louisville: Westminster/John Knox Press, 1998) 58-59.

[22]Paul Tillich, "Goethe on Reverence (5/1942)," *Against the Third Reich* (Louisville: Westminster/John Knox Press, 1998) 29-31.

it means reverence for everyone who is human, enemies and friends."[23] In this way, victims become human beings again, and the weak and vulnerable evoke appreciation for pain and suffering.[24] In another place, Tillich wrote, "With the German poets and philosophers, the stranger is the one who equally bears a human countenance and for whom we must, for that reason, have reverence. . . . Education for reverence toward the other person has been—from ancient times—education in reverence for the stranger."[25] Thus, Tillich exhorted his former compatriots, "Begin this training with your children today! Show them what a curse Germany has pulled down upon itself when it hunted down those whom it branded as strangers, who weren't strangers, and annihilated them within the borders of Germany."[26]

When he considered the cultural significance of education, Tillich believed that it either cultivated or demeaned humanity: "Human education awakens the joy in the riches of human possibilities, with regard to other nations, races, customs and capabilities. Inhuman education awakens contempt for everything that is unfamiliar, the unwillingness to understand it, and the will to fight and exterminate it."[27] Tillich called Germans, to begin the reeducation of their children: "give your children . . . the belief in their own personal worth, in the value of individual among them."[28]

On the ninth anniversary of the 1933 book-burnings, Tillich exalted in the power of human reason:

Book-burnings are as old as books. From the beginning onward, books were a power that was dangerous for the existing authorities. In the letters and sentences of a book, an explosive can lie hidden which destroys a world, and there can be locked up within it a spiritual force that constructs a new world! For this reason, books are sinister for all who want to maintain the old at any cost. For this reason, books are sinister for all who have a reason to fear the

---

[23]Paul Tillich, "Das neue Jahr—ein neues Zeitalter? (21/12/1943)" *An meine deutschen Freunde* (Stuttgart: Evangelisches Verlagswerk, 1973) 291.

[24]Tillich, "Goethe on Reverence (5/1942)," 30.

[25]Tillich, "Der Inhalt der künftigen deutschen Erziehung (21/6/1943)" *An meine deutschen Freunde* (Stuttgart: Evangelisches Verlagswerk, 1973) 223, 224.

[26]Tillich, "Der Inhalt der künftigen deutschen Erziehung (21/6/1943)" 224.

[27]Paul Tillich, "Die Nachkriegserziehung der Deutschen (27/10/1942)," *An meine deutschen Freunde* (Stuttgart: Evangelisches Verlagswerk, 1973) 122.

[28]Paul Tillich, "Erziehung zur neuen Freiheit (14/6/1943)," *An meine deutschen Freunde* (Stuttgart: Evangelisches Verlagswerk, 1973) 220.

truth. For this reason, tyrants are enemies of books, just as they have dread before thought-furrowed faces. Behind these furrows and behind the lines of books they smell the spirit of rebellion that they can dispel no longer, once it becomes word and letter. For this reason, books are sealed, suppressed and burned—sometimes with those who have written them, sometimes without them. But, again and again, the books are victorious. The thoughts, that have become embodied within them rise up out of their ashes, more powerful than before. The resurrection of thought through the fire of the spirit follows the destruction of the book through natural fire and burns the fire-starter.[29]

Ten months later, returning again to a discussion of the potency of human reason, Tillich offered this comment:

Reason in the human being means that the human being—and indeed *every* human being—has the predisposition to think and to act sensibly. No person, neither sex, and no race is excluded from this. Every person is capable of understanding the difference between true and false, between just and unjust, between good and evil, between believing and lack of belief. The significance of education today is to develop these talents and to turn all people into true human beings, into characters who follow reason, who listen to their consciences, who struggle for truth, who have a sense of the holy in life."[30]

In commenting on Germany's Germanic legacy, Tillich wrote of three gifts it had borne to German culture: chivalry, by which he meant strength combined with nobility; freedom, epitomized in the peasantry; and the spiritual depth of German culture.[31]

Nazism's Attack Upon Culture. Tillich saw Nazism as a tragic reversal of the cultural richness of the 1920s. The period of the Weimar Republic impressed him as a culturally exuberant one. It had been an immensely fruitful and successful period for Tillich personally. He reminded his audience:

You will remember how new beginnings were made in all spheres of life. Countless buds pressed towards the light. Much of that was certainly immature and premature. Much was so good that travelers from all over the world came to Germany in order to learn from the new thing which was bursting forth there, and to take it home with them. The first collapse removed many old

---

[29]Paul Tillich, "The Ninth Anniversary of Book-Burning (5/18/1942)," *Against the Third Reich* (Louisville: Westminster/John Knox Press, 1998) 33.

[30]Tillich, "The Human Legacy (3/16/1943)," 130.

[31]Tillich, "The Germanic Legacy (3/2/1943)," 122-23.

things, worthless things which had existed, and it generated many new things, valuable things. In spite of the misery of defeat, in spite of all the political defeats, it gave Germany possibilities like it had never before.[32]

During that period and before, Tillich argued that Germans would not have suspected the dreary prospects for their fate:

Had it been said to a German ten years before, indeed even five years before, that children would be murdered, that villages not lying in the battle zone would be wiped from the earth, that women would be carried off into slavery, that innocent people would be shot by the dozens, he would have turned away with horror. And now he has done all of that and doesn't even know what he's done. And if it had been said to the German people ten years ago, indeed even five years ago, that they would be turned into accessories of crimes, the like to which have seldom been seen even in the blood-stained pages of world history, the German people would have referred to its great past, to Meister Eckhardt and Luther, to Kant and Goethe, and would have declared themselves to be incapable of such horror, of even thinking of it. And now they've not only permitted it to be thought, but to be carried out in the name of the German people. All of that formed a part of the diabolical process with which National Socialism has led, and goes on leading, the German nation on the path of destruction.[33]

The blame for Weimar's failure lay in many quarters, in Tillich's view:

In the political as well as the social, in education as well as in the economy, in art as well as in ethical life, everything was undermined which would truly take new paths. *All* were to blame for that. Not only those who wanted to go back because they could no longer find themselves in the new, not only those who fought against the new because it threatened their selfish interests and customary positions, but also those who fought for the new, but without the necessary passion and devotion, and without the necessary clarity and foresight.[34]

While the Weimar Republic's great achievement was in overcoming the dismal attitude of post-World War I Germany by means of significant cultural achievements, Nazism intended the destruction of all this:

[32]Paul Tillich, "Zusammenbruch ohne Wiedergeburt? (30.10.1943)," *An meine deutschen Freunde* (Stuttgart: Evangelisches Verlagswerk, 1973) 273.
[33]Paul Tillich, Voice of America Speech 84 (11/1943) PTAH 603:001 (84).
[34]Tillich, "Zusammenbruch ohne Widergeburt? (30.10.1943)," 273-74.

Ten years of National Socialism have more sufficiently laid waste to this blossoming garden of culture than if wild beasts had broken in on it! And today the gardeners are dispersed into the world, on the stages of foreign cities, in the books of foreign languages, in the museums of foreign countries, in the concerts of foreign nations! One seeks German culture everywhere—except in Germany! In Germany it is destroyed by ten years of barbarity![35]

Tillich gave the German listeners this standard by which to measure the health of a cultural movement:

A new order of life, a new belief, has to prove itself, has to display its internal and external strength. A new order has to bring more happiness than the old, if it is to have a significance such that people will die for it. A new belief must open up new depths of life and make accessible new heights of living, if it is to awaken the enthusiasm which creates martyrs. Is the National Socialist order such an order? Is its belief such a belief?[36]

Nazism was the renunciation of the good in Germany's heritage: "Seldom in the history of the world has there been such a total renunciation of everything which was precious, great and holy in a nation."[37] Tillich compared the onset of Nazi rule to the signs of early spring: it promised life with the warmth of the sun, only to give way to the returning cold.[38] Hitler had promised much in terms of German culture.[39] Instead, Nazism was a manifestation of the worst in the German inheritance. He repeatedly associated poison and Nazism. In August 1942, he spoke of Nazi education as an imprisoning, "poisonous" reality.[40] The following December he wrote, "I believe that National Socialism was the outbreak and the concentration of nearly all of that which was diseased within the German soul. Long have these poisons accumulated within it. In the great crisis of the 1930's, they won the upper hand and shook the German nation in frightful, feverish

---

[35]Paul Tillich, "Zehn Jahre Nazi-Herrschaft (2.1943)," *An meine deutschen Freunde* (Stuttgart: Evangelisches Verlagswerk, 1973) 157.

[36]Paul Tillich, Voice of America Speech 78 (10/4/1943) PTAH 603:001 (78).

[37]Tillich, "The Germanic Legacy (3/2/1943)," 119.

[38]Paul Tillich, "Ein deutscher Frühling? (23.2.1943)" *An meine deutschen Freunde* (Stuttgart: Evangelisches Verlagswerk, 1973) 163-64.

[39]Tillich, "Ein deutscher Frühling? (23.2.1943)" 164.

[40]Paul Tillich, "Nachkriegsgestaltung als Neugestaltung (1.8.1942)," *An meine deutschen Freunde* (Stuttgart: Evangelisches Verlagswerk, 1973) 78.

convulsions. It was an illness that could have led to death."[41] Nazism meant the revival of monstrous, destructive forces from the past.[42] In the fall of 1943, Tillich again reflected on the nature of the cultural forces within Nazism:

> [T]he sacrifices of the First World War caused the most wretched, the most disastrous of the German inheritance to come to the surface and to result in the great game of the last ten years, to the ruin of Germany; the sense of being less than other nations, and at the same time, the opposite sense of being more; the misconception of having come off badly in the world, and the delusive belief of being the favored race which has developed from that; the servile disposition which a tyranny like that of National Socialism causes to be imposed, and the wish among the greatest and the least to have someone whom one can tyrannize, even if it be one's own family; the limitless belief in power and—over against power—the distrust of freedom and justice. National Socialism is the embodiment of all these qualities. In it and through it all these toxic substances came into the heart of the German nation and poisoned the entire body.[43]

Using the imagery of puppetry, Tillich described the way Nazi rulers functioned as puppeteers manipulating the wires of Mussolini, von Hindenburg, the Reichstag, the Reichs-bishop, university rectors, German youth, German soldiers ("machines driven by human machines"), Quisling in Norway, and Laval in France.[44] Then he turned to the Nazis themselves:

> [I]f you should look carefully, you would discover that at the deepest point, these puppeteers of National Socialism are themselves puppets. Behind them stand not human beings but dark, sub- and super-human forces by which they are driven. These forces are everything that is dark, distorted and desperate within the German soul and that has embodied itself within them. Look at them, how small and hollow they are as people, as personalities, how little they are free of the basest humanity quality! And then see how strong they are as

---

[41]Paul Tillich, "Where Hope Lies This Advent Season (12/8/1942)," *Against the Third Reich* (Louisville: Westminster/John Knox Press, 1998) 93-94.

[42]Paul Tillich, "A Guiding Light in the Darkness of the New Year (12/1942)," *Against the Third Reich* (Louisville: Westminster/John Knox Press, 1998) 101.

[43]Paul Tillich, "Der verzweifelte Spieler—das verlorene Spiel (13.9.1943)," *An meine deutschen Freunde* (Stuttgart: Evangelisches Verlagswerk, 1973) 262-63.

[44]Paul Tillich, "Puppets and Puppet-Masters (9/20/1943)," *Against the Third Reich* (Louisville: Westminster/John Knox Press, 1998) 193-95.

impersonal, dark powers driven by a demonic will, destroying whatever steps into their path and, in the end, destroying themselves. They are masks, behind which the powers of destruction hide, puppets on which the darkest sub strata of life draw, and which must, for that reason, turn all others into puppets. Pull off the mask! End the puppet show of darkness which has plunged you and the world into the greatest of all tragedies.[45]

Tillich characterized Nazism's cultural strategy as an attack on truth and its bearers: "Nazism rips to pieces the religious, intellectual, and ethical oneness of the human race and summons every part of humankind to an annihilating battle against every other part."[46] On the tenth anniversary of Hitler's rule, Tillich interpreted the despair of the German situation by calling it "a day of retrospect, but not a day of prospect."[47] He recounted the spheres of Hitler's destructiveness: the economy; the political system; the existence of diversity; legal rights; human prosperity and human life; and an ethics in which truth is "persecuted."[48] In short, Nazism was history's—not merely Germany's—"darkest period."[49]

Six weeks later, in a reversal of the stereotypical anti-Semitic use of the Passion Story of Christ, he used that story to characterize the Hitler regime as the perpetrators of the Passion Story of the Europe, specifically pointing to the persecution of the Jews. Recalling the biblical story of Jesus' encounter with the mourning women outside of Jerusalem, he called Germans to direct the words of Jesus to themselves, "Weep not for me, weep for your children." Yet, he exhorted them to have hope, given that defeat of the Nazis would mean rebirth and resurrection for Germany.[50]

Tillich wrote that Nazism was cursed because of its crimes against the Jewish people.[51] Tillich bemoaned Lutheranism's passivity in the face of Nazism. He saw it as part of its long tradition of renouncing its prophetic

---

[45]Tillich, "Puppets and Puppet-Masters (9/20/1943)," 196-97.

[46]Paul Tillich, "Der geistige Wiederaufbau in der Einheit von Wahrheit und Geist (8.8.1942)," *An meine deutschen Freunde* (Stuttgart: Evangelisches Verlagswerk, 1973) 85.

[47]Paul Tillich, "The Tenth Anniversary of Hitler's Regime (2/1943)," *Against the Third Reich* (Louisville: Westminster/John Knox Press, 1998) 115.

[48]Tillich, "The Tenth Anniversary of Hitler's Regime (2/1943)," 115-17.

[49]Tillich, "The Tenth Anniversary of Hitler's Regime (2/1943)," 118.

[50]Tillich, "The Passion Story of Nazism (Palm Sunday 1943)," 144.

[51]Tillich, "Zehn Jahre Nazi-Herrschaft (2/1943)," 158-59.

function.[52] In this, it failed to carry out religion's necessary struggle with the idolatrous: "In all countries of the world, the prophetic-Christian principle of life must defend itself against heathen-nationalist attacks. But, to be sure, nowhere as frequently, nowhere as fundamentally, nowhere till now has this been so great a battle of life and death as in the lands ruled by National Socialism."[53] In this, the church failed to see that Nazism had set in clear relief the contrast between a faith informed by the prophets and the teachings of Christ over against the paganism and neo-paganism of National Socialism.[54]

Nazism was the political betrayal of that past, Tillich argued. Nazism was not a return to primal human values: "It is wrong to characterize [the Nazi order] as a return to primitive stages of humanity. That would be an insult to the primitive peoples. It is much more an attempt to create, with every means of highest intelligence and technological maturity, a world in which that which is human disappeared."[55] Nazism is hostile to that which is human: "Humankind has grasped that with the Nazis it is not a question of the attack of one nation on another, but the attack of an enemy of all humanity on humanity itself."[56]

Nazism was also the betrayal of the future. In its worship of power, it lost the Christian teaching of the redeeming consequence of powerlessness: "German youth had no longer heard of the belief that the most fragile, the most helpless, and the most humble could be at the same time the highest, most creative, and most powerful. And if they heard it, they weren't allowed to accept it. And if they accepted it, they had to conceal it in a corner of their souls and had often completely forgotten it!"[57] Tillich saw the misguidance of the youth by the deceptive fraud of Nazism as one of its

---

[52]Paul Tillich, "Der Widerstand der norwegischen Kirche (27.4.1942)," *An meine deutschen Freunde* (Stuttgart: Evangelisches Verlagswerk, 1973) 33.

[53]Tillich, "Der geistige Wiederaufbau . . . (8.8.1942)," 83-84.

[54]Tillich, Voice of America Speech 39b (1/1943).

[55]Paul Tillich, "The Punishment of War Criminals (10/20/1942)," *Against the Third Reich* (Louisville: Westminster/John Knox Press, 1998) 79.

[56]Paul Tillich, "Auswege der Nazis—Gefahren für die deutsche Zukunft (13.3.1944)," *An meine deutschen Freunde* (Stuttgart: Evangelisches Verlagswerk, 1973) 328.

[57]Tillich, "Die fünfte Kriegs-Weihnacht (14.12.1943)," 284-85.

most serious legacies.[58]

Having heard of Goebbels's attempt to cultivate hatred for the Nazis' enemies, Tillich declared Nazism to be defined by hatred: National Socialism was "born in hatred, came to power in hatred, and exercised its power with hatred."[59] In the season of Advent, Tillich described the Nazi promulgation of an attitude of hatred as a unique crime against the Christ child:

> Only National Socialism has consciously and decisively placed itself on the side of those who persecuted the child in the manger, that is, the messenger of love. Only the National Socialists have advocated hatred and ridiculed love. Only they have consciously placed injustice on the throne and disdained justice. Only they have extolled falsehood, in print and in speech, and held the truth up to ridicule.[60]

The publication of a translation of a German soldier's letter in the American press led Tillich to comment on the dehumanizing impact of Nazism upon its soldiers:

> The terrible thing about [the letter] is the objective way with which something terrible is being communicated. No human outcry against the monstrous thing which is being done to innocent people in regions the size of Germany! Not once a word of passion against the hated enemy on whom one bestows all of this. Nothing of that: nothing human in the good and nothing human in the evil; complete inhumanity, destruction as an event that is as natural as a flood or a prairie fire. Nazism has brought the German people to this depth of dehumanization![61]

In contrast to this spirit, Tillich called for a return to the "new heroism . . . of sacrificial love."[62]

Under Nazism, the positions of tyranny and freedom had switched. Tillich reminded his listeners that at one time "Germany [had been] subject

---

[58]Tillich, "Ein deutscher Frühling? (23.2.1943)" 165.

[59]Paul Tillich, "How Should One View the Enemy (9/12/1942)" *Against the Third Reich* (Louisville: Westminster/John Knox Press, 1998) 62.

[60]Paul Tillich, "The Fourth War Christmas (12/15/1942)," *Against the Third Reich* (Louisville: Westminster/John Knox Press, 1998) 96.

[61]Paul Tillich, "A Soldier's Revealing Letter (12/27/1943)," *Against the Third Reich* (Louisville: Westminster/John Knox Press, 1998) 218.

[62]Tillich, "The Fourth War Christmas (12/15/1942)," 98.

to the French conqueror, and Germans [had] fought against the Napoleonic tyranny as saboteurs and guerrillas, with actions and writings. There was a time when German freedom fighters were shot dead for the same things for which the freedom fighters of the conquered nations are now being shot dead by the Germans."[63]

Renovation of German Culture. In the face of the devastating impact of Nazism upon German culture, Tillich called for renewal. While Germany could be liberated militarily and politically by outside forces, he argued that its spiritual renewal was work that had to be done from within.[64] Tillich described the path for Germany's cultural rehabilitation in various places in varied ways. In January 1944 he called for Germans to seek a balanced approach to their identity in the world:

> When the German nation ceases to swing to-and-fro between an outrageous arrogance and an absurd sense of inferiority, then a new Germany will be born. If the German nation, through the judgment which is passing on it, is healed of sometimes falling on its knees before power-without-spirit, sometimes fleeing into a thin, feeble spirituality, then greatness will have come to pass for it. If the German nation learns that it is not alone in the world and that it has something essential to contribute to the life of the human race, then all the immense suffering of these days has not been in vain. Then the path of judgment has become the path of salvation.[65]

The following month Tillich called the German people to challenge Hitler's feeble "culture" by using the treasures of Germany's Christian legacy— manifested in the prophets and gospels, poets and sages—as its guide: truth and justice; a knowledge of Germany's worth and limits; trust; the understanding that a nation can become guilty and must give compensation for its guilt; the fact that it is a valuable member of the human race as a whole, being both weak and gifted; the insight that every human being "must be valued as a reflection of the eternal," friend and foe alike; the belief in the common destiny of all nations; and the perception that humankind has meaning.[66]

---

[63]Paul Tillich, "Tyrannical Power Has Limits (4/6/1943)," *Against the Third Reich* (Louisville: Westminster/John Knox Press, 1998) 139.

[64]Tillich, "Nachkriegsgestaltung . . . (1.8.1942)," 81.

[65]Paul Tillich, "Judgment as Redemption (1/31/1944)," *Against the Third Reich* (Louisville: Westminster/John Knox Press, 1998) 228.

[66]Paul Tillich, "Der ‚Deutsche Glaube' und der Glaube der Deutschen

Even in their treatment of the Nazis, there was a moral limit on the behavior of German citizens. Tillich saw the absence of hatred as the barometer for differentiating themselves from the Nazis: "I am telling you in full awareness of what it means, and having the deepest conviction that it is true: you are superior to the National Socialists to the degree to which you keep yourselves free of hatred toward them! You are identical to them to the degree to which you permit yourselves to hate them."[67] To do this was to follow the pattern of Christ in loving one's enemies. One can have a passionate commitment to the cause, but fueled by the passion for salvation, not hatred. If this passion for salvation is a species of hatred, then it is a holy hatred aimed not at people but at "powers within the person for the sake of the salvation of the person."[68] However, to the call of the Nazis to sacrifice themselves, Tillich admonished his hearers to refuse to sacrifice *Germany* in order to preserve its Nazi leaders.[69]

A commitment to truth was central to Germany's cultural rehabilitation. Reflecting on the anniversary of the book-burnings of 1933, Tillich spoke on the weakness of falsehood and the dynamic strength of truth:

> Not all that was burned will rise again from the dead. Much has justly come to ashes, because it was not thought but babble, not depth but temptation. The truth must prove its worth through fire. What is false must burn. And much of that which was thrown from the ox-cart into the fire has no right to a resurrection. It was invalid even before it became ashes. In all of us was much nothingness which had to be burned away. In the entire world from which we came, there was much that was worthy only of rising up in flames. We all are implicated in the book-burning.[70]

Tillich called for a return to the unifying and spiritual renewing force of truth: "The truth is but one. When the truth is being distributed among different gods which contradict one another, then it is no longer truth; when nation or race is being made the standard of the truth, then the truth is sacrificed. And in Germany today, the truth lies bleeding on the altar of

---

(9.2.1944)," *An meine deutschen Freunde* (Stuttgart: Evangelisches Verlagswerk, 1973) 310-13.

[67]Tillich, "How Should One View . . . (9/12/1942)," 62-63.

[68]Tillich, "How Should One View . . . (9/12/1942)," 65.

[69]Paul Tillich, Voice of America Speech 26 (9/1942) PTAH 602:001(26).

[70]Tillich, "The Ninth Anniversary . . . (5/18/1942)," 34.

idolatrous sacrifice called national power worship."[71]

Much about facing the truth would be difficult, but it could be liberating as well. To clarify this, Tillich established a distinction between Nazism's portrait of a horrifying future and a more accurate picture of future:

> Germany will have to bear three things which are difficult; and everyone among you should be clear about them. The serious and honest truth chases away the pictures of horror with which they want to drive you to your death. And the truth looks like this: Germany will be weaponless at the end of the conflict; and Germany will be weak after the devastation of this war; and Germany will be smaller after its defeat. Each of these things is a difficult burden; it would be meaningless to dispute that. They must occur, and they must be borne. It will be the measure of the maturity of the German people, whether and how they are able to look this truth in the face. It really demands more strength and inner greatness to see and to bear the inevitable, than to avoid it with eyes closed and rush to one's death in the drunkenness of alleged heroism.[72]

Another element of truth-telling involved reversing the world's perception of German culture. Nazism's reversal of the world's positive perception of Germany cultivated during the Weimar period had created considerable confusion regarding German character.[73] Tillich was concerned about the caricaturing of Germans, specifically through the assumption that Nazism expressed the true German character. To him, the caricaturing of all Germans as Nazis was parallel to the Nazi caricature of the Jewish people, which had led to "the ruinous fate of the Jews."[74] However, he believed determined people wanted to prevent a German fate equal to the fate of the Jewish people. But, he also argued that Germans had to take their fate into their own hands, asserting that character is a combination of fate and decision. The German Opposition had to lead the way by decisively choosing to change Germany's fate. Militarism and

---

[71]Tillich, "Der geistige Wiederaufbau . . . (8.8.1942)," 85.

[72]Paul Tillich, "Weiterkämpfen oder Untergehen—Sterben oder Leben (28.2.1944)," *An meine deutschen Freunde* (Stuttgart: Evangelisches Verlagswerk, 1973) 323.

[73]Paul Tillich, "Zehn Jahre Nazi-Herrschaft (2/1943)," 157.

[74]Paul Tillich, "Germany's Past, Present and Future Fate (11/3/1942)," *Against the Third Reich* (Louisville: Westminster/John Knox Press, 1998) 82.

subservience had to be rooted out.[75]

As the Christian part of the world entered Advent 1943, Tillich led his listeners to embrace the hope characteristic of that season: "We stand in the Advent season, the season of hope and waiting. At the end of this waiting stands no military victory, no political achievement, but rather the birth of a child, the symbol of hope, the force of the rebirth of all humanity—even the German people!"[76]

Guilt

A second general focus of Tillich's speeches was the issue of guilt. Tillich saw personal and collective (or common) guilt as a part of Germany's despair.[77] This was not blanket guilt after the manner of Vansittart.[78] Rather,

---

[75]Tillich, "Germany's Past, Present and Future Fate (11/3/1942)," 83-85.

[76]Paul Tillich, Voice of America Speech 87 (12/1943) PTAH 603:001 (87).

[77]Paul Tillich, "Der Verzweiflung des deutschen Volkes (4.5.1942)," *An meine deutschen Freunde* (Stuttgart: Evangelisches Verlagswerk, 1973) 35.

[78]Lord Robert G. Vansittart wrote a series of pieces condemning Germans as a whole with no effort to interpret the levels of guilt or innocence within the German society or the world as a whole. They are published in his book, *The Black Record of Germany—Past, Present, and Future?* (New York: New Avon, 1944). Matthias Wolbold criticizes me for translating Tillich's *Gesamtschuld* as "collective guilt." Wolbold calls *Gesamtschuld* a neologism of Tillich's requiring a translation that distinguishes it from *kollektiv Schuld*, so as to distinguish it from Vansittartism. (Wolbold, "Against the Third Reich," 27.) I don't know whether Wolbold is correct in saying *Gesamtschuld* is Tillich's creation, but I question whether it is necessary or helpful to make the distinction he seeks. First, the German edition of Tillich's (or any author's) collected works uses the participial form of the word in its title, *Gesammelten Werken*. Second, if one looks at the definition of *gesamt* in *Langenscheidt* or *Cassell's* or *Wildhagen*, one has this range of options: "whole, entire, all, total" (*Langenscheidt*); "whole, entire, complete, united, joint, general, common, total, *collective*, aggregate, overall" (*Cassell's*); or "entire, total, aggregate, all, whole" and synonymous with *ganz* (*Wildhagen*). These deepen the degree of "collectivity" without negating it. Third, Tillich is profoundly critical of Germans in many ways and at many levels: no one is excluded from criticism. (He is also very critical of reactionary forces worldwide that supported Hitler's rise.) It is not very enlightening to choose "mass" or "common" guilt as opposed to "collective" guilt. And, to use "complete" or "entire" guilt would be to distort Tillich's subtle discussion of relative innocence and guilt. Fourth, Tillich used

it was a complicated and tragic guilt manifesting itself at many levels of society in and outside of Germany. No one was completely innocent in the rise of Nazi Germany:

> [N]ot the ones who out of folly, presumably in their own interest, propped up the ruling party in their struggle for power, and then changed positions, disillusioned and disappointed . . . [nor those] who stood aside and did nothing but greeted what was happening with hidden or open sympathy, out of political misunderstanding, out of narrowness based on nationalism, or out of class-based and race-based prejudice . . . [nor those] who saw what came with objection and horror, and still did not begin to do everything in a timely way to prevent its coming . . . [nor] the few who decided to do battle and who led it to the bitter end, escaped a share in the guilt: they led the struggle, but they did not lead it with a spiritual strength and depth and with the human greatness that alone would have been able to prevail over the frightening forces of opposition. . . . [Finally, guilt must be assumed by those who] drove Europe into disorder and Germany into despair through the false peace after the First World War, but also [the] wide circles within England, France and the smaller countries [who] behaved just like the Germans themselves.[79]

As a description of the levels of participation or nonparticipation in a political milieu, this sort of pattern occurs in all nation-states, according to Tillich. For the state of affairs at any point in time, there is a guilt/innocence distinction based on the choice that each person makes in each circumstance. In another place Tillich addressed the "levels of guilt" question with these words: "You will ask: are we the only guilty ones, then? Certainly not! In the divine words of wrath there is never only one guilty party. All are partly to blame, all suffered then and all suffer today beneath

---

gesamt in another context that conveys the sense of "collective." In "Es geht um die Methode," Tillich declared, "Ich habe bekämpft und werde weiter bekämpfen jede moralische Gesamtverteilung [collective or group condemnation] einer natürlich oder geschichtlich gewordenen Gruppe." (Tillich, "Es geht um die Methode," 280) At the end of the day, one is forced to read Tillich's discussion of guilt in the VOA speeches to see how significantly different his discussion is from Vansittart's, not simply depend on an etymological dispute on the term *gesamt*.

[79]Paul Tillich, "Guilt and Innocence (6/8/1942)," *Against the Third Reich* (Louisville: Westmnster/John Knox Press, 1998) 37-38. See also Tillich, "The German Tragedy (8/1942)," *Against the Third Reich* (Louisville: Westminster/John Knox Press, 1998) 48, for comments on the sense of guilt within Western democracies over the conclusion of World War I.

their shared guilt. But all are not equally guilty."[80]

Here we see the "tragic" touching the issue of guilt. Tillich contrasted "tragic guilt" with pure evil. Tragic guilt is guilt mixed with the good, exemplified in Great Britain's colonial relationship with India. Pure evil is seen in Nazism. India was placed in the unenviable position of choosing between British rule or Japanese oppression, the latter mirroring the pure evil of Nazism. Tragic, as well, was the German-Russian relationship in which contrasting responses to revolution ruptured the relationship.[81]

The Nazis themselves were easy to indict. In addition to the pure horror of their terrorizing policies, their attempts to shift guilt for the war from themselves to others was absurd. Contrary to their claims, Nazi attacks had been neither defensive nor preventative. The war had not been forced on Germany (by England and France) while Germany attempted to bring peace (after Poland) as proclaimed in their propaganda. Nazism was not a movement attacked without provocation by Allied reactionaries.[82] Yet, within Germany Tillich saw a guilt marked by the impact of authoritarianism:

> The German guilt is that the German nation has been turned into the instrument of a power that has diabolical traits: National Socialism. And this guilt is deeply rooted in the German character. It is the Germans' false sense of allegiance that has shattered every resistance to the National Socialist tyranny in the German nation. It is anxiety at the prospect of resistance to evil, when that evil comes from above and has the power and authority of the state behind it. It is the wavering between self-abasement and self-conceit that one finds everywhere in Germany. It is the worship of external power which has been fostered so long in Germany and which has become an idolatry more and more.[83]

Germans simultaneously abhorred the crimes of their Nazi leaders and

[80]Paul Tillich, "Retribution Unparalleled (11/23/1943)," *Against the Third Reich* (Louisville: Westminster/John Knox Press, 1998) 210.

[81]Paul Tillich, "The Tragic in the Evolution of History (8/14/1942)," *Against the Third Reich* (Louisville: Westminster/John Knox Press, 1998) 42-44.

[82]Paul Tillich, "Who Is Guilty? (1/1943)" *Against the Third Reich* (Louisville: Westminster/John Knox Press, 1998) 109-10.

[83]Paul Tillich, "Fate and Guilt (5/18/1943)," *Against the Third Reich* (Louisville: Westminster/John Knox Press, 1998) 156-57.

deferred to their authority.[84]

Tillich responded to simplistic declarations of innocence with this analysis of the guilt-innocence scale:

> No prophet and no apostle and no martyr ever maintained that he did not share responsibility for collective guilt, even for the guilt of those who persecuted him. No subtle conscience, no person of depth, will entirely exonerate himself from the responsibility for that which happened to him by way of injustice. But after he has done that, after he has placed himself and all the persecuted with him beneath the collective guilt, he will give testimony relating to the persecutors, with respect to his innocence, and now, with clear, good conscience. Compared to those who have dispersed us, robbed us, injured us, or slain us, we are innocent.[85]

Further, he argued that many Germans knew of the crimes of their leaders:

> All Germans have heard of the horrible crimes that have taken place in the concentration camps. But they hardened their hearts and did nothing and, as a result, made themselves culpable. Every German knew of the extermination campaign against the Jewish people. Everyone knew Jewish people about whom he felt sorry, but no protest arose. Not once did the churches take their place with the persecuted of the nation from which Christ came; and, thus, they all became culpable. The entire army saw, and keeps seeing, what is occurring in the occupied regions through the Gestapo's henchmen. Generals and soldiers know about it and turn their eyes away, often in shame, but never with action which could save Germany from this disgrace."[86]

In September 1943 Tillich turned to the biblical tradition as one way to ponder the issue of guilt. He used the Egyptian plagues as the pattern. First, he wrote that "the history of nations shows that nations always suffer for what their rulers do. And history shows that nations have to be struck so that the rulers are struck. So it was in ancient Egypt. . . . So it was in Napoleonic France. . . . So it was in prerevolutionary Russia. . . . So it now is in Germany."[87] Second, even with tyrants, the nation itself has a responsibility: "When a ruler has power over a nation, at that time the

---

[84]Tillich, Voice of America Speech 84 (11/1943).

[85]Tillich, "Guilt and Innocence (6/8/1942)," 38-39.

[86]Paul Tillich, "Collective Guilt (8/9/1943)," *Against the Third Reich* (Louisville: Westminster/John Knox Press, 1998) 181.

[87]Paul Tillich, "Egyptian Plagues and German Plagues (9/1943)," *Against the Third Reich* (Louisville: Westminster/John Knox Press, 1998) 189.

nation also has a joint responsibility, even if it hasn't elected the ruler. It has not elected him, but it has tolerated him."[88] In November 1943, he again wrestled with the relationship of a people's guilt to that of their leaders: "It is the guilt of the German nation that it has allowed itself to be made an accessory; not consciously, but also not entirely without approval; not out of wickedness, but out of weakness; not through a free decision, but through diabolical seduction."[89]

The Good Friday tradition led Tillich to deal with Nazism as crucifixion:

Millions have been nailed to the cross of the most profound suffering and the most agonizing death by the henchmen of National Socialism. And the German people stood by and looked on, just as in the old pictures of the crucifixion. No one became outraged over the suffering of the innocents. No German seized the German torturers by the arm. Only a few grasped what was taking place, and they had to look on silently as the innocents were slain and as a blood guilt was building up that, sooner or later, had to burst forth over the murderers, as well as over the spectators who were their accessories. They resemble the disciples and women who stand powerless and despairing beneath the cross. A few suspected what was happening. The masses permitted it to occur with indifference, and the murderers triumphed.[90]

Guilt had a specific impact on those fighting for the Nazi cause: "guilt destroys the roots from which all courage stems, the confidence to die for a value which is higher than life and fortune."[91] Tillich spoke of the personal responsibility of each soldier for saying "no":

It is difficult for the individual officer or man or civil servant, who has to carry out an order, to see that people want to make them guilty of complicity through that. But it isn't impossible for him to see that. When he feels that he is burdening his own conscience with the fulfillment of his order, then he shouldn't do it. When he sees that that which is commanded to him violates all human and divine laws, then he shouldn't allow himself to be made complicit. He should obey God more than humanity. He should 'fear God and nothing else in the world'—a phrase which is so frequently used in patriotic speeches

[88]Tillich, "Egyptian Plagues and German Plagues (9/1943)," 190.
[89]Tillich, Voice of America Speech Speech 84 (11/1943).
[90]Tillich, "A German Good Friday (3/28/1944)," 239.
[91]Paul Tillich, "Gottesfurcht und Todesfurcht (15.6.1942)," An meine deutschen Freunde (Stuttgart: Evangelisches Verlagswerk, 1973) 51.

and according to which action has been taken nowhere as infrequently as in Germany.[92]

Tillich questioned the hope for the German future, if the world was at the breaking point in tolerating further destruction and accepting different levels of guilt within Germany.[93] To encourage the German audience to embrace guilt, he placed it as but the first step on a three-stage path to salvation, a three-step law of guilt, atonement, and expiation. He wrote that expiation would happen when Germany atoned for its guilt by freeing itself from the Nazis. Tillich exhorted his listeners to show that expiation had begun.[94]

Freedom, Politics, and Resistance

Freedom and Politics. Tillich saw a contradiction between the courage of Germans to sacrifice militarily and the unwillingness to resist politically.[95] In April of 1944, Tillich stated that Germany's fate was due to "the inability of the German people to tolerate freedom."[96] Therefore, there had been no genuine revolution, and Germans "never sensed the breath of freedom to be the life-bestowing breath of humanism."[97] That same month he concluded that the saturation of German culture with intolerance of political freedom had led to this result:

> The upper-middle class aspired to be noblemen rather than free people, the lower middle class aspired to be upper middle class rather than develop a democracy, the laborers aspired to be lower middle class rather than fight for the liberation of their class. The civil servants preferred to have security than the right of free persuasion, the officers preferred human machines to true human beings. That is what went wrong for Germany, for centuries.[98]

Tillich distinguished democracy in the United States from his

---

[92]Tillich, Voice of America Speech Speech 84 (11/1943).

[93]Paul Tillich, "Zu spät für die Rettung Deutschlands? (30.3.1943)" *An meine deutschen Freunde* (Stuttgart: Evangelisches Verlagswerk, 1973) 184-85.

[94]Paul Tillich, "Guilt—Atonement—Expiation (8/16/1943)," *Against the Third Reich* (Louisville: Westminster/John Knox Press, 1998) 183-87.

[95]Paul Tillich, Voice of America Speech 94 (1/25/1944) PTAH 604:001 (94).

[96]Paul Tillich, "The Cost of Surrendering Freedom (4/18/1944)," *Against the Third Reich* (Louisville: Westminster/John Knox Press, 1998) 247.

[97]Tillich, "The Cost of Surrendering Freedom (4/18/1944)," 247.

[98]Tillich, "The Cost of Surrendering Freedom (4/18/1944)," 248.

experience of it in Weimar Germany. In the U.S., "Democracy is a human outlook, an interpretation of life, prior to being a system and a political method. . . . Defense of democracy means the defense of an interpretation of life, of a moral and religious outlook. The word has more of a religious than a political ring, although it includes the political."[99] The spirit of democracy is respect for the human dignity of all. It is not simply a matter of free expression, universal suffrage, or a parliamentary system, but rather "an interpretation of life [involving] . . . the acknowledgement of the human dignity within every person."[100] Therefore, freedom means the practice of respect for others, including the stranger: "Whoever is not free cannot respect himself and, for that reason, can also have no respect for others."[101] Without democracy, human dignity was oppressed; with it, human dignity was elevated.[102]

Tillich informed his listeners that twentieth century liberal democracy meant a step beyond the eighteenth century understanding of it, while Nazism was the rejection of the values of the French Revolution: freedom (liberty), equality, fraternity.[103] In the world outside of Nazi domination, "fraternity" had taken a step further, growing into the call for "social security for all . . . freedom from privation, want and fear."[104] While political freedom had matured outside of Germany in the modern era, Tillich told his audience that Germany's history of repressing political freedom had produced an internalized absence of freedom.[105] In June of 1943, he wrote of the dehumanizing impact of what he termed blind "cadaver-obedience" produced by this experience:

> [N]othing destroys humanity more than an obedience which no longer asks, no longer decides, and has no ultimate responsibility. For this reason, the ancients

[99]Paul Tillich, "Der amerikanische Glaube in die Demokratie (20.6.1942)," *An meine deutschen Freunde* (Stuttgart: Evangelisches Verlagswerk, 1973) 54.
[100]Tillich, "Der amerikanische Glaube in die Demokratie (20.6.1942)," 54.
[101]Tillich, "Der Inhalt der künftigen deutschen Erziehung (21.6.1943)," 222.
[102]Tillich, "Der amerikanische Glaube . . . (20.6.1942)," 54-55.
[103]Paul Tillich, "Nazism and the Ideals of the French Revolution (7/5/1943)," *Against the Third Reich* (Louisville: Westminster/John Knox Press, 1998) 170-71.
[104]Tillich, "Nazism and the Ideals of the French Revolution (7/5/1943)," 170-71.
[105]Paul Tillich, "Internal and External Freedom (4/20/1942)," *Against the Third Reich* (Louisville: Westminster/John Knox Press, 1998) 21-22.

said that the slave is no true person, that only the free person, who decides independently, can grow to full humanity. For this reason, one speaks of cadaver-obedience. A cadaver is a thing; the person who is no longer permitted to decide has become a thing. Like the cadaver, he has only the external appearance of the human. For this reason, everything depends on the German children being educated into inner freedom![106]

Alluding to Goethe's *Faust*, Tillich believed that just as the character, Gretchen, recognized the demonic to which she was tempted to surrender, so Germany had to recognize the demonic to which it had surrendered its freedom.[107]

For Tillich, the basic commitment to the free exercise of democratic rights was fundamental to political maturity. He saw fear of the unknown that a change toward democracy would involve as the basis for political immaturity in Germany:

The German nation is like a child who is courageous face-to-face with an opponent or a group which he knows. But as soon as something unknown appears—an unusual figure, the darkness of night, solitude—then dread breaks out and destroys reason and bravery. Horror in the face of the unknown seizes the child. It has also seized the German nation which, indeed, has never completely grown out of the stage of childhood politically.[108]

Mature and immature fear differ in this way: "Better the evil when it is known, than the unknown which one doesn't know, whether good or bad. The mind of the child operates in that way, but not that of a mature person. The mind of the inwardly subjugated, dread-filled classes of a nation operates in that way. The mind of free, courageous people isn't supposed to operate in that way."[109]

Political struggle is the key to political maturity in Tillich's thought. The reasons for political immaturity in Germany were religious and intellectual escapism. Here he was alluding to the tradition going back to Luther of the church's silence on political matters and his perception of pre-1918 academia as functioning in the realm of theory separated from

---

[106]Tillich, "Erziehung zur neuen Freiheit (14.6.1943)," 221.

[107]Paul Tillich, "To Whom Has Germany Surrendered? (9/24/1943)" *Against the Third Reich* (Louisville: Westminster/John Knox Press, 1998) 198-99.

[108]Tillich, Voice of America Speech 94 (1/25/1944).

[109]Tillich, Voice of America Speech 94 (1/25/1944).

existence.[110] He argued that "if the political is isolated from God, the devil takes it into its hand."[111] He indicted the intellectual leaders for their flight "into the inwardness of the heart from the external realm of political action."[112] This political immaturity was also due to the separation of nation from authority and of the human from the political.[113] Political immaturity had implications for both the world community and the intellectual community: "Without political responsibility and passion, intellectual life becomes one lacking in seriousness, and a nation without an earnest, politically responsible intellect is a danger to itself and to the rest of the nations."[114] Tillich wrote that political conflicts were normal for democracies, not a source of danger as within dictatorships: "In a democracy, they are a sign of internal strength, as long as they are being fought on democratic grounds and with democratic methods. In a dictatorship, where there are no such means to settle antagonisms, every division is a threat to the system and must be removed with violent means."[115] Tillich called the German opposition to fight the temptation to flee from the political.[116]

The failure of political freedom in this period of German history represented the deeper failure to grasp what it meant to be human. Tillich understood human existence to be a combination of freedom and fate. He turned to this formula in several instances in these speeches. Early on, he wrote that Germany's situation is a combination of destiny and guilt.[117] He reminded his audience that Hegel argued for the unity of all life such that one who attacks another, in fact, attacks himself or herself and launches fate—his or her own fate—against himself or herself.[118] Hitler had attacked

---

[110]Pauck, *Paul Tillich*, 41, 55.

[111]Paul Tillich, "Bringing Germany to Political Maturity (8/28/1942)," *Against the Third Reich* (Louisville: Westminster/John Knox Press, 1998) 54.

[112]Tillich, "Bringing Germany to Political Maturity (8/28/1942)."

[113]Tillich, "Bringing Germany to Political Maturity (8/28/1942)" 55.

[114]Tillich, "Bringing Germany to Political Maturity (8/28/1942)" 51.

[115]Paul Tillich, "Nicht Nation, aber Föderation (17.7.1942)," *An meine deutschen Freunde* (Stuttgart: Evangelisches Verlagswerk, 1973) 69.

[116]Tillich, "Nicht Nation, aber Föderation (17.7.1942)," 55.

[117]Tillich, "Verzweiflung des deutschen Volkes (4.5.1942)," 35-36.

[118]Paul Tillich, "Das große Gesetz allen Lebens: die Einheit alles Lebendigen (11.4.1944)," *An meine deutschen Freunde* (Stuttgart: Evangelisches Verlagswerk, 1973) 341.

life and provoked its response. When fate reacts against us, we must become reconciled to it by accepting it:

> It is its own fate by which the German nation is being subjugated, so the fear of this is not the fear of something foreign. It is not the fear of an avenging enemy or a punishing judge, but rather it is the decision to take the pain of injured life onto oneself. It is a courageous fear which includes the fortitude for a life which has only itself to blame. It is reconciliation with fate by accepting it as one's own fate. The fate which is being armed by the German people against themselves will be disarmed if it is understood and endured, not if is it treated as a strange thing or if it is outwitted. Wherever fate, whether of a person or of a nation, is acknowledged and endured as one's own, the first and decisive step towards reconciliation is taken.[119]

Were Germans to deny their fate, history would teach them. In a chilling reference to the fate to which Nazism had subjected the Jewish people, Tillich wrote these words in late 1943:

> [W]hen those of you on the ruins of the capital city and many other cities ask: 'Why did this have to strike us, particularly us?'—then perhaps you will hear a voice which repeats this question, a voice from the land of the dead, a voice composed of the despairing voices of hundreds of thousands of Jewish women and children and old people. And what this voice asks is like an echo of your question: are our people, above all others, predestined for suffering and misfortune? They are asking what you are asking, precisely the same question with precisely the same despair.[120]

Acting decisively against Nazism—exercising political freedom—was the way in which Germans could prevent being imprisoned by the diabolical caricature by which the Nazis had tarnished their national identity. Tillich wrote that national character, too, is a combination of fate and decision and that the German Opposition had to lead the way by decisively choosing to change Germany's fate, rooting out militarism and subservience.[121]

Resistance. Throughout the speeches, Tillich called for German people to resist the National Socialists. In his earliest speeches he called his

---

[119]Tillich, "Das große Gesetz allen Lebens: die Einheit alles Lebendigen (11.4.1944)," 344.

[120]Paul Tillich, "Breaking the Pact with the Nazis (11/30/1943)," *Against the Third Reich* (Louisville: Westminster/John Knox Press, 1998) 212.

[121]Tillich, "Germany's Past, Present and Future Fate (11/3/1942)," 84-85.

audience to resist Nazi lies by waking up to the truth of Christianity's indebtedness to Judaism,[122] to embrace sacrificial love and break loose from their death-bound leaders,[123] to see through Nazism's religiously garbed irreligion,[124] to assert their freedom inwardly and outwardly,[125] and to emulate the Norwegian church by reawakening the prophetic spirit within the church against injustice.[126] His diagnosis of Germany's malady was the absence of a resisting spirit:

> Many in Germany saw that it was wrong. Many resisted. Many were expelled, impoverished, killed for their resistance. But the German nation as a whole, its leaders and its masses, have not resisted. And that is what has gone wrong in Germany: some were too weak to accept the sacrifices of a serious resistance. Others were too apathetic . . . still others were too foolish to carry out resistance. They didn't think that the Nazis would take their own principles seriously. . . . But they gave money and the means of power into the hands of those whom they would have readily used for their aims, but by whom they, in fact, were used. They, above all, are responsible for the fact that something went wrong in Germany.[127]

Resistance meant basic self-preservation: "Everything depends on the world seeing, in this hour, that under the cover of tyranny a Germany has become mature, before which the hatred, which the messengers of the man-beast have aroused to an unimaginable degree, must remain silent. If that doesn't occur, hatred will have free play, then woe to you, Germany, woe to you, Europe."[128] This sensitivity to world perception is repeatedly present in his thoughts. In the summer of 1942 he wrote of the importance of manifesting a public opinion sympathetic to world community.[129] The next

---

[122]Tillich, "The Question of the Jewish People (3/31/1942)," 13-16.

[123]Paul Tillich, "The Death and Resurrection of Nations (4/1942)," *Against the Third Reich* (Louisville: Westminster/John Knox Press, 1998) 20.

[124]Paul Tillich, "Russlands religiöse Lage (13.4.1942)," *An meine deutschen Freunde* (Stuttgart: Evangelisches Verlagswerk, 1973) 25.

[125]Tillich, "Internal and External Freedom (4/20/1942)," 21-24.

[126]Tillich, "Der Widerstand der norwegischen Kirche (27.4.1942)," 33.

[127]Tillich, "The Cost of Surrendering Freedom (4/18/1944)," 246-47.

[128]Paul Tillich, Voice of America Speech 9 (5-6/1942) PTAH 602:001(9).

[129]Tillich, "Nicht Nation, sondern Föderation (17.7.1942)," and Paul Tillich, "Nachkriegsgestaltung als wirtschaftlich-soziale Neugestaltung (25.7.1942)," in *An meine deutschen Freunde* (Stuttgart: Evangelisches Verlagswerk, 1973) 69-77.

summer he wrote of the need for Germany to change the minds of the victims of Nazism by welcoming Germany's liberators (that is, the Allies) just as the liberated in other lands had welcomed them.[130]

He exhorted his listeners in May 1942 to assert their freedom by resisting: "[Take] the path of freedom, freedom from a tyranny whose destructive powers control body and soul, freedom from hopeless conflict, freedom from hopelessness and despair. Take this course! The only worthy course, the only saving course!"[131] He understood the dangers of action and, therefore, initially encouraged listeners simply to think with their supporters on the outside.[132] But this changed over time. Repeatedly, he spoke in terms like these: "[I]f many would take up arms in order to put an end to the internal siege, then it *would* be ended, suddenly, unexpectedly, and completely. That is now the one thing which has to be said over and over again: you have your fate in your hands!"[133]

Tillich believed that by understanding the roots of their predicament, Germans could find the courage to resist.[134] As noted before, this meant rejecting the temptation to flee from the political realm.[135] He challenged the radio audience to separate themselves from "those who have taken the freedom and dignity from the German people."[136] Along with fate and a supportive international community, Tillich saw the German resistance as a chief educator of the German people.[137] In a sense, he saw them to be a significant educator of the international community as well, persuading the world to believe in the existence of a better Germany true to its great cultural past.[138] By resisting, Germans would "become instruments of the moral, constructive world order, and not of the immoral, destructive world order."[139] He stated it in another way a year later: "To the extent to which

---

[130]Paul Tillich, "The Defeated Cheer the Victors (7/19/1943)," *Against the Third Reich* (Louisville: Westminster/John Knox Press, 1998) 175-77.

[131]Tillich, "Verzweiflung des deutschen Volkes (4.5.1942)," 37.

[132]Tillich, "Nachkriegsgestaltung (25.7.1942)," 74.

[133]Paul Tillich, Voice of America Speech 81 (10/1943) PTAH 603:001 (81).

[134]Paul Tillich, Voice of America Speech 10 (5-6/1942) PTAH 602:001 (10).

[135]Tillich, "Bringing Germany to Political Maturity (8/28/1942)," 53-54.

[136]Tillich, Voice of America Speech 26 (9/1942).

[137]Tillich, "Die Nachkriegserziehung der Deutschen (27.10.1942)," 124.

[138]Tillich, "Germany's Past, Present, and Future Fate (11/3/1942)," 84-85.

[139]Paul Tillich, Voice of America Speech 33 (11/1942) PTAH 602:001(33).

you yourselves use the sword of justice against those committing crimes against humanity, you prove before all the world that your hands are spotless and that there is still a German nation which can hear the voice of justice."[140] On another occasion, Tillich recalled a legend that embodied the bloody power motive of Nazism to motivate soldiers to cease the bloodletting:

> It is just as in the ancient legend, where the old tyrant had to bathe each day in the blood of a person in order to renew his strength and delay his end. *The same* day he found no sacrifice meant his end and the salvation of all further victims. *The same* day you, the German soldiers and laborers, refuse to offer the blood sacrifice for your tyrant would bring *his* end and your salvation.[141]

Though perhaps he did not know his radio project was coming to its end, the issue of resistance took on both urgency and resignation near the end of the project. In March 1944, as Germans did little to mitigate their fate, Tillich admonished his listeners:

> You surely know what kind of destiny the Nazis are leading Germany to. You have certainly seen that the end is the abyss and that there is no escape. Why, then, do you support them? What sort of responsibility do you have? A responsibility for Germany? Undoubtedly. But that surely means a responsibility over against the Nazis. Because it is they, indeed, who are making any German future impossible. It is your responsibility to get rid of the Nazis for the sake of Germany. You who know and yet don't want to know are the majority of the nation. Its fate depends upon you. If you know, then do what your knowledge tells you you must do. For the sake of your responsibility for Germany, take the responsibility on yourselves over against the Nazis. There is no loyalty toward those who knowingly allow German people to bleed to death for the sake of their power. Give up this war. It is no longer yours, it is no longer Germany's war. It is the Nazis' war, their war alone, and Germany and you, my German friends, are their instruments and their victims.[142]

Having chosen to deal with the devil, Germany would have to bear the consequences of that pact: "Didn't you know that a pact with the powers of evil first brings what is asked for, and that evil then insists on its right, the

---

[140]Paul Tillich, "Justice Rather than Vengeance (11/9/1943)," *Against the Third Reich* (Louisville: Westminster/John Knox Press, 1998) 207.

[141]Paul Tillich, Voice of America Speech 34 (11/1942) PTAH 602:001(34).

[142]Paul Tillich, "Rebellion and Loyalty (3/21/1944)," *Against the Third Reich* (Louisville: Westminster/John Knox Press, 1998) 236.

right to destroy the one with whom it has concluded a pact?"[143] Further, were Germans to embrace their just fate with bitterness, Tillich argued that this would be tragic. Using the Christian themes of Good Friday and Easter, he wrote that choosing bitter suffering meant "the true Good Friday has not come for the German people. Then you will again proceed among those who crucify others, and the end of this war will be a suffering without reconciliation and a death without resurrection."[144]

As the inevitable clouds of defeat were gathering, Tillich called the German people to look their fate of defeat in the eye, in order that it may be a source of hope.[145] Germany had to look into the mirror to see the truth about itself and find salvation.[146] It had to look into fate's dark face and consent to it, thereby taking away its sting and thereby changing its character.[147]

Justice and Economics

Nazism meant the menacing and vile disfigurement of justice.[148] Tillich stated that the German conscience testified to the truth that Germany's cause was not just. Germany had fought neither to protect Europe from Russia, nor to unify Europe, nor to maintain the existence of Germany.[149]

Tillich regretted the failure of intellectuals to understand their prophetic responsibility, their responsibility to ask questions of justice, particularly in Germany during this period. Technology may be morally neutral, but science must choose between good and evil. Germany had oppressed its intellectuals who understood this: "Everywhere there were some for whom the intellect meant life, struggle, revolution, mission. But where are they today? In exile, in the concentration camp, in seclusion, in the grave. They were betrayed by their colleagues . . . hated by the so-called intelligentsia

---

[143]Tillich, "Breaking the Pact . . . (11/30/1943)," 214.
[144]Tillich, "A German Good Friday (3/28/1944)," 240.
[145]Paul Tillich, "Dark Clouds Are Gathering (12/1942)," *Against the Third Reich* (Louisville: Westminster/John Knox Press, 1998) 86.
[146]Paul Tillich, "Blindness Precedes Ruin (4/27/1943)," *Against the Third Reich* (Louisville: Westminster/John Knox Press, 1998) 151.
[147]Tillich, "Fate and Guilt (5/18/1943)," 155.
[148]Tillich, "Zusammenbruch ohne Wiedergeburt (30.10.1943)," 274.
[149]Paul Tillich, "Who Stands on the Side of Justice? (5/2/1944)," *Against the Third Reich* (Louisville: Westminster/John Knox Press, 1998) 254-56.

... misunderstood by the masses."[150] Despite their technological know-how, German scientists were not asking deeper questions: "to what end? For whom? What happens to the human being who is doing all this? What does it look like to the masses? What does it look like within the souls of individuals?"[151] In failing to ask these questions within "the Holy of Holies of science . . . science ceased to be holy, let alone the Holy of Holies. It became neutral and fell, when the hour had come, to the power of destruction as welcome tools in its hand."[152] In short, the German intelligentsia "exalted when it should have condemned, it veiled when it should have unveiled; it kept silent when it should have spoken; it retreated when it should have fought; it betrayed when it should have tolerated."[153]

The response of the world order to Nazism was the response of justice at its very depths:

> The punishment of the war criminals, in the first place by the German people and then by all remaining enslaved and wounded nations, is the response of the divine world order attacked by the National Socialists. It is the response of human dignity which is trampled into the dust by the dehumanized instruments of National Socialism, first in Germany and then in all of Europe; it is the response of the community of human beings and of nations which is struck in its innermost being by the National Socialists. It is the response of that which is divine in the world to the attempt to distort it into that which is diabolical.[154]

Nazism had meant the revival of monstrous, destructive forces from the past. Allied victory meant a concrete justice: salvation from hunger, deprivation, and destruction; security with freedom; and a more just social order.[155] The world war was an embodiment of the world's justice responding to Nazism and Fascism. The bombing of Guernica in the Spanish Civil War symbolized Fascism's "war against the rest of the world."[156] What was happening in the subsequent world war was the world's retribution against the crimes of Fascism, a retribution consistent

---

[150]Tillich, "The Intelligentsia and Germany's Conquest (9/4/1942)," 58.
[151]Tillich, "The Intelligentsia and Germany's Conquest (9/4/1942)," 59.
[152]Tillich, "The Intelligentsia and Germany's Conquest (9/4/1942)," 59.
[153]Tillich, "The Intelligentsia and Germany's Conquest (9/4/1942)," 59.
[154]Tillich, "The Punishment of War Criminals (10/20/1942)," 80.
[155]Tillich, "A Guiding Light in the Darkness of the New Year (12/1942)," 101, 102-103.
[156]Tillich, "Retribution Unparalleled (11/23/1943)," 208-209.

with that spoken of by the prophets of the Bible.[157]

The Jewish prophetic tradition was a keystone to Tillich's understanding of justice in the Voice of America speeches.[158] Each nation was to bring the perpetrators [of Nazi crimes] to justice in accordance with the laws of each given land. Yet, it was to be a global justice. There was to be no place to hide for perpetrators, but justice was to be the goal, rather than vengeance, justice for the perpetrators, not vengeance against German innocents.[159]

It was easy for Nazism to dismiss Russian communism by branding it as atheism. However, Tillich tried to get his listeners to interpret the Russians as possessing a commitment—an "ultimate concern"—directed toward the "communist social order" and toward "the mission of the Russian people as bearers of the idea of a new justice": this was what he believed motivated Russian soldiers.[160]

Thus, Tillich called Germans to engage actively in the struggle for justice. He wrote in the spring of 1943, "No one is as powerful as the one who fights for justice with good conscience."[161] The following winter, he offered this standard for measuring national behavior: "[T]rue and correct is every belief, every step into the unknown, which a nation takes, when it turns away from injustice and turns toward justice."[162] Nazism was the revival of nationalistic tribalism rooted in tribal gods promoting international conflict. The prophetic spirit should have been the motivation for political leaders to stand against nationalism. Prophetic and Christian tradition lifted up the one God who transcends national boundaries: "the one God and the one people of God, beyond all tribes and nations."[163] The prophetic and apostolic tradition "proclaimed the one divine law, the one

---

[157]Tillich, "Retribution Unparalleled (11/23/1943)," 210.

[158]Tillich, "The Question of the Jewish People (3/31/1942)," 14-15.

[159]Tillich, "Justice Rather than Vengeance (11/9/1943)," 204-206.

[160]Tillich, "Russlands religiöse Lage (13.4.1942)," 23, 24.

[161]Paul Tillich, "Two Kinds of Defeatism (5/25/1943)," *Against the Third Reich* (Louisville: Westminster/John Knox Press, 1998) 161.

[162]Paul Tillich, "Schritte ins Dunkel—Schritte des Glaubens (4.1.1944)," *An meine deutschen Freunde* (Stuttgart: Evangelisches Verlagswerk, 1973) 298.

[163]Paul Tillich, "The Defeat of Nazi Belief (6/1/1943)," *Against the Third Reich* (Louisville: Westminster/John Knox Press, 1998) 164.

truth and the one justice for all."[164] Tillich encouraged his listeners to seek the greatness of Germany by the just path: to see their defeat as just; to admit complicity in their rulers' crimes; to ensure that their leaders face the consequences of their crimes; and to "establish justice within Germany itself."[165]

As described in previous chapters, Tillich was persuaded by Marx's writings to take economic justice seriously. In the Voice of America speeches he spoke to this matter on many occasions. In the summer of 1942 he declared, "[T]here can be no doubt that democracy, even in its best and most effective forms, is constantly threatened by economic antagonisms."[166] Whether in its democratic or totalitarian forms, Good Friday death without Easter hope was the recipe for class warfare: "a nation in which one class exploits the others is opening its doors to the conqueror and dies in class hostility."[167] He saw the cause of the war to be primarily economic: the capitalist system could "no longer give the masses of the people the security and the material prosperity which the people could demand in the period of limitless productive powers. And because that is so, the world is not able to come to rest, until its economic foundations are rebuilt."[168] An Allied victory would mean a more just social order.[169] Tillich saw Nazism as the most tragic consequence of the dehumanizing impact of capitalism. The downfall of capitalism had opened up a power vacuum into which the irrational forces of National Socialism had flowed, according to Tillich's reading of history. At this point, he was optimistic that a restructuring of the Western social order under more just terms was still a possibility, terms based upon socialism's concern to fight against the estrangement of people

---

[164]Tillich, "The Defeat of Nazi Belief (6/1/1943)," 164.

[165]Paul Tillich, "Das deutsche Volk: Größe durch Gerechtigkeit (18.1.1944)," *An meine deutschen Freunde* (Stuttgart: Evangelisches Verlagswerk, 1973) 305-306.

[166]Paul Tillich, "Gerechte Wirtschaftsordnung durch eine gerechte Gesellschaftsordnung (28.6.1942)," *An meine deutschen Freunde* (Stuttgart: Evangelisches Verlagswerk, 1973) 56.

[167]Paul Tillich, "The Tolling of Easter Bells (Easter Sunday 1943)," *Against the Third Reich* (Louisville: Westminster/John Knox Press, 1998) 147.

[168]Tillich, "Nachkriegsgestaltung als wirtschaftlich-soziale Neugestaltung (1.8.1942)," 76.

[169]Tillich, "A Guiding Light in the Darkness of the New Year (12/1942)," 103.

by the economic system.

Tillich took the impact of economic justice seriously because economic stability is a component of what it means to be human. Economic security with democracy preserves human dignity. Economic security with dictatorship leads to dehumanization. To Tillich, Roosevelt's New Deal modeled economic stability within democracy. He believed that Western liberals within the Allied leadership connected economic insecurity with the rise of Nazism. Thus, the Atlantic Charter and the Declaration of the Allied Nations called for reform of the economic order to eliminate "freedom from fear" and "freedom from want."[170] As alluded to before, Tillich declared these to be steps beyond the high aspirations of the French Revolution: "[T]oday, we know that freedom and equality before the law are lost if they are not borne by freedom from want and equal opportunity for everyone."[171]

Tillich understood that the struggle for economic justice was not unique to Germany. He described how labor parties and churches were working together for social reorganization in Britain. In the United States, the task was always a challenging one: "Every foot of social justice must be fought for here, just as in England, just as everywhere in the world. Everywhere there are powerful interest groups which want to sacrifice none of their privileges. Everywhere there is indifference which does not want to fight, and foolishness which does not want to see. And everywhere the battle for justice is a more difficult and perilous battle."[172]

Tillich spoke of the transformation of churches into advocates for social and economic justice during the previous two decades. Formerly, "the word justice was used in commentaries and sermons in every period, but people didn't think that practical conclusions could be drawn from it. The workers' parties and struggling trade unions were abhorred in church circles. They were interpreted as ungodly and subversive."[173] Testimony to the awakening of the social justice-conscience in the church was found in an issue of a New York paper at the time in which there were three church position

---

[170]Tillich, "Gerechte Wirtschaftsordnung durch eine gerechte Gesellschafts-ordnung (28.6.1942)," 57.

[171]Tillich, "Nazism and the Ideals of the French Revolution (7/5/1943)," 171.

[172]Tillich, "Nachkriegsgestaltung als wirtschaftlich-soziale Neugestaltung (1.8.1942)," 75-76.

[173]Paul Tillich, "Die Kirchen im Kampf für soziale Gerechtigkeit (3.7.1942)," *An meine deutschen Freunde* (Stuttgart: Evangelisches Verlagswerk, 1973) 60.

statements published inspired by the prophetic spirit: one was a protest by American church leaders about the racist treatment of workers; the second was a call for a living versus a minimum wage by British Roman Catholic bishops; and the third was the Archbishop of Canterbury William Temple's warning that victory could lead to the exploitative use of freedom for the sake of greed and economic dominance.[174] Tillich concluded, "It is astonishing to discover over and over again to what degree the thoughts of religious socialism, which were suppressed in Germany, have gained acceptance in the rest of the world."[175]

A few weeks later, Tillich admonished the German Opposition to think with others on the postwar structure of the world. He told his German listeners that in the larger world, "[i]n leading circles of all churches, people grasp that it is useless to preach of divine grace and the love of neighbors on Sunday, if at the same time the people are handed over to the spiritual and bodily destitution of unemployment, or they are allowed to live in continuous anxiety and uncertainty."[176] This meant that both international and economic reorganization were necessary following the war. In this spirit, he exhorted the radio audience to "[a]llow the Protestant protest to become strong among you, as it did among your fathers in their time. Internal and external freedom have proven to be one. The struggle for both is what your time requires of you."[177]

Nationalism and World Community

Nationalism. Inspired by his central European experience, Tillich portrayed Europe as a unifying force in world history. That unifying force was built upon Christianity and modern culture. While this may sound like a naïve romanticization of Europe's past, Tillich used the idea as a provocative tool for condemning Hitler's destruction of world unity.[178] He believed that with the rise of Nazism and the onset of war, the idea of "nation" had advanced

---

[174]Tillich, "Die Kirchen im Kampf für soziale Gerechtigkeit (3.7.1942)," 60-62.

[175]Tillich, "Die Kirchen im Kampf für soziale Gerechtigkeit (3.7.1942)," 64.

[176]Tillich, "Nachkriegsgestaltung als wirtschaftlich-soziale Neugestaltung (25.7.1942)," 74-75.

[177]Tillich, "Internal and External Freedom (4/20/1942)," 24.

[178]Paul Tillich, "Die Bedeutung Europas in Vergangenheit und Zukunft (4.5.1943)," *An meine deutschen Freunde* (Stuttgart: Evangelisches Verlagswerk, 1973) 194-95.

and been victorious over international entities, such as the Roman Catholic Church, the cosmopolitan spirit in science and culture, and the labor movement.[179] He argued that just as truth cannot be divided, so the world cannot legitimately be divided.[180]

The period of prewar isolation under Nazism had been a time for this nationalistic idolatry to germinate. Tillich contrasted healthy isolation with pathological isolation. The first is the solitude of greatness: "Completely great people are always, somehow or other, solitary people, because they bring something new for which others are still not ready. Even nations which bear within themselves something great, something new, go through such periods of solitude."[181] He saw such greatness in ancient Israel and Greece, in Great Britain, in revolutionary France and Russia, and in classical German culture.[182] Thus, there is a healthy faith in self and nation.[183] In contrast to this is destructive solitude with its international consequences. The Germany of Nazism rejected international community, looking "on every foreign nation only to see if and when it can be successfully attacked. This is the frightful, not creative, but rather destructive solitude into which the German nation has been driven by its rulers."[184]

Nazism had used technology—practical truth—to divide the world. At a time when technology had accomplished the physical and technological connection of the human race, Nazism had distorted these means for the division of the human race:

> All that the human spirit has created in the great overcoming of space has been placed into the service of division, of enmity, of hatred, and of destruction. The implements of community—in the air, on water, on earth—have been turned into implements of discord. The airplane carries the deadly bomb, the ship the deadly torpedo, the truck the deadly missile; the electric wave connects the

---

[179]Paul Tillich, "Die nationale Idee und der nationale Götzendienst (10.7.1942)," in *An meine deutschen Freunde* (Stuttgart: Evangelisches Verlagswerk, 1973), 64-68.

[180]Tillich, "Der geistige Wiederaufbau (8.8.1942)," 85.

[181]Paul Tillich, "Deutschlands Einsamkeit (23.8.1943)," *An meine deutschen Freunde* (Stuttgart: Evangelisches Verlagswerk, 1973) 256.

[182]Tillich, "Deutschlands Einsamkeit (23.8.1943)," 256-57.

[183]Tillich, "'Der 'Deutsche Glaube' . . . (9.2.1944)," 310-11.

[184]Tillich, "Deutschlands Einsamkeit (23.8.1943)," 255-59.

continents by word, spreads falsehood and hatred, and the oneness it creates is being simultaneously destroyed! The human race has not been matched to creations of its own spirit. They have become a curse for it, because there was no unified human race which had been able to use them—for a blessing instead of a curse.[185]

Tillich saw the only unity pursued by Nazism as nationalism. Nazism's nationalist idolatry contradicted the prophetic tradition's universalism,[186] choosing the path of paganism and neo-paganism over that of the prophets and the Christ.[187] The idea of nation had become the poison" of nationalistic idolatry in Germany.[188] Idolatry spreads like an epidemic: "As hate gives birth to hate, so nationalism gives birth to nationalism, and national idolatry to national idolatry."[189] Nazism promoted a diabolical, nationalistic and idolatrous faith:

It is the idolatrous belief in the mission of the Germans to redeem the world, in the greater sanctity of the German soil, in the saving strength of German blood. It is the belief in the *Führer*, through whom a special providence speaks to the Germans, through whom a divine preference exalts the German nation above all other nations. It is the belief that power is the secret to life and that truth and justice must serve power. It is the belief in whose name its fanatical priests, the S.S. and the Gestapo, have slaughtered hundreds of thousands and offered them to the idol for a sacrifice. It is the belief which has torn everything which is human out of the souls of its adherents and has brought the horrors of primeval barbarity upon the human race in the twentieth century. The belief which has been forced on the German people looks like that.[190]

German youth were nurtured into the nationalistic ideology "that power

[185]Paul Tillich, "Weihnachtsbotschaft für Alle (21.12.1942)," *An meine deutschen Freunde* (Stuttgart: Evangelisches Verlagswerk, 1973) 136. See also Paul Tillich, Voice of America Speech 80 (10/20/1943) PTAH 603:001 (80) regarding technology as a force for uniting the world.
[186]Tillich, "The Question of the Jewish People (3/31/1942)," 14-15.
[187]Tillich, Voice of America Speech 39b (1/1943).
[188]Tillich, "Die nationale Idee . . . (10.7.1942)," 65.
[189]Tillich, "Die nationale Idee . . . (10.7.1942)," 66.
[190]Tillich, ",Der ,Deutsche Glaube' . . . (9.2.1944)," 311. See also Paul Tillich, Voice of America Speech 1 (12/1942 or 12/1943) PTAH 604:001 (I), a fragment in which Tillich declared that giving glory to self and to nation was the basis for Germany's undoing.

is everything and justice nothing; that blood is everything and spirit nothing; that the nation is everything and the individual nothing."[191] This was a matter of patriotism gone wrong, patriotism in the extreme. Tillich distinguished between blind and seeing patriotism:

> What is genuine love for one's fatherland? It is seeing, not blind, love. Blind love overrates everything peculiar to itself and underrates everything strange. And for that reason it is incapable of adapting to the rest of humanity. Nothing has become so difficult for the German nation than this adaptation to the spirit of other nations. It has always swayed between senselessly overrating another nation and senselessly overrating itself.[192]

In short, Fascism and Nazism faced their downfall because they sacrificed the eternal and exalted the temporal: nation, military power, *Führer*, youth, technology and the past.[193]

In Tillich's view, nationalism is power untamed, predestined to be imperialistic. As in all periods of his thought, power in itself was not the difficulty for Tillich. In February 1944 he spoke of the legitimate relationship between power and community:

> [C]ommunity needs power to be able to live. That is so with all living entities; also with the life of a national community. It needs power in order to keep from decaying. It needs power to keep from being destroyed. It needs internal and external power. Every community of living cells within a body requires a power that holds the cells together, directs their growth, and protects them against harmful influences from without. A community of human cells, a national community, also needs such a uniting, directing, and protecting power.[194]

---

[191]Paul Tillich, "Ziel und Zerbrechen der nationalsozialistischen Erziehung (7.6.1943)," *An meine deutschen Freunde* (Stuttgart: Evangelisches Verlagswerk, 1973) 215.

[192]Paul Tillich, "Der Widerstand gegen den Terror und die Vaterlandsliebe (26.7.1943)," *An meine deutschen Freunde* (Stuttgart: Evangelisches Verlagswerk, 1973) 240.

[193]Paul Tillich, "Faschismus und Nationalsozialismus (2.8.1943)," *An meine deutschen Freunde* (Stuttgart: Evangelisches Verlagswerk, 1973) 242-46, and Paul Tillich, ",Not lehrt beten' (10.1.1944)," in *An meine deutschen Freunde* (Stuttgart: Evangelisches Verlagswerk, 1973) 299-300.

[194]Paul Tillich, "Community in the Service of Power (2/15/1944)," *Against the Third Reich* (Louisville: Westminster/John Knox Press, 1998) 229-30.

However, the dangers of power without justice were a perpetual concern for him. In the late spring of 1942 he put the issue in the form of a question:

> Shall human beings be creatures who are moved by will-to-power, hatred, contempt, falsehood, hostility, dominion, and slavery? Or shall they be creatures who put their passions into the service of justice, the recognition of that which is human in human beings, truth, the desire for freedom and equality? Shall that which is bestial or that which is divine in humanity triumph? When it submitted to the present rule, Germany chose in favor of the bestial in humanity.[195]

The dehumanizing impact of Nazism was the demonic corruption of humanity. Tillich's concerns about nationalism were related to the way it embodied power: "The secret of pure nationalism is that it has no essence and, therefore, is revealed to be pure will-to-power. The empty self-deification of the nation takes effect in an unending striving for self-expansion."[196] In a speech on power politics in October 1942, Tillich wrote that justice is the effective adversary of Nazi power-idolatry. The significance of legitimate power is that it is life-giving.[197] On the other hand, power without justice is sadistic.[198] It is both dangerous and illusory: "Power which is not united with justice is only apparently power, and is, in reality, the deepest powerlessness; and justice which possesses no outward power is only apparently powerless, but is, in reality, an invincible power."[199] In a speech on tyrannical power in the spring of 1943, Tillich called Nazism a tyrannical machine of oppression. Though it was using increasingly oppressive methods, it was simultaneously provoking and strengthening resistance, eventually even attacking its own minions and instruments.[200] He concluded, "Tyrannical power has limits because it develops forces of self-destruction, and it has limits because humanity is created with freedom."[201] In October 1943 he declared that Nazism's ascent

---

[195]Tillich, Voice of America Speech 9 (5-6/1942).

[196]Tillich, "Die nationale Idee . . . (10.7.1942)," 66-67.

[197]Paul Tillich, "Power Politics (10/13/1942)," *Against the Third Reich* (Louisville: Westminster/John Knox Press, 1998) 72, 74.

[198]Tillich, Voice of America Speech 34 (11/1942).

[199]Tillich, "Power Politics (10/13/1942)," 73.

[200]Tillich, "Tyrannical Power Has Limits (4/6/1943)," 138-39.

[201]Tillich, "Tyrannical Power Has Limits (4/6/1943)," 139.

to power meant will-for-justice was replaced by will-to-power: "[T]he old which they restored was something ancient. It was primitive barbarity, idolatry and desire for plunder and conquest, the belief in the tyranny of the one and the enslavement of the others, it was education for death and killing."[202] Nazism had coerced a living nation into becoming a lifeless machine:

> In place of community walks coercion; in place of love, fear; in place of the free interrelation of free people, the forced arrangement of everyone into an enormous, all- entangling machine. But a machine is not a community. And a nation which has turned into a machine has lost everything which can be called national community. With the misused term, national community, a coercive machine has been created which is kept in motion with terror, a machine through which any remnant of national community is being destroyed.[203]

Nazi nationalism was the extreme example of a phenomenon Tillich saw to be particularly flawed, that of national sovereignty.[204] Tillich was hopeful that "the national idea—after it has celebrated its last, mad triumph in Germany—will have lost its power and will have to yield to another, higher idea."[205] This was not to deny the value of particular cultural identities or the richness they grant the world, "But no nation, neither German nor any other, shall retain the possibility of a politically powerful nationalism."[206]

Seeking to understand the meaning of Good Friday and Easter for international life, Tillich interpreted nationalism as death without hope of resurrection:

> Many of the fighting, suffering, nearly dying nations of this war have understood the great law of life, of Good Friday and Easter. . . . They have grasped that a nation which lives only to itself, and which scorns the community of nations, perishes in its isolation. . . . They have grasped that a nation which acknowledges no ultimate religious values but seeks only the penultimate—power and money—squanders its inner strengths and

[202]Tillich, "Zusammenbruch oder Wiedergeburt? (30.10.1943)," 274.

[203]Tillich, Voice of America Speech 10 (5-6/1942).

[204]Tillich, Voice of America Speech 39b (1/1943). In another speech, Tillich characterized it as "a recipe for irresponsibility and inactivity." Tillich, "Nicht Nation, sondern Föderation (17.7.1942)," 72.

[205]Tillich, "Die nationale Idee . . . (10.7.1942)," 67.

[206]Tillich, "Die nationale Idee . . . (10.7.1942)," 68.

disintegrates.[207]

He called for Germans to experience a true Easter:

> Easter does not speak of the victory of weapons, it doesn't speak of the defeat
> of death through national power seizures and political concentrations of power.
> The victory over death does not happen in the palace of Augustus who had
> united the world. It doesn't happen in the victorious battles of the Romans who
> made this unification possible. Not once does it happen through the power and
> position of the high priests and the splendor of their temple. The victory over
> death occurs there where no one expects it, where no one can hope for it.
> Easter becomes living where a genuine Passiontide, a genuine Good Friday has
> preceded it. And for this reason there can be Easter in Germany today better
> than in the days when it was only a spring festival or a pleasant custom.
> Because there is a genuine Good Friday in Germany today, there is also a
> genuine Easter.[208]

By the summer of 1943, Tillich was posing the question as Germany's
choice between two paths: the abysmal path of continued war or the
hopeful, life-giving path of "community with others."[209] Taking the latter
path meant separating from the Nazis; concluding the war; returning self-
determination to the people and returning to the community of nations.[210]

World Community. Tillich believed the German people stood against
Hitler's approach to the world: "The German nation wants to live, like other
nations and with other nations. The German nation doesn't want to rule the
world. But it also doesn't want to perish."[211] Tillich admonished his
listeners to act from this viewpoint: "Say no to the fearful choice which the
National Socialists have set before you! Say no to world rule, say no to
destruction. Say yes to the community of nations, say yes to life, to the
future of the German nation."[212] He called the German people to speak a
profound word on world community: "The last word is a word of
reconciliation and of the new community of nations beyond crime, curse

---

[207]Tillich, "The Tolling of Easter of Bells (Easter Sunday 1943)," 147.

[208]Paul Tillich, "The Ancient and Eternal Message of Easter (4/4/1944),"
Against the Third Reich (Louisville: Westminster/John Knox Press, 1998) 242.

[209]Paul Tillich, Voice of America Speech 73 (8/1943) PTAH 603:001 (73).

[210]Tillich, Voice of America Speech 73 (8/1943) PTAH 603:001 (73).

[211]Paul Tillich, Voice of America Speech 66 (7/1943) PTAH 603:001(66).

[212]Tillich, Voice of America Speech 66 (7/1943) PTAH 603:001(66).

and punishment."[213] In another place he urged, "Speak of that which national-being means—that it means community, and the path to take is the community of all people."[214] Germany's story could become an Easter resurrection story:

> [T]he German resurrection . . . depends on whether the German nation becomes a new nation, a people that loves justice and not power, that loves truth and not deceit, that wants not to destroy but to build, that does not wish to exist unless it does so within the community of nations. The resurrection of such a Germany would be an Easter message for Germany and for the world. And it would be an Easter message even over the death fields in all lands.[215]

Tillich argued, on the one hand, that "Germany cannot live without the human race, not economically, not intellectually, not politically."[216] In May 1943, he called Germany to become a legitimate force for both European and world unity. To do this it must recognize and act upon four bases for world unity: it must have a desire for unity; it must seek the preservation of "the particular nature of the individual nations"; it must conquer the forces of self-destruction, particularly the vengeful spirit; and it must proceed beyond continental unity to world unity.[217] Tillich's assertion was that the "struggle for the unity of Europe should not become a struggle for an isolated Europe. . . . Europe should only signify this, that the hearth of two world wars has eliminated within itself the preconditions for a third world war. Europe should signify that a great common past has again become present."[218] In February 1944, he described the requisites of community as "common destiny, mutual trust, and the same goals."[219]

On the other hand, the world needed Germany as well. There is a necessary unity that forms a part of international relations. Peace or war in one locality has worldwide implications. Therefore, "A peace which does

---

[213]Paul Tillich, "Zehn Jahre Nazi-Herrschaft (2/1943)," 159.

[214]Tillich, "Das neue Jahr—ein neues Zeitalter? (21.12.1943)," 291.

[215]Tillich, "The Ancient and Eternal Message of Easter (4/4/1944)," 244.

[216]Tillich, "Zu spat für die Rettung Deutschlands? (30.3.1943)," 183.

[217]Paul Tillich, "Die Bedingungen für eine europäische Einigung (11.5.1943)," *An meine deutschen Freunde* (Stuttgart: Evangelisches Verlagswerk, 1973) 198, 199, 200, 201.

[218]Tillich, "Die Bedingungen für eine europäische Einigung (11.5.1943)," 201-202.

[219]Tillich, "Community in the Service of Power (2/15/1944)," 230.

justice to the necessities of life of all Germans must be granted by the victors, for the sake of themselves and for the sake of the world which must otherwise fall to ruin."[220]

Further, he endorsed the idea of a world federation over against the post-World War I pattern of the League of Nations. In July 1942, Tillich discussed forward-seeing representatives of nations occupied by Germany, now in exile, who sought regional federations and a world federation: "[T]hey want to hand over their military and diplomatic sovereignty to this united entity and retain only their cultural and internal-political standing. Even the economic questions shall be handled in the first place by the large, united entity, the federation."[221] The amount of focus on "world" throughout the world gave him reason to believe that there would be less particularism and provincialism after the war. "World" in this sense equals unity, not in the sense of a mechanistic or repressive unity, but rather a unity that is "special, unique, free, and creative."[222] Tillich saw the meaning of World War II to be the creation of a broader world community.[223] In such a world, there could "no longer be any external freedom, in the sense of the sovereignty of the individual states after this war. No nation will be free in this sense. All nations of the world will join together in an all-embracing unity."[224] Tillich pointed to the world movement toward unity within Christianity as a basis for hope in the prospect of international community. He advocated the overcoming of "the pernicious results of national sovereignty" by means of a community of nations, contending that "God's objective is *humanity* and not any particular nation."[225] Tillich wrote this at a time during which he still held out hope for a united Germany with a legitimate voice in a world, not one dominated by three or four powerful nations.

In one of his earliest speeches, Tillich had offered his hope that the

---

[220]Tillich, Voice of America Speech 80 (10/20/1943).

[221]Tillich, "Nicht Nation, sondern Föderation (17.7.1942)," 70.

[222]Paul Tillich, "Die Welt nach dem Krieg (29.9.1942)," *An meine deutschen Freunde* (Stuttgart: Evangelisches Verlagswerk, 1973) 106.

[223]Paul Tillich, "Gemeinschaft der Völker—Gemeinschaft der Menschen (22.2.1944)," *An meine deutschen Freunde* (Stuttgart: Evangelisches Verlagswerk, 1973) 317.

[224]Paul Tillich, "What Is Worth Defending? (10/6/1942)" *Against the Third Reich* (Louisville: Westminster/John Knox Press, 1998) 69.

[225]Tillich, Voice of America Speech 39b (1/1943).

German people would soon "see through and shake off the religious packaging of their nationalism, without falling to the level of genuine irreligion, namely to despair and to indifference to any meaning in life."[226] As a remedy for their nationalistic idolatry, he called for Germany to turn to the eternal: "It can happen that the German people—turning to the eternal—learns what place it occupies within the temporal: where it belongs, what it means for the human race, what its limits are, and what its true greatness is."[227]

Conclusion

On the occasion of his one hundredth speech over the Voice of America, Tillich explained the purposes of his speeches: "What I have attempted, week after week over the last two years, is to lead the German people to a new, genuine hope. . . . What I have said to you and pondered with you in these two years was the inner preparation for the German future. . . . Separate yourselves from those who are bringing you to ruin: that tone was missing from none of the speeches."[228] As this chapter has shown, Tillich engaged in a rich and wide-ranging discussion of issues in his pursuit of this goal. The thematic treatment of the content of the speeches has illustrated both the evolution as well as the constancy of Tillich's thought. The principle elements of the Voice of America speeches to be included in an ethic of religious internationalism are these:
1. National identity within international community and world unity must be cultivated, rather than isolated nationalism and tribalism;
2. Creativity within cultures should be embraced; critical thinking must be unrelenting; reverence for human beings must be practiced (democracy as respect for human dignity; free decision as the expression of one's humanity);
3. Socioeconomic justice should be pursued;
4. Power with justice is the goal;
5. Political resistance is necessary when it functions as an instrument of justice ("instruments of the moral, constructive world order, and

---

[226]Tillich, "Russlands religiöse Lage (13.4.1942)," 25.
[227]Tillich, ",Not lehrt beten' (10.1.1944)," 302.
[228]Paul Tillich, "One Hundred Speeches on Liberation from Nazism (3/7/1944)," *Against the Third Reich* (Louisville: Westminster/John Know Press, 1998) 262-63.

not of the immoral, destructive world order");

6. The destructive idolatry of power worship should be rejected;
7. Nations will be struck for the international guilt of their leaders;
8. Nations must accept responsibility for the crimes of their leaders; and
9. Technology is morally neutral, but science must make moral choices.

Chapter 5

World War II—Tillich's Message
to His Audience in the United States:
Social Renewal
and International Reconstruction

Introduction

Paul Tillich wrote many articles and lectures for the English-speaking community during World War II which addressed the meaning of this historical crisis and which advocated various strategies. The discussion here is structured under three general areas: philosophy of history; Protestantism and its principle(s); and postwar reconstruction. Tillich's philosophy of history takes seriously the reality of human being as finite freedom exercised in sensitivity to periods ripe for action. Through it Tillich interpreted the times to be characterized by cultural disintegration, widely experienced but most tragically experienced by the Jewish people. Tillich's collection of Protestant principles push toward the possibility of what he variously called an "eternal Protestantism" or a "post-Protestantism" or a "Protestant Catholicity." His thoughts on postwar reconstruction are rooted in the religiously socialistic spirit, mustered to bring about social renewal and mined to construct an ethical basis for international action and organization.

Philosophy of History

General Comments. Tillich's philosophy of history is anchored in his religious socialism. Religious Socialism posed a way for religion to influence social outlook that avoided overemphasizing either human essence (and thereby losing human existence) or human existence (losing humanity's essential nature). The way of religious socialism kept essence and existence in tension.[1] Religious socialism maintained belief in the downfall of—and estrangement embodied within—the bourgeois period,[2]

---

[1] Paul Tillich, "Trends in Religious Thought that Affect Social Outlook," in *Religion and the World Order*, F. E. Johnson, ed. (New York: Harper, 1944) 17-19.

[2] This was consistent with Marx's description of the outcome of untrammeled capitalism. "In him the experience of estrangement reached explosive power, and

the rise of a collectivistic period, and the religious understanding of this collectivistic period.[3] Religious socialist anthropology distinguished human being from God (infinite freedom) and nature (finite necessity): "The structure of man is the structure of 'finite freedom.' "[4] Thus, utopianism is false: "The perfect never appears," however, "Man is able to act without Utopianism because he is able to realize the infinite meaning of a creative act to which he gives his finite existence."[5]

Tillich clarified that the social group does not equal the person:

> Social groups are not organic or personal beings. They are personalized by analogy, but this analogy is not only vague but also dangerous, because it hides the power structure of every social group and asks for free decisions of a group which can be asked only of those who act for the group. . . . [It] is always the individual person who decides and acts and not a mythological collective which is dressed up as a person.[6]

Further, he questioned whether creative freedom equaled political freedom, given that political freedom and pathological economic insecurity can exist

---

the demand for reconciliation reached revolutionary strength." Paul Tillich, "Estrangement and Reconciliation in Modern Thought (Presidential address to the American Theological Society, April 14, 1944), *Review of Religion* [New York] 9/1 (November 1944): 14.

[3]Paul Tillich, "Man and Society in Religious Socialism (Paper presented in the Philosophy Group at the 'Week of Work,' National Council on Religion in Higher Education," *Christianity and Society* (New York) 8/4 (Fall 1943): 10.

[4]Tillich, "Man and Society in Religious Socialism," 13.

[5]Tillich, "Man and Society in Religious Socialism," 15. Tillich challenged Friedrich Pollock's support for the possibility of human fulfillment within history, given the right economic conditions. When Pollock and Adolph Löwe accused him of replacing an earthly utopia with a transcendental one, Tillich declared that "we know nothing of human beings in a better social climate. Are they blessed beasts or blessed angels? . . . Isn't the presupposition of a classless society much more fantastic than the transcendent solution." Paul Tillich, "Symposium on Philosophy of History (1940s)" PTAH 206:034, 4. As noted previously, in citing sources from the Paul Tillich Archive at Harvard, I will use the notation created by Erdmann Sturm: the acronym PTAH designating the Paul Tillich Archive at Harvard; the first number designating the box number; and the number following the colon designating the file number within the box.

[6]Tillich, "Man and Society in Religious Socialism," 15, 16.

simultaneously.[7] Finite freedom was Tillich's alternative and challenge to the metaphysical loneliness of religious individualism, the detached humanism of cultured individualism and the atomization of rational individualism. In finite freedom, human creativity occurs within the collective and within the other structural limits of history.[8]

Tillich made two concrete applications of this formulation of finite freedom: the future of Germany; and the future of Jewish-Christian relations. He saw hope for the future of Germany as dependent upon groups capable of giving "ingenious leadership which is in creative agreement with the historical situation."[9] He believed any future action on the relationship of Judaism and Christianity as a matter of acting within the "gaps" that fate permitted.[10]

Finite freedom defines the limits and possibilities for historical action. From the viewpoint of religious socialism, historical dialectics was "a union of waiting and acting," captured by the biblical position of "the Kingdom of God is 'at hand.'"[11] History is dynamic, ever changing, and always potentially creative.[12] The optimal place from which to interpret history is out of broken finitude. In place of the detached "mere observer" and the unreflective "mere activist," broken finitude is "opened for the infinite by suffering."[13] Occupied by the prophets in ancient Israel, the socially vulnerable in the time of Christ, and the proletariat for Marx, religious socialism saw it to include the "'broken' people in all groups."[14] In a March 1944 sermon, Tillich pointed to both Cyrus of Persia and the suffering servant of Isaiah as such people: Cyrus, in ignorance; the suffering servant, the

---

[7]Tillich, "Man and Society in Religious Socialism," 18. Tillich believed that becoming a U.S. citizen had granted him the freedom to create, a freedom he valued at least as highly as political freedom. Paul Tillich, "I Am an American," *Protestant Digest* (June-July 1941): 26.

[8]Tillich, "Man and Society in Religious Socialism," 18-20.

[9]Paul Tillich, "Theses on the Peace Treaty" (PTAH 404:038), 6.

[10]Paul Tillich, "The Religious Relation between Christianity and Judaism in the Future (Early 1940s)" PTAH 416:011, 1.

[11]Tillich, "Man and Society in Religious Socialism," 20.

[12]Paul Tillich, "The Protestant Approach to the Present World Situation: The Special Difficulties of the Protestant Approach," PTAH 406B:033, 1-6.

[13]Tillich, "Man and Society in Religious Socialism," 21.

[14]Tillich, "Man and Society in Religious Socialism," 21.

prototype of "all those who are innocently sacrificed for the future, to be *one* small stone in the building of the divine Kingdom."[15]

The activism of religious socialism—the expectation of the possibilities for exercising freedom—was founded on its *kairos* doctrine. As previously described, *kairos* is "the right moment of time, in which eternity breaks into history and demands a decisive step, without assuming that this step will lead into an immanent or transcendent stage of perfection."[16] It "unites in a special way theological optimism and pessimism and overcomes the alternative," that is, the alternatives of "utopianism as well as historical indifference."[17]

Cultural Disintegration. Tillich argued that the European situation—particularly, the destruction of the bourgeoisie and the entry into a period of "radical transformation"—was not accidental. It was a logical consequence of the bourgeois fallacy of harmony and the utopian belief in the capacity of reason to grant that harmony. Both intra-class and ideological splits had arisen.[18]

Economic security, employment status, the position of the proletariat, lack of academic posts, disintegration of the bourgeoisie, and the relationship of politics and religion led to splits within the leading bourgeoisie, organized labor, the intelligentsia, the bureaucratic-military complex, and Protestantism.[19] The internationalism of the League of Nations had been contradicted by nationalistic divisiveness. Anti-Semitic and antialien policies had undermined the emancipation of the Jews and the freedom of

---

[15]Tillich, "The God of History (1944)," 6. Tillich saw Marx to be wrong in isolating the proletariat as the sole vehicle of societal reconciliation: "Those who fight successfully for reconciliation against estrangement must have experienced reconciliation within their estranged situation, as had the Jewish prophets and the revolutionary movements in Christianity." (Tillich, "Estrangement and Reconciliation in Modern Thought," 14, 15-16.)

[16]Tillich, "Trends in Religious Thought," 28.

[17]Tillich, "Trends in Religious Thought," 28.

[18]Marx foresaw class struggle but not split within classes. Paul Tillich, "The Causes of the European Situation" PTAH 406A:003, 2, 5-6; Paul Tillich, "Our Disintegrating World," *Anglican Theological Review* 23/2 (April 1941): 135; and Paul Tillich, "The World Situation," 1945, in *The Christian Answer*, ed. Henry P. Van Dusen (New York: Scribner's, 1948) 2, 4, 6.

[19]Tillich, "The Causes of the European Situation," 7-9.

aliens.[20] Nietzsche, Kierkegaard, Stirner, Dolstoyevsky, and Jacob Burck-
hardt had all shared Marx's sensitivity to disintegrating trends within
European culture.[21]

Tillich wrote that this collapse was civilizational, not restricted to
Germany.[22] The German situation had simply become the most pathological. Germany's interwar conditions led to Nazism: "political oppression
from outside, social insecurity from inside, intellectual disintegration everywhere."[23] If such conditions arose again, the consequences would again be
negative. Tillich spoke to the question of whether National Socialism
represented the true spirit of Germany. While Germany could not be
completely separated from Nazism, the same was true of Europe and the
world as a whole: "*All* were complicit: an *epoch* is complicit; and *this epoch*
is now going up in flames."[24] In a July 1942 article, Tillich responded quite
sharply to publisher Emil Ludwig's call for a fight against the people of

[20]Tillich, "Our Disintegrating World," 140.

[21]Paul Tillich, "Nietzsche and the Bourgeois Spirit," *Journal of the History of
Ideas* 6/3 (June 1945): 308. Of Nietzsche Tillich argued, "No interpretation . . .
should neglect his grand and tragic war against the spirit of his age, the spirit of
bourgeois society." (Tillich, "Nietzsche and the Bourgeois Spirit," 309.) In a review
of Jacques Maritain's *The Rights of Man and Natural Law*, Tillich expressed
appreciation for the richness of its content. At the same time, Tillich believed
Maritain's presentation of political principles neglected an adequate treatment of
the historical context in which they would operate: "Is it possible to state political
principles without applying historical dialectics 'to the situation for which they are
used'?" Paul Tillich, "Book Review: Jacques Maritain's *The Rights of Man and
Natural Law*," *Religion in Life* 13/3 (Summer 1944): 465-66. See also Tillich, "Our
Disintegrating World," 143, and Tillich, "The World Situation," 9-12.

[22]The American Friends of German Freedom (Reinhold Niebuhr was chairman;
its thirty-nine-member National Committee included Paul Tillich and Thomas
Mann), *Germany Tomorrow* (New York: American Friends of German Freedom,
undated, but between 6/1941 and 4/1945) 1-6.

[23]Tillich, "Theses on the Peace Treaty," 4.

[24]Tillich called his listeners to reject the illusions of returning to "the old
Europe, the old Germany, that which one loved." Paul Tillich, "Läuterndes Feuer"
(Rede auf dem "Goethe-Tag 1942" im Hunter College von New York [original
Title: "Verbranntes Buch—Unzerstörbare Kultur"], veranstaltet von der *Tribüne für
freie deutsche Literatur und Kunst in Amerika*, 18 May 1942) *Aufbau/
Reconstruction* (New York) 8/22 (29 May 1942) 10, *GW XIII*, 277, 278.

Germany, particularly Ludwig's declaration that Hitler was Germany and that Germany was a warrior nation.[25] To Tillich, this was group defamation: "I have fought against, and will continue to fight against any moralistic collective condemnation of a natural or historical existing group."[26] He saw group stereotype as contrary to prophetic justice.[27] Further, it undermined both of the goals for which the war was being fought: to motivate Germans to resist Hitler's regime and to bring about a unified Europe in which each nation surrendered parts of its sovereignty in a regional system of accountability.[28]

In the realm of ideas, there were splits between the Marxist and Nietzschean criticisms of the bourgeois system, rationalism and irrationalism, classical world-bourgeois liberalism and nationalist racialism, Wilsonian pluralism and national sovereignty, and humanistic rationalism and traditional religious forms.[29] Protestantism experienced a parallel development during the period: unmediated access to the divine Spirit and to the sacred texts were consistent with the belief of the power of reason in all people. Reason dominated the period: "Adaptation of religion to reason, but to a reason which was based on religion."[30] Tillich attributed the failure of the principle of harmony (one of reason's optimistic expectations) to "an economic, a political, and a spiritual exhaustion of this principle."[31] In economics, the middle class had broken down and permanent unemployment had arisen. In politics, world power struggles had destroyed any sense of a united world. In spirituality, the simultaneous decline of religious conformity and the onset of secular emptiness created a "spiritual vacuum."[32] Tillich

[25]Paul Tillich, "Was soll mit Deutschland geschehen?" 6, *GW XIII*, 278.

[26]Paul Tillich, "Es geht um die Method—Antwort Paul Tillichs an die Kritiker im ‚Aufbau,' " *Aufbau/Reconstruction* (New York) 8/32 (7 August 1942), 7-8, in *GW XIII*, 280.

[27]Tillich, " Es geht um die Method—Antwort Paul Tillichs an die Kritiker im ‚Aufbau,' " 280-81.

[28]Tillich, " Es geht um die Method—Antwort Paul Tillichs an die Kritiker im ‚Aufbau,' " 281.

[29]Tillich, "The Causes of the European Situation," 9-11.

[30]Paul Tillich, "Protestantism and Moral Anarchy (early 1940s)," PTAH 406A:026, 4-5.

[31]Tillich, "Protestantism and Moral Anarchy (early 1940s)," 11.

[32]Tillich, "Protestantism and Moral Anarchy (early 1940s)," 11.

expressed this tragic breakdown as an undeniable reality:

> Nobody can deny any more the end of economic expansion, especially in Europe, indirectly all over the world, the consequent loss of fixed capital, the deepening of the economic crisis, the increased danger of imperialistic clashes as a consequence of the narrowing down of the world market, the tremendous speed of technological development as one of the main causes of structural unemployment which can be reduced only by a full or half-dictatorial war economy, the monopolistic-bureaucratic trends towards the centralization of economic power and ultimately towards state capitalism, the psychological effects of economic and social insecurity, expressed in indifference to freedom and democracy, especially in the younger generation, and in readiness to follow anyone who promises a greater amount of security, the intellectual emptiness leading either to cynicism or to a tragic will to death as the meaning of life—all this is a reality nobody can overlook.[33]

Elsewhere he attributed Western civilization's collapse to basic superficiality:

> The noise of these shallow waters prevents us from listening to the sounds out of the depth, to the sounds of what really happens at the base of our social structure, in the longing hearts of the masses, in the struggling minds of those who are sensitive to historical changes. Our ears are deaf to the cries out of the social depth as they are deaf to the cries out of the depth of our soul. We leave the bleeding victims of our social system alone as we leave our bleeding souls alone after we have hurt them, without hearing their outcries in the noise of our daily lives.[34]

In Tillich's view, moral anarchy had become manifest. The vacuum was ripe to be filled by irrational forces.[35] Fascism was able to replace "religion" with "nation" as the source of values. Russian communism combined rationalism with nationalism. Tillich believed that Western powers failed to acknowledge that "[t]hey have created Communism by the social injustice they defended with all their power and they have nourished Fascism in order to use is as a tool against Communism."[36] The spiritualist groups

---

[33]"Our Disintegrating World," 136-37.

[34]Paul Tillich, "Depth," *Christendom* (New York) 9/3 (Summer 1944): 321.

[35]Tillich, "Our Disintegrating World," 141; Paul Tillich, "Spiritual Problems of Past-War Reconstruction." *Christianity and Crisis* (New York) 2/14 (10 August 1942): 3-4.

[36]Paul Tillich, "Why War Aims?" *Protestant Digest* (June-July 1941): 36.

maintained their nonpolitical positions: Tillich included Karl Barth within this group. Neo-Catholicism perpetuated the authority within the church over all realms, but with less power than before. Cynicism was the natural consequence for those unpersuaded by any of these options.[37] As the postwar period approached, a double disintegration—of personality and community—signaled the loss of meaning.[38] Tillich called the church to face this disintegration and to use its structure to interpret the world situation.[39]

The Jewish People. Tillich proceeded along various lines to understand the impact of Nazism and Western civilization upon the Jewish people. He was asked by the American government to write on the relationship of Catholicism and Protestantism to the Jewish Question during the war years. Tillich saw Catholicism and Judaism as two systems competing to provide a comprehensive understanding of existence, two unrelenting and exclusive world views. The exclusiveness of their worldviews made Catholic Anti-Judaism and Jewish Anti-Catholicism almost inevitable.[40] Tillich reviewed the biblical roots of anti-Judaism and the combination of rejection and protection that was present in the period of the Church Fathers.[41]

In certain cases, the line between of anti-Judaism and anti-Semitism was blurred by the behavior of clerics. Interestingly, when Catholicism took the path of anti-Semitism, it became more vulnerable. As Tillich put it, "Catholic anti-Semitism can be fought, Catholic anti-Judaism cannot."[42] He seemed to have been commenting on the comparative difficulty of fighting a doctrinal battle rooted in the sacred texts of Christianity (anti-Judaism)

---

[37]Tillich, "Protestantism and Moral Anarchy," 11-14.

[38]Tillich, "Spiritual Problems of Past-War Reconstruction," 3. Tillich clearly appreciated Nicolas Berdyaev's work on dehumanization, depersonalization, alienation and objectivation of human beings ontologically and theologically, as well as in the realms of nature, society, civilization and self. However, Tillich would have liked Berdyaev to apply his theory of objectivation to concrete historical movements, bourgeois capitalism, for instance. Tillich, "Book Review of Nicolas Berdyaev's *Slavery and Freedom*," *Theology Today* 2/1 (April 1945).

[39]Tillich, "The World Situation," 143, 144.

[40]Paul Tillich, "Catholicism and Antijudaism (early 1940s)," PTAH 416:009, 1-2.

[41]Tillich, "Catholicism and Anti-Judaism (early 1940s)," PTAH 416:009, 6-7.

[42]Tillich, "Catholicism and Anti-Judaism (early 1940s)," PTAH 416:009, 9.

over against a social justice struggle against the stereotyping of the character of any person because of their membership in a racially defined group.

Tillich's discussion of Protestantism and Anti-Semitism was structured around Lutheranism and comparisons between Lutheranism and Catholicism as well as between German Lutheranism and American sectarian, post-Reformation Protestantism. While Lutheranism had no political ethic,[43] Protestant sectarianism's belief in "the presence of the divine in the ground of every human soul," as well as the principle of tolerance which logically arises from this belief, placed Christians and Jews on equal footing in terms of human dignity.[44] However, when the notion of "the inner light" within all people slid over into a rationalistic secularism devoid of anything feeding the nonrational dimension of human beings, irrational anti-Semitic movements could move in, allegedly to meet that nonrational need while doing their destructive and oppressive work.[45]

In a 1942 article, Tillich discussed the nature of faith in the Jewish and Christian traditions, part of his intermittent "project" of placing Christianity and Judaism in relation to one another. In prophetic Judaism, God *"reverses the imminent order of human possibilities. The acceptance and confidence in this transcendent order is faith* [Tillich's italics]."[46] God's ways are deeper than the explicit power circumstances of history. The achievement of the Protestant Reformation was the rediscovery of this paradox of biblical faith. Luther saw faith as a nonrational, intellect-transcending gift: faith as "a living, restless power,"[47] faith as "the acceptance of the transcendent order which contradicts the order to which we belong. . . . Faith is the triumphant paradox of life."[48]

In his response to Emil Ludwig's rhetoric cited above, Tillich criticized

---

[43]Paul Tillich, "Protestantism and Anti-Semitism (early 1940s)," PTAH 416:010, 4.

[44]Tillich, "Protestantism and Anti-Semitism (early 1940s)," PTAH 416:010, 8-11.

[45]Tillich, "Protestantism and Anti-Semitism (early 1940s)," PTAH 416:010, 12.

[46]Paul Tillich, " 'Faith' in the Jewish-Christian Tradition," *Christendom* (New York) 7/4 (Autumn 1942): 520-21.

[47]Tillich, " 'Faith' in the Jewish-Christian Tradition," *Christendom* (New York) 7/4 (Autumn 1942): 525.

[48]Tillich, " 'Faith' in the Jewish-Christian Tradition," *Christendom* (New York) 7/4 (Autumn 1942): 526.

Ludwig for using stereotype in the same way as the Nazis were doing at the time. Germans of integrity had chosen emigration in the face of such distortion of the truth by National Socialism. Now, the same distorting method was being used by members of the Jewish community against Germans.[49] In place of group defamation, Tillich called for a common struggle for that for which he had advocated in his "war aims" pamphlets: a Europe in which each nation surrendered parts of its sovereignty in a regional system of accountability.[50]

In another instance, in his capacity as President of the Council for a Democratic Germany, Tillich received a letter from Rabbi Stephen S. Wise *"as to the attitude of the members of the Council . . . toward the problem of anti-Semitism and the persecution of the Jews,"* given the absence of comments on the matter in the Council's first policy statement.[51] In response, Tillich noted that no reference to anti-Semitism was present in their policy statement because it was an assumption taken as a given by a Council with members who had previously articulated their positions on the matter.[52] In this same spirit, and much more explicitly, the Council sent a telegram to the very first meeting of the World Jewish Congress, supporting full rights of citizenship and reparations in a future democratic Germany.[53] The World Jewish Congress gave a warm response, published in a subsequent issue of the Council's *Bulletin*.[54]

Protestantism and Its Principle(s)

Tillich wrote that religion's word to the people of his time combined the classic viewpoints of religious reservation and religious obligation: "Religion is, first, an open hand to receive a gift and, second, an acting hand to distribute gifts. Without coming from the religious reservation, carrying with us something eternal, we are of no use in working for the religious

---

[49]Tillich, "Gegen Emil Ludwigs," 278.

[50]Tillich, "Es geht um die Method," 281.

[51]Paul Tillich, "An Important Letter," *Bulletin of the Council for a Democratic Germany* 1/2 (25 October 1944): 1.

[52]Tillich, "An Important Letter," 4.

[53]Paul Tillich, "A Telegram," *Bulletin of the Council for a Democratic Germany* 1/3 (1 January 1945): 3.

[54]Stephen S. Wise and Nahum Goldmann, "World Jewish Congress," *Bulletin of the Council for a Democratic Germany* 1/5 (May 1945): 2.

obligation to transform the temporal. . . . The vertical line must become actual in the horizontal line."[55] Tillich called on the United States to avoid the dangers of a vacuous, unrooted religious obligation when the end of the war would finally come.[56] The two sides of religion's word unite in hope: "Hope is the opposite of utopianism. . . . Hope unites the vertical and horizontal lines, the religious reservation and the religious obligation. Therefore, the ultimate word that religion must say to the people of our time is the word of hope."[57]

A Protestantism deeply rooted within the prophetic tradition fueled Tillich's religious understanding. The prophetic spirit—rooted in universal monotheism—is a force standing against the rule of particularity and provincialism. The prophets of the Old Testament bore the message of peace and justice as the meaning of history over against nationalism. Tillich once again pointed to Abraham as the archetype of the prophetic spirit, "called out of his home and family and blood and soil to become *the* nation of history, the nation in which all other nations are blessed."[58] This spirit challenged Nazism and challenges any nation's claim to ultimacy.[59] Protestantism provides the persistently critical judgment against claims to ultimacy by any human being or institution.[60]

In politics, Tillich again honed in on the prophetic spirit embodied in early Marxism, which explains his religious socialism and his carefully defined affiliation with Marxist thought: "Marxism never has been accepted indiscriminately and without a serious criticism by the Religious-Socialist movements . . . partly a rejection, partly an acceptance and an essential transformation of the Marxist teachings."[61] For him, Marxism and biblical

[55]Paul Tillich, "The Word of Religion to the People of This Time," *The Protestant* 4/5 (April-May 1942): 43-48, in *The Protestant Era* (Chicago: University of Chicago Press, 1948): 186-88. See also Paul Tillich, "What Strategy Should the Church Adopt with Reference to Communism?" (PTAH 408:031), 6.

[56]Tillich, "The Word of Religion," 189-90.

[57]Tillich, "The Word of Religion," 191.

[58]Paul Tillich, "The Purpose that Unites (1944)," PTAH, 406:008, 5.

[59]Tillich, "The Purpose that Unites (1944)," 6.

[60]Tillich, "The Purpose that Unites (1944)," 20-21.

[61]Paul Tillich, "Marxism and Christian Socialism (Symposium with Eduard Heimann: 'Marxism and Christianity')," *Christianity and Society* (New York) 7/2 (Spring, 1942): 13. See also Tillich, "What Strategy Should the Church Adopt . . . "

prophecy shared similarities with regard to their understandings of history and humanity. History is meaningful as a realm of conflict between good (justice) and evil (injustice). The present state of society, and the escape from it into personal piety, are together seen as evil; a catastrophic breakdown of the present order will occur prior to the rise of a period dominated by justice; and specific vehicles of history will move it toward its culmination in a just order.[62] Humanity within history is estranged from its true destiny. A human being's individual existence does not tell the full story of human meaning, and truth cannot be sought by means of the separation of theory and practice.[63] Thus, Marx was led to combat economically and sociologically destructive ideologies, and Christian Reformers were compelled to combat idolatry.[64]

Realistic though he may have been, Marx's inner historical understanding of fulfillment was utopian to Tillich's thinking: Tillich and religious socialism saw fulfillment within history as unrealistic.[65] Further, communism secularized the prophetic spirit, dissipating its dynamism.[66] Nonetheless, Marxism offered religious socialism its existentialism (tying truth to theory and practice), its historical materialism (taking history seriously), and its dialectical method (negotiating the ambiguities of both life and the search for truth).[67]

With this framework in hand, I turn to a range of principles Tillich assembled during this period which he attributed to Protestantism. Tillich began to describe these in relation to the mission of the journal, *The Protestant*, in the article, "Our Protestant Principles."[68] Here, the discussion starts there and then gleans the additional ones from other sources.

Principle one affirms God's unchallengeable authority and protests all

(PTAH 408:031), 2-3; and Tillich, "What Strategy Should the Church Adopt with Reference to Communism?" (PTAH 416:007) 6-8.

[62]Tillich, "Marxism and Christian Socialism," 13-14.

[63]Tillich, "Marxism and Christian Socialism," 14.

[64]Tillich, "Marxism and Christian Socialism," 15.

[65]Tillich, "Marxism and Christian Socialism," 15-16.

[66]Tillich, "What Strategy Should the Church Adopt?" (PTAH 408:031) 3; Tillich, "What Strategy Should the Church Adopt?" (PTAH 416:007) 6.

[67]Marxism and Christian Socialism," 17.

[68]Paul Tillich, "Our Protestant Principles (Editorial in explication of "Protestant Principles")," *The Protestant* (New York) 4/7 (August-September 1942).

ecclesiastical and secular attempts to give absoluteness to human truth-claims.[69] Tillich's unrelenting point was to challenge the false absoluteness of religion with a small "r" (religious institutionalism) with the legitimate absoluteness of Religion with a capital "R" (Religion as the depth of meaning beneath the illegitimate distinction between sacred and secular). In his sermon, "Flight to Atheism," Tillich described the dual attitude we have to our relationship with God: hatred and dependence. God is "[t]he eyes of the witness which we cannot stand" and "the eyes of infinite wisdom and supporting benevolence."[70] Tillich wrote that Protestantism "is a spirit which expresses one central point of the prophets and apostles: the spirit of humility of Christ and the majesty of God alone."[71] Tillich called justification by faith "the un-understandable abbreviation of the Protestant principle: the unconditional character of the divine which has to be accepted, which is always the *prius*."[72] In "Protestantism and Moral Anarchy," he called for a "Post-Protestantism" that would offer three "immortal" principles, "not natural laws, but dynamic forces," the first of which is "the unconditional and uncomparable [*sic*] majesty of the divine' which has always—and will always—counter any ultimate claim by human authorities."[73]

Principle two rejects Catholicism's reduction of divine imminence to hierarchical authority.[74] In "The Problem of Protestantism in a Collectivistic

[69]Tillich, "Our Protestant Principles," 8-9.

[70]Paul Tillich, "Flight to Atheism," *The Protestant* (New York) 4/10 (February-March 1943): 45, 47.

[71]Paul Tillich, "Lecture at Meadville (1943)," PTAH 421:001, 15-16.

[72]Paul Tillich, "The Protestant Principle and the Next Stage of History (mid 1940s)," PTAH 406B:036, 4.

[73]Tillich, "Protestantism and Moral Anarchy," 16.

[74]Tillich, "Our Protestant Principles," 9-10, 11-12. See also Tillich, "Lecture at Meadville," 15-16 and Tillich, "The Protestant Principle and the Next Stage of History," 4-5. In the review of Jacques Maritain's *The Rights of Man and Natural Law*, Tillich noted Maritain's failure to explain how his idea of a "spiritually Catholic state" (as an alternative to authoritarian states) could itself avoid authoritarianism. Tillich, "Book Review," 465, In "The Problem of Protestantism in a Collectivistic Age," Tillich declared, "The sin of the Roman Catholic system is not its rejection of historical Protestantism but its exclusion of Eternal Protestantism by a hierarchical, half-totalitarian collectivism." Paul Tillich, "The Problem of Protestantism in a Collectivistic Age (mid-1940s)," PTAH 406B:037, 12-13.

Age," Tillich declared, "The sin of the Roman Catholic system is *not* its rejection of historical Protestantism but its exclusion of Eternal Protestantism by a hierarchical, half-totalitarian collectivism."[75] On the other hand, principle three indicts Protestantism for an institutionalism that results in ethical and doctrinal rigidity and for a hyper-critical spirit that exchanges the power of religious symbolism, ritual and doctrine for an empty and superficial individualism, subjectivity, and rationalism.[76]

Principle four rejects the sacred and secular distinction and argues for the imminence of God within cultural acts: "The secular realms are no more secular if they penetrate to their own ground and aim. They have their second quality in themselves and need no ecclesiastical sanctification."[77] Further, religious institutions are heavily penetrated by "the secular" through the various ways they are dependent "on the special cultural situation in which [they have] appeared."[78] Principle five is closely connected to the fourth and affirms the legitimacy of culture apart from ecclesiastical authority.[79] Principle six challenges a spiritless secularism. Since "God is directly related to every realm of life, no cultural creation can be cut off from this relation without losing its ultimate meaning, ground and aim."[80] Tillich spoke of a spirit of self-critique—"eternal Protestantism"—as "the acknowledgment of the divinity of the divine which is neither identical with nor dependent on any of our achievements."[81] This provokes dangerous responses from power-holders. He wrote, "Eternal Protestantism is the divine protest against the world," particularly its rootedness in sub- or penultimate concerns.[82] Tillich had been committed to helping Protestantism embody this critical voice ever since "the first world war threw me out of the ivory

---

[75]Tillich, "The Problem of Protestantism in a Collectivistic Age (mid-1940s)," 12-13.

[76]Tillich, "Our Protestant Principles," 10-11.

[77]Tillich, "Our Protestant Principles," 12. See also Tillich, "Lecture at Meadville," 15-16 and Tillich, "The Problem of Protestantism in a Collectivistic Age," 17-18.

[78]Tillich, "Our Protestant Principles," 12. See also Tillich, "The Protestant Principle and the Next Stage of History," 7-8.

[79]Tillich, "Our Protestant Principles," 13.

[80]Tillich, "Our Protestant Principles," 13.

[81]Tillich, "The Problem of Protestantism," 12.

[82]Tillich, "The Problem of Protestantism," 12-13.

tower of philosophical idealism and religious isolationism."[83] Out of the soil of "an empty secularism" and "an autonomous culture" grew cultural self-destruction and "an antidivine heteronomy. This is the story of our time."[84] Principle seven is based on *kairos*, the notion that history provides openings for well-timed, creative, constructive, and salvific (healing) action. It asserts that "creativity in the historical dynamics" is possible. It is the second "immortal" principle of "Post-Protestantism."[85]

Principle eight declares that in place of a distinctively Protestant politics or ethics, the Protestant principle of prophetic and loving critique is perpetually relevant: "Protestantism is not bound to its past; therefore it is free for its future, even if this future should deserve the name: 'Post-Protestant Era.' "[86]

Principles nine and ten came in his 1943 "Lecture at Meadville." In that lecture, he described, on the one hand, Protestantism's "open[ness] to both sides" of the East/West divide within Christianity and, on the other hand, its "lay character . . . [enabling it] to embody itself in innumerably different forms in individuals, in accidental movements, in secular groups, in esoteric seclusion."[87]

Yet, Tillich also pointed to the impotency of Protestantism without Catholic mysticism. In "The Permanent Significance of the Catholic Church for Protestantism" he wrote, "A Protestantism which has no more place for meditation and contemplation, for ecstasy and 'mystical union' has ceased

---

[83]Paul Tillich, "Tillich Challenges Protestantism" (speech given at a dinner in Dr. Tillich's honor by friends of *The Protestant*, 9 February 1942) *The Protestant* 4/4 (February-March 1942): 2-4.

[84]Tillich, "Our Protestant Principles," 13.

[85]Tillich, "Protestantism and Moral Anarchy," 17.

[86]Tillich, "Our Protestant Principles," 14 and Tillich, "Lecture at Meadville," 15-16.

[87]Tillich, "Lecture at Meadville," 15-16. "The Protestant minister is not a priest but a layman who has the job to preach the Gospel. He has no authority whatsoever, beyond the authority of the content of his preaching." Thus, it is not out of the ordinary for the church's official (yet, practically, nonauthoritative) position to be in direct contradiction to the behavior of the parishioners. Tillich, "Protestantism and Anti-Semitism," 7. In "The Protestant Approach to the Present World Situation," Tillich spoke of the tolerance required by its criticism of absolute claims. Tillich, "The Protestant Approach to the Present World Situation."

to be religion and has become an intellectual and moral system in traditional religious terms."[88] However, he also warned that mysticism on its own is vulnerable to distortion: "mysticism, separated from prophetic Christianity, is in danger to become pantheistic and naturalistic, and . . . the doctrine of the unity of God and man can be abused by the claim of man to be God himself."[89] A "Protestant Catholicity" would take seriously the collective unconscious and address the adequacy of its symbols, seeing its sacramental life as "a means of collective healing."[90] Thus, principle eleven is the practice of the mysticism and sacramentalism of the ancient church.

Principle twelve applies to the church's relationship to other religions and cultures, in which Tillich advocated the use of the Protestant principle as a tool for critical assessment,[91] "finding a kind of Old Testament in all religions."[92] Principle thirteen is the one lying behind all experiences of reunion and reconciliation within existence: love. Love is the process of "creating unity in a concrete situation."[93] It is the third "immortal" principle of "Post-Protestantism."

Tillich noted that while history was moving towards collectivism, Protestantism is personalistic. He distinctly distinguished personalism from individualism. Individualism is the final, dehumanizing product of technological culture and involved "the loss of a spiritual center."[94] On the other hand, "Protestant personalism"—principle fourteen—includes both piety and decision: personal decision triumphs over collective responsibility. Here, the subconscious is no longer "a bearer of grace," and "ritual activities" are replaced by "world-transforming activities."[95] As mentioned before, Tillich was careful not to equate the social group with the person.[96]

---

[88]Paul Tillich, "The Permanent Significance of the Catholic Church for Protestantism," *Protestant Digest* 3 (February-March 1941): 30.

[89]Paul Tillich, "Book Review: Meister Eckhart. A Modern Translation made by Raymond B. Blakney," *Religion in Life* 11/4 (Autumn 1942): 626.

[90]Tillich, "The Protestant Principle and the Next Stage of History," 23.

[91]Tillich, "The Protestant Principle and the Next Stage of History," 25-26.

[92]Tillich, "Lecture at Meadville," 18.

[93]Tillich, "Protestantism and Moral Anarchy," 17.

[94]Tillich, "The Protestant Principle and the Next Stage of History," 10.

[95]Tillich, "The Protestant Principle and the Next Stage of History," 10. See also Tillich, "The Protestant Approach to the Present World Situation."

[96]Tillich, "Man and Society in Religious Socialism," 15, 16.

The sectarian mysticism and the rationalism at the heart of orthodox theology—both within Protestantism—creates a bridge between personalism and individualism.[97] Religion and democracy are connected at their deepest level by their understanding that respect for human dignity—for the person—is the outcome of perceiving human existence and meaning in their ultimate sense.[98] Tillich pointed to the fragility of democracy, arguing that it "is always dependent on a willingness of the struggling groups. . . . It is more dependent on historical grace than any other system."[99] While culture expresses meaning within the collective, the individual is always the creative force in culture. The creations of the individual are either their own personal product or the product of the collective by means of the individual.[100]

According to Tillich, Protestantism's personalism stood in tension with collectivism, a social pattern in which the identity of individuals within the group is more influenced by the group's identity than the individual's.[101] Collectivism does not mean the complete suppression of individual self-determination as in totalitarianism. Totalitarianism is imposed conformism, not self-determined collectivism. Authority is different in totalitarianism than it is in collectivism. In totalitarianism, it is a force external to the individual; in collectivism, it arises almost automatically within its bearers.[102]

In contrast, Protestantism is "the principle of eternal and essential non-conformism, because God is never conform[ed] with the world,"[103] Protestantism in the West had conformed politically, leading to religious wars, apoliticality, and an uncritical and persecuting institutionalism.[104] While historical Protestantism had compromised with the conformist, progressive ideology of technical civilization, "The Protestant principle is able to detach the Church from every form and attach it preliminarily to every still creative form. The solution under the Protestant principle [is] the dialectical,

[97]Tillich, "The Protestant Principle and the Next Stage of History," 11-12.

[98]Paul Tillich, "Democracy and Religion (early 1940s)," PTAH, 409:003, 2-3.

[99]Tillich, "Democracy and Religion (early 1940s)," 5. See also Tillich, "The Protestant Approach to the Present World Situation," 4-6.

[100]Tillich, "The Problem of Protestantism in a Collectivistic Age," 6.

[101]Tillich, "The Problem of Protestantism in a Collectivistic Age," 1.

[102]Tillich, "The Problem of Protestantism in a Collectivistic Age," 2-3.

[103]Tillich, "The Protestant Principle and the Next Stage of History," 17.

[104]Tillich, "The Protestant Principle and the Next Stage of History," 17, 19, 20.

nonutopian type of Religious Socialism."[105] This is the fifteenth and final principle in the present interpretation of Tillich's Protestant thought.

Tillich assessed the period culminating in World War II as "reality seen in the light of the sacred 'void,' as the sacred not-having, a not-yet."[106] This was one of his early expressions of his sense of history's entry into a period of a-kairotic vacuum. His conclusion was that the twentieth century did not mean the end of Christianity or Protestantism and its principle. However, it did mean the end of its dominance.[107] He pondered whether a Protestant Catholicity—inaugurating a post-Protestant Era—was necessary to cope with "the fever within the body Protestant."[108] He wrote, "I love the Protestant church, but I love more the Protestant principle for the sake of which the Protestant church may lose its significance in the next stage of history."[109] Tillich saw Protestantism as "the continuation of the Christian Church, the group which carries the historical consciousness of mankind. It is the reception of the New Being as manifest in Jesus as the Christ."[110] As opposed to security rooted in the transient, Protestantism stands for security in the transcendent.[111] Tillich concluded, "Protestantism *will* live as eternal principle. Protestantism *can* live as a self-transforming historical reality representing the New Being in history."[112]

Postwar Reconstruction

Based on his understanding of the failure of Western civilization and his construction of the content of Protestantism, Tillich turned to the shape of the postwar world. He directed his attention to social renewal and international organization.

The Religiously Socialistic Spirit. Tillich advocated a social transformation which is "the development in human existence of that species which socially produces and reproduces being with dignity."[113] That is, Tillich

[105]Tillich, "The Protestant Principle and the Next Stage of History," 12, 15.
[106]Tillich, "The Protestant Principle and the Next Stage of History," 20.
[107]Tillich, "The Protestant Principle and the Next Stage of History," 21-22.
[108]Tillich, "The Protestant Principle and the Next Stage of History," 22.
[109]Tillich, "The Protestant Principle and the Next Stage of History," 26.
[110]Tillich, "The Problem of Protestantism in a Collectivistic Age," 15.
[111]Tillich, "The Problem of Protestantism in a Collectivistic Age," 16.
[112]Tillich, "The Problem of Protestantism in a Collectivistic Age," 18.
[113]Paul Tillich, "Christian Basis of a Just and Durable Peace (1943)," in

sought a path of human existence in which all of humanity was committed to the perpetuation of just societies, i.e., societies that allow their members to live in dignity. He believed vocation should be the basis for all human creative activity, not merely theological work.[114] To permit continued dehumanization was to sanction a human species vulnerable to manipulation by tyrannical powers, with the Hobbesian Leviathan state as the consequence.[115] After the fall of the Enlightenment's liberating reason, capitalism's technological reason, and Marxism's revolutionary reason, Tillich argued for planning reason: "We must go forward under the direction of planning reason toward an organization of society which avoids both totalitarian absolutism and liberal individualism."[116] By endorsing planning reason, Tillich showed his distrust of an untrammeled free market economy, believing some degree of government oversight was required to prevent exploitation by economic power holders.

Tillich used the biblical and Hobbesian image of Leviathan to describe the multiple forms dehumanization can take, the three-faced Leviathan of late medieval authoritarianism, bourgeois capitalism, and totalitarianism. He believed that "Christianity must give its message to a world in which Leviathan in its different aspects threatens all human existence to its very roots,"[117] rejecting the paths of both a reactionary and conservative Catholicism and a weak and compromising Protestantism. Instead, it was compelled to bear the methods—and embody the truths—of concrete justice and unifying love, operating in a nonutopian way in the world.[118]

The Nazi crimes against the Jewish people and his own friendships with Jewish colleagues led Tillich to repeated consideration of the future of the relationship between Jews and non-Jews. He observed two paths on which

---

Theology of Peace, ed. Ronald H. Stone (Louisville: Westminster/John Knox Press, 1990) 79.

[114]Tillich, "Christian Basis of a Just and Durable Peace (1943)," 80-81.

[115]Tillich, "Christian Basis of a Just and Durable Peace (1943)," 81-82.

[116]Tillich, "The World Situation," 8.

[117]Tillich, "The World Situation," 8.

[118]Paul Tillich, "Power and Justice in the Postwar World (1944)," in *Theology of Peace*, ed. Ronald H. Stone (Louisville: Westminster/John Knox Press, 1990) 101, 103; Paul Tillich, "The Christian Churches and the Emerging Social Order in Europe," *Religion in Life* 14/3 (Summer 1945): 334-39; and Tillich, "The World Situation," 43-44.

Christians and Jews met and could continue to meet in contributing to social renewal: the prophetic and the mystical. Along the prophetic path, the demand is for justice, with idolatries of thought and religion, of politics and economics constantly questioned, with "the Jews always emphasizing the 'not yet' and the horizontal line towards the Kingdom, the Christians the transcendent 'already' and the vertical line."[119] Along the mystical path, Tillich saw a meeting point in the transcendence of Christ, with its roots in the hiddenness of God to which Hellenistic Judaism gave particular attention.[120] Despite the genocidal crimes committed by Germans against Jews, Tillich described parallels in German and Jewish experience:

> No nation has more contributed to the cruelty of the Jewish fate in our time and— nevertheless—no nation shows more similarities in character and destiny within Judaism than the Germans. Both have experienced tremendous catastrophes in their history on religious or ultimate grounds. Both are lacking that balance in historical existence and human attitude which is the gift of destiny to more favored nations. Both show a sociological split and psychological wound which produce highly creative and highly destructive forces at the same time.[121]

Together, Tillich believed, Jews and non-Jews captured by the prophetic spirit could be bearers of both "a period of justice and peace" as well as "cultural interpenetration and cross-fertilization."[122] He had hopes that Jews living in their own homeland or homelands would become "reservoirs of the special gifts and the special spirit of this nation,"[123] i.e., possessing a prophetic spirit that suppresses nationalistic separatism and promotes world unity.[124] In his general hope for the rise of a broader,

---

[119]Tillich, "The Religious Relation Between Christianity and Judaism in the Future," 4.

[120]Tillich, "The Religious Relation Between Christianity and Judaism in the Future," 5. Tillich's contemporary and acquaintance, Martin Buber, wrote of the hiddenness of God as a way to begin understanding the Holocaust event. Martin Buber, "The Dialogue between Heaven and Earth," On Judaism (New York: Shocken Books, 1972).

[121]Paul Tillich, "The Role of Judaism in Postwar Reconstruction (mid 1940s)," PTAH 405A:001, 1.

[122]Tillich, "The Role of Judaism in Postwar Reconstruction (mid 1940s)," 4.

[123]Tillich, "The Role of Judaism in Postwar Reconstruction (mid 1940s)," 4.

[124]Tillich, "The Role of Judaism in Postwar Reconstruction (mid 1940s)," 3.

internationalist viewpoint, Tillich seemed to offer the specific hope that the Jewish people may become a vehicle for intercultural relationships. However, it would probably go too far to say that Tillich was asserting the equality of all religious traditions, in light of his general Christocentrism.

Social Renewal. While Europe was the stated object of Tillich's comments, Germany in particular and Western civilization as a whole were always in the background of his discussion of social renewal. He described the following as elements necessary for that renewal: a convincing sense of life's meaning; symbols adequate to that meaning; reinvigoration of personality and community, " a community which overcomes loneliness by a more collectivistic form of life without sacrificing the meaning and right of the individual"; sociopolitical transformation, specifically, societal renewal based on central planning that promotes individual spontaneity, yet not dominated by the private decisions of economic-industrial power-holders; "a centralized State power with democratic correctives," authority without oppression, and security; a spiritual vanguard of youth; religious people intellectually and spiritually unbound by religious institutions; creative representatives of the secular realm; prophetic parties committed to social justice; and the mobilization of public opinion in America, England and Europe to prevent a reactionary, "so-called *Ordnungspolitik* (policy for maintaining order)" from being executed by occupying authorities.[125]

With regard to Germany, Tillich argued that the following was

---

[125]Tillich, "Spiritual Problems of Past-War Reconstruction," 4, 5; Paul Tillich, "War Aims—II. What War Aims?" *Protestant Digest* (August-September 1941): 16-18; Tillich, "Storms of Our Times": 31; Paul Tillich, "Die Weltgeschichtliche Zukunft Europas" (PTAH 201:015) 9-10; Paul Tillich, "The Future of Germany," PTAH 404:007 George Thomas of Princeton University remarked saliently, relevantly, and gently critically to Tillich's views. First, he saw American politics in less need of change than its economic system. Second, he believed the relationship with Russia should not blind us to the profound weaknesses of its bureaucratic system. Third, in opposition to Tillich's notion of an organic society as the framework for politics and economics, he favored a "middle way, in which individual enterprise is taken advantage of and extended so that labor has a partnership in the management as well as the profits of industry." Frederick C. Grant, Angus Dun, Joseph F. Fletcher, George F. Thomas, and Paul Tillich, "Panel Discussion of Tillich's "Storms of Our Times." *Anglican Theological Review* 25/1 (January 1943): 41-43.

necessary: the punishment and removal of all Nazi elements and their pre-1933 supporters; stable German economic production—in an economy of peace—under a "directed European economy"; the revival democratic movements combined with patience towards Germany as its democracy developed; the guarantee of basic civil rights, restoring and protecting religious freedom and expression; elimination of racial policies; inclusion of Germany in any international security arrangement; and the establishment of collective security within a European federation.[126]

He repeatedly expressed his disgust at the Allied rhetoric regarding the reeducation of Germany. To the question, "Is it possible to reeducate the Germans?" Tillich forcefully declared, "It should not even be tried! A nation is not a schoolboy. The only real education is fate and nothing else!"[127] He questioned the integrity of such a strategy: would it "mean that American teachers teach the German adults the American way of life under the guns of the tanks and a censorship of radio, newspapers, magazines, books, public speeches by the American censors? Does anyone believe that this is an educational situation?"[128] However, if reeducation occurred, it had to be sensitive to certain realities: the nature of a victor-vanquished relation-

---

[126]American Friends of German Freedom, *Germany Tomorrow*, 11-16; Paul Tillich, "A Program for a Democratic Germany (A statement by the members of the Council for a Democratic Germany, Paul Tillich, chairman)," *Christianity and Crisis* (New York) 4/8 (15 May 1944): 3-4; Council for a Democratic Germany, "Germany's Collapse and the Hope for a Workable Peace," *Bulletin of the Council for a Democratic Germany* 1/5 (May 1945): 4; and Council for a Democratic Germany, "Emergency Measures in Germany," *Bulletin of the Council for a Democratic Germany*, 1/5 (May 1945): 5. Tillich's first demand failed to acknowledge both the complicated nature of the relationship of Nazism to German culture and Tillich's own understanding of the levels of guilt within German society. The American Friends of German Freedom's *Germany Tomorrow* describes five matters which stood in the way of a transition to democracy in Germany: the dependence of such a revolution upon invading armies overturning Nazism; the period of more than a decade without democratic organizations; hatred caused by the war initiated by Hitler; the destruction wreaked by the war; and the dynamics that make international federation difficult without the Nazi factor (American Friends of German Freedom, *Germany Tomorrow*, 6).

[127]Paul Tillich, "Can the Jew Return to Germany?" (early 1940s) PTAH 416:008, 7.

[128]Tillich, "The Future of Germany," 14.

ship; the counter-productiveness of oppressive policies by occupiers; the necessity of creative, constructive measures by means of a secure social system; and the class and cultural factors that influence education.[129]

With respect to the Jewish community, Tillich specifically addressed these matters: the nature of the peace concluded at war's end; the possibility of restitution; and the nature of the German anti-Semitism which was the basis for the war. If peace were brought about through negotiation with either the German opposition or with the pre-World War I status quo, the dynamics for effective cultural change would not be present: only a peace through communist revolution or through "autonomous German revolutionary movements" able to set up "a socialist and humanist Germany within a more or less federated world" could bring the change necessary for the return of Jews to be a real possibility.[130] Tillich was vague regarding who or what would bring about such a revolution, but the esoteric, religious-intellectual orders he described in the interwar period would likely have provided the ideological justification for revolutionaries. The restitution of private property would be impossible under any scenario. However, restitution in terms of "the symbols of [anti-]Nazi future" would not only be possible but a point of honor within "a socialist and humanist Germany."[131] Symbols such as synagogues, hospitals, schools, and old people's homes conveyed an openness to receiving the impoverished Jews back into German society and to welcoming Jews back into German cultural life.[132] With respect to anti-Semitism, Tillich did not accept the notion of an exclusively German guilt for anti-Semitism, arguing that Europe as a whole (including Germany) was anti-Semitic by tradition, but that Germany (under Nazism) was even more so through the additional element of indoctrination.[133]

Tillich summed up his vision of Europe in this way:

My vision for the spiritual reconstruction of Europe is a large number of anonymous and esoteric groups consisting of religious, humanist and socialist

---

[129]Paul Tillich, "The Post-War Education of the German People (early 1940s)" PTAH 404:008, 2-8.

[130]Tillich, "Can the Jew Return to Germany?" 1-2.

[131]Tillich, "Can the Jew Return to Germany?" 3-4.

[132]Tillich, "Can the Jew Return to Germany?" 4.

[133]Tillich, "Can the Jew Return to Germany?" 5.

people who have seen the trends of our period and were willing to resist them, who have contended for personality and community (many of them under persecution), and who know about an ultimate meaning of life even if they are not yet able to express it.[134]

The Religiously International Spirit. In his 1943 lectures before the Federal Council of Churches Commission on a Just and Durable Peace, chaired by future Secretary of State John Foster Dulles, Tillich declared that anyone seeking a lasting solution had, first, to understand the meaning of the war: not merely a war among nations, but "a war of world revolution under the cover of a war among nations."[135] Tillich described the theological bases for Christian engagement with this and other political realities in three "formal principles": God's "absolute transcendence," God's "paradoxical imminence," and "the universal reference" of all things to God. The first halts any claims to absolute truth by any human entity. The second means that history is the story of the presence of the transcendent God in a way that will not eliminate human freedom and the evil consequences thereof. The third means that the holy can be found anywhere and will not be limited by human constraints.[136] To these could be added the four elements of prophetic spirit, universal wisdom, collectivism, and the Protestant principle of self-critique which he would assemble in May 1944.[137] As a result, Tillich disputed the goal of the commission, "argu[ing] the necessity of destroying the moralistic arrogance of the concept of a just and durable peace in a situation in which tragedy and possibly grace are the only categories that can be applied to the present disrupted world."[138] He asserted that a peace had to be sought that was cognizant of the dynamic context within which justice must be sought, a context unavoidable, ambiguous, and fragmented, rather than a final, just order out of touch with the nature of life ("the peace of the cemetery").[139]

---

[134]Tillich, "Spiritual Problems of Past-War Reconstruction," 6. Again, see Tillich's discussion of secular-Protestant religious orders in chapter 3.

[135]Tillich, "Christian Basis of a Just and Durable Peace," 73.

[136]Tillich, "Christian Basis of a Just and Durable Peace," 74-75.

[137]Tillich, "The Purpose that Unites," 17, 20.

[138]Tillich, "Christian Basis of a Just and Durable Peace," 87.

[139]Tillich, "Christian Basis of a Just and Durable Peace," 78-79. In "Power and Justice in the Postwar World," from the summer of 1944, Tillich interpreted the dynamics which would dictate the postwar conditions of the world. He did this by

In contrast to this, he characterized the work of the Council for a Democratic Germany of a year later as a voice of realism in the face of historical and cultural distortions.[140]

The next direction Tillich took in the "Just and Durable Peace" speeches harked back to his speech, "Ethics in a Changing World," delivered in 1940 for the bicentennial of the University of Pennsylvania and presaged an essay from the summer of 1944, "Power and Justice in the Postwar World." They are three thought-projects in which Tillich honed key concepts necessary for a depth-analysis of the international situation.

In "Ethics in a Changing World," Tillich described the inadequacy of three prior solutions to ethics in a period of profound change: the static supra-naturalistic solution of Catholicism; the dynamic-naturalistic solution of life-philosophy, positivism, pragmatism and (in a distorted way) Nazism; and the progressive-rationalistic solution dominant during the Enlightenment. In their place Tillich posed an agapeic-kairotic solution implied in Christian ethics. This solution combines eternal principle with temporal application. Agapeic love provides the "eternal, unchangeable element, but makes its realization dependent on continuous acts of creative intuition."[141] *Kairos*, the qualitative understanding of time, speaks to a sense of timing necessary for specific acts rooted in love, acts incited by a prophetic spirit. In this construction, "love is the principle of ethics and *kairos* the way of its

---

outlining the relationship of the three metaphysical bases for understanding reality (power, justice and love) and applied these to the international arena. Power is simply the power of being, the power to be, which all entities within existence with varying strength. Justice is the ordering of these power dynamics within each entity and among entities. Love is the primary structure of existence, the drive toward unity which dictates the shape which the ordering process of justice should take. One sees the impact of justice upon power by the fact that "[a] just order is an order in which every part gets what its deserves according to the structure of power it represents." One sees the role of power in justice in that "no order has existence without an ordering power." Love tames power and quickens justice. (Tillich, "Power and Justice in the Postwar World," 90, 92, 94.)

[140]Paul Tillich, "A Statement," *Bulletin of the Council for a Democratic Germany* 1/1 (1 September 1944): 4.

[141]Paul Tillich, "Ethics in a Changing World," in *Religion and the Modern World* (Philadelphia: University of Pennsylvania Press, 1941) 56.

embodiment in concrete contents."[142] Tillich asserted, "Love realizing itself from *kairos* to *kairos* creates ethics which is beyond the alternative of absolute and relative ethics."[143] Agapeic-kairotic ethics is neither antilaw nor and anti-institution: "Love demands laws and institutions, but love is always able to break through them in a new *kairos* and to create new laws and new systems of ethics."[144] Justice is Tillich's term for "the laws and institutions in which love is embodied in a special situation."[145] For Tillich, the task of ethics was this: "to express the ways in which love embodies itself and life is maintained and saved."[146]

In the "Just and Durable Peace" lectures of three years later, Tillich returned to these themes. He focused his thoughts on what he termed three "material principles": love, life, and justice.[147] Thus, agapeic love remained, and kairos was the implied basis for his consideration of life (or life-force) and justice. By love, Tillich meant "the movement from the one to the complete otherness and the reunion of the remaining otherness."[148] Politically, it is "the fundamental structure on which the others [, i.e., life and justice] are dependent."[149] By life, he meant "the dynamic might of the individual center to be" which insists that power be taken seriously in politics, for "being expresses its power character in dynamic self-realization."[150] By justice, Tillich meant "the uniting form of being . . . [which is] the expression of the substance of being: namely, love."[151] In politics, "It points to the limits in which individual self-realization is compatible with the unity of the whole or with love."[152] In criticizing the work of the commission, Tillich related life to justice: "Life without justice is chaos and therefore not the power of being. Justice without life is dead

---

[142]Paul Tillich, "Ethics in a Changing World," 60.

[143]Paul Tillich, "Ethics in a Changing World," 57.

[144]Paul Tillich, "Ethics in a Changing World," 60.

[145]Paul Tillich, "Ethics in a Changing World," 61.

[146]Paul Tillich, "Ethics in a Changing World," 61. The present discussion will return to Tillich's agapeic-kairotic approach in chap. 7.

[147]Tillich, "Christian Basis of a Just and Durable Peace," 76-77.

[148]Tillich, "Christian Basis of a Just and Durable Peace," 76.

[149]Tillich, "Christian Basis of a Just and Durable Peace," 76.

[150]Tillich, "Christian Basis of a Just and Durable Peace," 77.

[151]Tillich, "Christian Basis of a Just and Durable Peace," 77-78.

[152]Tillich, "Christian Basis of a Just and Durable Peace," 78.

law and therefore strange to being."[153] This means that justice is a dynamic concept involved in "the dynamic shaking of the durable," calling into question attempts to restrict and dilute its significance within a formulation assuming life to be persistently "just" or "durable."[154]

By the summer of 1944, when he wrote "Power and Justice in the Postwar World," Tillich had arrived at the structural elements which remained a part of his analysis of reality in subsequent periods: love, power, and justice. Thus, by interpreting the postwar dynamics in this way, he was perceiving the international arena through the relationship of the three metaphysical bases for understanding reality as a whole. Here, power is simply the power of being, the power to be which all existing entities have with varying strength. Justice is the ordering of these power dynamics within each entity and among entities. Love is the primary structure of existence, the drive toward unity which dictates the shape which the ordering process of justice should take. One sees the impact of justice upon power by the fact that "[a] just order is an order in which every part gets what its deserves according to the structure of power it represents." One sees the role of power in justice in that "no order has existence without an ordering power." Love tames power and quickens justice.[155] Kairos is again implied as the background of well-timed existential action.

Thus, in three writings over four years, the Tillich of the World War Two years constructed an agapeic-kairotic ontology to undergird ethical thought in international relations. From the metaphysics of the religiously international spirit, I will turn to Tillich's thoughts on the significance of two matters related to boundaries: immigration and cross-cultural fertilization.

The boundary situation so important to much of his thought led Tillich to reflect occasionally on the significance of forced inhabitants of the boundary during international crises: refugees and immigrants. As one who moved from the status of refugee to immigrant and citizen (on March 4, 1940), Tillich wondered whether refugees in the United States would be seen as bearers of "cultural cross-fertilization" as history had shown them to be or, he asked, was "the same spirit growing in this country, antialien,

---

[153]Tillich, "Christian Basis of a Just and Durable Peace," 78.
[154]Tillich, "Christian Basis of a Just and Durable Peace," 78.
[155]Tillich, "Power and Justice in the Postwar World," 90, 92, 94.

anti-Semitic, antihumanistic, anti-Christian, finally," as had developed in Germany?[156] In a mid-1941 article, Tillich expressed his belief that becoming an American citizen had forced him to transcend a nationalistic, provincial bias he perceived within European culture.[157] At a 1942 event, he reflected on migration as characteristic of, and necessary for, significant world transformation.[158] In a May 1944 speech, he wrote, "Wherever there is particularity preserving itself, there is not freedom, there we are slaves of the special drives and urges of our being, there we are slave drivers of ourselves. And he who is slave and slave driver of himself is always slave and slave driver of others at the same time. *The realm of freedom is the realm of conquered particularity.*"[159] Further, particularity is defeated through encounters with other particularities: "The more community, the more freedom. They do not contradict each other. They are interdependent. The purpose that unites expresses man's very nature: his freedom from and his communion with all things."[160]

Tillich evaluated religion's capacity to catalyze inter-civilizational cross-fertilization. At the fourth symposium of the Conference on Science, Philosophy and Religion in Their Relation to the Democratic Way of Life, held at Columbia University in September 1943, he wrote, "the spiritual unity of mankind is a matter of an existential union of the big cultural groups on the basis of decisions they make for one ultimate existential truth."[161] While religions had been successful in creating civilizational unity, world unity had eluded religion. Consistent with his realistic but hopeful tone, Tillich wrote, "It is not impossible that, in connection with the present religious and cultural cross-fertilization, movements may develop— perhaps under the leadership of a profoundly transformed Christianity— which lead to a unity of cooperation between the world religions, and later,

---

[156]Paul Tillich, "Refugees: The Consequences of a Half-Religious War Raging in Europe," 404:003, 7-8.

[157]Tillich, "I Am an American," 25.

[158]Tillich, "Tillich Challenges Protestantism," 1-2.

[159]Tillich, "The Purpose that Unites," 10.

[160]Tillich, "The Purpose that Unites," 11, 12.

[161]Paul Tillich, "Comment," in *Approaches to World Peace: Fourth Symposium*, Bryson, Finkelstein, and Maciver, eds. (New York: Harper & Bros., 1944) 685.

on this basis to a unity of symbols and existential truth."[162]

International Organization. Even before the entry of the United States into the war, Tillich did not support world government or even world federation, both of which he saw to be unrealistic. Yet, he called for a European federation that was more than a vassal of the United States and Great Britain: "America can and should support the creation of a European federation, completed by some kind of a free, intercontinental union."[163] After failed efforts to unite based on religion and humanism, he asked whether there might be "a third foundation of European unity, also not in the political sense, whose bearers will be a new, yet unknown group which will arise out of the subsoil/ underground of the European tragedy."[164] By 1943, given the dominance of the Allied powers, he saw that such a federation was unlikely.[165]

To Tillich, a realistic assessment of power realities was necessary to escape illusory hopes for the postwar shape of the world. Having given up any hope for a European federation which had parity with other world powers or in which Germany would have a role on par with its European partners, Tillich spoke frankly of the probable outcome of a "dependent, internally pacified, economically calm, asiatic peninsula," a European entity dominated by outside forces: this seemed inescapable.[166] He commented in 1943, "We should not in our plans go beyond the chances that are presented by the constellation of power,"[167] In the 1944 essay, "Power and Justice in the Postwar World,," he wrote:

> It is meaningless to demand structures of justice not implied in the described structures of power, at least as possibilities. It is, for instance, meaningless to demand a continental European federation, an idea which was very near to my heart and to which I gave literary expression in an early stage of the war. The

---

[162]Tillich, "Comment," in *Approaches to World Peace,* 685.

[163]Paul Tillich, "War Aims—III. Whose War Aims?" *Protestant Digest* (October-November 1941): 27. See also Tillich, "Storms of Our Times," 31.

[164]Tillich, "Die Weltgeschichtliche Zukunft Europas," 15.

[165]His friend and colleague, Adolph Löwe believed that "some kind of functional federalism instead of a regional federalism" could be the basis for European unity. Paul Tillich, "Discussion on Post-War Reconstruction in Europe" (1940s), PTAH, 206:033.

[166]Tillich, "Die Weltgeschichtliche Zukunft Europas," 14-15.

[167]Tillich, "Die Weltgeschichtliche Zukunft Europas," 2.

Big Three will by no means admit the creation of a fourth big power in terms of a new world power: "Europe."[168]

To him, to maintain such an illusion was to endorse a lifeless, abstract, irrelevant notion of justice: "This justice is abstract, not real justice; it lacks the power of creating community. It fails to fulfill the demand of love, in which power and justice are united."[169]

Thus, Tillich could be impatient with illusory proposals. On March 1, 1943, the Commission on a Just and Durable Peace arrived at six propositions or "pillars" that it argued would provide for a just and durable peace: (1) International political collaboration based on the present unity of the United Nations; (2) Control of economic and financial acts which may disturb international peace; (3) Establishment of an organization to adapt the treaty structure to changing conditions; (4) Autonomy for subject peoples; (5) International control of armaments; and (6) Religious and intellectual liberty.[170] Religious leaders were divided on the usefulness of the list.[171] Because of their vagueness and lack of realism, Tillich concluded

---

[168]Tillich, "Power and Justice in the Postwar World," 97.

[169]Tillich, "Power and Justice in the Postwar World," 98.

[170]The Witness, "Six Pillars of Peace Issues by Church," *The Witness* 26/43 (25 March 1943): 4.

[171]Joseph F. Fletcher of the Graduate School of Applied Religion argued that the principles were too general to be effective: "we can't just spout broad principles and leave it to diplomats to make the vital choices." Joseph F. Fletcher, "Comment on the Report of 'The Commission on a Just and Durable Peace,' " *The Witness* 26/45 (8 April 1943): 3. Rev. John Gass of St. Paul's Church of Troy NY saw the six pillars as "adequate to support a structure of society which holds out the hope of stability, the promise of peace and the achievement of justice." Gass, "Comment on the Report of 'The Commission on a Just and Durable Peace,' " *The Witness* 26/45 (8 April 1943): 4. Professor Harry F. Ward of Union Seminary called them "worse than a disappointment. . . . The people want bread and the learned doctors of the law, sacred and secular, give them a stone—that is, form syllable generalities." Harry F. Ward, "Comment on the Report of 'The Commission on a Just and Durable Peace,' " *The Witness* 26/45 (8 April 1943): 4. Rev. C. Leslie Glenn, a chaplain in the U.S. Navy, saw them as helpfully moderate, neither too general to be irrelevant nor too specific to go beyond the expertise of the commission. C. Leslie Glenn, "Comment on the Report of 'The Commission on a Just and Durable Peace,'" *The Witness* 26/45 (8 April 1943): 4. Rev. Phillips E. Osgood of Emmanuel Church, Boston, saw the pillars to be ineffective generalities.

that "No German would even listen to one of the six pillars. They would not give him the slightest hope for the post-war world."[172] Yet, until the end of the war he staved off cynicism. While he understood comments of a prominent leader regarding the prospects of the postwar world—"We have got neither the grace nor the virtue nor the wisdom to handle the present world situation' "[173]—he would declare, nonetheless, "In spite of the tension between the East and West we shall fight for a world-wide solution on the basis of the collaboration between the East and the West."[174]

In early 1945, he and the Council for a Democratic Germany expressed their satisfaction with published positions taken at the Crimea Conference: its demand for cooperation between East and West in the organization of Europe; its position towards the free and independent participation of nonfascist national governments in a European organization; and its distinction between Germans and Nazis.[175] At the same time, he knew that the future required a serious reckoning with the strengths and weaknesses

---

He called for the statement of a program "definitely workable and potently realistic," declaring, "If Christianity (in the large) is at all the conscience of society then something more than principles must be enunciated fine as those principles are." (Phillips E. Osgood, "Comment on the Report of 'The Commission on a Just and Durable Peace,' " *The Witness* 26/46 (15 April 1943): 5. Professor Adelaide Case of the Episcopal Theological School—observing that the pillars for peace were presented at a luncheon including leaders of capitalism and college presidents—noted the absence of the voice of labor: "It is obviously absurd for the Church to talk about this problem except in conference with the workers' representatives. Where were the labor leaders?" (Adelaide Case, "Comment on the Report of 'The Commission on a Just and Durable Peace,' " *The Witness* 26/46 (15 April 1943): 5. Professor Russell Bowie of Union Seminary had mixed feelings. The peace pillars were not a problem for him. His concern was with antilabor and pro-big business trends that could hijack their implementation. W. Russell Bowie, "Comment on the Report of 'The Commission on a Just and Durable Peace,' " *The Witness* 26/46 (15 April 1943): 5-6.

[172]Tillich, "Comment on the Report of 'The Commission on a Just and Durable Peace' ": 4.

[173]Paul Tillich, "Outlook for 1945," *Bulletin of the Council for a Democratic Germany* 1/3 (1 January 1945): 1.

[174]Tillich, "Outlook for 1945," 1.

[175]Paul Tillich, "The Crimea Concept and the Council," *Bulletin of the Council for a Democratic Germany* 1/4 (February 1945): 1.

of democracy and collectivism. He wrote, "You cannot have a working democracy built on ruins and you cannot have it if the masses prefer death in a revolution to starvation and economic slavery under so-called democratic government."[176] Capitalistic democracy without justice and without a commitment to social security must be rejected. In fact, Tillich saw Europe moving in the direction of "something new which could be called collectivistic and authoritarian without the primitivistic connotations of the former and the absolutistic connotations of the latter."[177]

Tillich acknowledged that these facts would characterize the postwar lay of the land: the dominance of the Big Three of the United States, Great Britain, and Russia; the maintenance of the monopoly capitalism which he saw to be the deepest reason for the war; and the growth in antidemocratic centralized and authoritarian nations.[178] Nonetheless, changes in international relations had to occur. Tillich saw a range of shorter and longer term issues to be important: the fair adjudication of the guilt within Germany; the brokering of any division of Germany only as part of a wider

---

[176]Tillich, "The Christian Churches and the Emerging Social Order in Europe," 331, 332.

[177]Tillich, "The Christian Churches and the Emerging Social Order in Europe," 332. Context should be given for Tillich's comment here. He was speaking about the post-Nazi social upheaval in Germany: "The relations of parents and children, of the sexes, of friends, of the classes, of experts and laymen, of everybody to everybody, have undergone such a change that a man of the late nineteenth century would hardly recognize our present world. . . . In destroying the authority of the parents and teachers for the sake of the Party, in subjecting the sexual life to the demands of the state, in equalizing (contrary to their archaistic theory) male and female in the service of total war, in removing any independent economic or intellectual power, in introducing a universal, technical consciousness, they have created a generation which has no approach to the individualism of the nineteenth century." Tillich, "The Christian Churches . . . ," 332. In the earlier article, "Ethics in a Changing World," Tillich argued that equality had become "a mere ideology to cover the exclusive chance for a few" and, in so doing, had become "a contradiction of love." In place of this understanding of equality, Tillich spoke for one meaning "equal security of everyone, even if much political equality must be sacrificed." In short, while liberal democracy too often contradicted love, perhaps more collectivistic solutions could approximate it more fully. Tillich, "Ethics in a Changing World," 59.

[178]Tillich, "Power and Justice in the Postwar World," 95-97.

strategy for a European federation; a renunciation of military autonomy by all European nations, not simply by Germany; the prospect of Germany's movement to the East or West as dependent upon which side posed the more creative policies for a secure future; the presence of reactionary nationalism beyond German borders; the shape of Europe; social security for all Europeans as a crucial basis for lasting peace; a nonexploitative approach to Europe; the role of Russia as a future, equal partner; calls for national sovereignty by smaller nations; India's independence; the rejection of a return to the balance of power of sovereign nations in favor of independence of national cultures, combined with economic and military interdependence; a constructive world unity embodied in an international organization involving political and socioeconomic concerns; the United States as a prospective center for world organization; the role of the church; and an Asian policy neither racially nor imperialistically motivated.[179]

Conclusion

Paul Tillich took a nonutopian approach to action within the dynamic flow of history. He had a deep sensitivity to the operation of power within international politics, Tillich gave much effort to enunciating principles—whether termed Protestant, eternally Protestant, Protestant-Catholic, or immortally Post-Protestant—that he saw to facilitate the timely embodiment of agapeic justice in the world. With all of these considerations in mind, his message to his audience in the United States included these elements relevant to religious internationalism:

1. Religion understood as the grounding and subjection of all things to a transcendent, ultimate source of meaning should be encouraged. Such religion is characterized by the following: depth (and, conversely, criticism of spiritual superficiality in both the "sacred" and "secular" realms); openness (ecumenical,

---

[179]Tillich, "Christian Basis of a Just and Durable Peace," 87; Tillich, "Die Weltgeschichtliche Zukunft Europas," 11-13. In "Power and Justice in the Postwar World," Tillich pointed out that the limits imposed upon justice did not mean the elimination of justice. He saw the prospects in the area of economic and social security, what he called "an inroad for justice in the power jungle of the postwar situation." Tillich, "Power and Justice in the Postwar World," 101. See also Tillich, "Theses on the Peace Treaty," 7-11; Tillich, "The Future of Germany," 9, 11-13; and Tillich, "Storms of Our Times," 31.

interreligious, ideological); creative criticism of that which is unloving, unjust, and destructive as manifested in the self or the other; creative participation in history; and pursuit of world transformation;

2. Action should be in "creative agreement with the historical situation," consistent with dynamic, ever-changing, and potentially creative historical circumstances, making new applications of traditional, past formulations, i.e., practice "agapeic- kairotic" ethics;

3. Groups or "orders" of intellectuals motivated to "contend for personality and community" must be cultivated;

4. Consistent with religious socialism, history and socioeconomic structure is crucial to meaning in human existence;

5. The dialectic between personalism and collectivism should be acknowledged as reflecting the definition of human existence as freedom and finitude;

6. Social transformation which leads to being with dignity should be a perpetual goal;

7. Economic security that enables creative freedom should be pursued;

8. Group stereotype is wrong, whether practiced by international criminals or the formal bearers of international justice;

9. Nations are to be the vehicles for international blessing;

10. Regional federations should be sought;

11. "Cultural interpenetration and cross-fertilization" should be pursued; and

12. The dehumanizing, Hobbesian Leviathans of history must be confronted.

Chapter 6

The Cold War: Venturing Courage
in the Face of Historical Vacuum

Introduction

The final period for considering Tillich's thoughts on war and peace is the longest one, stretching over two decades. The most important project during this period was his magnum opus, the *Systematic Theology*. Published in three volumes (and five parts) over a period of twelve years, the work is an apt symbol for the period, manifesting Tillich's goal of communicating—as comprehensively as he could—his interpretations of the wide reach of humankind's questions and what he took to be the profoundly meaningful depth of theology's answers. Here and in a dozens of other writings of varying length, strands of his political thought from earlier times colored the fabric of his thinking. However, by the time of the Cold War, Tillich's thinking had been shaped by two world wars, a profoundly tumultuous quarter century of German and world history, and emigration to the United States. Thus, continuity and change were intriguingly combined in this period.

Tillich continued to frame his understanding of the interpenetration of religion and culture around the dynamics of autonomy, heteronomy and theonomy.[1] The dialectical method—now the method of correlation—

---

[1]Paul Tillich, *Systematic Theology*, vol. 1 (Chicago: University of Chicago Press, 1951) 83-86, 147ff. Hereafter, this volume is referred to as *ST I*. Paul Tillich, *Systematic Theology*, vol. 3 (Chicago: University of Chicago Press, 1963) 157-61, 250-74. Hereafter, this volume is referred to as *ST III*. See also Paul Tillich, "Religion and Secular Culture (1946)," in *The Protestant Era* (Chicago: University of Chicago Press, 1948) 56-57, 58; Paul Tillich, "The Conquest of Theological Provincialism (1952)," in *Theology of Culture* (New York: Oxford University Press, 1959) 171-72; Paul Tillich, "Christian Criteria for Our Culture" (edited and shortened version of address to the Yale Christian Association, Dwight Hall, Yale University, 19 October 1952) *criterion* (New Haven) 1/1 (October 1952): 3; Paul Tillich, "Beyond the Dilemma of Our Period," *The Cambridge Review* (Cambridge MA) 4 (November 1955): 210; Paul Tillich, "Religious and Secular Bases of Culture and Politics" (1953) [PTAH, 408:024], 2, 2-9, 10; Paul Tillich, "Religion (A broadcast talk, 28 November 1954: 'Religion as an Aspect of the Human Spirit')"

remained the engine for distilling truth from existence for him.[2] He maintained his commitment to embrace history with deep seriousness, eschewing any theory that minimized its import through escape:[3] life and history were ambiguous;[4] kairos remained, but with an important turn;[5] and progress was

---

in *Man's Right to Knowledge*, 2nd ser.: "Present Knowledge and New Directions" (New York: Herbert Muschel, Box 800, Grand Central, 1955) 80l; repr. "Religion as a Dimension in Man's Spiritual Life," in *Theology of Culture* (New York: Oxford University Press, 1959); Paul Tillich, "Aspects of a Religious Analysis of Culture (1956)," in Paul Tillich, *Theology of Culture* (London: Oxford University Press, 1959) 41, 42 (repr. from *World Christian Education* [2nd quarter 1956]); Paul Tillich, "Religion and Political Ideologies (Early 1960s)," PTAH 408:020, 8. As noted previously, in citing sources from the Paul Tillich Archive at Harvard, I will use the notation created by Erdmann Sturm: the acronym PTAH designating the Paul Tillich Archive at Harvard; the first number designating the box number; and the number following the colon designating the file number within the box.

[2]Tillich, *ST I*, 30-31, 64-66; Paul Tillich, *Systematic Theology*, vol. 2 (Chicago: University of Chicago Press, 1957) 13-16, 90-92. Hereafter, this volume is referred to as *ST II*. See also Paul Tillich, "The Present World Situation and the Christian Message," (1945) [PTAH, 406A:014], 1-6; Paul Tillich, "The Problem of Theological Method" (Symposium with E. A. Burtt at the American Theological Society, New York, Spring 1946)," *Journal of Religion* (Chicago) 27/1 (January 1947): 25; Tillich, "Autobiographical Reflections (1952)," 13; Paul Tillich, *My Search for Absolutes* (New York: Touchstone, 1967) 40-41; and Paul Tillich, *The New Being* (New York: Scribner's, 1955) 102.

[3]Tillich, *ST III*, throughout. See also Paul Tillich, "Historical and Nonhistorical Interpretations of History: A Comparison," in *The Protestant Era* (Chicago: University of Chicago Press, 1948) 20, 26-27; Paul Tillich, "The Political Meaning of Utopia (1951)," in *Political Expectation* (New York: Harper & Row, 1971; repr. Macon GA: Mercer University Press, 1981) 142, 144, 145, 146, 147, 149, 149-50, 150-51, 152, 153; Paul Tillich, "Victory in Defeat: The Meaning of History in Light of Christian Prophetism," *Interpretation* (Richmond) 6/1 (January 1952): 26; and Tillich, "Christentum und Marxismus (1953)," *GW III*, 174, 175.

[4]Tillich, *ST III*, 30-110.

[5]Tillich, *ST III*, 140ff., 369ff. See also Tillich, *The New Being*, 120, 168, 169; Paul Tillich, "Kairos," in *A Handbook of Christian Theology: Definition Essays on Concepts and Movements of Thought in Contemporary Protestantism*, Marvin Halverson and Arthur A. Cohen, eds. (New York: Meridian Books, 1958) 194, 196; Paul Tillich, "Kairos and the Awareness of the Historical Moment," in *Kairos and Utopiua* (Rauschenbusch Lectures [1959]) PTAH 408:026, 9, 11, 13-15, 18-22, 23,

questioned.[6] The voice of religious socialism,[7] though quieter and perhaps subtler, remained as a dialectical tool for negotiating the tension between the mystical, "vertical," Catholic substance of religion[8] and the prophetic,

---

25-26; Paul Tillich, "Judging and Misjudging an Historical Situation," in *Kairos and Utopia* (Rauschenbusch Lectures [1959]) PTAH 408:026, 11-13, 14-15, 16-17, 24-27, 29-30; Paul Tillich, "The Present Kairos as Problem and Task," in *Kairos and Utopia* (Rauschenbusch Lectures [1959]) PTAH 408:026, 2, 3, 4.

[6]Tillich, *ST III*, 333-39, 352, 354, 365; Paul Tillich, *The Shaking of the Foundations*, (New York: Scribner's, 1948) 22; Paul Tillich, "Die philosophisch-geistige Lage und Protestantismus," *Philosophische Vorträge und Diskussionen* (Bericht über den Mainzer Philosophen-Kongress 1948), ed. Georgi Schischkoff Sonderheft 1 der *Zeitschrift für philosophische Forschung* (Wurzach/Württ.: Pan Verlag, 1948) 120; and Paul Tillich, "The Decline and the Validity of the Idea of Progress," (1964), in *The Future of Religions* (Westport CT: Greenwood Press, 1966) 71.

[7]Tillich, *ST I*, 76, 87, 92, 265-66; Tillich, *ST III*, 310, 329-30, 356, 369; Paul Tillich, "Martin Buber and Christian Thought: His Threefold Contribution to Protestantism (1948)," in *Theology of Culture* (New York: Oxford University Press, 1959) 198, 199; Paul Tillich, "How Much Truth Is in Karl Marx?" *Christian Century* (Chicago) 65/36 (8 September 1948): 906, 907; Tillich, "Autobiographical Reflections," (1952) 12-13; Tillich, *My Search for Absolutes*, (1967) 40; Tillich, "Christian Criteria for Our Culture," (1952) 3; and Paul Tillich, "Der Mensch im Christentum und im Marxismus" (Vertrag, gehalten am 29 July 1952 im Robert-Schumann-Saal zu Düsseldorf), Düsseldorf: "Schriftreihe des Evangelischen Arbeitsausschusses Düsseldorf," no. 5 (1953) *GW III*, 198, 203-208; Paul Tillich, *The Courage to Be*, (New Haven CT: Yale University Press, 1952) 136; Paul Tillich, "Religion in Two Societies (1952)," in *Theology of Culture* (New York: Oxford University Press, 1959) 182, 183-84, 186; Paul Tillich, "Marx's View of History: A Study in the History of the Philosophy of History," in *Culture in History: Essays in Honor of Paul Radin*, ed. Stanley Diamond (New York: Columbia University Press, 1960) 631, 633, 634, 636, 638, 639, 640. For an analysis of the continuing presence of Marx in Tillich's thought, see Donnelly, *The Socialist Émigré*.

[8]Tillich, *ST III*, 236-41, 245. See also Paul Tillich, "Vertical and Horizontal Thinking," Symposium, with Raphael Demos and Sidney Hook, in the American scholar Forum: "The Future of Religion," *American Scholar* (New York) 15/1 (Winter 1945–1946): 103; Paul Tillich, *Types of Man's Self-Interpretation in the Western World: 3 Lectures*, "Lecture 2: The Vertical Self-Interpretation of Man in the Late Ancient and the Medieval Period," (early 1960s), PTAH, 402:016; Paul Tillich, "Visit to Germany," *Christianity and Crisis* (New York) 8/19 (15 November 1948): 149; Tillich, "Protestantische Vision. Katholische Substanz,

"horizontal," Protestant protest of religion,[9] with the goal of defending creative freedom, personhood, and justice[10] against the onslaught of the idolatrously and ideologically demonic forces of existence,[11] chief among

---

Protestantisches Prinzip, Sozialistische Entscheidung" (Vortrag, gehalten am 8 Juli 1951 im Robert-Schumann-Saal zu Düsseldorf), Düsseldorf: *Schriftenreihe des Evangelischen Arbeitsausschusses Düsseldorf 3* (1951): 4, 5, 6 (PTAH BX4827, T 53, A1, #26).

[9]Tillich, *ST III*, 78ff, 169, 177ff, 208-210, 213-14, 223-24, 239, 245, 262ff, 331ff, and 368ff. See also Tillich, "Vertical and Horizontal Thinking," 103; Paul Tillich, "Theologians and the Moon," *Christianity Today* 3/1 (13 October 1958): 31; Paul Tillich, *Types of Man's Self-Interpretation in the Western World: 3 Lectures*, "Lecture 3: "The Horizontal Self-Interpretation of Man in the Modern Period" (early 1960s) PTAH, 402:016; Tillich, *The Shaking of the Foundations*, 7; Tillich, "Die philosophisch-geistige Lage und Protestantismus," 122-23; Tillich, "How Much Truth Is in Karl Marx?" 907-908; Tillich, "Protestanische Vision," 9, 10, 11; Tillich, "Autobiographical Reflections," 12-13; Tillich, *My Search for Absolutes*, 40; Paul Tillich, "Jewish Influences on Contemporary Christian Theology," (The Milton Steinberg Lecture in Jewish theology, delivered at the Park Avenue Synagogue, New York) *Cross Currents* (New York) 2/3 (Spring 1952): 41-42; Tillich, "The Conquest of Theological Provincialism," 169; Tillich, "Religion in Two Societies," 182, 183-84, 186, 187; Paul Tillich, "The Prophetic Element in the Christian Message and the Authoritarian Personality," *McCormick Quarterly* 17/1 (November 1963): 24-25; Paul Tillich, "Funeral Address at Pope John XXIII's Death," (1963) PTAH, 415:011, 1; Tillich, *The Shaking of the Foundations*, 89-90; Tillich, "Martin Buber and Christian Thought," 194, 195; Paul Tillich, "The Present Theological Situation in Light of the Continental European Development," *Theology Today* (Princeton) 6/3 (October 1949): 308; and Tillich, "The Conquest of Theological Provincialism," 168.

[10]Tillich, "Nietzsche and the Bourgeois Spirit," 308; Paul Tillich, "The Cultural Situation After the Second World War" (1945) PTAH 406A:009, 1; Paul Tillich, "What Has the War Done to Us? Culturally!" (1945) PTAH, 406A:010, 1; Paul Tillich, "Die Philosophie der Macht" (Zwei Vorträge, gehalten im Juni 1956 an der Deutschen Hochschule für Politik Berlin), *Schriftenreihe der Deutschen Hochschule für Politik Berlin* (Berlin: Colloquium, 1956), in *GW IX*, 64; Tillich, "Victory in Defeat," 22; Tillich, *The Courage to Be*, 86-91, 160-63; and Tillich, *The New Being*, 71.

[11]Tillich, *ST III*, 76-81, 89-92, 258-68, 402-19. See also Tillich, *The Shaking of the Foundations*, 5; Paul Tillich, "Existentialism and Religious Socialism," in Symposium: "The Meaning of Existentialism," *Christianity and Society* (New

them the economically oppressive and culturally disintegrating and
dehumanizing elements of Western, capitalistic, industrial civilization.[12] It

York) 15/1 (Winter 1949–1950): 10; and Tillich, "Religion and Political
Ideologies," 2.

[12]Tillich, "The Cultural Situation," 9; Tillich, "The Present World Situation,"
10-14a; Paul Tillich, "The Revolutionary Character of the Struggle Going on in the
World Today" (1945) PTAH, 406:015 3, 5, 6; Paul Tillich, "The Contemporary
Spiritual and Moral Situation," (1946) PTAH, 406:004, 1-3; Tillich, "Die
philosophisch-geistige Lage und Protestantismus," 119; Paul Tillich, *The Eternal
Now* (New York: Scribner's, 1963) 135-44; Tillich, "Nietzsche and the Bourgeois
Spirit," 308; Paul Tillich, "Cultural Roots of the Present World Crisis" (late 1940s)
PTAH 406:005, 5, 9-12; Tillich, *The Shaking of the Foundations*, 79; Tillich,
"Martin Buber and Christian Thought," 189; Paul Tillich, "Address at the
Commemoration of the University of Marburg" (1948) PTAH 206:037, 6-7, 9, 11,
12, 13, 17; Paul Tillich, "Christianity and the Problem of Existence," (Three
lectures delivered in Andrew Rankin Chapel, Howard University, April 24, 1951),
Washington DC: Henderson Services, 1951. [Andover-Harvard Microfilm 281n,
#26], 23-24; Tillich, "Protestanische Vision," 13-15; Paul Tillich, "Communicating
the Christian Message: A Question to Christian Ministers and Teachers," in
Theology of Culture (New York: Oxford University Press, 1959) 210; Tillich,
"Christian Criteria for Our Culture," 3; Tillich, *The Courage to Be* (New Haven CT:
Yale University Press, 1952) 61, 137, 138; Paul Tillich, "The Person in a Technical
Society," in *Christian Faith and Social Action: A Symposium*, ed. John A.
Hutchison (New York/London: Scribner's, 1953) 127, 131, 132, 133, 134-35, 138;
Paul Tillich, "Schelling and the Beginnings of the Existentialist Protest,"
(Translation of "Schelling und die Anfänge des existentialischen Protestes,"
Gedächtsnisfeier zum 100.Todestag von Friedrich Wilhelm Joseph von Schelling
am 26.September 1954, *Zeitschrift für philosophische Forschung*
[Meisenheim/Glan] 9/2 [1955], 197-208) PTAH, 203A:023, 10-11; Tillich, *The
New Being*, 94; Tillich, "Aspects of a Religious Analysis of Culture," 42-43, 44-45;
Tillich, "Die Philosophie der Macht (1956)," 216, 219; Paul Tillich, "Christianity,
Democracy and the Arts (1957)" PTAH 401A:005, 4-5; Paul Tillich, "Das
christliche Verständnis des modernen Menschen," (Vortrag, gehalten im
Süddeutschen Rundfunk am 19 Dezember 1958, in *Das ist der Mensch. Beiträge
der Wissenschaft zum Selbstverständnis des Menschen* [Stuttgart 1959], Kröners
Taschenausgabe Bd. 292), *GW III*, 191; Paul Tillich, "Creative Integrity in a
Democratic Society," (1960) PTAH, 517:006, 1, 4; Paul Tillich, "How Has Science
in the Last Century Changed Man's View of Himself?" A lecture for the centennial
celebration of the Massachusetts Institute of Technology on 8 April 1961, *The*

is difficult to overemphasize the import power continued to possess in this period.[13] The nature of a world order remained on Tillich's mind, stripped of illusions regarding the potential for formal organization.[14] In general terms, Tillich summarized the continuity with the earlier periods as follows: the importance of participation in "the fight for the fragmentary actualization of the Kingdom of God in history"; the assertion that individual and social salvation or healing are intermingled; and the call to point to the demonic as it raises its head in "the special historical situation of the West" and its industrial society, producing "misery . . . meaninglessness . . . accommodation . . . [and] subjection."[15]

Yet, even in the face of this continuity, there was a definite change with the evolution toward cold war. At the conclusion of the Second World War, Tillich's active participation in directly political activity lessened significantly. The Council for a Democratic Germany had failed to reach its goals. Germany had been divided by the Allied powers. In 1949 he wrote, "I see a vacuum which can be made creative only if it is accepted and endured and, rejecting all kinds of premature solutions, is transformed into a deepening 'sacred void' of waiting. This view naturally implies a decrease of my participation in political activities."[16] A few years later he recalled, "After the Second World War I felt the tragic more than the activating elements of our historical existence, and I lost the inspiration for, and the contact with, active politics," despite his declaration that "politics remained, and always will remain, an important factor in my theological and philosophical

---

Current 6/1-2 (1965) repr. in Tillich, *The Spiritual Situation in Our Technical Society* (Macon GA: Mercer University Press, 1988) 80; and Tillich, *The Eternal Now*, 69, 71-72, 119.

[13]Tillich, *ST III*, 308-10, 355ff., and 385ff.

[14]Tillich, "The Cutural Situation," (1945), 7-8; Tillich, "What Has the War Done to Us? . . . ," (1945), 6-7; Paul Tillich, *Love, Power and Justice* (New York: Oxford University Press, 1954) 104-106; and Tillich, "Die Philosophie der Macht," (1956) 230, 231.

[15]Paul Tillich, "Past and Present Reflections on Christianity and Society" (1955) PTAH 409:005, 2-3.

[16]Paul Tillich, "Beyond Religious Socialism." *Christian Century* (Chicago) 66/24 (15 June 1949): 733. He was also less active politically because of the failures of the Council for a Democratic Germany.

thought."[17] By 1960, Tillich admitted that the perception that there was in his thought a partial "turn from the social problems to aesthetic and psychological questions . . . [was] not altogether wrong."[18] There were four reasons for this. First, he wrote, "I felt that for a German-born American citizen for whom political activity was difficult and perhaps inappropriate, who was practically without political activity, it was more fruitful to try to relate religion to culture in realms in which one could work without those barriers imposed by the political climate of the times."[19] Second, "Beyond this there was a feeling which I probably share with many people in our time, that we are in the hands of small power groups who, by their very existence, exclude most people from bringing influence to bear on actual decisions."[20] Third, Tillich perceived the post-World War II period to be one of vacuum (dominated by trend) versus kairos (dominated by historical opportunities). Fourth and finally, Tillich sensed a yearning among his students for "a transcendent security in a world in which neither social nor spiritual security is guaranteed."[21] As a consequence, the Cold War period saw a series of changes between post-World War I religious socialism and "the later point of view": (1) the goal was no longer to change the system; (2) historical necessity no longer dictated the way problems were seen; (3) no longer was there a belief in a saving vanguard; and (4) no longer was there a comprehensive world view.[22] Religious socialism was transformed "in America into a movement of protest against the loss of the person in the objectifying society."[23]

Neither of Tillich's self-descriptions—a thinker of politics while

---

[17]Tillich, "Autobiographical Reflections," 19. Tillich, *My Search for Absolutes*, 50.

[18]Tillich, "How My Mind Has Changed in the Past Decade" (November 1960) PTAH 517:008, 5.

[19]Tillich, "How My Mind Has Changed in the Past Decade" (November 1960) 5.

[20]Tillich, "How My Mind Has Changed in the Past Decade" (November 1960) 5-6.

[21]Tillich, "How My Mind Has Changed in the Past Decade" (November 1960) 6.

[22]Tillich, "Past and Present Reflections on Christianity and Society," 2.
[23]Paul Tillich, "The Present Social Structure and the Christian Church" (1958) PTAH 409:006, 3.

remaining political inactive, or one who had turned from the social and political to the psychological and aesthetic—do justice to his labors during this period. The evidence overwhelmingly attests to his ongoing commitment to the dialectical task of regularly and comprehensively taking the existential pulse of his time and giving dogged pursuit of the meaning of—the answers to the questions posed by—existence: from the 1920s to his death in 1965, Tillich was attentive to "the crying of the situation" of existence.[24] Culture and politics were not the only concern of Tillich in this project, but they were always present in his larger effort to interpret existence in its totality. In the discussion here, I will first turn to two broad areas that informed Tillich's thought on politics, peace, and justice during this period: historical vacuum and existentialist estrangement. From there, I will point to the bases for hope Tillich offered during this perplexing period in history.

Vacuum and Estrangement

Historical Vacuum as a Result of Inner Disintegration. Tillich characterized the post-World War II period as an historical vacuum. He believed that Western technological thought had led to the disintegration of the spiritual center of its culture.[25] Tillich wrote, "It was truly symbolic for the collapse of our secular autonomy when the atom scientists raised their voices and preached the end, not unconditionally but with conditions of salvation which present-day humanity is hardly willing to fulfill."[26] A vacuum of vitality within German Protestantism had rendered it impotent in the face of Nazism.[27] This vacuity in German Christianity was embodied by leaders whose actions showed that "Christian generals and statesmen are in no way a guarantee for the Christian character of political decisions."[28]

---

[24]Paul Tillich, "The Ambiguities of the Moral Law" (1960) PTAH 403:017, 10.

[25]Tillich, *The Shaking of the Foundations,* 41, and Paul Tillich, "The Disintegration of Society in Christian Countries," in *The Church's Witness to God's Design: An Ecumenical Study Prepared under the Auspices of the World Council of Churches, Amsterdam, August 22–September 4, 1948,* vol. 2: "The Amsterdam Assembly Series" (New York: Harper & Brothers, 1948) 59.

[26]Tillich, "Religion and Secular Culture," 61.

[27]Tillich, "The Present Theological Situation," 302.

[28]Paul Tillich, "World War II and the Younger Churches" (1946), PTAH 514:022, 11.

Tillich's sense of a *kairos* following World War I was profoundly shaken by the onset of Nazi tyranny, the subsequent war, and the postwar East-West division of the world.[29] Recent history had shown that totalitarianism is able to fill the voids left in life fostered by the rationalistic myth of harmony.[30] In the face of a cultural vacuum,[31] paganism was ever prepared to fill such vacuums in history.[32] Tillich wondered whether the post-World War II vacuum would lead to the destructiveness to which the post-World War I power vacuum had ultimately led.[33]

According to Tillich's reading of history, Western civilization had lost its center of meaning.[34] Spiritual life required a center of meaning as "the ultimate principle of understanding existence and the ultimate purpose for acting in existence."[35] In his view, the absence of an adequate spiritual center was the basis for the difficulties of the time: the spiritual center is to be unitary (over against metaphysical pluralism); it is to be absolute (over against metaphysical relativism); and it is to be ultimate (over against metaphysical pragmatism).[36] Personalities and communities require spiritual centers: the problem was that there was a "psychology without an Ego-Self" and a "sociology without a We-Self."[37] A healthy spiritual center maintains unity, as against the disunity that he saw to be current at the time.[38] Creativity and culture arise from the spiritual center, as opposed to using means for the penultimate ends which dominated Western industrial civilization.[39] The meaning of existence is to arise out of the spiritual center: instead, positivism was successfully emphasizing facts over meanings.[40] In

------

[29]Tillich, "Beyond Religious Socialism," 732; Tillich, "Vertical and Horizontal Thinking," 104; and Tillich, "Religion and Secular Culture," 60.

[30]Tillich, "The Disintegration of Society in Christian Countries," 54-55.

[31]Tillich, "The Cultural Situation," 5.

[32]Tillich, "World War II and the Younger Churches," 9.

[33]Paul Tillich, "The Dangers of a Spiritual Vacuum" (1945) PTAH, 406A:011, 1-2.

[34]Tillich, "The Present World Situation," 7.

[35]Tillich, "The Present World Situation," 7.

[36]Tillich, "The Present World Situation," 8.

[37]Tillich, "The Present World Situation," 8.

[38]Tillich, "The Present World Situation," 8.

[39]Tillich, "The Present World Situation," 9.

[40]Tillich, "The Present World Situation," 9.

interpreting time, the present is to be united with past and future in a spiritual center, over against the concern for mere memory in historicism and mere expectancy in utopianism.[41]

While Christianity proclaimed the message of an ultimate center who stands against the structure of the time,[42] Christian institutions—as part of that vacuous structure—had lost their true center.[43] Christian symbols—rooted in the existentially particular, and cut off from the ultimate center—were without truth.[44] Christian activities—reduced to moralism and con-formity—lost the grace of the spiritual center.[45] Christian churches—intended to be places for the vital presence of the ultimate center in activities and symbols—conformed to, rather than criticized, the cultural structure.[46] Christian faith—as "the reception of the center of all centers" in self-transcendence—had become a disparate, un-centered group of experiences. Therefore, Christianity had lost its spiritual center and was a tool for "monopolistic production and self-destruction."[47]

Human Anxiety in the Face of Estrangement from Human Essence. Tillich's concern about the dehumanizing impact of modern civilization upon people informed his existentialist orientation. According to Tillich, the Marburg period of his work (1925) was the beginning of his serious encounter with existentialism.[48] He exalted existentialism as the best philosophy for which to understand culture. He saw the method of correlation as the best theological approach for bridging the divide between supernaturalism and naturalism,[49] opening theology to the subjective, existential

---

[41]Tillich, "The Present World Situation," 9.
[42]Tillich, "The Present World Situation," 15.
[43]Tillich, "The Present World Situation," 15.
[44]Tillich, "The Present World Situation," 16.
[45]Tillich, "The Present World Situation," 16.
[46]Tillich, "The Present World Situation," 16.
[47]Tillich, "The Present World Situation," 17.
[48]Tillich, *My Search for Absolutes*, 42. See also Tillich, "Autobiographical Reflections," 14.
[49]Tillich, "Beyond Religious Socialism," 733. See also Tillich, "The Religious Situation in Post-War Era" (1962) PTAH, 406:007, 3-4; Paul Tillich, "The Nature and Significance of Existentialist Thought," (Symposium with George Boas and George A. Schrader, Jr.: "Existentialist Thought and Contemporary Philosophy in the West") *Journal of Philosophy* (New York) 53/23 (8 November 1956): 740; and Paul Tillich, "Existential Analyses and Religious Symbols," in *Contemporary*

element.[50] Together, Christian theology and existentialist philosophy fully embraced the world.[51]

Existentialism poses "the question of the meaning and possibility of human existence."[52] According to Tillich, "[The existentialists] ask a question and insist that this question is asked profoundly. It is the old religious question of the human predicament, man's finitude and self-estrangement, his anxiety and despair":[53] anxiety as "the existential awareness of non-being";[54] and anxiety in the face of death (ontic anxiety), meaninglessness (spiritual anxiety), and condemnation (moral anxiety).[55] Tillich affirmed the existentialist protest present in Kierkegaard's call for religious liberation, Marx's call for political liberation, and Nietzsche's call for liberation through the self-affirming will. All three struggled against the forces of technical society.[56] Pointing to his spiritual father, Schelling, he maintained that "behind all existential descriptions of the human situation, from Pascal to Heidegger, stands that which Schelling has expressed in poetic-philosophical form, namely, the perception of anxiety and melancholy in all creaturely life, the alienation between man and nature, as well as that of man from himself, and the vision of the unity of the creative and destructive elements in every being."[57] Reaching back further in history, he pointed to Augustine's description of humanity's threefold Angst based on his life experiences: "The Angst before fate including death, the Angst of guilt and despair over guilt, and the Angst of meaninglessness."[58]

Tillich's view was that existentialism and religious socialism shared a sense that human existence (what humanity is) contradicts human essence

---

Problems in Religion, ed. Harold Albert Basilius (Detroit: Wayne State University Press, 1956) 37ff.

[50]Tillich, "The Problem of Theological Method," 25. On existentialism and anxiety, see also Tillich, *ST I*, 191ff. and 206-10, and Tillich, *ST II* as a whole.

[51]Tillich, *The New Being*, 111-12.

[52]Tillich, "Ethische Normen und Geschichtliche Relativitat" (1948) PTAH 202:002, 2.

[53]Tillich, "Religion in Two Societies," 186.

[54]Tillich, *The Courage to Be*, 35.

[55]Tillich, *The Courage to Be*, 41.

[56]Tillich, "The Person in a Technical Society," 121-26.

[57]Tillich, "Schelling and the Beginnings of the Existentialist Protest," 8.

[58]Tillich, "Protestanische Vision," 3.

(what humanity ought to be).[59] In philosophy, literature, and art, it expressed the loss of meaning in the face of the breakdown of harmonious rationalism.[60] Tillich wrote that existentialist intellectuals "can express the despair of existence artistically or philosophically, and can create a meaning of the meaningless. The heroism of despair transcends despair through the power of the intellectual of expressing it, not in outcries but in creative forms."[61] Of the existentialist project, he wrote:

> They revolt against the increasing transformation of man into a thing, a cog in the universal system of organized production and organized consumption. They react against the education of adjustment which tries to press everyone into a pattern by exposing him day and night to centrally directed means of communication. Although in antireligious, atheistic, often cynical, often despairing terms, they represent an ultimate religious concern; they see the truth about the human predicament universally and in every particular situation.[62]

In the immediate postwar period, Tillich observed the "fanatical absolutism and skeptical relativism" of young Germans[63] and a generation in America asking Brecht's question, " 'Is there nothing to which one can hold?' "[64] It led him to wonder "whether the twentieth century must forever totter between fanaticism and despair."[65] Space exploration in the late 1950s and early 1960s provoked him to speak of humanity's feeling of "vertigo in relation to infinite space"[66] and of "the anxiety of being a meaningless bit of matter in a meaningless vortex of atoms and electrons."[67] In short, with the twentieth century, humanity could escape the full force of the demonic

---

[59]Tillich, "Existentialism and Religious Socialism," 8.
[60]Tillich, "Christianity and the Problem of Existence," 13-17, 18-21.
[61]Paul Tillich, "Religion and the Intellectuals" [1950] PTAH, 515:011, 2.
[62]Tillich, "Religion in Two Societies," 186-87.
[63]Tillich, "Ethische Normen und Geschichtliche Relativitat," 1.
[64]Tillich, "Ethische Normen und Geschichtliche Relativitat," 1.
[65]Tillich, "Ethische Normen und Geschichtliche Relativitat," 2.
[66]Tillich, The Eternal Now, 70.
[67]Tillich, The Eternal Now, 77 See also Paul Tillich, "Has Man's Conquest of Space Increased or Diminished His Stature?" in The Great Ideas Today 1963, ed. R. M. Hutchins and Mortimer J. Adler (Chicago: Encyclopedia Britannica, 1963) repr. in Tillich, The Spiritual Situation in Our Technical Society (Macon GA: Mercer University Press, 1988) 189.

no longer, specifically the angst of finitude and estrangement.[68] Tillich proclaimed, "*Existence is separation!*"[69]

Tillich saw a correspondence between the Augustinian and Marxist doctrines of split or estrangement: "This idea seems to me to be, in fact, an idea which is so fundamental that there can scarcely be anything [else] which can express reality, which can express the human situation for both Catholicism and Protestantism and, over and above this, for socialism."[70] Elsewhere, he noted, "What is estranged existence in Marxism is fallen existence in Christianity," estranged and fallen as individuals but also as a group.[71] Existentialism and religious socialism shared a sense that the industrial situation was a basis for human estrangement and objectification and that socialism was a protest against the repression of creative freedom.[72]

Beyond the Western industrial and economic reality, the decision for nationhood was the shattering of humanity, to Tillich: "in that decision we excluded mankind and all symbols expressing the unity of all men. The former unity was broken, and no international group has been able to reestablish it."[73] The inevitable consequence was international estrangement: "The most irrevocable expression of the separation of life from life today is the attitude of social groups within nations towards each other, and the attitude of nations themselves towards other nations. The walls of distance, in time and space, have been removed by technical progress; but the walls of estrangement between heart and heart have been incredibly strengthened."[74]

The Holocaust experience of the Jewish people was a crisis of cultural and international estrangement arguably without comparison in the modern era. Tillich analyzed it in Berlin lectures delivered in 1953. There he noted

---

[68]Tillich, "Das christliche Verständnis des modernen Menschen," 190.

[69]Tillich, *The Shaking of the Foundations*, 155. See all Tillich, *The Courage to Be*, 48, and Tillich, *The Eternal Now*. Tillich's emphasis.

[70]Tillich, "Protestanische Vision," 3. See also Tillich, "Der Mensch im Christentum und im Marxismus," 196.

[71]Tillich, "Der Mensch im Christentum und im Marxismus," 199.

[72]Tillich, "Existentialism and Religious Socialism," 9. On estrangement, see Tillich, *ST II* as a whole. On freedom and finitude, see Tillich, *ST I*, 200ff., Tillich, *ST II*, 31ff., 126ff., 148ff., and Tillich, *ST III*, 230ff.

[73]Tillich, *The Shaking of the Foundations*, 180.

[74]Tillich, *The Shaking of the Foundations*, 157.

operative factors in the German-Jewish situation common to Europe as a whole: (1) Jews were protected as long as they were useful to the ruling classes as "brokers of capital"; (2) religious anti-Semitism was used as a diversionary tactic by the rulers when it was advantageous to do so; (3) political anti-Semitism used stereotypes of Jews which removed the personal responsibility and, in the process, the personhood of Jews, consistent with the dehumanizing pattern of industrial society.[75]

As a German problem, Tillich saw the fate of the Jews as related to the notion that similarity breeds both strong attraction and strong revulsion: (1) both groups "experienced a prophetic movement of reform: the Jews in Prophecy, the Germans in the Reformation";[76] and (2) both possessed a "spiritual inner strife . . . a mixture of self-hatred and self-overestimation."[77] He then wrote of what he judged to be the response of Germans to the stranger within, over against the stranger without: "We have seen that Germans love that which is foreign, partly because they want to be rid of themselves by losing themselves in what is strange. But they cannot tolerate the foreign elements alive among them, because it wrenches them from their unquestioning self-affirmation, and because their self-realization is so weak that it cannot admit anything foreign."[78] As an existential problem for the Jewish people, Tillich believed that the lack of national space for Jews had led either to assimilation or to Zionism. This created complexity in understanding the identity of the Jewish people in history.[79] Formerly, he exalted the status of the Jewish people as the people of history. Initially, this had led him to have reservations about the establishment of a Zionist state, something which emphasized the physical-spatial significance of Jewish existence over against its time-historical dimension. But Tillich eventually

---

[75]Paul Tillich, "The Jewish Question: a Christian and a German Problem," trans. Marion Pauck, *North American Paul Tillich Society Bulletin* 30/3 (Summer 2004): 12-13 (originally published as *Die Judenfrage, ein christliches und ein deutsches Problem: Vier Vorträge, gehalten an der Deutschen Hochschule fr Politik Berlin*, "Schriftenreihe der Deutschen Hochschule für Politik Berlin" [Berlin: Gebrüder Weiss, 1953], *GW III*, 128-70).

[76]Tillich, "The Jewish Question," 9.

[77]Tillich, "The Jewish Question," 10; see also 12. Tillich gives no supportive reasoning or documentation for the latter statement.

[78]Tillich, "The Jewish Question," 13.

[79]Tillich, "The Jewish Question," 19-20.

came around to Zionism: "we must ask ourselves whether it makes sense to condemn the average Jew in the world for wanting to escape the fate of dispersion or for refusing to belong to the nation of time, the nation without its own space."[80] Further, he wondered, "is it possible that the space Israel has found as its own space may lead to new embodiments of the prophetic spirit, and that from this new impulses will arise for Israel, as well as for the Diaspora?"[81] He posed the other option as well, "that modern nationalism will triumph completely, that Israel will become a nation that is only a nation, and that the element of the religious community will be lost."[82]

Turning in another direction, Tillich saw in the East and the West the onset of collectivism, conformity, and patternization, that is "[t]he transformation of the present world into a new collectivism as the structural trend in all realm[s] of life."[83] Within the enigma of economic security he saw the problem of conformity, perceiving "fear as the main problem."[84] He asked whether security without slavery was possible.[85] As for religion, he saw certain elements of institutional religion working against freedom and in favor of conformity: conservatism, authoritarianism, intolerance, and transcendentalism.[86]

In the United States, the church's responses to societal patterns had involved either withdrawal into doctrinal formulations of the past or conformity to industrial society.[87] Conformity was not negative *per se*.[88] However, it was when it became what Tillich termed patternization, when

---

[80]Tillich, "The Jewish Question," 20.

[81]Tillich, "The Jewish Question," 20.

[82]Tillich, "The Jewish Question," 21.

[83]Tillich, "The Jewish Question "The Revolutionary Character of the Struggle," 1.

[84]Tillich, "The Jewish Question "Beyond the Dilemma of Our Period," 211.

[85]Tillich, "The Jewish Question "The Revolutionary Character of the Struggle," 7.

[86]Paul Tillich, "Freedom and the Ultimate Concern," (Lecture delivered in the Seminar on Religion and the Free Society, May 9, 1958, World Affairs Center, New York; sponsored by the Fund for the Republic) in *Religion in America: Original Essays on Religion in a Free Society*, ed. John Cogley (New York: Meridian Books, 1958) 274-77.

[87]Tillich, "Aspects of a Religious Analysis of Culture," 45.

[88]See Tillich, *The Courage to Be*, 103-107, 112.

"the individual form that gives uniqueness and dignity to a person is subdued by the collective form."[89] He believed the causes of conforming patternization to be technological civilization, mass manipulation by economic, advertising, and mass cultural power-holders, and the yearning for security by the young which leads to surrender to the group at the cost of individual dignity.[90]

Tillich noted that in Russia, "The Communists in spite of their prophetic background, their valuation of reason, and their tremendous technical productivity have almost reached the stage of tribal collectivism."[91] He saw the evolution of communism in Russia as an understandable source of disappointment for utopian liberals worldwide: "it cannot be denied that this widespread repudiation of human rights had a depressing affect on those who, like myself, without being utopian, saw the dawn of a new creative era in a moment which actually presaged a deeper darkness."[92] As a consequence, Tillich wrote, "It is by far the greatest tragedy of our century that this fight has produced a political system in which man's creative freedom is even more lost than in the economic system over which it has triumphed."[93] A year later he reiterated this concern:

> It is the great tragedy of our time that Marxism, which had been conceived as a movement for the liberation of everyone, has been transformed into a system of enslavement of everyone, even of those who enslave the others. . . . The courage to be was undermined in innumerable people because it was the courage to be in the sense of the revolutionary movements of the nineteenth century. When it broke down, these people turned either to the neocollectivist system, in a fanatic-neurotic reaction against the cause of their tragic disappointment, or to a cynical-neurotic indifference to all systems and every content.[94]

Socialism had become widely discredited because of communism's transformation of it into this system of dehumanization.[95] Tillich attributed this

---

[89]Paul Tillich, "Conformity" (1957), *The Spiritual Situation in Our Technical Society* (Macon GA: Mercer University Press, 1988) 145.

[90]Paul Tillich, "Conformity" (1957), 146-47, 149.

[91]Tillich, *The Courage to Be*, 98.

[92]Tillich, "Beyond Religious Socialism," 733.

[93]Tillich, "Existentialism and Religious Socialism," 9.

[94]Tillich, *The Courage to Be*, 153.

[95]Tillich, "Protestanische Vision," 12. Tillich noted the inability of Americans to distinguish between socialism and communism. See also Tillich, "Christentum

to a hole in Marx's system. While Marx's concern was "the freely creative person who forms the world of things and who has not become a thing," this must be gleaned from Marx's description of estranged humanity. It is not explicitly stated as such.[96] The vacuum in Marx's description opens the way for the subjection of humanity in the communist revolution.[97]

Another example of the patternizing consequence of mass manipulation to which Tillich pointed was the East-West political situation of the Cold War:

> The schizophrenic split of mankind into East and West, and the secrecy connected with it, makes an independent political judgment almost impossible for most people. It prevents the rise of fresh political philosophies, since every nonconformist political thought is denounced as neutralist or worse. Courage is demanded for the expression of serious political disagreement even by a student, because it may later wreck his career.[98]

Tillich wondered whether there would be a third way that could unite the "freedom thoughts" (*Freiheitsgedanken*) of the West and "the radical faith in security" in the east.[99]

With this description of Tillich's pessimistic portrayal of Cold War existence, I now turn to the prospects for just action which Tillich saw in such a situation, rooted in the boundary perspective and leading to venturing courage.

Bases for Hope and Healing

The Boundary Perspective. As I have noted before, the boundary functioned as a symbol of significance for Tillich throughout most of his creative life.[100] In war and peace, from politics to theology, as a refugee, emigrant, and citizen, he was existentially marked and defined by the boundary situation. With the arrival of the cold war period, the boundary became a place from which Tillich addressed important issues related to national identity and international behavior relevant to the period. In 1946, he wrote

---

und Marxismus," 170-71.

[96]Tillich, "Der Mensch im Christentum und im Marxismus," 197.
[97]Tillich, "Der Mensch im Christentum und im Marxismus," 197.
[98]Tillich, "Conformity," 147.
[99]Tillich, "Die philosophisch-geistige Lage und Protestantismus," 124.
[100]See chap. 3.

of how serious people could function as a bridge between the Germany of
that time and other cultures: "The only possibility of influencing them is to
have fellowship with them, not to come as a judge or educator, nor to speak
of revenge, but as a friend who is willing to receive gifts from them in
exchange for what he tries to bring them."[101] By 1952, the reality of the iron
curtain between East and West moved him to ask about American cultural
identity, "Will America remain what it has been to us, a country in which
people from every country can overcome their spiritual provincialism?"[102]

Tillich admitted to possessing a theological provincialism when he had
arrived in the United States in the early 1930s: "It was our feeling that only
in Germany was the problem of how to unite Christianity with the modern
mind taken absolutely seriously."[103] The collapse of German culture into
Nazi rule shook this provincialism profoundly: "Neither my friends nor I
myself dared for a long time to point to what was great in the Germany of
our past. If Hitler is the outcome of what we believed to be the true philosophy and the only theology, both must be false."[104] Following World War
Two, he had several opportunities to travel and lecture in Germany. Both
in his lectures as well as in his reports on these journeys, Tillich functioned
as a mediator of the boundary.[105] Tillich made a distinction between living
on the boundary and analysis from the boundary. He described his perspective as rooted in "the experience of someone who came from without this
country, lives now here for twenty-four years, but still has at least in some
corners of his being the observer attitude—and I think for observation it is
useful to live on the boundary line between these cultures. For living, it's
not good; it splits. But for observation, it's good."[106]

It is not surprising that in 1962, on the occasion of receiving the Peace
Prize from the Marketing Association of the German Book Trade in
Frankfurt, Tillich spoke of the centrality of what was previously described
as the dynamic boundary: "Existence on the frontier, in the boundary
situation, is full of tension and movement. It is in truth no standing still, but

---

[101]Tillich, "Visit to Germany," 148.
[102]Tillich, "The Conquest of Theological Provincialism," 176.
[103]Tillich, "The Conquest of Theological Provincialism," 161.
[104]Tillich, "The Conquest of Theological Provincialism," 164.
[105]Paul Tillich, "The Social and Spiritual Forces in Germany Today" (1946)
PTAH, 404:005 and Tillich, "Visit to Germany," 147-49.
[106]Tillich, "Christianity, Democracy, and the Arts," 4.

rather a crossing and return, a repetition of return and crossing, a back-and-forth—the aim of which is to create a third area beyond the bounded territories, an area where one can stand for a time without being enclosed in something tightly bounded."[107]

The boundary was clearly a place of risk and courage to Tillich. When one arrives at the boundary, one can either fall back or transcend self. In falling back, resentment or disappointment in failing to "meet" the boundary moment can lead to fanaticism. Fanaticism can also arise in a new bounded situation following a boundary crossing.[108] Tillich saw the *petit bourgeois* as incapable of successfully negotiating the anxiety of the boundary where in "seeing themselves in the mirror of the different, can never risk rising above the habitual, the recognized, the established. They leave unrealized the possibilities which are given to all from time to time to rise up out of themselves."[109] He summoned the church to regain relevance by "return[ing] to the boundary, to cross over it and wrestle for the Beyond in the to-and-fro between church and culture."[110] Relating this specifically to the matter of peace, Tillich emphasized the importance of possessing courage to cross boundaries:

> Only he who participates on both sides of a boundary line can serve the Comprehensive and thereby serve peace—not the one who feels secure in the voluntary calm of something tightly bounded. Peace appears where, in personal as well as in political life, an old boundary has lost its importance and thereby its power to occasion disturbance, even if it still continues as a partial boundary. Peace is not side-by-side existence without tension. It is unity within that which comprehends, where there is no lack of opposition of living forces and conflicts between the Old and the sometime New—yet in which they do not break out destructively but are held in the peace of the Comprehensive. If crossing and reversing the boundaries is the way to peace, then the root of disturbance and of war is the anxiety for that which lies on the other side, and the will to eliminate it which arises from it.[111]

Tillich saw boundaries as crucial for establishing identity: "the one who

---

[107]Paul Tillich, "Boundaries" (1962) in *Theology of Peace*, ed. Ronald H. Stone (Louisville: Westminster/John Knox Press, 1990) 163.
[108]Tillich, "Boundaries" (1962) 164, 165.
[109]Tillich, "Boundaries" (1962) 166.
[110]Tillich, "Boundaries" (1962) 165.
[111]Tillich, "Boundaries" (1962) 163.

has found his identity and thereby the boundary of his nature does not need to lock himself in or to break out. He will bring to fruition what his nature is. Of course, in that realization all the questions of border crossings come back, but accompanied now by a consciousness of himself and his own potential."[112] Among nations, this consciousness of boundary and identity is expressed in "the consciousness of calling, in which the identity, and with it the essential limit, of a nation expresses itself."[113] The danger arises when power is detached from calling in national identity, when power is detached from its "essential limit."[114] Tillich saw peace to be possible under conditions in which "power stands in the service of a genuine consciousness of calling and where knowledge of the essential limit limits the importance of the factual limits."[115] The danger in the East-West divide was that the consciousness of calling "on both sides has the character of exclusiveness and therefore, given the circumstances of contemporary technology, threatens humanity with self-destruction."[116] Therefore, Tillich saw it as "most important for the possibility of peace [to be] the acceptance of their own finitude by the nations—of their time, of their space, and of their worth. The temptation not to accept finitude, but rather to lift oneself to the level of the Unconditioned, the Divine, runs through all history."[117] Contemplating the Berlin crisis and the debate live at the time about the appropriateness of using nuclear weapons, Tillich reminded his audience, "There is no human group which has the right, for the sake of its boundaries, to begin something whose continuation must lead to the destruction of itself and of all other human reality."[118]

Utopia, Kairos, and Movement toward Reunion. As he reflected on the state of Protestantism at the close of World War Two, Tillich expressed the belief that when both the utopian hope of the post-World War I period and the cynical realism of the post-World War II period were judged by the Protestant principle, it led to the conclusion that history should be

---

[112]Tillich, "Boundaries" (1962) 168.
[113]Tillich, "Boundaries" (1962) 169.
[114]Tillich, "Boundaries" (1962) 170.
[115]Tillich, "Boundaries" (1962) 170.
[116]Tillich, "Boundaries" (1962) 171.
[117]Tillich, "Boundaries" (1962) 172.
[118]Tillich, "Boundaries" (1962) 173.

approached with a realism of hope.[119] In this spirit Tillich framed the decade of the 1950s with two series of lectures addressing the theme of utopia and kairos: his 1951 Berlin lectures at the Deutschen Hochschule für Politik, *The Political Meaning of Utopia*; and his 1959 Rauschenbusch lectures at Colgate Rochester Divinity School, *Kairos and Utopia*.[120]

The Berlin lectures focused on the nature of utopia. Tillich argued that being—specifically human being—is the beginning of the discussion of utopia.[121] In the distinction between human essence (what humanity ought to be) and human existence (what humanity actually is), there is the tendency of human beings to posit their essential self as existing in an ideal period in the past and making this ideal the basis for what humanity could become.[122] He distinguished between those lines of thought which either denied utopia (the pessimistic Protestantism of a Karl Barth and existentialism) from those that affirmed utopia (the revolutionary spirit and victorious revolutionary progressivism).[123]

---

[119]Tillich, "Author's Introduction," xxix.

[120]See Tillich, "The Political Meaning of Utopia." The four lectures of this series are "The Root of Utopia"; "Historical and Unhistorical Thinking"; "Religious and Secular Utopia"; and "Critique and Justification of Utopia." See also Tillich, "Kairos and Utopia," (1959). The four lectures are "Between Utopianism and Escape from History"; "Kairos and the Awareness of the Historical Moment"; "Judging and Misjudging an Historical Moment"; and "The Present Kairos as Problem and Task." Lecture 1 ("Between Utopianism and Escape from History") is published in *Colgate Rochester Divinity School Bulletin* 31/2 (1959). Lectures 2 and 3 ("Kairos and the Awareness of the Historical Moment"; "Judging and Misjudging an Historical Moment") are found as handwritten manuscripts in the Harvard Archive, PTAH 408:026. Lecture 4 is found as a handwritten outline in the Harvard Archive, PTAH 408:026.

[121]Tillich, "The Political Meaning of Utopia," 125-32, 140. See also Tillich, *ST III*, 345-46, 353-60, and 398 on utopia. Tillich lectured at the Deutschen Hochschule für Politik for three summers, beginning in 1951. For details, see O. H. Gablentz, "Paul Tillich in der Deutschen Hochschule für Politik." [PTAH, 901E:087].

[122]Tillich, "The Political Meaning of Utopia," (1951), 133-36, 141. This is captured in Tillich's discussion of the relationship between the German word, *Wesen* ("essence") and its cognate, the participle *gewesen* ("been"), capturing the notion of human essence being a phenomenon of the past (141).

[123]Tillich, "The Root of Utopia," in "The Political Meaning of Utopia," 136-40, 141.

He saw utopian patterns in both historical and unhistorical thinking. In historical thinking (in which time rules space), time "runs ahead—inescapable, irreversible, nonrepeatable—time that moves toward what is new. . . . The new [which] comes to birth in history."[124] Tillich found the utopian in Zoroastrianism's victory of good over evil, the eighteenth century middle class' vision of the harmonious age of reason, and socialism's proletarian revolution iniating "the utopia of the classless society."[125] Tillich called Marxism "the radicalization of the utopian Christian sect in its secular form."[126] In the vision of Zionism, the political agenda of Roman Catholicism, and the crusading spirit of Protestantism, Tillich saw the utopian as expressed by movements representing a more balanced tension between time and space.[127] In unhistorical thinking (in which space dominates time) Tillich pointed to classical mysticism where history is deterioration and utopia is in the past.[128] He highlighted naturalism in which "the eternal return as one observes it in nature (or believes he can) [is] the foundation for denying all significance to history,"[129] In Stoicism's past Golden Age and Nietzsche's anticipation of the Great Noonday of the Superman or Overman,[130] in the lines of existentialism exemplified by Heidegger's idea of "the 'revelation of pure being'" and Sartre's involvement in the French resistance, he found "the expectation that in the individual, through his struggle for freedom of decision, the system of objectification and authority will one day be overcome."[131]

Tillich wrote of every utopia as fundamentally a "negation of the negative," a stand against nonbeing, manifested in finitude and estrangement under the conditions of existence. This is seen in utopias related to the conquest of death through myths of immortality or present participation in the eternal,[132] the overcoming of estrangement through the various levels of healing, including the technological conquering of nature and remedies for

[124]Tillich, "Historical and Unhistorical Thinking," 147, 153.
[125]Tillich, "Historical and Unhistorical Thinking," 149-50.
[126]Tillich, "Cultural Roots of the Present World Crisis," 2.
[127]Tillich, "Historical and Unhistorical Thinking," 150-51.
[128]Tillich, "Historical and Unhistorical Thinking," 142.
[129]Tillich, "Historical and Unhistorical Thinking," 144.
[130]Tillich, "Historical and Unhistorical Thinking," 145.
[131]Tillich, "Historical and Unhistorical Thinking," 146, 147.
[132]Tillich, "Religious and Secular Utopia" [1951] 156-58.

illness,[133] the overcoming of the social ills of authority and exploitation by social restructuring,[134] the return to the Ground of being through the absorption of humanity identity in mysticism, and the unity with the Ground (without losing human identity) in prophetic visions.[135] Tillich stressed:

> In every religious hope, the Christian as well, reunion with the divine ground of being is strived for. But the form of reunion is different. It can emphasize the arising of the individual into the eternal more and it can emphasize existing within the eternal more. The first is the form of hope in mystically influenced religions; the second is the form of hope in prophetically influenced religions. It is no simple either-or. But often a different emphasis has immeasurable historical results for ultimate human insights. And so it is with the symbols of hope. The valuation of history, of the individual in personality, of the transformation of the actual in service of the ultimate goal: all of that belongs to the consequences of the prophetic hope for world history. And when the great religions in the near future are engaged in spiritual competition, then the symbols of Christian hope—eternal *life* and *kingdom* of God—will be of decisive significance. Their actuality in the world, in our world as well, be it openly or secretly, be it directly or indirectly, cannot cease."[136]

Within utopia, positive and negative meaning were combined. Utopia was truthful in expressing the essence of humanity, fruitful in opening up possibilities for humanity, and powerful in enabling transformation of the present state of affairs.[137] However, it was untruthful in being blind to human existence as estranged from human essence (undercutting fulfillment of essence within existence), unfruitful in concealing the impossibility of some of the possibilities it posed (ignoring the nature of reality as the "oscillation between possibility and impossibility") and impotent (given the ambiguousness of existence and its possibilities, leading to disillusionment).[138]

---

[133]Tillich, "Religious and Secular Utopia" [1951] 159-63.

[134]Tillich, "Religious and Secular Utopia" [1951] 163-66.

[135]Tillich, "Religious and Secular Utopia" [1951] 166-67.

[136]Tillich, "Christliche Hoffnung und ihre Wirkung in der Welt" (1960s) PTAH 204:048, 10-11.

[137]Tillich, "Critique and Justification of Utopia," 168-70.

[138]Tillich, "Critique and Justification of Utopia," 170-73. On the relationship of utopia to international relations, see Ronald H. Stone, "Utopianism and International Relations," Unpublished paper delivered before the "Tillich: Issues

Thus, Tillich called for the transcendence of utopia. He wrote of the structural principle of life that "Every living thing drives beyond itself, transcends itself."[139] He argued that World War I had taught his generation two things about utopia: "[F]irst, that a utopia of simply going forward [a horizontal utopia] did not grasp the human situation in its finitude and estrangement, and that it must lead necessarily to metaphysical disillusionment; and second, that a religion for which utopia is exclusively transcendent [a vertical utopia] cannot be an expression of the New Being, of which the Christian message is witness."[140]

The consequence was that post-World War I religious socialism saw its period as a time of *kairos*—as a time in which something new could happen—but that any new order would be an ambiguous one, not an absolute one.[141] Therefore, Tillich advocated a doctrine of two orders including "both historical reality and transhistorical fulfillment" in which there is "the vertical, where alone fulfillment is to be found, yet precisely where we are unable to see it but can only point to it" as well as "the horizontal, where fulfillment is realized in space and time but where just for this reason it can be found only in an anticipatory, fragmentary way—in this hour, in that form."[142] He concluded, "In whatever way we describe the situation, what is important is the idea that overcomes utopia in its untruth and makes it manifest in its truth. Or, as I could perhaps say in summation of all four lectures on utopia: *it is the spirit of utopia that conquers utopia*."[143]

In the Rauschenbusch lectures at the close of the decade, Tillich turned to utopia once again, but this time he gave extensive attention to the role of kairos. As in other areas and at other times, the visual arts provided a powerful stimulus for Tillich's thinking on these matters. The Renaissance masters presented a dual message of anticipated and realized utopia.[144] The German expressionists "were seismographs who announced the coming

---

in Theology, Religion and Culture Group" (A18-125), American Academy of Religion, San Diego CA (18 November 2007).

[139]Tillich, "Critique and Justification of Utopia," 173.

[140]Tillich, "Critique and Justification of Utopia," 176-77.

[141]Tillich, "Critique and Justification of Utopia," 177.

[142]Tillich, "Critique and Justification of Utopia," 179.

[143]Tillich, "Critique and Justification of Utopia," 180.

[144]Tillich, "Between Utopianism and Escape from History," 36.

earthquakes" within history.[145] For Tillich, the latter were inspired by the spirit of utopia, rooted in "man's existential dissatisfaction with everything that is, his striving beyond the given and his anticipation of a fulfillment which is not yet actual."[146]

Regarding the religious roots of utopia, Tillich argued that in prophetism's anticipation of fulfillment at history's end, in apocalypticism's momentous, concluding and perfecting inbreaking of the divine into history, and in the Christian Trinitarian understanding of the relation of the Holy Spirit to the future he perceived the religious foundations underlying religious and secular utopias.[147] From Tillich's perspective, "The immense world-conquering and nature-subduing dynamic of the West cannot be understood without its source in the hope of the Jewish prophets and the Christian proclamation of the coming Kingdom." The utopian hope of the Renaissance, eighteenth century reason, the nineteenth century belief progress, socialism's classless society: all are "dependent on the religious expectation of the kingdom of God"; yet, "the more distant from their religious roots, the more technical, dubious, empty, and disappointing became their innerworldly hopes."[148]

With regard to the most prominent secular utopia, socialism, Tillich noted Marx's rejection of a utopian socialism in which the transformation from capitalism to socialism would naturally evoke peace and harmony. Yet, he believed Marx's allegedly scientific socialism failed to avoid the same trap with its ultimate goal of a classless society. As I noted before, history, for Tillich, involved the interplay of trend (fate or finitude) and chance (freedom). In Marxist thought, history is driven by trend. Since history requires the participation of freely acting people—the proletariat as the embodiment of chance, the classless society—it is perpetually vulnerable to failure.[149]

Tillich interpreted escapism as a response to failed utopia. Luther represented a tradition which went back to the disappointment of the apocalyptic visionaries about the unfulfilled prophetic expectations, to the disappointment of the early Christians about the delay of the second coming of Christ,

---

[145]Tillich, "Between Utopianism and Escape from History," 35-36.
[146]Tillich, "Between Utopianism and Escape from History," 36.
[147]Tillich, "Between Utopianism and Escape from History," 36-37.
[148]Tillich, "Christliche Hoffnung und ihre Wirkung in der Welt," 8.
[149]Tillich, "Between Utopianism and Escape from History," 38-39.

to the disappointment of the church leaders about the spirit movements and their promises, and to Augustine's rejection of the third stage in history.[150] For Lutherans, history must be endured rather than transformed. The emphasis on the afterlife in German Lutheran and Russian Orthodox traditions led them to be without prophetic criticism of worldly powers.[151] Tillich was led to ask whether this was the death knell for the spirit of utopia: "Is it possible to save the spirit of utopia while dismissing utopianism? . . . are there, we now ask, prophetic spirits among us, spirits of utopia who can resist the temptation of the coming utopianism?"[152] The boundary between utopianism and escapism on which Tillich stood was the spirit of utopia.

To answer the question regarding the fate of the spirit of utopia, Tillich first rejected progressivism (which was contradicted by history's inevitable barriers to progress)[153] and historicism (which was ignorant of prophet criticism and the situation of the oppressed).[154] Instead, he returned to a familiar theme in his philosophy of history: Tillich turned to kairos as "the answer to the question of utopianism."[155] He defined it as "a moment of time in which something can happen and in which something can be done which is impossible at any other time"[156] pointing to "unique moments in the temporal process, moments in which something unique can happen or be accomplished. In the English word 'timing' something of the experience which underlies the term kairos is preserved."[157] It is the "breakthrough of an eternal potentiality of being which now becomes actual as something new."[158] In *The New Being*, Tillich wrote, "the eternal can also cut into the temporal by affirming it, by elevating a piece of it out of the ordinary context of temporal things and events, making it translucent for the Divine

---

[150]Tillich, "Between Utopianism and Escape from History," 40.

[151]Tillich, "Christliche Hoffnung und ihre Wirkung in der Welt," 7.

[152]Tillich, "Between Utopianism and Escape from History."

[153]Tillich, "Kairos and the Awareness of the Historical Moment," 2, 3-4, 5, 9-10.

[154]Tillich, "Kairos and the Awareness of the Historical Moment," 8, 10.

[155]Tillich, "Kairos and the Awareness of the Historical Moment," 9.

[156]Tillich, "Kairos and the Awareness of the Historical Moment," 11.

[157]Tillich, "Kairos" (1958) 194.

[158]Tillich, "Kairos and the Awareness of the Historical Moment," 13.

glory."[159] Again, "When the finger of the clock turns around; not one vain moment is replaced by another vain moment, but each moment says to us: The eternal is at hand in *this* moment."[160] And yet again, "When eternity calls in time, then activism vanishes. When eternity calls in time, then pessimism vanishes. When eternity times us, then time becomes a vessel of eternity. Then we become vessels of that which is eternal."[161] Theologically, it is providence. Anthropologically, it is the convergence of conditions necessary for an act or event.[162] For humankind as a whole, human history is itself a kairos, a "cosmic kairos."[163] The world's religions have central, i.e., history-centering, "world-historical" kairotic events: for Christians, the earthly life of Jesus; for Jews, the Mt. Sinai covenant; for Muslims, the rise of Mohammed; and for Persians, the appearance of Zoroaster.[164] Nonetheless, Tillich argued that Christianity "most conspicuously and most successfully" functioned as history's center:

> Conspicuously insofar as here the distinction of the old and the new eon determines the name Christ and the self-consciousness of the early church to life in the final eon. And it is here most successfully, insofar as even the most secular foe of Christianity accepts the division of historical time into the time before and the time after the appearance of the Christ, even if it does not mean anything for him religiously. Nobody actually escapes the centrality of the figure of Jesus for historical consciousness, even if he does not accept him as the Christ."[165]

The secular world does not escape the kairological understanding of history with its sense of profoundly significant historical occurrences: for the Roman Empire, the founding of Rome; for the bourgeoisie, the Enlightenment; and for socialists, the rise of the proletariat.[166] Tillich spoke of religious socialism's nonutopian understanding of kairoi or moments fruitful for the fragmentary creation of a new reality.[167] These history-

---

[159]Tillich, *The New Being*, 120.
[160]Tillich, *The New Being*, 168.
[161]Tillich, *The New Being*, 169.
[162]Tillich, "Kairos and the Awareness of the Historical Moment," 11.
[163]Tillich, "Kairos and the Awareness of the Historical Moment," 13.
[164]Tillich, "Kairos and the Awareness of the Historical Moment," 13-15, 18.
[165]Tillich, "Kairos and the Awareness of the Historical Moment," 15.
[166]Tillich, "Kairos and the Awareness of the Historical Moment," 16.
[167]Tillich, "Kairos" (1958) 196.

centering kairoi giving meaning to all of history for their "adherents." Thus, for example, in a Christ-centered history, "the beginning of history is the indefinite development in which man became aware of his predicament of estrangement and misery and was grasped by expectations of a better existence. . . . In the same way, the end of history is determined by the center, namely the actualization of what is potentially given in the center, the new principle of being."[168] What would be termed smaller kairoi can happen at every moment in history, moments at which the prophetic spirit is "the center of a smaller or larger stretch of the historical process . . . always [these serve as a] kairos *for* somebody in a concrete situation."[169] What is occurring at such points in time is "the work of the spirit of utopia working in somebody and giving him the certainty of a qualified moment in the flux of quantitative time."[170]

Kairos answers the question of utopia—treads the boundary between utopianism and escapism, and avoids falling to either—by doing two things. First, rather than escaping history, it takes history seriously. Within a kairos moment, the eternal enters history, not to bear information, but to be present: "the divine presence which changes reality" in a way that matters to us, bearing both "announcement and appeal . . . a promise and a threat."[171] Recognition of kairoi is a matter of timing. Often missed by the privileged, they are fruitful moments for the spirit of utopia to function among those "on the negative side of life" whose dissatisfaction with the present and dreams for a better future can be at the root of a prophetic spirit.[172]

The second way kairos answers the question of utopia is by rejecting utopianism by means of "the transcendent foundation of the prophetic spirit."[173] As deep as dreams for the future may be, they are never adequately fulfilled within history. Tillich uses the distortion of the Kantian

---

[168]Tillich, "Kairos and the Awareness," 17. Here, cognizant of Bultmann's presence at the event, Tillich makes parenthetical reference to "Bultmann's eschatological Christ."

[169]Tillich, "Kairos and Awareness," 18-19. Here Tillich parenthetically refers to "Bultmann's existential interpretation of history."

[170]Tillich, "Kairos and the Awareness," 19.

[171]Tillich, "Kairos and the Awareness," 19-20.

[172]Tillich, "Kairos and the Awareness," 21-22.

[173]Tillich, "Kairos and the Awareness," 23.

idea of *eternal* peace into *everlasting* peace as an example. Understood as "everlasting," the notion sets up pacifists for perpetual disappointment and takes away human freedom, namely, the freedom to contradict. On the other hand, understood as eternal, it is the symbol for human fulfillment. The confusion of a symbol of fulfillment with actual fulfillment is utopianism.[174] This leads to the positive task enabled by kairos.

Kairos-periods are occasions when the utopian spirit demands and empowers people to stand against the demonic. Tillich saw the Roman Empire, Nazism, Western industrial capitalism, and communism as examples of this ambiguous reality known as the demonic.[175] The key is to maintain a spirit of utopia that risks decisive action against the demonic at times of kairos, without falling into utopianism.[176]

Again, decision involves risk. The sense of a kairos after World War I was both correct and incorrect. This is consistent with prophetic consciousness.[177] False prophecy is "the demonic distortion of truth." True prophecy contains divine truth "independent of the errors of those who represent it."[178] True prophets judge everything that is finite. False prophets proclaim something finite to be superior to all other finite things: a nation, a social class, "the elected race, blood, soil, as in Nazism," a particular human cultural activity or cultural institution.[179] False prophets prophesy events incapable of bringing fulfillment.[180]

As noted above, trend and chance are key to historical interpretation, trend representing necessity and chance representing contingency. Trend enables kairos-consciousness to exist.[181] Chance speaks to the inevitability of error. Tillich described their interrelationship:

> The trend or the element of necessity is based on the relatively perpetual structures of historical existence. The nature of historical man, its sociological and psychological character, generally and particularly, the natural structures outside of man, the unique constellation of all these elements in a special

---

[174]Tillich, "Kairos and the Awareness," 25-26.
[175]Tillich, "Kairos and the Awareness," 29-32.
[176]Tillich, "Kairos and the Awareness," 32.
[177]Tillich, "Judging and Misjudging an Historical Situation," 3-4.
[178]Tillich, "Judging and Misjudging an Historical Situation," 4-5.
[179]Tillich, "Judging and Misjudging an Historical Situation," 6-7.
[180]Tillich, "Judging and Misjudging an Historical Situation," 7-8.
[181]Tillich, "Judging and Misjudging an Historical Situation," 11.

moment. But in opposition to these structural necessities are the contingencies which bring in the element of chance. They result from the spontaneity of everything alive, from the freedom of man as centered personality, from the incalculability of the moving whole of being which is effective in every part of being [from the original quality of contingency, namely the fact that there is something and not nothing]. In this way structural necessities and genuine contingency interpenetrate each other in every historical process, producing the polarity of trend and chance.[182]

The knowledge necessary for determining a moment to be a true kairos goes beyond scientific knowledge.[183] In order to judge a period to be a kairos, "one must have been grasped by the historical situation in the dimension of the ultimate. . . . Only he who participates in an historical situation in its deepest meaning can speak of a kairos," a participation involving "one's total being."[184] Pronouncing a kairos requires courage and seriousness.[185] The very pronouncement of a kairos is part of that kairos: "He who asserts a kairos *makes* it, to a certain degree, a kairos. He himself is an element in the whole situation."[186] In such a person, potential kairos becomes actual. The horizontal-vertical distinction becomes operable here, as well. Horizontally, error is possible in describing future events. Vertically—when dealing with the meaning of an historical moment—judgments do not involve error or truth, but relation to the demonic or the divine.[187] Horizontal judgments are theoretical judgments subject to the conditions of all theory. Kairos-consciousness "trespasses the subject-object structure of theory."[188]

Because it is captive to the horizontal dimension, utopianism is "open to the misjudgments of future events," leading to profound disappointment, having confused the horizontal and vertical dimensions.[189] The Kingdom of God is central to the problem. The Kingdom of God has "an innerhistorical

---

[182]Tillich, "Judging and Misjudging an Historical Situation," 12-13.
[183]Tillich, "Judging and Misjudging an Historical Situation," 14-15.
[184]Tillich, "Judging and Misjudging an Historical Situation," 16.
[185]Tillich, "Judging and Misjudging an Historical Situation," 16-17.
[186]Tillich, "Judging and Misjudging an Historical Situation," 17.
[187]Tillich, "Judging and Misjudging an Historical Situation," 18-19.
[188]Tillich, "Judging and Misjudging an Historical Situation," 20.
[189]Tillich, "Judging and Misjudging an Historical Situation," 21-22.

and a transhistorical dimension."[190] It is both "at hand" in kairotic moments of history and beyond history, "the eternal fulfillment of what remains unfulfilled in the historical process."[191] Utopianism arises when the innerhistorical understanding overwhelms the transhistorical one. Escapism results when the transhistorical dominates.[192] The spirit of utopia as embodied in the prophetic spirit entails both dimensions: "The ultimate unity of things in the eternal life of God remains the criterion of every moment of innerhistorical fulfillment . . . [present in] the ambiguous structures of historical existence."[193]

Kairotic breakthroughs "reveal and weaken" demonic structures and manifest another familiar element of Tillich's thought, theonomy: "there is always theonomy in history, but always in struggle against both empty autonomy and demonic heteronomy."[194] As "the supporting power of history" theonomy is always present: "as long as there is history there is hidden or open theonomy."[195] Of the dynamics of theonomy, autonomy, and heteronomy, Tillich wrote:

> The interplay of these forces is nowhere in our known history as evident as in the Western world. Nowhere do we find such a radical secularism, produced by an almost unrestrained autonomy. Nowhere do we find such fanatical reactions against it, in the name of divine authority or human-totalitarian substitution for it. And nowhere is the longing for new theonomous symbols as strong as in the ancient and modern West. One could write a story of the intellectual development of the West in terms of the interplay of these three

---

[190]Tillich, "Judging and Misjudging an Historical Situation," 24.

[191]Tillich, "Judging and Misjudging an Historical Situation," 24.

[192]Tillich, "Judging and Misjudging an Historical Situation," 24. The this-worldly understanding of the Kingdom of God/Heaven influenced the Roman world church, the sects, and lay movements of the Middle Ages, and Reformed and Sectarian Protestantism. God's rule is mediated by hierarchy in Catholicism and by Christian preachers and laity in Protestantism. "The establishment of God's rule over all the earth according to the model of Calvin's Geneva, Cromwell's England, Puritan and Pietistic America is the goal of innerworldly Christian hope." This was the basis of Rome's political claims and the Anglo-Saxon crusading spirit. Tillich, "Christliche Hoffnung und ihre Wirkung in der Welt," 7-8.

[193]Tillich, "Judging and Misjudging an Historical Situation," 25.

[194]Tillich, "Judging and Misjudging an Historical Situation," 26.

[195]Tillich, "Judging and Misjudging an Historical Situation," 27.

forces. . . .[196]

It is toward a new theonomy that the spirit of utopia—the prophetic spirit—is driving:

> Theonomy is not fulfillment but it is the image of fulfillment in history. It is not the removal of the demonic, but it is the victory over special demonic structures, it is not the establishment of peace on earth, but it is the establishment of symbols of the unity of mankind, it is not the final state of justice and harmony, but it is an ever varying manifestation of the principle of love, it is not the guarantee of social or cultural progress, but it is an ultimate motive for acting into the future, it is not the Kingdom of God, but it is its fragmentary, anticipatory, endangered image in a particular period of human history.[197]

As a consequence of this analysis, Tillich was led to conclude that he and his contemporaries were the preparers of—not bearers of—a kairos.[198] In fact, the post-World War II period was an a-kairos.[199] Trend seemed to dominate chance. Resignation was combined with an "anger 'at large'."[200] Escapist mysticism was stronger than the prophetic spirit. The trend was toward security, "'success' conquered by 'security.'"[201] The conquest of space led to space "taken as a reality of its own."[202] The prospect of an "atomic end" provoked an "anti-prophetic and anti-utopian" eschatology.[203] Yet, humanity is not captive to existential paralysis. This is seen in Tillich's treatment of love, power, and justice.

Love, Power, and Justice. The capacity to act at the well-timed moment

---

[196]Tillich, "Judging and Misjudging an Historical Situation," 29-30.

[197]Tillich, "Judging and Misjudging an Historical Situation," 31-32.

[198]Tillich, "The Present Kairos as Problem and Task."

[199]Tillich, "The Present Kairos as Problem and Task," 2. Tillich writes, "If there is a kairos it should be a tellmic kairos!" Tillich, "The Present Kairos as Problem and Task," 1. I have not successfully found the word "tellmic" in a dictionary or any other reference works, but Tillich equates it with "a-kairos," i.e., the opposite of kairos or opportune time. Later, he uses "tellmic" in reference to the division nationalism creates in the international arena, a demonic "tellmic split" in the world. Tillich, "The Present Kairos as Problem and Task," 6.

[200]Tillich, "The Present Kairos as Problem and Task," 2.

[201]Tillich, "The Present Kairos as Problem and Task," 3.

[202]Tillich, "The Present Kairos as Problem and Task," 3.

[203]Tillich, "The Present Kairos as Problem and Task," 4.

was rooted in the centered person or group. One line that Tillich took to describe the substance at the center of what it means to be human—to get at that from which humanity was estranged, to refill the vacuum created by the processes of Western, industrial civilization—was to consider the elements of human relationships expressed by the concepts of love, power, and justice. For more than a decade, Tillich had been using this conceptual framework to analyze existence. In several places at about this time—but particularly in the short book, *Love, Power and Justice*—Tillich outlined the essential, the ontological, relationship of the three components of that book's title. In this way, he gave a sketch of the center out of which religion calls people to participate in community as individuals and groups.

In Tillich's construction, power is the power of being[204] possessed by all existing things in a dynamic process of separation and return.[205] It is "the possibility of self-affirmation despite inner and outer negation, it is the possibility to take up into itself and to overcome nonbeing without limitation."[206] Love is the reunion of the separated.[207] It enables the "returning" element within power to occur, and it requires the presence of power in its struggle against that which stands against love. Tillich wrote, "Love, in order to exercise its proper works, namely charity and forgiveness, must provide for a place on which this can be done, through its strange work of judging and punishing. In order to destroy what is against love, love must be united with power . . . compulsory power."[208] Justice gives

---

[204]Tillich, "Die Philosophie der Macht," 207. Tillich saw Nietzsche's will-to-power as the quintessential formulation of the relation of being to power: "the self-affirmation of life, of the life which dynamically reaches beyond itself, which overcomes internal and external resistance," the resistance of nonbeing. Tillich, "Die Philosophie der Macht,", 208, 209.

[205]Tillich, *Love, Power and Justice*, 48-49. "Life is the dynamic actualization of being." Tillich, *Love, Power and Justice*, 41.

[206]Tillich, "Die Philosophie der Macht," 209.

[207]Tillich, *Love, Power and Justice*, 28. See also Tillich, "Being and Love," in *Moral Principles of Action: Man's Ethical Imperative*, ed. Ruth Nanda Anshen (New York: Harper & Brothers, 1952) 666-68; Tillich, "Love, Power, and Justice" (A broadcast talk on the BBC's Third Programme, based on the Firth Lectures delivered in Nottingham) *The Listener* (London) 48/1231 (2 October 1952): 544; and Tillich, *The Eternal Now*, 55-56.

[208]Tillich, *Love, Power, and Justice*, 49.

forming shape to power and love,[209] enabling them to exist.[210] Justice prevents power from being oppressive and gives backbone to love: "A love of any type, and love as a whole if it does not include justice, is chaotic self-surrender, destroying him who loves as well as him who accepts such love."[211] With this ontological structure, Tillich paints a picture in which power is inimical to neither love nor justice. All three are basic elements necessary for existence.

Love, power and justice all occur in encounters with other beings in Tillich's approach.[212] The capacity for being is determined through conscious and unconscious decisions in encounters with other beings.[213] In all positive and negative encounters there is "unconsciously or consciously a struggle of power with power, of potential with potential."[214] Politically, it includes the capacity to have space[215] as well as economic and technical expansion.[216]

As in his discussion about the difficulty of determining guilt among the German people in the face of Hitler's murders, Tillich warned against the false analogy between the individual person and the social group.[217] The group possesses no personal center[218] over against the individual person who is "the battlefield of the powers which struggle in every cell of his body and in every movement of his thought for or against his human being."[219] Power centers in groups are the power-holders who work within

---

[209]Tillich, "Die Philosophie der Macht," 215. Tillich called love *personal holiness* and justice *social holiness* in the 1957 *Dynamics of Faith*, 56.

[210]Tillich, *Love, Power, and Justice* (1954) 56, 67. See also Tillich, "Love, Power, and Justice," 545.

[211]Tillich, *Love, Power, and Justice*, 68.

[212]Tillich, "Die Philosophie der Macht," 215.

[213]Tillich, "Die Philosophie der Macht," 210.

[214]Tillich, "Die Philosophie der Macht," 220.

[215]Tillich, "Die Philosophie der Macht," 228.

[216]Tillich, "Die Philosophie der Macht," 229.

[217]Paul Tillich, "Shadow and Substance: A Theory of Power (1965)," in *Political Expectation* (New York: Harper & Row, 1971; repr.: Macon GA: Mercer University Press, 1981) 116, 117; Tillich, *Against the Third Reich*, 37-39, 109-110, 156-57, 183-87, 189, 210.

[218]Tillich, "Shadow and Substance: A Theory of Power," 117.

[219]Paul Tillich, "Humanität und Religion," *Hansischer Goethe-Preis* 1958, Gedenkschrift zur Verleihung des Hansischen Goethe-Preis 1958 der

a structure requiring both acknowledgement and enforcement.[220] The power and being of such a social organism requires geographic space, radiation of power through economic and technical expansion, self-expression through symbols and ideas, and a sense of vocation.[221]

Force and compulsion are necessary tools of group power: "Power actualizes itself through force and compulsion. But power is neither the one nor the other. It is being, actualizing itself over against the threat of nonbeing. It uses and abuses compulsion in order to overcome this threat. It uses and abuses force in order to actualize itself. But it is neither the one nor the other."[222] The demonic and, thus, ambiguity enter in when coercion is brought into consideration. Coercion and force are inescapable in the estranged condition of human existence. They are present in all three elements of group power: will, space, and growth.[223] Coercion is tragic in dehumanizing its human object, depriving human beings of freedom. It dehumanizes both the forced and the enforcer.[224]

Much of Tillich's concern with power focused on its embodiment in the form of authority. His main concerns surrounded the impact of authority upon personhood, the accountability of authority to those subject to it, and the tendency towards idolatry to which power was prone. He was interested in preventing authority from becoming authoritarian. Therefore, he distinguished between legitimate and illegitimate authority. Illegitimate authority he variously called principled, vested, hypostasized or unjust. It was presumed to be absolute and beyond criticism, yet "every hypostasized authority is unjust authority in its essence, because it takes something away from the capacity for being of the individual and submits him to that which

---

gemeinnützigen Stiftung F.V.S. zur Hamburg an Professor D. Dr. Paul Tillich (Hamburg: Stiftung F.V.S., 1958) 25-35, Tillich, *GW IX*, 111.

[220]Tillich, *Love, Power, and Justice*, 94-95.

[221]Tillich, *Love, Power, and Justice*, 100-101. "[I]n all power encounters of groups an indistinguishable unity of power-drive and consciousness of calling finds itself." The combining of these two occurred in historical developments in all periods: the conflict at the time between Russia and the United States presented this combination. Tillich, "Die Philosophie der Macht," 229-30.

[222]Tillich, *Love, Power, and Justice*, 47.

[223]Tillich, "Shadow and Substance: A Theory of Power," 119-20, 123.

[224]Tillich, "Shadow and Substance: A Theory of Power," 121.

for the time being must be freely received by him."[225] An authority is illegitimate "which breaks humanity and which breaks consciousness of truth."[226] It is demonic in denying its finitude, provoking and justifying prophetic criticism:

> The way in which the true prophet tries to liberate them from the demonic power and to heal the authoritarian personality is the message of an ultimate security beyond insecurity and security; he reveals the demonic character of unconditional bondage to any vested authority and communicates the power of the Spirit which unites ecstasy with order, creativity with community, freedom from and for all authorities which can stand under the prophetic judgment.[227]

Tillich admonished that the God who is Spirit "does not isolate us from the community to which we belong and which is a part of ourselves. But he denies ultimate significance to all these preliminary authorities, to all those who claim to be images of His authority and who distort God's authority into the oppressive power of a heavenly tyrant."[228] Tillich pointed to "history, a book, a priest, a king or a leader (*Führer*) or a commissar," the Pope, the Bible (for orthodox/fundamentalist Christians), dictators, parents (in patriarchal families) and patriarchal models of teaching as examples of illegitimate authority.[229] Tillich was particularly concerned that social upheaval made authoritarianism attractive.[230]

Legitimate or factical authority "expresses what the truth of the ground of being is."[231] For Tillich, cultural and specifically political authorities "are tools through which the Spiritual qualities of mutuality, understanding, righteousness, and courage can be mediated to us."[232] Just authority and power of being go together: "Just authority rests on the fact that everyone has a *de facto* power of being and can for that reason take part in it. In this

---

[225]Tillich, "Die Philosophie der Macht," 222-23.
[226]Tillich, "Protestantische Vision," 7.
[227]Tillich, "The Prophetic Element in the Christian Message," 24-25, 26.
[228]Tillich, *The New Being*, 89-90.
[229]Tillich, "Protestantische Vision," 6; Tillich, "Die Philosophie der Macht," 222-23.
[230]Tillich, "The Prophetic Element in the Christian Message," 18-19, and Tillich, "Beyond the Dilemma of Our Period," 211, 212.
[231]Tillich, "Protestantische Vision," 7.
[232]Tillich, *The New Being*, 90.

sense we are all authorities for one another."[233]

There are three levels of justice in Tillich's understanding: (1) "the intrinsic claims for justice of everything which has being . . . raised silently or vocally by a being on the basis of its power of being";[234] (2) tributive forms of justice which are calculating and proportional, granting what is determined to be the justice due to a person or thing;[235] and (3) transforming or creative justice.[236] There are four principles of justice: adequacy; equality (acknowledging the equal dignity of each person); personality (which prohibits treating people like things); and liberty ("political and cultural self-determination").[237] Justice, for Tillich, necessarily went beyond strict, calculating, proportional justice to creative, productive or transformative justice. Proportional justice is that which is calculated to be a person's due. Productive or creative justice is dependent upon love (the reunion of that which belongs together and is separated).[238] Tillich spoke of the ultimate meaning of justice as "creative justice, and creative justice is the form of reuniting love."[239] It is rooted in forgiveness.[240] Forgiveness manifests love to be the principle of justice.[241] Tillich argued:

Only love can transform calculating justice into creative justice. Love makes justice just. Justice without love is always injustice because it does not do justice to the other one, nor to oneself, nor to the situation in which we meet. For the other one and I and we together in this moment in this place are a unique

---

[233]Tillich, "Die Philosophie der Macht," 223.
[234]Tillich, Love, Power, and Justice, 63.
[235]Tillich, Love, Power, and Justice, 63-64.
[236]Tillich, Love, Power, and Justice, 64-66.
[237]Tillich, Love, Power, and Justice, 57, 58, 59-60, 61.
[238]Tillich, "Die Philosophie der Macht," 221.
[239]Tillich, Love, Power, and Justice, 71.
[240]"[N]othing greater can happen to a human being than that he is forgiven. For forgiveness means reconciliation in spite of estrangement; it means reunion in spite of hostility; it means acceptance of those who are unacceptable, and means reception of those who are rejected." Tillich, The New Being, 7-8. "Forgiveness is an answer, the divine answer, to the question implied in our existence." The New Being, 9. "But genuine forgiveness is participation, reunion overcoming the powers of estrangement" The New Being, 10.
[241]Tillich, Love, Power, and Justice, 71.

unrepeatable occasion, calling for a unique unrepeatable act of uniting love.[242]

Injustice is not a matter of the superiority of one person's power of being over another's. "Injustice occurs in the moment in which the inner claim, which every single essence has through that which it essentially is, is overlooked or denied and its potential for being is reduced or destroyed."[243] Nationalism is innately unjust: "Nationalism denies justice and is afraid of the prophetic attack on its consecration of injustice. This explains the weakness of the resistance Protestantism showed against the Nazis and the almost complete lack of criticism of their attempt to eradicate the Jewish people."[244] Thus, rather than centered action in which love, power, and justice coalesce in a humanizing, life-giving way, untrammeled power crushed human beings.

With this understanding of the Tillichian triumvirate of love, power, and justice in hand, I now turn to Tillich's approach to action apt for the cold war context. To face the historical vacuum, Tillich argued that Christianity must combine expectation with action. On the one hand, Tillich confessed, "I see a vacuum . . . ,"[245] and "my own personal feeling is that today we live in a period in which the Kairos, the right time of realization, lies far ahead of us in the invisible future, and a void, an unfulfilled space, a vacuum surrounds us."[246] On the other hand, the position of waiting meant active waiting. He believed that all peoples are rooted in a center that "serves to orient its philosophy of history and posits its beginning and its end."[247] He wrote, "An integrated state of society is one in which creative forces are held in balance by the power of an embracing and determining principle."[248] He admonished his coreligionists, "Christianity has the power of resistance against paganism only if it is rooted in the message of the divine paradox, namely that Jesus is the Christ."[249] Therefore, rejecting inward, utilitarian, or escapist patterns in Christianity,[250] Tillich built upon

[242]Tillich, *The New Being*, 32.

[243]Tillich, "Die Philosophie der Macht," 222.

[244]Tillich, "Jewish Influences on Contemporary Christian Theology," 41-42.

[245]Tillich, "Beyond Religious Socialism," 733.

[246]Tillich, "Critique and Justification of Utopia," 180.

[247]Tillich, "Historical and Unhistorical Thinking," 152.

[248]Tillich, "The Disintegration of Society in Christian Countries," 53.

[249]Tillich, "World War II and the Younger Churches," 10.

[250]Tillich, "The Present World Situation," 18, 19.

that stream of his tradition that embraced existence and called for Christianity to proclaim Christ as the absolute center of meaning and "the center of all centers."[251] It points to the divine in its symbolism.[252] It seeks connection to the ground through ritual.[253] Its moral and social actions are touched by the transformative power of the absolute.[254] It takes depth psychology's goal of connecting people to "their subconscious vitality" to the next step of connection to the absolute, in order to have centered personalities.[255] And it asserts the necessity of a "church"[256]—apart from complicit "organized Christianity," or demonic "ecclesiastical, national and utopian absolutism," or culturally infertile institutions[257]—that represents "the center of meaning for the totality of life . . . the center and basis of all creative life," that is the core of transformative revolutionary movements,[258] and that is, therefore, composed of "venturing individuals or groups . . . able today to carry the revolutionary movements towards a new, centered or theonomous world-structure."[259]

Venturing Courage. Just as Augustine called for "a courage which was born out of participation in a new reality,"[260] Tillich summoned forth courage to face estrangement. In summarizing the message of his book, *The Courage to Be,* he spoke of offering courage in the face of existential Angst, "But a very special kind of courage. . . . Not the courage of the soldier but the courage of the human being who feels all the riddles and all the meaninglessness of life and who is nevertheless able to say 'yes' to life."[261] When true to its identity, the church's most adequate answers to reality's

---

[251]Tillich, "The Present World Situation," 21-22, 22-23.

[252]Tillich, "The Present World Situation," 23.

[253]Tillich, "The Present World Situation," 24.

[254]Tillich, "The Present World Situation," 24.

[255]Tillich, "The Present World Situation," 25.

[256]Tillich, "The Present World Situation," 25, 26.

[257]Tillich, "The Present World Situation," 26, 27, 28.

[258]Tillich, "The Present World Situation," 25, 26, 27.

[259]Tillich, "The Present World Situation," 28.

[260]Tillich, "Protestanische Vision," 4.

[261]Paul Tillich, "Paul Tillich: Interview with Werner Rode" (1955) Andover-Harvard Library Microfilm 281, PTAH, bMS 621, p. 165. See also Paul Tillich, "Human Fulfillment," in *Search for America,* ed. Huston Smith (Englewood Cliffs NJ: Prentice-Hall, 1959) 164-74, on the courage to face the anxieties of existence.

questions are both "the good news of the conquest of the law by the appearance of a new healing reality . . . [arising from] the ground and meaning of our existence and of existence generally,"[262] as well as prophetic criticism against the demonic.[263]

Tillich attempted to embody this centered, venturing courage in concrete ways. I will now consider how he practiced this in relationship to six issues: the Jewish question; personhood versus patternization; the nuclear question and the Berlin crisis; the Cuban missile crisis; the papal encyclical, *Pacem in Terris*; and interreligious community.

Applying this to the healing of German crimes against the Jews and the continuing presence of anti-Semitism, Tillich stated the necessity for courage on the Germans' part to do the following: assume responsibility without distractions over guilt and punishment—"If one were able to apply the concepts of depth psychology to groups, one would say that the German people must undergo a collective analysis that would raise up the past into consciousness"[264]; embrace sober judgment over against arrogant overreaction; and reintegrate Germany into Western civilization.[265] On the other hand, the rest of the world had to combine proportionate justice with creative justice in its treatment of the Germans, enabling the reunion of parties separated by injustice, a reunion that neither forgets the violation nor considers it settled: creative justice and remembering reunion.[266]

While sparse in detailed instruction with regard to collectivism and conformity, Tillich called both the East and the West, first, to make any "new collectivism a humanized one and to prevent its antihuman form,"[267] and, second, to take action against mass conformity that smothers individual spontaneity.[268] He saw hope for resistance to patternization in the boredom among the masses that motivated their manipulators to innovate, in the artistic exposure of patternization, and in "the spirit of rebellion which . . . is the courage to say yes to one's birthright as a unique, free, and

---

[262]Tillich, "Aspects of a Religious Analysis of Culture," 49, 50.
[263]Tillich, "Aspects of a Religious Analysis of Culture," 51.
[264]Tillich, "The Jewish Question," 21, 22.
[265]Tillich, "The Jewish Question," 22.
[266]Tillich, "The Jewish Question," 5-6.
[267]Tillich, "The Revolutionary Character of the Struggle," 1-2.
[268]Paul Tillich, "Man Against Mass Society" (1955) PTAH, 409:001.

responsible individual."[269]

Asked to comment on the development of the hydrogen-cobalt bomb, Tillich shared these thoughts: (1) its development awakens the notion than humankind may be destroyed through its own devices rather than by "a cosmic event"; (2) history's meaning is independent of its actual end and is beyond history;[270] (3) the eternal dimension of life and history call for humankind's unrelenting struggle "against man's suicidal instincts";[271] (4) this struggle must be conducted at all levels; and (5) this struggle "must be done in acts which unite the religious, moral, and political concern, and which are performed in imaginative wisdom and courage."[272]

For a discussion with Secretary of State Dean Rusk, Max Freedman, future Secretary of State Henry Kissinger, and journalist James Reston on Eleanor Roosevelt's television program, "Prospects for Mankind," Tillich constructed seven theses regarding the Berlin crisis of 1961. First, political decision is rooted in ethics.[273] Second, social ethics is rooted in creative justice, "a justice whose final aim is the preservation or restitution of a community of social groups, subnational or supranational."[274] Third, steps toward creative justice must be conducive to that goal.[275] Fourth, war is only justifiable as an instrument of creative justice. Fifth, atomic warfare is inconsistent with creative justice. Sixth, given the preceding theses, certain consequences necessarily follow: self-defense and defense of those who

---

[269]Tillich, "Conformity," 149.

[270]Paul Tillich, "The Hydrogen-Cobalt Bomb," Symposium in a Special Issue of *Pulpit Digest* (Great Neck NY) 34/194 (June 1954): 32.

[271]Tillich, "The Hydrogen-Cobalt Bomb," 32, 34.

[272]Tillich, "The Hydrogen-Cobalt Bomb," 34. See also Helmut Thielicke, "Christians and the Prevention of War in an Atomic Age," in *Religion and Culture: Essays in Honor of Paul Tillich*, ed. Walter Leibrecht, 335-40 (New York: Harper & Row, 1959).

[273]Paul Tillich, "Seven Theses concerning the Nuclear Dilemma" in *The Spiritual Situation in Our Technical Society* (Macon GA: Mercer University Press, 1988) 197. Originally published as "Contribution to 'The Nuclear Dilemma' Discussion," *Christianity and Crisis* 11/19 (1961): 203-204. See also the reprint of this piece as "The Ethical Problem of the Berlin Situation," in *Theology of Peace*, ed. Ronald H. Stone (Louisville: Westminster/John Knox Press, 1990) 160-61. See PTAH 905A:003 for further details of this panel discussion.

[274]"Seven Theses," 197.

[275]"Seven Theses," 197.

share the threat is ethically required; the impotency of conventional weapons does not lift the prohibition against the use of atomic weaponry, defensive or otherwise; the possession of atomic weapons is permitted as a message to the other side regarding the potential consequences of a first use of atomic weapons by the other side; no first use of atomic weapons is permitted; and should this mean withdrawal from territory, this is a tolerable short term consequence. Seventh, the distinction between conventional and atomic weapons is crucial. Again, no first use of atomic weapons is permissible.[276] Tillich saw the first use of nuclear weapons as unethical, because "Its result is mutual destruction and neither the preservation of freedom nor the victory of Communism."[277]

Tillich joined several other academics and church leaders in responding to the Cuban missile crisis in 1962. Together they appealed to "resolution and courage" rather than "rash or reckless" action.[278] They believed in unwavering "determination to defend freedom," but admonished that "we must never act so as to defeat the very ideals we seek to defend . . . [acting] not for prestige but for the principles on which our nation was founded."[279] Therefore, they argued that no military steps would be appropriate without exhausting all possible routes of negotiation.[280]

In response to the papal encyclical, *Pacem in Terris*, Tillich gathered thoughts on realism and peace. He appreciated the commitment to justice expressed in the encyclical.[281] However, he made several points that reveal his judgment that the document was utopian. To its call for the defense of human dignity, Tillich noted that there are cultures in which this is not a first concern and that, therefore, freedom and equality would be of little significance to these cultures. To the encyclical's call for resistance to those who attack human dignity, Tillich questioned the assumption that such a

[276]"Seven Theses," 198.

[277]Paul Tillich, "The Cold War and the Future of the West" (1962) PTAH 518:004, 1.

[278]Paul Tillich, John C. Bennett, Jerald C. Brauer, Angus Dun, Samuel Miller, Reinhold Niebuhr, and Francis Sayre, "The Cuban Missile Crisis: A Joint Statement" (1962) PTAH 522:021.

[279]Tillich et al., "The Cuban Missile Crisis: A Joint Statement" (1962).

[280]Tillich et al., "The Cuban Missile Crisis: A Joint Statement" (1962).

[281]Paul Tillich, "On 'Peace on Earth' " (1965) *Theology of Peace*, ed. Ronald H. Stone (Louisville: Westminster/John Knox Press, 1990) 174.

path was unambiguous.[282] Tillich believed that power, correctly understood, had to be taken more seriously in questions of peace than the encyclical did.[283] Further, he warned that the personification—and the call to moral accountability—of groups carries with it the fallacy of equating the moral agency of an individual with that of a group.[284] He questioned the encyclical's appeal to "men of good will." Rather, it should have been understood as an appeal to people in whom good and evil are mixed.[285] In addition to this series of criticisms, Tillich offered constructive alternatives to the document's utopianism, what he believed to be an antiutopian basis for hope to address both the ambiguities of technological progress and the destructive realities of the age atomic weapons and totalitarianism.[286] He pointed to what he saw as the true seeds for peace into the future: (1) a sense of common destiny—the ambiguous fact of "a community of fear" under the atomic shadow; (2) the world-shaking impact of technology which increases hostility, but which can also dissipate both the sense of the strangeness of the other and the perception of danger; (3) growth in cross-national and cross-cultural cooperation and collaboration; (4) the limited, but present, structure of legal accountability internationally;[287] and, finally, (5) the reality of intermittent successes. Tillich wrote, "we cannot hope for a final stage of justice and peace within history; but we can hope for partial victories over the forces of evil in a particular moment of time."[288]

Beyond the ecumenical discussions illustrated by Tillich's thoughts on *Pacem . . .* , Tillich engaged in interreligious work,[289] making an effort to understand those religions with whom he believed Christianity shared "the moving depth" of the divine. Tillich came to speak of the Ground of Being

---

[282]Tillich, "On 'Peace on Earth' " (1965) 175.
[283]Tillich, "On 'Peace on Earth' " (1965) 176.
[284]Tillich, "On 'Peace on Earth' " (1965) 177.
[285]Tillich, "On 'Peace on Earth' " (1965) 177.
[286]Tillich, "On 'Peace on Earth' " (1965) 179.
[287]Tillich, "On 'Peace on Earth' " (1965) 179-80.
[288]Tillich, "On 'Peace on Earth' " (1965) 181.
[289]On Tillich's approach to other religions, see Geffré, "Paul Tillich and the Future of Interreligious Ecumenism"; Kitagawa, "Tillich, Kraemer, and the Encounter of Religions"; Takeuchi, "Buddhism and Existentialism"; and Thomas, Terence, "On Another Boundary: Tillich's Encounter with World Religions."

as the God transcending theism[290] or the God above God:

> Absolute faith, or the state of being grasped by the God beyond God, is not a state which appears beside other states of the mind. It never is something separated and definite, an event which could be isolated and described. It is always a movement in, with, and under other states of mind. It is the situation on the boundary of man's possibilities. It *is* this boundary. Therefore it is both the courage of despair and the courage in and above every courage. It is not a place where one can live, it is without the safety of words and concepts, it is without a name, a church, a cult, a theology. But it is moving in the depth of all of them. It is the power of being, in which they participate and of which they are fragmentary expressions.[291]

Tillich valued his relationship with Martin Buber personally and profession-ally.[292] His papers reveal his interest in Islam.[293] He saw both his trip to Japan in 1960 and his collaboration with religious historian Mircea Eliade on a course in comparative religion at the University of Chicago as important ways to broaden his perspective. Of the Eliade partnership he wrote, "Nothing is better for overcoming every theological provincialism."[294]

His most important effort in interreligious thinking was his book, *Christianity and the Encounter of the World Religions*. In this short book, Tillich gave particular attention to what he designated quasi-religions and to a comparison of Christianity to Buddhism. In fact, he saw the primary interreligious encounter of the early 1960s as that between religion and the quasi-religions of fascism and communism.[295] He made the provocative

---

[290]Tillich, "Christianity and the Problem of Existence," 33.

[291]Tillich, *The Courage to Be*, 188-89.

[292]Tillich, "Martin Buber and Christian Thought," 199.

[293]Paul Tillich, "Notes from a Book about Islam" (early 1960s) PTAH 545:001; Paul Tillich, "Notes on Islam" (early 1960s) PTAH 422:018; and Paul Tillich, "The Relationship Between Islam and Christianity" (early 1960s) PTAH 422:019, 4.

[294]Paul Tillich, "Rundbrief" (1964) PTAH 802:055, 2.

[295]Tillich, *Christianity and the Encounter of the World Religions*, 5-6, 12, 15. lectures in this book were originally delivered at Columbia University in 1961 as the fourteenth in the series known as the Bampton Lectures in America. See also Tillich, "Dialogues East and West: Conversations between Dr. Paul Tillich and Dr. Hismatsu Shin'ichi," in *The Encounter of Religions and Quasi-Religions*, ed. Terence Thomas, Toronto Studies in Theology 37 (Lewiston NY: Edwin Mellen,

judgment that liberal humanism did not rise to the status of quasi-religion with the potency to defend against communism or fascism, unless it defied its own tenets to be successful.[296]

Setting the context for his discussion of the Buddhism-Christianity comparison, Tillich observed that Christianity's historic relationship to other religions had alternated between tolerance and rejection, with the dominant pattern being exclusivist intolerance.[297] He saw himself as approaching non-Christian religions dialectically, the "union of acceptance and rejection, with all the tensions, uncertainties, and changes which such dialectics implies."[298] His dynamic typology for interpreting religion isolated "type-determining elements."[299] To assemble these elements in a way that enabled interreligious understanding, Tillich posed four presuppositions: (1) "both partners acknowledge the value of the other's religious conviction"; (2) "each of them is able to represent his own religious basis with conviction"; (3) "common ground . . . makes both dialogue and conflicts possible"; and (4) "openness of both sides to criticisms directed against their own religious basis."[300] With these ground rules in mind, he compared Christianity's and Buddhism's treatment of the purpose of each religion, their "valuation[s] of existence," their approaches to the holy, and their anthropologies.[301]

The soundness of Tillich's interpretation of Buddhism has been roundly challenged. What is important here is Tillich's interpretation of Christianity's mindset as it enters into interreligious dialogue. For Tillich, criteria for assessing itself, other religions, and quasi religions had to be rooted in "the appearance and reception of Jesus of Nazareth as the Christ," in whom particularity was sacrificed on behalf of the universal, freeing "his image from bondage both to a particular religion . . . and to the religious sphere as such; the principle of love in him embraces the cosmos, including

---

1990) 5-141.

[296]Tillich, *Christianity and the Encounter of the World Religions*, 9-10.

[297]Tillich, *Christianity and the Encounter of the World Religions*, 32-33, 34-36, 37-38, 44.

[298]Tillich, *Christianity and the Encounter of the World Religions*, 30.

[299]Tillich, *Christianity and the Encounter of the World Religions*, 57.

[300]Tillich, *Christianity and the Encounter of the World Religions*, 62.

[301]Tillich, *Christianity and the Encounter of the World Religions*, 63-71.

both the religious and the secular spheres."[302] Therefore, the criteria at which he arrived were these: "particular yet free from particularity"; and "religious yet free from religion."[303]

With these two criteria in hand, Christianity could be shaped by other religious streams, gaining (as examples) a wider sense of the presence of the holy from polytheism, the criticism of its cultural flaws from Judaism, a broader knowledge of the non-West from Islam, a deeper sense of evil from Zoroastrianism, and a greater understanding of the transpersonal and personal dimensions of the holy from the religions of India.[304]

Tillich believed that these possibilities should lead Christianity to seek dialogue rather than conversion, gaining the insight that in every religion, "that to which it points breaks through its particularity, elevating it to spiritual freedom and with it to a vision of the spiritual presence in other expressions of the ultimate meaning of man's existence."[305]

Conclusion

The final stage in Tillich's life and intellectual output proved him to be the continued practitioner of the boundary perspective. Many earlier themes were maintained. However, the disappointments of the post-World War II order and the descent of the atomic age upon history led Tillich to take older themes more deeply and to discover new ones responsive to the existential needs of the age. The postwar fate of Germany, the existence of the state of Israel and its relation to the lives of the Jewish people, the stifling bipolarity of the Cold War international structure, the oppressive distortion of Marx's thought (particularly in Russian communism), and the increasing power of humanity's capacity for destruction through the development of ever more powerful nuclear weapons were specific issues to which Tillich applied his thinking in this last period of his life and career.

As a consequence, the following are the elements of an ethic of religious internationalism that can be derived from the period.

1. International action must not contradict the values upon which just democracies are built;
2. Courageous, venturing risk is necessary for creative international

---

[302]Tillich, *Christianity and the Encounter of the World Religions*, 81-82.
[303]Tillich, *Christianity and the Encounter of the World Religions*, 82.
[304]Tillich, *Christianity and the Encounter of the World Religions*, 85-89.
[305]Tillich, *Christianity and the Encounter of the World Religions*, 95, 97.

relationships;

3. A sense of historical timing to be able to assess whether a moment or period is a kairos or an a-kairos should be developed;

4. A spirit of utopia—versus utopianism—is necessary to risk decisive action at moments of kairos;

5. Serious, self-aware, self-critical, open and receptive cross-cultural dialogue, involving the regular crossing of cultural boundaries, reduces the ignorance of the cultures on the other side of those boundaries;

6. A nation's knowledge of the limits of its cultural and national identity prevents it from intruding upon other national and cultural identities; and

7. Creative justice that bears love, appropriately trammels power, and maintains an antiauthoritarian bias must be sought.

Chapter 7

Religious Internationalism: Ethics of War and Peace

Construction

Paul Tillich took specific intellectual paths in his analysis of matters of war and peace during each of the five periods of his work. I have attempted to distill elements of his thought from each period that I have judged to be relevant to ethical international behavior. My next task will be to assemble those elements into the ethic of war and peace termed here religious internationalism. I will use Tillich's approach to ethics in general as the framework within which to present his ethics of religious internationalism in particular. Following this, I will assess Tillich's approach and apply it to current issues displaying the relationship of religion and culture to international relations.

Tillich's Ethics: Ethical Theory and Moral Act. Tillich argued that religion and morality were inseparable: "the relation of religion and morality is not an external one . . . morality is religious in its very essence."[1] Ethics was inextricably embedded within Tillich's existentialist theological discourse: "The ethical element is a necessary—and often predominant—element in every theological statement" given that "the doctrines of finitude and existence . . . are equally ontological and ethical in character."[2] Here, Tillich's general approach to ethics will be briefly outlined, primarily using one of his last books, *Morality and Beyond*.[3]

---

[1]Tillich, *ST I*, 31. In 1963, John E. Smith wrote, "American Protestantism has moved back and forth between the extremes of a sentimental piety and a social liberalism; there have been few attempts to hold a genuinely ethical and well-grounded theology related to both personal and social life. Tillich has tried to show the intimate connections between theology and the religious life; he has been unwilling to accept a divorce between the two." (John E. Smith, "Paul Tillich," in *Thirteen for Christ*, ed. Melville Harcourt [New York: Sheed and Ward, 1963] 79.)

[2]Tillich, *ST I*, 31.

[3]Paul Tillich, *Morality and Beyond* (New York: Harper and Row, 1963; repr. Louisville: Westminster/John Knox Press, 1995). As with several other books by Tillich, it is one whose chapters come from different periods. The first three

In arguing for its religious basis, Tillich called the moral imperative "the command to become what one potentially [or essentially] is, a *person* within a community of persons . . . a completely centered self, having himself as a self in the face of a world to which he belongs and from which he is, at the same time, separated."[4] It is the religious imperative, "the silent

---

chapters—"The Religious Dimension of the Moral Imperative," "The Religious Source of the Moral Demands," and "The Religious Element in Moral Motivation"—were written near the time of the book's publication in 1963. The fourth and fifth chapters were published in the 1948 *The Protestant Era* (another collection of writings from different periods) but had their first publications in 1945 (chapter 4, "The Transmoral Conscience") and 1941 (chapter 5, "Ethics in a Changing World"). Tillich gave attention to the general theme of ethics (versus ethical discourses on particular issues) on several other occasions: a 1948 lecture for Göttingen and Berlin, „Ethische Normen und geschichtliche Relativität" (the typewritten German manuscript is in the Harvard Tillich Archive, PTAH 202:002); a chapter entitled "Moralisms and Morality: Theonomous Ethics," written for a 1955 book edited by Iago Galdston (*Ministry and Medicine in Human Relations*) and reprinted in Tillich's *Theology of Culture*; a 1957 lecture published in 1959 as "Is a Science of Human Values Possible?"; a March 1960 lecture for the Brandeis Lawyers' Guild in Philadelphia, "The Ambiguities of the Moral Law" (for which there are handwritten notes in the Harvard Archive, PTAH 403A:017); a 1962 lecture series in Texas, "Problems of Christian Ethics," for which there are merely sparse notes for the first of four lectures (PTAH 403A:024); and a 1962 lecture not published until 1987 as "Ethical Principles of Moral Action," both of which will be cited below. (See Paul Tillich, "Is a Science of Human Values Possible?" in *New Knowledge in Human Values*, ed. Abraham H. Maslow [New York: Harper & Brothers, 1959] 189-96; and Paul Tillich, "Ethical Principles of Moral Action (1959)," Appendix to *Being and Doing: Paul Tillich as Ethicist*, ed. John J. Carey [Macon, Ga.: Mercer University Press, 1987] 205-17.)

[4]Tillich, *Morality and Beyond*, 19. See also Tillich, *The Courage to Be*, 54; Tillich, *My Search for Absolutes*, 95; and Tillich, *ST III*, 38-44, 157-61, 266-75. In "Is a Science of Human Values Possible?" Tillich argued against the philosophy of values in insisting that human values cannot be derived from existence (via pragmatism) but that they can be derived from the essential structures of being, from the essential nature of humanity. (See Tillich, "Is a Science of Human Values Possible?") Konrad Glöckner has examined Tillich's ethics as an expression of his theological understanding of personhood. See Glöckner, "Personenhaftes Sein." Glenn Graber has argued that Tillich's ethics are materialistic (having a content arising out of humanity's essential nature) rather than formalistic (consistent with

voice of our own being which denies us the right to self-destruction," that is, "the awareness of our belonging to a dimension which transcends our own finite freedom and our ability to affirm or negate ourselves," an awareness which possesses an "unconditional character . . . [which] is its religious quality."[5] The unconditional moral imperative is embodied in, and imposed by, conditioned moral authorities. These are social and institutional authorities interpreted by the conscience in enabling a person to negotiate his or her way to becoming what he or she essentially is. Because of this, "every moral act includes a risk . . . True morality is a morality of risk. It is a morality which is based on the 'courage to be,' the dynamic self-affirmation of man as man."[6] Sometime later Tillich wrote, "In the smallest decisions you make in your classes, or in your homes, or wherever it may be, there is the same problem of ethical decision which is found in the crudeness of the cavemen; you are not better than they."[7] Tillich saw the unwillingness to risk decision to be beyond the tragic: "if there were not people of this character who take this risk, then our culture would come to

---

Kant's understanding of moral principles as formally categorical or unconditional). Terence O'Keeffe has added the subtlety that while Graber has correctly characterized Tillich's American period, he has not acknowledged the shift from his German period (of formalism) to his American period (of materialism). See Glenn Graber, "The Metaethics of Paul Tillich," in *Being and Doing: Paul Tillich as Ethicist*, ed. John J. Carey (Macon, Ga.: Mercer University Press, 1987) 32ff. and Terence O'Keeffe, "The Metaethics of Paul Tillich: Further Reflections," in *Being and Doing: Paul Tillich as Ethicist*, ed. John J. Carey (Macon, Ga.: Mercer University Press, 1987) 57-58, 66-67. Louis Midgely questions Tillich's success in grounding his "science of values" in ontology. See Midgley, "Politics and Ultimate Concern." As noted previously, in citing sources from the Paul Tillich Archive at Harvard, I will use the notation created by Erdmann Sturm: the acronym PTAH designating the Paul Tillich Archive at Harvard; the first number designating the box number; and the number following the colon designating the file number within the box.

[5]Tillich, *Morality and Beyond*, 25. See also Tillich, „Die Philosophie der Macht," 218 and Tillich, "The Christian Message and the Moral Law: Three Lectures (1957)," PTAH 403:027, 29-31.

[6]Paul Tillich, "Moralisms and Morality: Theonomous Ethics (1952)," in *Theology of Culture* (New York: Oxford University Press, 1959) 140, 141.

[7]Tillich, "The Decline and the Validity of the Idea of Progress," 72.

a miserable standstill and end."[8] Tillich posited the religious basis for moral "demands" as "love under the domination of its *agape* quality."[9] This love is to be unified "with the imperative of justice to acknowledge every being with personal potential as a person."[10] To do this, it is to be "guided by the divine-human wisdom embodied in the moral laws of the past, listening to the concrete situation, and acting courageously on the basis of these principles."[11] Such love-rooted, wisdom-guided decisions have the potential to "transform the given tables of laws into something more adequate for our situation as a whole as well as for innumerable individual situations."[12]

---

[8]Paul Tillich, "Grounds for Moral Choice in a Pluralistic Society (1963)," PTAH 403:030, 13.

[9]Tillich, *Morality and Beyond*, 46.

[10]Tillich, *Morality and Beyond*, 46.

[11]Tillich, *Morality and Beyond*, 46. This same framework—(1) love as ultimate principle, (2) wisdom derived from religious, national, and societal law, through which one interprets how to (3) embody love in the concrete situation—arises in the lecture from the same period, "Ethical Principles of Moral Action." Joseph Fletcher argued that Tillich's thought supported Fletcher's situation ethics. Fletcher quoted Tillich's *My Search for Absolutes* to support this claim: "Let us suppose that a student comes to me faced with a difficult moral decision. In counseling him I don't quote the Ten Commandments, or the words of Jesus in the Sermon on the Mount, or any other law, not even a law of general humanistic ethics. Instead, I tell him to find out what the command of *agape* in his situation is, and then decide for it even if traditions and conventions stand against his decision." (Fletcher, "Tillich and Ethics: The Negation of Law": 36.) Fletcher also cited conversations with Tiullich in which he gleaned Tillich's ethical theory: "He would say that we move from *agape*, the imperative, through the *sophia*, general principles, to the *kairos*, the concrete decision. In this way 'love is the principle of ethics' and '*kairos* is the means of its embodiment in concrete contents.'" It is a bit startling that Fletcher saw the changing situation as the priority in these instances, when Tillich clearly made a constant—love—the guiding principle. On negotiating ethics in pluralistic societies, see Tillich, "Grounds for Moral Choice in a Pluralistic Society (1963)," 9-10, 12.

[12]Tillich, *Morality and Beyond*, 46. See also Tillich, "The Christian Message and the Moral Law: Three Lectures," PTAH 403:027, 8; Paul Tillich, *Problems of Christian Ethics: 4 Lectures*, "First Lecture: Basic Considerations. Job and Vocation (1962)," PTAH, 403:024, 2-3; Paul Tillich, "Second Lecture: Sex-Relations, Love and Marriage (1962);" Tillich, "Grounds for Moral Choice in a Pluralistic Society," 7; Tillich, *ST I*, 280-82; and Tillich, *ST III*, 129-38, 177ff, and 272ff.

Tillich designated grace as the theological motive for moral behavior. He declared, "it is not the moral imperative in its commanding majesty and strangeness that is morally motivating, but the driving or attracting power of that which is the goal of the moral command—the good."[13] To establish an even tighter connection between grace and motivation, Tillich turned to the *eros* quality of love: "*Eros* is a divine-human power. It cannot be produced at will. It has the character of *charis, gratia,* 'grace'—that which is given without prior merit and makes graceful [the one] to whom it is given."[14] Tillich wrote about this at a later point in this way: "He who makes a moral decision . . . and doesn't prefer the security of following moral convention . . . which is of course a questionable security . . . he risks to fall into error and guilt . . . And he must have in himself the certainty that there is a power of forgiveness, overarching all that we do and making possible for us to decide without anxiety about falling into error, but with courage to risk it . . . And perhaps by doing so, become representatives of a deeper understanding of man and his relationship to others."[15]

Tillich weighed the contributions of philosophy and theology to the discussion of human conscience and was led to call for a "transmoral conscience." Revealing the influences of both his Christian tradition as well as an analytic psychotherapy to which he was sympathetic, Tillich described the transmoral conscience as a transcendence characterized "by the acceptance of the divine grace that breaks through the realm of law and creates a joyful conscience," as well as "by the acceptance of one's own conflicts when looking at them and suffering under their ugliness without an attempt to suppress them and to hide them from oneself."[16]

Tillich noted that moral living is life concretizing ethics in a world of change, ethics as "the expression of the ways in which love embodies itself, and life is maintained and sustained."[17] Tillich tied his thoughts to his interpretation of *kairos* as an inspired "sense of timing" which characterizes historic, prophetic figures. Connecting *kairos* to his interpretations of the nature of *agape* and *eros*, Tillich wrote, "Love, realizing itself from *kairos* to *kairos,* creates an ethics that is beyond the alternatives of absolute and

---

[13]Tillich, *Morality and Beyond,* 60.

[14]Tillich, *Morality and Beyond,* 61.

[15]Tillich, "Grounds for Moral Choice in a Pluralistic Society," 8.

[16]Tillich, *Morality and Beyond,* 81.

[17]Tillich, *Morality and Beyond,* 95.

relative ethics."[18]

Therefore, the elements of Tillich's approach to ethical theory and moral action from *Morality and Beyond* are these:

(1) The moral act is the embodiment of one's essential—transcendent and religious—nature in personhood;

(2) The movement is from (a) the principle of agape, through (b) the wisdom found in the moral laws of the past, to (c) courageous decision in the concrete situation;

(3) The divine-human power of love as eros is the grace-based drive toward the good: grace stimulates gracious or grace-bearing action;

(4) This law-overwhelming grace enables humanity to confront brokenness; and

(5) The embodiment of love occurs amidst change, from *kairos* to *kairos*.

The specific ethics of religious internationalism can be placed within the general framework of Tillich's ethics by rooting the "religious" part in humanity's essential nature, the agape principle, wisdom, and grace-eros, and then by anchoring the "internationalism" part in courageous decision, grace-borne confrontation of brokenness, and constructive and well-timed agape-love. Thus, as religious internationalism unfolds within the thought of Paul Tillich, it shows itself to be (1) founded upon a handful of religious "givens," (2) propelled to face certain perpetual problems, and (3) led along specific routes to remedy these problems. Here it is argued that the religious givens for Tillich were religion per se, power, and history (particularly culture and economics). The problems that an internationalism fueled by religion must confront are idolatry and nationalism on the one hand and ideology and injustice on the other hand. The constructive work of religious internationalism involves the dialectically dynamic boundary perspective, the promulgation of an agapeic-kairotic ethics, and the concrete manifestation of love and justice.

Religious Internationalism Embraces Religion, Power, and History. In religious internationalism, religion grounds and subjects all things to a transcendent, ultimate source of meaning which is characterized by depth. It is

---

[18]Tillich, *Morality and Beyond*, 90. See also Tillich, "The Ethical Teachings of Lutheranism (late 1940s)," PTAH 403:019, 16, 19-20; Tillich, "Moralisms and Morality: Theonomous Ethics," 135, 136, 137; and Tillich, "The Ambiguities of the Moral Law," 10.

the criticism of spiritual superficiality in both the "sacred" and "secular" realms. As a consequence, it is the basis for ecumenical, interreligious, ideological openness. It enables creative criticism of that which is unloving, unjust, and destructive in the self or the other to occur. It empowers creative participation in history. It inspires the pursuit of world transformation. Religion calls autonomy to acknowledge its theonomous depth, empowering autonomy's rejection of heteronomy.[19]

Power has ontological significance for religious internationalism. It is a morally neutral reality that is the creative force and supportive element behind and within existence. Everything that is has some lesser or greater degree of power. In the political realm, the bearers and institutions of power assert power claims to carry out policies. Some of these assertions have the potential to bring about justice. Others carry the perpetual risks of cultivating political idolatry and/or exploiting the vulnerable.

By taking existence seriously, religious internationalism takes history seriously. Culture and economics are of particular significance to it. The state of a nation's cultural health directly affects its decisions regarding war and peace. People choose between various alternatives. They can embrace the creative or the destructive streams within their respective cultures. They can practice critical thought in an unrelenting way or passively accept prevailing currents. They can be reverent toward human beings or engage in dehumanization. They can embody human dignity expressed in democracy and free decision or bow to authoritarian subjection. Healthy cultures cultivate dynamics with a trajectory toward being with dignity. Such cultures fight against the dehumanizing, Hobbesian Leviathans of history intranationally and internationally. This requires that they know their limits, reject exclusivist claims to power and truth, and practice ongoing, self-aware boundary crossing that leads to "cultural interpenetration and cross-fertilization."

Economics both transcends and is immersed within cultures. It is a central gauge for measuring a nation's cultural health. For religious inter-

---

[19]Glenn Graber believes that Tillich wrongly rejects the possibility of an heteronomous ethics with the assumption that "outside powers are barred from pronouncing principles truly based on man's essential nature." See Graber, "The Metaethics of Paul Tillich," 39. David Novak offers a helpful discussion of Tillich's theonomous ethics, particularly in relationship to analytic philosophy, Judaism, and natural law. See Novak, "Theonomous Ethics": 436-63.

nationalism, this includes a socioeconomic justice which takes seriously the economic structures of society, working toward economic security as a basis for creative freedom.

Religious Internationalism Confronts Idolatry and Ideology. Two of the most intransigent and perplexing problems facing decisions on war and peace are idolatry and ideology. For religious internationalism, penultimate views that claim divine authority—that make claims alleging ultimacy, but that contradict the norms of love and justice—are either idolatrous or irreligious. Cultures have vulnerabilities to idolatry which must be unveiled and confronted. Perhaps the most destructive form of this idolatry is power worship. The form of power worship posing the greatest danger to the world's peace is nationalism.

As the deceptive cloak for falsehood, ideology is another significant difficulty faced by any ethics of war and peace. Religious internationalism calls for a wary attentiveness to ideology, whether in the ideological manipulation of capitalism in the western political and economic system, the ideological bastardization of Marx in communism, or the ideological distortion of the institutions and doctrines of religion. Ideology can become a powerful basis for injustice against the poor and powerless.

Both idolatry and ideology involve the reign of a heteronomy that violates theonomously rooted human autonomy. Religious internationalism, as expressed in the Protestant principle, is both critical and creative. Biblical prophecy gives it its primal source of legitimacy. Its critical function is to hold all human claims up to unyielding scrutiny, bearing the "suspicion of ideology" against all holders and institutions of power, gauging the justice of socioeconomic structures, and measuring all truth claims—including those involving culture and politics (as a subset of culture)—by the standards of love and justice.

War results from idolatrous power claims, the ideological corruption of culture, or a combination of the two, according to religious internationalism.

Religious Internationalism Practices Ethics and Justice from the Boundary. The constructive work of religious internationalism is based upon a boundary perspective from which to exercise well-timed agapeic moral action leading to justice. The perspective most conducive to a truthful interpretation of history is the dynamic boundary.[20] From the boundary it

---

[20]Roger Shinn argues for the centrality of the boundary for Tillich's ethics. See Roger Shinn, "Tension and Unity in the Ethics of Paul Tillich," in *Being and*

is possible to have greater clarity with regard to any given situation, to have dynamic openness to the future, to new understandings, and to new applications of traditional, past formulations. It embodies self-transcending realism ("believing realism") and rises above a sacred-secular or holy-profane distinction by seeing all realms of existence as potentially ripe for creative, theonomous activity. Religious internationalism must be cultivated by groups of intellectuals motivated to "contend for personality and community," willing to approach the boundaries of their disciplines, ready to engage in the practice of dialectical thinking.

In religious internationalism, moral action is consistent with a *kairos*, working in "creative agreement with the historical situation," cognizant of the dynamic, ever-changing, and potentially creative historical circumstances. It involves a sense of timing for historically fruitful action. This points to the significance of periods of *kairos* as well as to the distinction between *kairotic* and a-*kairotic* periods. In the flow of history, there is power as the primal force which enables being (historical existence), and there is the demonic, i.e., power destructively divorced from the creatively ordering dynamics of history. A *kairos* is a moment or period ripe for creative action as against demonic distortion. It is these *kairotically* opportune periods for just and loving action (the *kairoi* of history) to which participants in history can attune their actions for maximum creative impact.[21] It

---

Doing: Paul Tillich as Ethicist, ed. John J. Carey (Macon, Ga.: Mercer University Press, 1987) 10-11.

[21]By characterizing Tillich's understanding of Protestantism as only prophetic critique, Peter Slater forgets Tillich's attempt to speak to the formative impact of Protestantism. More than this, in arguing for the necessity of ritualizing forgiveness—set times for acknowledging *kairos*—Slater needlessly diminishes as "business as usual" acts of justice and love and forgiveness which are repeated opportunities to experience the fullness of time. Perhaps it is an expression of the perpetual sacramental-ethical tension within Christianity for Roman Catholic thought to assume that "the logical and psychological effect of declaring every moment a time for forgiveness is to make no specific moment *that* time," while Protestant thought revels in embodying continuous action in response to continuous—though not constant—and repeated moments of "*that* time." See Slater, "The Relevance of Tillich's Concept . . . ," 50, 51. In this context, perhaps Ronald Stone's statement is apt: "Tillich was primarily a theoretician of practice." (Stone, *Paul Tillich's Radical Social Thought*, 156.)

requires a readiness for courageous, creative, decisive, and venturing risk. In other words, religious internationalism practices "agapeic-kairotic" ethics. Moral behavior embraces "world," affirms human dignity, advocates active participation in history, and is rooted in "the beyond self and world."

As stated above, and as guided by the Protestant principle, religious internationalism measures all truth claims by the standards of love and justice.[22] Love and justice require that the self-world correlation be kept in balance, rejecting both arrogant imposition of *self* as well as the crushing domination by *world*, cultivating new possibilities for community through creative justice. It seeks justice for the vulnerable. It stands against injustice and hatred, including the unjust, space-bound, and dehumanizing provincialisms of nationalism, racism, and capitalism. It demands that democracy act according to its noblest principles. It pursues social transformation leading to being with dignity. It supports political resistance when resisters are allies of justice, "instruments of the moral, constructive world order, and not of the immoral, destructive world order."[23] It rejects the destructive idolatry of power worship. It rejects group stereotype as wrong, whether practiced by international criminals or the formal bearers of international justice. The love-and-justice-forged-Protestant principle works toward national identities committed to international community. Its

----

[22]Jerome Arthur Stone has examined the notion of responsibility as rooted in rational thought (using Gert and Gewirth) or experience (Tillich and Maguire). He has argued that Tillich's use of *agape*, in which "listening, giving, and forgiving are unlimited in character" can be strengthened and accepted as a persuasive basis for moral action in moral philosophy by emphasizing *agape*'s strong connection to the cultivation of personhood and by conceding that personhood can be understood in a naturalistic rather than a transcendent (or religious) way. (Jerome A. Stone, "A Tillichian Contribution to Contemporary Moral Philosophy: The Unconditional Element in the Content of the Moral Imperative," in *Being and Doing: Paul Tillich as Ethicist*, ed. John J. Carey (Macon, Ga.: Mercer University Press, 1987) 72, 85. Peter Slater notes that Tillich "explicitly subordinated justice to love, interpreting justice by reference to conceptions of natural law and love as the absolute demand for *agape* in the *kairos* or time of fulfillment." (Slater, "The Relevance of Tillich's Concept . . . " 50.)

[23]Informed by Tillich's formulation of love, power, and justice, Ronald Stone argues that the twenty-first century places before humankind the challenge to resist four demonic trends: "fundamentalism, violence, greed, and domination." (Ronald Stone, "The Religious Situation and Resistance in 2001," 57.)

members have equal integrity, meaning the just balancing of claims of nations in the international arena and, thus, world unity rather than isolated nationalism and tribalism. Religious internationalism affirms international organization, looks on national sovereignty with deep suspicion, and pursues regional federations that enable international accountability to be practicable. It calls nations to accept responsibility for the behavior of their national leaders, including the crimes of their leaders. It is committed to addressing the dehumanizing, Hobbesian Leviathans of history that operate at a level transcending nations. Religious internationalism is informed by the teaching of Genesis 12 that nations are to be the vehicles for international blessing.

In the end, peace arises among just societies brought about through weaving together the countless strands of well-timed actions of justice along the trajectory towards human dignity. These actions are taken only after considered deliberation from the perspective most conducive to truth, the boundary.

Critique

One may seek to fight back the religious language and confessional perspective within which Paul Tillich couched his thought on these matters of war and peace. One may regret some of the limitations of his arguments. One may suggest that the material possesses a soundness which remains after the apparent theological shell has been removed. However, for Tillich, theology and confessional standpoint and religious orientation formed the life blood of his thought. Perhaps his best known expression of that fact is this: "Religion as ultimate concern is the meaning-giving substance of culture, and culture is the totality of forms in which the basic concern of religion expresses itself. In abbreviation: religion is the substance of culture, culture is the form of religion."[24] What this means is that Tillich's writing is innately religious and that it is almost redundant to append adjectives making this explicit: when Tillich wrote or spoke, religion was implicitly present. Further, for the purpose of assessing his contribution to international relations, I will use his own definition of religion ("meaning-giving substance") as a way to prevent the term "religion" from being a barrier. The discussion will even go so far as to question occasions in which

---

[24]Tillich, *Theology of Culture*, 42.

Tillich's use of terminology similar to this (i.e., theonomy, theonomous, Protestant, etc.) may have been an unnecessary barrier.

Here, my comments in critique of the religious internationalism constructed in the previous pages will surround these issues: the boundary; culture and meaning-giving substance; kairos and ethics; "world," Marx, and capitalism; the Jewish people; and contemporary relevance.

The Boundary: Boundary Theologian and Boundary Crosser. In his later years, Tillich must have grimaced as he read some of the words he penned as an army chaplain, unabashedly proclaiming Germany as Christ's righteous sword in a world sinfully directing its power against the German Empire. The pre-World War I and World War I period were ones in which Tillich was occupied with academic training and held his first church positions. He was an inexperienced young man who later characterized himself as living his life and carrying out his ministry in a way consistent with the values of his culture. Obedience to authority was the norm for him. As a chaplain, he preached sermons consistent with this norm. These sermons were intended to comfort the soldiers amidst the stresses of war. However, they go further. They present a consistently nationalistic perspective.

At the same time, at least according to Tillich's own accounts, his superiors were not always pleased with the content of his theology and sermonizing. In later years, he spoke of one officer who criticized him for a theology that was too liberal[25] and asserted that a number of superiors admonished him for not cultivating sufficient patriotism among the soldiers through his preaching.[26] There does not seem to be independent documentation of these incidents. Thus, we are left with the content of his public sermons and his private correspondence. In these we see a tension between private thoughts which were growing in radicality and public preaching that maintained the conservative, imperial values of the government and that manifested no apparent growth in political perspective during the course of the war. This unquestioning consent manifested a perspective strikingly inconsistent with his later thought.

Further, Tillich's military career molded his views on the inescapable reality of power in several general ways. Positively, it often kept him from

---

[25]Pauck, *Paul Tillich*, 50.
[26]MacLennan, "World War I and Paul Tillich," 5; Ratschow, *Paul Tillich*, 17; Tillich, *GW XIII*, 71.

being utopian and Pollyannaish about the motives and capabilities of power holders. It remained a strength of his political theory that power had foundational import. Negatively, Tillich was impressed by power. During the First World War, this made him vulnerable to mouthing the uncritical endorsements of his government's policies cited above which slid over into idolatry: in sum, he displayed a nationalism with clearly idolatrous traits. In his case, it was a clear German chauvinism which used theological arguments to raise the nation to the level of the divine. The impressiveness of power made him vulnerable to manipulation by power holders and the promulgators of that chauvinism. That he shared this trait with many of his generation in and outside of Germany highlights that it was a characteristic of that period. However, this fact neither excuses the characteristic nor denies the significant continuing strength and danger of nationalistic chauvinism into the twenty-first century.

Tillich's nationalism can be attributed to the personalistic piety he practiced at the time which produced a spirituality of inwardness that served as a barrier to the consideration of broader questions. His life at this point illustrated the correspondence between theological and spiritual inwardness and the passive toleration of government policy: government was left with no theologically rooted moral check on its behavior. Therefore, his life at the time showed the consequences of the silence of the stewards of religious ethics and—by its absence—confirmed the necessity to persistently question government policies, tenaciously weighing the arguments posed for their execution.

At the same time, it is significant that there were points at which Tillich followed lines of reflection which could have saved him from the closed perspective of those war years. His thoughts on the obligation to love brother and to become reconciled with enemies prior to sharing the Eucharist could have been broadened to a more universal scope. His rejection of personal hatred for enemy soldiers in favor of commitment to one's cause could have become the theological basis against self-righteous nationalism. Schelling taught him that humanity's moral sensibility should be broadened to something closer to "the greatness of the divine," yet Tillich's ethical framework remained imprisoned in the provincial, not yet liberated through transcendence.

Therefore, the period first functions as a negative example for international thought. It illustrates that provincial cultural and theological ideology are conducive to passive submission to power, including powers that can be prone to war. Once again, circumstances of the twenty-first century reveal that this is a perpetual danger with which justice must cope. Secondly, and perhaps more importantly, this period effectively threw Tillich onto the boundary. He was sent to the actual boundary of his nation in the war. He was driven to the boundary of sanity by the destructive experiences of war and his duty to salve the impact of that destruction upon others. He was driven to question the bounds of a traditional, personalistic bourgeois ethic by his first wife's adultery while he was away at war, including her conception of two children to a friend. He saw himself to be forced from an academic perspective separated by traditional boundaries from the rest of existence. And he was driven beyond the bounds of a conservative, inwardly looking political perspective to one saturated in social and cultural concern.

As painful as the transition was for Tillich, and as troubling as the documents are to read with the benefit of historical distance, they present another feature of the practice of international relations that can make it more truthful: the practice of transcending one's culture in order to see broader truths. Post-World War I, Tillich sought to make this transcendence core to his approach. In contrast to this are present-day approaches, like that of the late Samuel Huntington, which cultivate intercultural hostility on the one hand, while white-washing the history of his own country on the other hand.[27] This makes evident the continuing importance of this work. Tillich not only became a theologian of the boundary but was forced to become a boundary crosser as an immigrant. The example he set through his thought—between 1933 and 1945—showed a person unwilling to tolerate the self-righteousness of a nation which had become his safe haven. He was also greatly moved by the story of the great biblical immigrant, Abram, and the divine command to Abram in Genesis 12 to bring about a nation with the mission to become a blessing on behalf of all the peoples of the world. This is an important insight for immigration and border policy in a world much more closely intertwined, economically, than in Tillich's day. At the least, it calls the international relations discipline to question the justice of any nation's policies with regard to their impact upon the populations of

---

[27]Huntington, "The Clash of Civilizations? (1993)"; Huntington, *The Clash of Civilizations and the Remaking of World Order* (1996); and Samuel P. Huntington, *Who Are We? The Challenges to America's National Identity* (New York: Simon & Schuster, 2004).

other nations. Even if "blessed" is unpalatable to the discipline, "just" should not be.

Culture and Meaning-Giving Substance. The experience of World War I and the German revolution transformed Tillich from an antisocialist into a religious socialist. The church's significance for him changed as well. It became both smaller and larger in its significance for him. No longer simply the bearer, protector, and embodiment of a restricted set of Christian doctrine and values, the church became but one part of the cultural reality which served as the outer form of the deeper substance of religion. The church was one element of religiously understood reality, part of a project far broader in scope than Tillich had formerly believed, the project of seeking out the depth of that religious reality in all spheres of existence. From the boundary perspective, no sphere of reality was out of bounds.

Liberated from nationalism, Tillich interpreted existence as a theologian of culture. His example in this offered a way to release subsequent theologians of culture from being intellectually and institutionally bounded in two senses. First, as an existentialist in the broadest sense of the word, the theologian of culture is responsible for directing his or her ultimate concern toward all of existence, rather than merely one sphere of it. The thought-work of a theologian of culture is not restricted to traditional doctrinal questions but is, in theory, infinite in the scope of questions for which it can provide answers. This fact not only permits, but even requires, dialogue with practitioners of areas of study beyond the traditional theological realm. Second, the cultural theologian is unrestricted by boundaries as a thinker on the boundary. The boundary perspective is intended to be an intellectual location, a location from which to transcend existence in order to see existence better. Tillich made this clear in specifying it as a perspective from which to theorize as opposed to a place in which to live.

War drove Tillich into cultural analysis. The implication is that for him a nation's culture determines its bases for considering the prospect of war. His indictment against post-Enlightenment western civilization is that autonomous reason had misled humankind into the arrogant presumption that educational progress would bring about universal harmony. It minimized the significance of power and the unjust and unloving use of power. Tillich's solution was theonomy and the depth-giving dimension of theonomy. Secular theorists may find this as an unnecessary leap to take. However, if theonomy is translated from living God-consciously into living meaningfully (consistent with Tillich's previously stated definition of religion), it can become a less divisive call to living with a sense of depth.

For instance, the autonomous perspective need not be equated with arrogant overestimation of human possibilities or blindness to human limits, as Tillich wrote of autonomy, i.e., as devoid of "meaning giving substance." There is a broader range of possibilities for defining autonomy. Considering its most basic meaning, autonomy (combining the Greek words αυτός, or "self," and νόμος, or "law") is the "law of the self." Obviously, the content of that law can be the subject of endless debates over the plethora of views regarding what it fundamentally means to be human. Among the numerous possibilities, it is imaginable that many of these would include some rendition of human imperfection, for example, "part of what is means to be human is to be imperfect and vulnerable to error." This is a meaningful statement calling for humility. Another element of the law of the human self may be the view that peace is the result of societies in which justice is sought and love is a significant presence. For adherents of religious groups, God may be centrally related to this. They may argue that their experience of human existence compels them to believe that any definition of autonomy requires the inclusion of an acknowledgement of God with whom human beings should be ultimately concerned and a theonomy as the root of the yearning for justice and love. However, it is possible to conceive of human beings who have been the victims of the deepest injustice and most cruel hatred and who are driven to renounce all faith in God and "theonomy," yet as a consequence of the most nightmarish experiences are provoked to demand that love and justice be seen as central to the "law of the self," i.e., it provides part of the meaning giving substance of their lives. Thus, there are both theistic and nontheistic ways to transcend the expectations of harmonious utopias in existence and to acknowledge the inescapability of oppression and hatred. Adequate autonomies with apparently penultimate concerns can reach for the same goal. Tillich's "meaning giving substance" as a goal for policy can carry weight in both secular and religious approaches thereto.

Tillich's formulation of the Protestant principle provides another way to consider the matter. One is led to this question: does an affirmation of the centrality of justice and love require the Pauline doctrine of justification by grace through faith? Further, conceding—for the sake of argument—the necessity of this doctrine (which is shared by Christianity at large), does this successfully argue for the priority of Protestantism over Roman Catholicism or Eastern Orthodoxy in the face of the perpetual violation of justice and love by Christians of all stripes over the two millennia of its existence?

The affirmation of Paul's doctrine of justification by faith is not a necessary move to make in order to assemble principles consistent with a culture with meaning giving substance. One can see this by comparing the list of assertions assembled as Tillich's Protestant principles in chapter 5 to a version of them assembled without the confessional bias.

Protestant Principles	Principles of Meaning-Giving Substance
1. God's unchallengeable authority over truth and the rejection of absolute truth claims by humanity	1. The rejection of absolute claims by humanity
2. The rejection of Catholicism's reduction of divine immanence to hierarchical authority	2. The rejection of hierarchical power
3. The rejection of Protestant ethical rigidity, doctrinal rigidity, and hypercritical spirit, as well as the Protestant endorsement of secular individualism, absent spiritual depth	3. The rejection of ethical rigidity, a hypercritical spirit, and individualism
4. The rejection of the secular-sacred distinction; divine depth in all things	4. The affirmation of the inherent dignity of all things
5. Culture as legitimate without ecclesiastical authority	5. The inherent dignity and meaning of culture
6. The rejection of spiritless secularism	6. The rejection of superficiality
7. Creativity as possible in history, consistent with kairos	7. The affirmation of creative potential attuned to historical context
8. The Protestant principle of prophetic, loving critique as always relevant	8. The perpetual relevance of just, loving critique
9. Protestant ecumenism	9. The openness to dialogue among competing ideologies
10. The lay character of Protestantism	10. A limited anarchy
11. A Protestant-Catholicity cognizant of collective unconscious	11. The cognizance of the unconscious
12. A Protestant openness as a basis for interreligious relations	12. [See #9]
13. Love as the principle of unity within history	13. Love as the principle of unity within history
14. Protestant personalism that triumphs over collective	14. A personhood that trumps collectivism

responsibility	
15. A Protestant collectivism that maintains the dignity of personalities by means of a dialectical, nonutopian religious socialiam	15. Just, realistic communities that support personhood

If either the theonomous or the Protestant designation of Tillich's cultural analysis is removed, nonetheless his thought makes a significant contribution to the broader thought on international relations: a commitment to the centrality of dignified human existence is the primary characteristic of healthy cultures and is the condition undermining the possibility of war. While rooted in Tillich's peculiar engagement of the world out of his Protestant Christian tradition, it transcends Protestant Christianity. It levels the challenge to produce culture with meaning-giving substance.

Kairos and Ethics. The doctrine of kairos in Tillich's thought is a particularly difficult concept to evaluate. Kairos involves the metaphors of ripeness and maturity and timing as applied to history in general. For Tillich, it was further related to his ethical framework. To him, ethics was thought and theory regarding moral behavior. Behavior is moral when it follows the imperative to become a complete person and to promote fullness of personhood. It is the embodiment of love, informed by the wisdom of the past, but creatively and decisively enacted in a way consistent with the qualities of the moment, i.e., consistent with kairos. With experience, one can learn with a fairly high degree of accuracy when to pluck an apple or when to eat an avocado.

With experience, one can learn the moods of a partner and, as a consequence, generally determine the point at which a word would be helpful or an action would be healing. With experience, one can gain some level of mastery over the timing necessary to tell a story or a joke well or to perform a work of music persuasively. However, can this notion of timing be transferred to action within history, especially history understood from a religious standpoint?

Tillich seems to have drawn this term from the Greek Testament, in which it is used eighty-eight times. In fifty-five of these cases, kairos is used in ways relevant to Tillich's conception of it. On fourteen occasions, it refers directly to God's timing.[28] In nine places, it designates "the coming

---

[28]John 5:4 (a verse absent in the most authoritative manuscripts); Acts 1:7;

age" or "the time" or "the time of judgment."[29] At seven points, the term is found in parables in reference to harvest time or the "proper" time.[30] On thirteen occasions, it refers to the fulfillment of Jesus' time.[31] In all of these places, the actor is God. In contrast to these examples, there are five places in which kairos refers to periods when evil forces are operative.[32] At seven points, kairos characterizes human behavior: warning of the risk of bad timing;[33] calling for a timely alertness;[34] exhorting service to the kairos (a usage absent from the most authoritative manuscripts);[35] indicating that the faithful will reap at harvest time;[36] exhorting the faithful to work at an opportune time;[37] calling the faithful to make the most of the time;[38] and describing the prophetic inquiry into the time of salvation.[39]

Whether in reference to God's timing or to times dominated by evil or to conditions propitious for human action, the circumstances making a time ripe for action combine matters under the human agent's control and those beyond that control. It can be argued that the significantly larger proportion of the circumstances fall into the latter category.

Further, Tillich characterized the prophetic spirit as one possessing a sense of—even a genius for—kairos. Extensive exegetical work would be necessary to assess the degree to which the broad variety of prophetic behavior and prophetic literature (particularly from the Hebrew Testament)

3:20; 17:26; Romans 5:6; 9:9; 13:11; 1 Corinthians 4:5; 7:29; 2 Corinthians 6:2 (twice); Ephesians 1:10; 1 Thessalonians 5:1; and 1 Peter 5:6.

[29]Matthew 8:29; Mark 10:30; 1 Timothy 4:1; Hebrews 9:10; 1 Peter 1:5; 4:17; Revelation 1:3; 11:18; and 22:10.

[30]Matthew 21: 34, 41; 24:45; Mark 11:13; 12:2; Luke 12:42; and 20:10.

[31]Matthew 16:13; 26:18; Mark 1:15; 13:33; Luke 1:20; 12:56; 19:44; John 7:6, 8; 2 Thessalonians 2:6; 1 Timothy 2:6; 6:15; and Titus 1:3.

[32]Luke 4:13 (the devil); 21:24 (the Gentiles); 2 Timothy 3:1 ("distressing times"); 4:3 ("times of unfaithfulness"); and Revelation 12:12 (the devil's sense of timing).

[33]Luke 21:8.
[34]Luke 21:36.
[35]Romans 12:11.
[36]Galatians 6:9.
[37]Galatians 6:10.
[38]Colossians 4:5.
[39]1 Peter 1:11.

was in accord with all elements of Tillich's heroic treatment of prophets.[40] The specific use of the term, kairos, in the Septuagint (the Greek translation of the Hebrew text) is generally rare, rarer still in reference to the qualitative meaning of time, and never used to characterize a prophet's sense of timing.[41] Therefore, Tillich's transference of kairos to the prophetic spirit communicates his sense of the significance of those people who felt moved to offer what they took to be God's Word to a given time, people Tillich took to be attuned to the transcendent meaning of a specific period of time. This is perhaps enough to know in order to assess the relationship between Tillich's kairos doctrine to the prophetic spirit.

There is substantial merit in calling actors in history to the practice of historical-contextual awareness. This historical-contextual awareness could be defined as the continuous assessment of the conditions within oneself, within one's culture, within the world, and within history—therefore, conditions within and beyond one's control—which affect the possibilities for—and the outcomes of—decisions.

Tillich rightly drew attention to the significant factor of risk in decisions made in general and in decisions taken in light of a perceived kairos. The risk factor is inescapable, no matter how much empirical data one can muster and no matter how many intangibles one senses at the nonrational level in relation to the decision at hand. Further, it is credible to assume that there are peculiarly gifted personalities who possess such awareness to a greater degree than others. In the biblical cases cited which referred to timely human action, human agents had to be exhorted to grasp the opportunity for such action. If one goes beyond the seven examples

---

[40]There is not much ambiguity in Tillich's use of biblical prophecy. Yet, justice is not always paired with timing in the Bible. Nathan was heroic in calling King David to task for the murderous abuse of power (2 Samuel 11-12), but Nathan also functioned as a political insider and powerbroker (1 Kings 1). Alongside the universal concerns of Amos and Micah are the nationalist tones of Obadiah, Jonah, and Nahum. In each case, they offered their messages at the time they felt called to do so.

[41]Gerhard Delling, "καιρός," in *Theological Dictionary of the New Testament* 3 (Θ-K), ed. Gerhard Kittel, trans./ed., Geoffrey W. Bromiley (Grand Rapids, Michigan: Eerdmans, 1965): 458-59. Further, in the case of John the Baptist, it is the Jesus of Mark's gospel uses the occasion of John's arrest to pronounce the "fulfillment of time." It is not John who expresses this. (Mark 1:15)

cited in the Greek Testament to prophetic behavior in the Hebrew Testament, one sees Elijah and Jeremiah hesitant to bear the prophetic mantel, with God presented as pushing them to undertake the prophetic task.[42] Even the gifted personalities had to be literally inspired to act. The difficulties and flaws in Tillich's formulation of kairos are revealed in the broader scriptural bases of kairos, his own efforts to sense periods of kairos amidst the storms of the early and mid-twentieth century, as well as a certain presumptuousness about the doctrine.

The picture drawn of kairos in the Greek New Testament is different from that Tillich draws on the matter of an inherently positive moral significance which he attributes to it. In the fifty-five instances in which kairos is used in the Greek Testament to indicate qualitatively significant time, the matter of timing does not have exclusively positive moral qualification. God acts in a way to render conditions conducive for creative action in some instances. However, evil forces can also gain mastery of the ability to time when conditions are ripe for destructiveness. Further, Jesus' assessment of the right time largely surrounds his reading of the time to enter into a drama mixing good and evil. As a consequence, the moral element must be added to kairos: kairos is not accurately understood as inherently moral. Rather, moral behavior is that class of activity which is aware of the historical context and which moves in the direction of full personhood.

Turning to Tillich's own story, it becomes clear that he judged different points in history during his lifetime to be characterized either by kairos (the "fullness of time") or vacuum (the "emptiness of time") under the assumption that kairos designated time ripe for creative and just action. The problem is that he was repeatedly wrong in this judgment. At the end of the World War I and again near the end of the interwar period, Tillich judged Germany to be ripe for social democracy or for a cultural decision in favor (religious) socialism. Yet, much of the German culture seemed perpetually hostile to social democracy during the period, eventually crumbling in the face of National Socialism. Decades later, Tillich judged World War II to be a kairotic turning point toward world-wide social reconstruction and a more unified, world-wide political reorganization. In fact, the events of that period precipitated four-and-a-half decades of Cold War. Tillich judged the Cold War period to be vacuous—empty—of creative international political

---

[42]1 Kings 19; Jeremiah 1.

activity. Yet, history continued to push forward with its ambiguous mixture of steps forward in justice—for instance, the beginning of the dismantling of colonialism—and steps backward into hegemony—as seen in the behavior of superpowers turning significant parts of the world into arenas for their power struggles. Further, Tillich himself made creative forays into interreligious dialogue during this period. In doing so, he addressed a central dynamic in contemporary international relations: the religious impact upon culture and the religious motivations for policies of war and peace. This was not vacuous work, but work full of significance.

This leads to the final point on the doctrine of kairos: it is presumptuous to render any moment or period distinctively ripe for action to the exclusion of other moments or period. To do so empties these latter moments of meaning and assumes a comprehensive knowledge of history at all times and in all places which no person and no civilization can have: it is impossible to possess the existential knowledge to affirm particular periods as historically fertile for action and to reject other periods as historically barren. Tillich's Christianity led him to place Christ at the center of history. This approach raises barriers to interreligious discussion and to interreligious community, not to mention minimizing the significance of other paths of spirituality. To avoid this move need not imply a denial of the intense significance of the Christ event for Christianity. However, avoiding Christo-centrism is simply following Tillich (at his best) to the boundary where one's inner vision may well see an ongoing condition of fullness of time, rooted in a plethora of events intensely significant for different peoples, a vision experienced in unpredictable places and times by surprisingly inspired personalities.

Thus, Tillich's doctrine of kairos can be placed within two wider contexts. The first is that of human decision. This is a context which is filled with the moral ambiguity of human existence and in which both the good and the bad can become competent in reading the signs of the times. The second context is that of human spirituality untied to confessional bias. It could be summed up in Tillich's phrase, "meaning giving substance." If these two contexts are considered, Tillich's thinking provokes international thought to understand the necessity of the ongoing practice of intense historical-contextual awareness, particularly with regard to the degree that any period buttresses or undermines the meaning giving substance of human existence. It is a timely awareness filled with potential for errors and requiring cross-cultural community to mitigate ignorance and misunderstanding.

It is an awareness which is as vulnerable to evil purposes as it is to good ones.

"World": Marx, Capitalism, Globalization. Tillich's awakening to Marx during the post-World War I years began a lifelong consciousness of the importance of a just economic order. At the same time, the boundary perspective gave Tillich several insights regarding socialism. From 1918 forward, Tillich was hostile toward self-isolating individualism. However, he was significantly concerned with personhood. The self-world correlation which he eventually enunciated was an attempt to express human wholeness as a balance between the richness of human solitude and the cultural importance of human society. As a product of an authoritarian period of German history, Tillich treated socialism in a way that indicated a real shift in his thought. His socialism was not a call to submission of the person to the culture but a call to responsible social behavior and just social structures on behalf of the dignity and creativity of the person.

It is curious, however, that an intellectual who characterized himself as a thinker on the boundary rarely gave written expression to his views on movements inspired by Marx beyond the bounds of Germany. On those occasions when he did give attention to non-German movements fueled by Marxist thought, he referred (often romantically) to the Russian Revolution.[43] It was clear that Tillich shared the dissatisfaction of others with the Social Democrats during the Weimar—particularly in light of their alliances with representatives of what Tillich called political romanticism. However, as a theologian of culture, it would have made sense for him to inquire whether there were parallels between the actions, alliances, and policies of the Social Democratic Party in the German context and the Labor Party in British context, on the one hand, or socialist movements within the Swedish context, on the other hand. Such comparative work may have revealed insights to Tillich that would have given him the confidence to participate more fully in the political processes of the United States, that would have been useful for his late World War II work with the Council for a Democratic Germany, or that would have persuaded him to believe he could have a role in the reconstruction of post-World War II Germany.

Further, the boundary perspective may have led Tillich to be more

---

[43]The fact that Tillich referred to postrevolutionary Russia as Russia, rather than as the U.S.S.R. or the Soviet Union, may imply a similar romanticism.

realistic about the Soviet Union. It was certainly fair for him to disparage the ignorance of U.S. citizens regarding the difference between communism and socialism. However, Tillich was quite shocked by news of Stalin's purges of communist leaders in 1936, characterizing it as a "shattering revelation."[44] On the other hand, his Voice of America addresses—perhaps in deference to the U.S.S.R. as an ally—was silent on conditions within Soviet society. In one speech, Tillich maintained a romantic regret over the rupture of the historical relationship between Germany and "Russia": the speech is weak on the tragedy of a Germany under Hitler's sway and a Soviet Union under Stalin's iron hand. He dealt with the latter repeatedly elsewhere, but he was silent about it throughout twenty-six months of speeches.[45] In another speech, Tillich castigated Nazism's assertion of Soviet communism's atheism, arguing that the Soviets bore an "ultimate concern" as "bearers of a new justice": this was nearly six years following news of the purges.[46]

Perhaps the thought only arises from benefit of hindsight, but Tillich sounded a bit naïve in asserting the possibility of German revolutionary movements leading to societies promoting dignified human existence apart from encroachment by the Soviets from the East. Yet, given Soviet territorial demands as conditions of their initial treaty with the Nazis upon the start of World War II, Soviet aggression following such a revolution sounds like a logical expectation.

During the Cold War, Tillich finally gave full vent to his deep disappointment in the crushing of human rights in the U.S.S.R. However, he attributed Soviet communism's repression of human dignity to a hole in Marx's system, i.e., the absence of a fully developed anthropology. Once again, the boundary perspective could have provided a comparative perspective, sensitive to a cultural context more logically the basis for the failure of Marxism rather than Marxist thought. In that way, for example, Tillich would have been able to compare the New Deal social policies meant to protect U.S. citizens from an unregulated market economy with Soviet social policies.

Tillich argued for democracy as a corrective tool for other forms

---

[44]Tillich, *My Travel Diary*, 167.
[45]Tillich, *Against the Third Reich*, 42-44.
[46]Tillich, *Against the Third Reich*, 23, 24.

governance. The question is whether that formulation works. Does it work to begin with monarchy or aristocracy or oligarchy as the constitutive foundations for governance and then, secondarily, to bring in democracy as the corrective factor? Tillich was perpetually suspicious of democracy. Freedom to vote does not guarantee freedom against oppression, given the victory of an oppressor. German democracy of the 1920s was weak and led to Nazism. However, this does not argue for removing democracy as a constitutive factor in the formation of a government. In the spirit of Tillich's dialectical, boundary perspective, it makes sense to bring to the table those elements which strike prudent minds as necessary to bring into the mix of sound government, holding them in appropriate tension with one another. Some of the elements of such a government are effective instrumentalities for exercising power, democratic processes for establishing and maintaining those instrumentalities, the access of citizens to those instrumentalities, respect for human rights in the operation of those instrumentalities, and protections against the violation of those rights.

These discussions remain brimful of relevance. The new millennium still manifests the broad context of capitalist dominance in a world with a perplexing array of cross-cultural forces within a dynamic and unstable international arena. Cultural and, more specifically, economic globalization has provoked a confusing mixture of receptiveness and hostility toward wealthy nations on the part of the less wealthier ones. It is a tension based on competing economic philosophies, fueled by political manipulated religious and civilizational identities.

If Tillich's discussion of Marx and economic justice is more fully placed within his thinking on "world," his thought brings to international relations a demand for just economic systems cognizant of cultural context, aware of the factors embedded within cultures at any given time which facilitate or prevent justice. The perpetual mission then becomes the cultivation of a world community in which people are liberated for lives possessing meaning giving substance, the constitution of which requires broad, intercultural inquiry and debate.

The Jewish People: Time and Space. The Holocaust took place in the middle years of Tillich's adult life. It unavoidably marked him, given that he was a sensitive and serious person, a person of German descent, an existentialist thinker committed to the importance of history, and an adherent of the religious tradition which was used to justify the Holocaust. One senses real Angst in Tillich's struggle with issues related to the life situation of Jewish people. Yet, his argumentation strikes one as significant overcompensation that risks doing unintended injustice to Jews and limiting the more universal implications of his thought.

In *The Socialist Decision* of 1932, Tillich set the corrective function of Jewish prophetism over against the parochial and expansive threat of political romanticism. He was challenging entrenched, exclusivist cultural chauvinism. As one metaphor in the argument for justice over against oppression, the biblical example of the prophetic tradition works. As the only metaphor, it both reduces the scope of the argument and traps a human group within a metaphor.

Twenty years later in Berlin, a similar weakness arose in Tillich's lectures on the Jewish question. Here, among other matters, Tillich spoke of both the commonalities between Germans and Jews as well as the purported difficulty of Germans with "foreign" elements. While his point was the parallel he perceived in the historical experiences of Germans and Jews, Tillich seemed unaware that by posing the comparison between Germans and Jews he evoked a surely unintended questioning of the "German-ness" of the Jews. For example, while it was undeniable that German Christianity and ancient Israel each experienced reform movements (the former in the Protestant Reformation, the latter in the prophetic tradition), Tillich does not catch the subtlety that the Protestant Reformation changed nations in which both Jews and Christians were present. When Tillich condemned the German pattern of intolerance of "the foreign," he did not take time to question the whole notion of foreignness. Again, the myth of the failure of Jews to assimilate was communicated.

There is also the difficulty of Tillich's vision for the role of the Jewish people in history. In both his high expectations for modern Israel to be a nation embodying the prophetic spirit and his perpetual insistence that the Jewish people were the people of history, there is an unreasonable expectation that denies the Jewish people the right to be simply a people and nation. Once again, Tillich embraced the Jewish people as the metaphor for justice (the bearers of the prophetic spirit), for a time even to the point of rejecting the option of a Jewish nation. When he conceded the necessity of the existence of the state of Israel, he advocated it seriously, but also saw it as a concession to the average Jewish person not ready for their historical role. In the end, one begs Tillich simply to permit Jews to be considered as mere human beings and to allow the state of Israel to be a nation among the community of nations.

When Tillich's thoughts on the Jewish question are released from the space/time preoccupation, his contributions to international and cultural thought here become more apparent. International relations occur among nations in which the political dynamics involve the dialectical balance between old "truths" and new possibilities, between status quo and innovation, and between cultural institutions and the demand for justice. Further, in the act of balancing, minorities are vulnerable to exploitation and destruction. It is the task of all nations to protect their vulnerable minorities as they pursue the goal of promoting ways of life possessing meaning giving substance.

Contemporary Relevance. This critique has considered these issues that have arisen in the discussion of Paul Tillich's ethics of war and peace: the boundary; culture and meaning-giving substance; the historical-contextual awareness of one's own nation or of a hostile nation or of a potentially hostile nation, and the relation of this awareness to just policies; international economics and its relation to a just world order; and the vulnerability of unprotected minorities. All of these issues are relevant in varying degrees to policy discussions at the beginning of the twenty-first century.

The boundary perspective and boundary consciousness could aid the United States in its economic policy toward the rest of the Americas. It could help the United States more honestly assess its corporate and governmental development policies. It could lead the U.S. to more compassionately respond to the understandable attraction of its immense wealth to the poor of Latin America and the consequent legal and illegal immigration of Latin Americans into the United States.

Intra- and international clashes all over the world attest to the relationship of religion to politics. There are a plethora of ways within and among nations that the religious search—the pursuit of the meaning-giving substance of life—impinges on governmental policy. Among the contexts in which this has occurred in recent memory are these: Palestinian and Israeli relations; the war between pro- and anti-Taliban forces in Afghanistan; clashes between Pakistan and India; France and Germany in relation to Islamic immigrant workers; the political culture-wars of the United States; post-Saddam Hussein Iraq's efforts to build a nation dealing justly with Shiites, Sunnis, and Kurds; and clashes between Myanmar's military dictatorship and Buddhist monks at home and natural-disaster responders abroad. Tillich's approach teaches that efforts to bring about peace within cultures and among cultures requires a far thicker knowledge of cultures, and a far deeper and more respectful awareness of the historical-context than governments generally achieve. The nature of the United States government's war and post-invasion policy in Iraq exemplifies the consequences of thin knowledge, just as it did in Vietnam. The issue of accountability to the world-at-large informs the controversies over the policies of the United States there as well as Iran's approach to its nuclear energy program. The decision of the former to go to war and the decision of the latter to develop its uranium enrichment capacity were made in contradiction to world opinion. Both decisions traded the cultivation of the meaning-giving substance of the populations involved for the expansion of their power. There is at least some level of hypocrisy that would permit either government to comment on the other's decision.

Finally, Rwanda in the last decade of the previous millennium and Darfur in the first decade of the present millennium attest to the continuing depravity of power without morality in dehumanizing and murdering vulnerable people and the necessity for the powerful to cultivate the world's character and muster the world's conscience to protect them: it is difficult to defend the meaning-giving substance of life, unless nations and peoples are first willing to defend life itself.

Because of his willingness to ponder these sorts of issues, and because the world continues to face the perplexing problems they pose, the thought of Paul Tillich remains a relevant source of thought in international relations.

Conclusion

Paul Tillich wrote and thought on issues of culture and conflict, war and peace for most of his life. Those strands of thought can be woven together to form the fabric of an ethic of war and peace that is appropriately called religious internationalism. The lines of thought I have highlighted here are derived directly from Tillich's deep experience of existence.

To be grasped by the religious dimension meant for Tillich that nothing within existence had ultimate import. Therefore, all is open to question. No nation can make claims and no leader can set policy with the assumption that they will not be questioned. If nations and leaders are attuned to the religious dimension, the questioning of others is neither resented nor disdained, but is seen as a path toward truth and towards the goal of a just society: religiously informed leaders are grateful for the truth-seeking dialectics of debate. Tillich was nurtured from birth within the confines of the Prussian Lutheran Church. Yet, he came to find liberation in the ongoing dialogue with atheists and agnostics, scientists and rationalists, and positivists and pragmatists, because his search was for ultimate meaning. To him all of reality is transparent—or, at least, translucent—for the divine.[1] This confused, and continues to confuse, some of his fellow Christian adherents and would lead to antagonism with religious and nonreligious people unable or unwilling to take the culturally and interculturally comprehensive path he took.

Tillich was driven to the boundary. The German Empire sent had him to the geographic boundary to fight in World War I. There he would be driven to the boundary of sanity on at least two occasions. But he was also forced to the boundary between worker and aristocrat that launched him to the spiritual and intellectual boundary following the war. Collaborations of different kinds and research projects on different topics along this dynamic boundary would open him up to insights from sources beyond those of traditional theology. Hitler would throw him beyond the bounds of Germany, compelling him to navigate existence in a new land as immigrant, refugee, and, ultimately, citizen. It was a position of risk but also great fruitfulness. Yet, it was open to controversy. Tillich's positions on a humane, healing postwar structure for Germany and Europe, his continued embrace of religious socialism (as distinct from its distortion within Russian

---

[1] *Theology of Culture*, 43.

communism), his stand against the use–particularly the first use–of nuclear weapons all placed him in tension with the prevailing winds of policy of his day. Nonetheless, they were positions that showed him to be unwilling to cave in to views with which he disagreed and which clamored for endorsement on either side his boundary position.

Life taught Paul Tillich about the riddles of *kairos* and vacuum. He firmly believed that the post-World War I period was a time of *kairos*. He deeply hoped that the close of World War II would provide for a *kairos* in Europe, his former homeland, and the world as a whole. Yet, he never held these positions in any strict or rigid way. Rather than a promise of perfect fulfillment, a *kairos* was a time that summoned people to fruitful, strategic action, with no guarantees for the outcome. While the Cold War was a period characterized by particularly strong bipolarity, it is an interesting question whether Tillich was justified in calling even this period an *a-kairos*. Such a period may not strike one as possessing a necessarily strong ripeness for action, but that may be because of either lack of data or the reality that it is not ripe for action in one's own part of the world. The liberation of the colonial empires of Europe in the decades following the war exemplified the great ambiguity of attempts to read the times. To the degree that Africa and Asia experienced liberation, it was fullness of time for historical action. To the degree that the great powers acted in a way to abort liberation and evolution, the descent of a historical vacuum could be considered justified. One would suspect that Tillich would have accepted such a position as pointing to the ambiguity of history: it is neither totally kairotic nor totally a-kairotic.

The affirmation of life and its dynamism was central to Tillich's political thinking. The image of his reading *Thus Spake Zarathustra* in the woods of the French countryside during World War I as well as the reality of mental breakdowns pointed to a will that refused to see war–the apex of estranging human action--as truth-bearing and affirmed it as the depth of human tragedy, not to be embraced and only to be entered when all else failed. This life affirmation was also, of course, power affirmation. Tillich clearly saw pacifism as a combination of the prophetic and the utopian. It is prophetic in calling humanity from the powerful temptation of war. It is utopian in refusing to face the demonic rising up against the innocent who will die, absent the action of those who stand for just, humane existence. Love cannot bear its fruit without the power of being necessary to manifest itself. Power is potent and dangerous. Power is not evil. However, the challenges of competing powers of being means that fulfillment will always be fragmentary. Justice will always be under threat. Institutions of world organization will always have to struggle against the demonically parochial and to see their gains significantly mitigated by the parochial. Peace will be broken by the destructive streams of injustice borne by nations and non-governmental entities which will have to be fought by those bearing the cause of creative justice. In short, the religious internationalism of Paul Tillich was existentially realistic.

Prophetic criticism resulted from two God-given phenomena: humanity's capacity to think and humanity's courage to act upon its thought. Tillich saw it as Protestantism's contribution to the modern period. That designation is probably not a helpful one in ecumenical, interreligious and interideological discourse. However, the defense and exaltation of the human being's capacity and responsibility to think combined with the freedom to act is central to what it means to have human dignity. This is at the heart of Tillich's approach to political action and theory. It represents the nonutopian side of classical liberalism which he valued. It also reveals the reason he saw the structure of economic systems as a crucial point of inquiry and Marx's criticism of capitalism's dehumanizing processes as one with the prophetic tradition of scripture: justice and creative freedom cry out for existence in the lives of human beings.

In raising Protestantism as the bearer of the prophetic spirit beginning with the Christian Reformation, Tillich affirmed the centrality of history in his thought. Both the affirmation of life and the enunciation of prophetic criticism raise the call for the action of free people within the confines of history. History matters. Religious people often forget this. Religion is not escape from history, but the dialectic of transcending and actively reentering history through now inspired participation in history. In religious internationalism, the transcending move is away from the perpetual temptation to exalt the historical to ultimacy. The religious-transcendent side of the dialectic bears continuous questions against everything within existence. Religious nationalism is always blasphemous and idolatrous. Religious internationalism is a move in the right direction, never wholly devoid of the temptation of idolatry within existence, but always bearing a fragment of self- and nation-denying justice.

The biographer of Tillich's Harvard years, Grace Cali, tells of a conversation with him about his practice of the centuries old German tradition of trimming the Christmas tree with lit candles. Thinking of the wariness of

Americans to this tradition as well as the cautiousness of his students, Tillich commented, "I have never seen such slavery to security and the avoidance of all risks such as I find among the young Americans. Where is the love of adventure? . . . So many of the students just out of college seek jobs without risks and with only questions about retirement plans, fringe benefits–and all at the age of twenty-two!"[2] Tillich had been tempered by dangers to his life on the battlefield, threats to his career in choosing socialism, and consequences for his life, career and family for his stand against National Socialism. To him, courageous decision moved history forward. Cowardly indecision severs the lifeline to dreams, to cultures, and to the future. Courageous, venturing decisiveness articulates the reconciling and life-giving power of creative justice, giving hope to the innocent and the guilty: it inspires dreams, deepens cultures, builds the future. Tillich's probes into interreligious dialogue were a later example of that risk taking and of self and communal transcendence.

Indian-born film maker Mira Nair, commenting on the impact of the September 11, 2001 attacks on the United States, spoke of the resulting impact upon the world and the consequent responsibility for creative people, in her case, a film artist:

> Now, in this post-9/11 world where the schisms of the world are being cemented into huge walls between one belief and way of life and another, now more than ever–I feel–we need cinema to reveal our tiny local worlds in all their glorious particularity. In my limited experience [it's when film has] done full-blown justice to the truths and idiosyncracies of the specifically local that it crosses over to be surprisingly universal."[3]

These words capture the mission of all creative people, and they express the constructive approach of religious internationalism in Paul Tillich's thought: by attempting to do "full-blown justice to the truths and idiosyncracies" of his own approach to the world, he expressed a way to think that turns out to be surprising in its universality.

---

[2]Grace Cali, *Paul Tillich First-Hand: A Memoir of the Harvard Years* (Chicago: Exploration Press, 1996) 58.
[3]Mira Nair, "Bollywood Meets Hollywood," *The Arts, Creativity and the Common Good* at the Westminster Town Hall Forum, Minnesota Public Radio's "Midday with Gary Eichten," Thursday, 22 September 2005, hour 2, <http://news.minnesota.publicradio.org/programs/midday/listings/md20050919.shtml>.

Bibliography

Primary Sources by Paul Tillich

In citing sources found at the Paul Tillich Archive of the Harvard-Andover Library at Harvard Divinity School, the notation created by Erdmann Sturm is used: the acronym PTAH designates the Paul Tillich Archive at Harvard; the first number (occasionally followed by a letter) designates the box number; and the number following the colon designates the file number within the box.

"Address at the Commemoration of the University of Marburg." 1948. PTAH 206:037.

Against the Third Reich: Paul Tillich's Wartime Radio Broadcasts into Nazi Germany. 1942–1944. Translated by Matthew Lon Weaver. Louisville: Westminster/John Knox Press, 1998.

"The Ambiguities of the Moral Law." 1960. PTAH 403A:017.

An meine deutschen Freunde: Die politischen Reden Paul Tillichs während des Zweiten Weltkriegs über die "Stimme Amerikas" [1942–1944]. vol. 3 of *Ergänzungs- und Nachlassbände zu den Gesammelten Werken von Paul Tillich*. Stuttgart: Evangelisches Verlagswerk, 1973.

"Aspects of a Religious Analysis of Culture." *Theology of Culture*, 40-51. London: Oxford University Press, 1959. First published in *World Christian Education* (2nd quarter, 1956).

"The Attack of Dialectical Materialism on Christianity." *Student World* (Geneva) 31/2 (2nd quarter, 1938): 115-25.

"Author's Introduction." *The Protestant Era*, ix-xxix. Chicago: University of Chicago Press, 1948.

"Autobiographical Reflections." In *The Theology of Paul Tillich*, ed. Charles W. Kegley and Robert W. Bretall, 3-21. New York: Macmillan, 1952.

"Basic Principles of Religious Socialism." In *Political Expectation*, ed. James Luther Adams and trans. James Luther Adams and Victor Nuovo, 58-88. New York: Harper & Row, 1971. Repr.: Macon GA: Mercer University Press, 1981. First published as "Grundlinien des Religiösen Sozialismus," *Blätter für Religiosen Sozialismus* 4/8 (1923). Also in *Christentum und Soziale Gestaltung: Frühe Schriften zum Religiöse Sozialismus*, vol. 2 of *Gesammelte Werke*, ed. Renate Albrecht, 91-119. Stuttgart: Evangelisches Verlagswerk, 1962.

"Die Bedeutung der Gesellschaftslage für das Geistesleben." Lecture at the Dresden Civil Service Academy. June 1927. In *Christentum und Soziale Gestaltung: Frühe Schriften zum Religiöse Sozialismus*, vol. 2 of *Gesammelte Werke*, ed. Renate Albrecht, 133-38. Stuttgart: Evangelisches Verlagswerk, 1962. First published in *Philosophie und Leben* 4 (1928): 153-58.

"Der Begriff des christlichen Volkes. 1. und 2. Version." Habilitation Lecture outline and text. January 1916. In *Religion, Kultur, Gesellschaft—Unveröffentlichte Texte aus der Deutschen Zeit (1908–1933), Erster Teil*, vol. 10 of *Ergänzungs- und Nachlassbände zu den Gesammelten Werken von Paul Tillich*. ed. Erdmann Sturm, 114-26. Berlin/New York: de Gruyter, 1999.

"Being and Love." In *Moral Principles of Action: Man's Ethical Imperative*, ed. Ruth Nanda Anshen, 661-72. New York: Harper & Brothers, 1952.

"Between Utopianism and Escape from History." *Colgate Rochester Divinity School Bulletin* 31/2 (1959): 32-40.

"Beyond Religious Socialism." *Christian Century* (Chicago) 66/24 (15 June 1949): 732-33.

"Beyond the Dilemma of Our Period." *The Cambridge Review* (Cambridge MA) 4 (November 1955): 209-15.

"Book Review: Alexeiev's *Die marxistische Anthropologie*." 1920s. PTAH 209:045.

"Book Review: Eildermann's *Urkommunismus und Urreligion*." 1921. PTAH 209:009.

"Book Review: The Soul of a Revolution—Fedor Stepun's, *The Russian Soul and Revolution*." *Christendom* (New York) 1/2 (Winter, 1936): 366-67.

"Book Review: Hirsch's *The Kingdom of God*." 1922. PTAH 209:017.

"Book Review: Jacques Maritain's *The Rights of Man and Natural Law*." *Religion in Life* 13/3 (Summer 1944): 465-66.

"Book Review: Karl Barth's *The Church and the Political Problem of Our Day*." 1939. PTAH 522:026.

"Book Review: Meister Eckhart. A Modern Translation made by Raymond B. Blakney." *Religion in Life*, 11/4 (Autumn 1942): 626.

"Book Review: Nicolas Berdyaev's *Slavery and Freedom*." *Theology Today* 2/1 (April 1945).

"Boundaries." Address delivered upon receiving Peace Prize of the Marketing Association of the German Book Trade in Frankfurt. 1962. In *Theology of Peace*, ed. Ronald H. Stone, 162-73. Louisville: Westminster/John Knox Press, 1990.

"Can the Jew Return to Germany." Early 1940s. PTAH 416:008.

"Catholicism and Anti-Judaism." Early 1940s. PTAH 416:009.

"The Causes of the European Situation." Early 1940s. PTAH 406A:003.

"Christentum als Ideologie." Stellungnahme zur Regierungserklärung des Kabinetts von Papen. 1932. *Impressionen und Reflexionen: Ein Lebensbild in Aufsätzen, Reden und Stellungnahmen*, vol. 13 of *Gesammelte Werke*, ed. Renate Albrecht, 179-81. Stuttgart: Evangelisches Verlagswerk, 1972.

"Christentum, Sozialismus und Nationalismus. Ein Auseinandersetzung mit der 'Marburger Erklärung' des Wingolf." In *Impressionen und Reflexionen: Ein*

Lebensbild in Aufsätzen, Reden und Stellungnahmen. vol. 13 of *Gesammelte Werke*, ed. Renate Albrecht, 161-65. Stuttgart: Evangelisches Verlagswerk, 1972. First Published in *Wingolf-Blätter* 53 (1924): 78-80.

"Christentum und Marxismus." Lecture at the Rias-Funkuniversität. 4 May 1953. In *Das Religiöse Fundament des Moralischen Handelns: Schriften zur Ethik und zum Menschenbild*, vol. 3 of *Gesammelte Werke*, ed. *Renate Albrecht, 170-77. Stuttgart: Evangelisches Verlagswerk, 1965. First published in Politische Studien* 11/119 (1960).

"Christentum und Sozialismus (II)." In *Christentum und Soziale Gestaltung: Frühe Schriften zum Religiöse Sozialismus*, vol. 2 of *Gesammelte Werke*, ed. Renate Albrecht, 21-34. Stuttgart: Evangelisches Verlagswerk, 1962. First published in *Das neue Deutschland* (Gotha) 8/6 (15 December 1919): 106-110.

"Christentum und Sozialismus. Bericht an das Konsistorium der Mark Brandenburg." 1919. In *Impressionen und Reflexionen: Ein Lebensbild in Aufsätzen, Reden und Stellungnahmen*, vol. 13 of *Gesammelte Werke*, ed. Renate Albrecht, 154-60. Stuttgart: Evangelisches Verlagswerk, 1972.

"The Christian and the Marxist View of Man." Universal Christian Council for Life and Work. December 1935. PTAH 402:017.

"Christian Basis of a Just and Durable Peace." Three Lectures for the Federal Council of Churches Commission on a Just and Durable Peace. 1943. In *Theology of Peace*, ed. Ronald H. Stone, 73-87. Louisville: Westminster/John Knox Press, 1990.

"The Christian Churches and the Emerging Social Order in Europe." *Religion in Life* (New York) 14/3 (Summer 1945): 329-39.

"Christian Criteria for Our Culture." *criterion* (New Haven) 1/1 (October 1952): 1, 3-4.

"The Christian Message and the Moral Law: Three Lectures." 1957. PTAH 403A:027.

"Christianity and Emigration." *Presbyterian Tribune* (New York) 52/3 (29 October 1936): 13, 16.

"Christianity and Modern Society." In *Political Expectation*, trans. John C. Modschiedler and Victor Nuovo, 1-9. New York: Harper & Row, 1971. Repr.: Macon GA: Mercer University Press, 1981. First published as "Das Christentum und die moderne Gesellschaft," in *Student World* (Geneva) 21/3 (July 1928): 282-290; summary, in English, 290-92. Also in *Die Religiöse Deutung der Gegenwart: Schriften zur Zeitkritik*, vol. 10 of *Gesammelte Werke Band*, ed. Renate Albrecht, 100-107. Stuttgart: Evangelisches Verlagswerk, 1968.

Christianity and the Encounter of the World Religions. New York: Columbia University Press, 1963.

"Christianity and the Problem of Existence." Three lectures delivered in Andrew Rankin Chapel, Howard University. 24 April 1951. Washington DC:

Henderson Services, 1951. Andover-Harvard Microfilm 281n, #26.

"Christianity, Democracy and the Arts." 1957. PTAH 401A:005.

"Christliche Hoffnung und ihre Wirkung in der Welt." 1960s. PTAH 204B:048.

"Das christliche Verständnis des modernen Menschen." Lecture given over the South German Radio. 19 December 1958. In *Das Religiöse Fundament des Moralischen Handelns: Schriften zur Ethik und zum Menschenbild*, vol. 3 of *Gesammelte Werke*, ed. *Renate Albrecht, 188-93. Stuttgart: Evangelisches Verlagswerk, 1965. First published in Das ist der Mensch. Beiträge der Wissenschaft zum Selbstverständnis des Menschen*. Stuttgart, 1959.

"The Church and Communism." *Religion in Life* (New York): 6/3 (Summer, 1937): 347-57.

"Church and Culture." 1924. In *The Interpretation of History*, 219-41. New York: Scribner's, 1936.

"Church and State: Lecture Two from Three Lectures at Union Seminary." 1938. PTAH 408:009.

"The Church and the Third Reich: Ten Theses." 1932. In *Paul Tillich: Theologian of the Boundaries*, ed. Mark Kline Taylor, 116-18. London: Collins, 1987.

"The Class Struggle and Religious Socialism." 1929. In *Paul Tillich on Creativity*, by Jacqueline Ann K. Kegley, 95-118. Lanham MD: University Press of America, 1989.

"The Cold War and the Future of the West." 1962. PTAH 518:004.

"Comment." In *Approaches to World Peace: Fourth Symposium*, ed. Bryson, Finkelstein, and MacIver, 684-85. New York: Harper & Bros., 1944.

"Comment on 'The Report of the Commission on a Just and Durable Peace.' " *The Witness* 26 (8 April 1943): 4.

"Communicating the Christian Message: A Question to Christian Ministers and Teachers." In *Theology of Culture*, 201-13. New York: Oxford University Press, 1959. First published in *Union Seminary Quarterly Review* 7/4 (June 1952).

"Conformity." Paper delivered at the commencement of the New School for Social Research. 1 June 1957. In *The Spiritual Situation in Our Technical Society*, 145-50. Macon GA: Mercer University Press, 1988.

"The Conquest of Intellectual Provincialism." In *Theology of Culture*, 159-76. New York: Oxford University Press, 1959. First published in *Cultural Migration*, ed. W. Rex Crawford. Philadelphia: University of Pennsylvania Press, 1952.

The Construction of the History of Religion in Schelling's Positive Philosophy: Its Presuppositions and Principles. 1910. Trans. Victor Nuovo. Lewisburg PA: Bucknell University Press, 1974.

"The Contemporary Spiritual and Moral Situation." 1946. PTAH 406A:004.

The Courage to Be. New Haven CT: Yale University Press, 1952.

"Creative Integrity in a Democratic Society." 1960. PTAH 517:006.

"The Crimea Concept and the Council." *Bulletin of the Council for a Democratic Germany* 1/4 (February 1945): 1.

"Critical and Positive Paradox: A Discussion with Karl Barth and Friedrich Gogarten." In *The Beginnings of Dialectical Theology*, trans. Keith R. Crim and ed. James M. Robinson, 133-41. Richmond VA: John Knox Press, 1968. First published as "Kritisches und positives Paradox. Ein Auseinandersetzung mit Karl Barth und Friedrich Gogarten." *Theologische Blätter* (Leipzig) 2/11 (November 1923): 263-69.

"Cuban Missile Crisis, The: A Joint Statement." 1962. (Cosigned by Paul Tillich, John C. Bennett, Jerald C. Brauer, Angus Dun, Samuel Miller, Reinhold Niebuhr, and Francis Sayre.) PTAH 522:021.

"Cultural Roots of the Present World Crisis." Late 1940s. PTAH 406A:005.

"The Cultural Situation After the Second World War." 1945. PTAH 406A:009.

"The Dangers of a Spiritual Vacuum." 1945. PTAH 406A:011.

"The Decline and the Validity of the Idea of Progress (One of the Edwin and Ruth Kennedy Lectures at Ohio University, Athens, Ohio, 19 May 1964)." In *The Future of Religions*, 64-79. Westport CT: Greenwood Press, 1966.

"Democracy and Religion." Early 1940s. PTAH 409:003.

"The Demonic: A Contribution to the Interpretation of History." In *The Interpretation of History*, trans. Elsa L. Talmey, 77-122. New York: Scribner's, 1936. First published as "Das Dämonische, ein Beitrag zur Sinndeutung der Geschichte." Tübingen: Verlag S.C.B. Mohr, 1926.

"Depth." *Christendom* (New York) 9/3 (Summer 1944): 317-25.

"Dialogues East and West: Conversations between Dr. Paul Tillich and Dr. Hismatsu Shin'ichi." In *The Encounter of Religions and Quasi-Religions*, Toronto Studies in Theology 37, ed. Terence Thomas, 5-141. Lewiston NY: Edwin Mellen Press, 1990.

"Discussion on Post-War Reconstruction in Europe." 1943. PTAH 206:033.

"The Disintegration of Society in Christian Countries." In *The Church's Witness to God's Design*, vol. 2: "The Amsterdam Assembly Series," 53-64 (New York: Harper & Brothers, 1948.)

Dynamics of Faith.. New York: Harper & Row, 1957.

"The End of the Protestant Era." *Student World* (Geneva) 30/1 (First Quarter 1937): 49-57.

"The End of the Protestant Era ?" In *The Protestant Era*, 222-33. Chicago: University of Chicago Press, 1948. First published as "Protestantism in the Present World-Situation." *American Journal of Sociology* 43/2 (1937).

"Estrangement and Reconciliation in Modern Thought." *Review of Religion* (New York) 9/1 (November 1944): 5-19.

The Eternal Now. New York: Scribner's, 1963.

"Ethical Principles of Moral Action (A Lecture Delivered at Florida State

University, 2 March 1962)." Appendix to *Being and Doing: Paul Tillich as Ethicist*, ed. John J. Carey, 205-17. Macon GA: Mercer University Press, 1987.

"The Ethical Teachings of Lutheranism." Late 1940s. PTAH 403:019.

"Ethics in a Changing World." In *The Protestant Era*, 150-60. Chicago: University of Chicago Press, 1948. First published in *Religion and the Modern World. Philadelphia: University of Pennsylvania Press, 1941.*

"*Ethische Normen und Geschichtliche Relativitat.*" 1948. PTAH 202A:002.

"*The European War and the Christian Churches.*" Direction (Darien CT) 2/8 (December 1939): 10-11.

"An Evaluation of Martin Buber: Protestant and Jewish Thought." In *Theology of Culture*, 188-99. New York: Oxford University Press, 1959. First published as "Martin Buber and Christian Thought: His Threefold Contribution to Protestantism." In *Commentary* (New York) 5/6 (June 1948): 515-21.

"Die evangelische Kirche und der Mensch der Gegenwart." Mid-1920s. PTAH 112:002.

"Existential Analyses and Religious Symbols." In *Contemporary Problems in Religion*, ed. Harold Albert Basilius, 37-55. Detroit: Wayne State University Press, 1956.

"Existentialism and Religious Socialism." In Symposium: "The Meaning of Existentialism." *Christianity and Society* (New York) 15/1 (Winter 1949–1950): 8-11.

" 'Faith' in the Jewish-Christian Tradition." *Christendom* (New York) 7/4 (Autumn 1942): 518-26.

"Feldpredigten 1914–1918." In *Frühe Predigten (1909–1918), vol. 7 of Ergänzungs- und Nachlassbände zu den Gesammelten Werken*, ed. Erdmann Sturm, 355-645. Berlin/New York: de Gruyter, 1994.

"Flight to Atheism." In *The Shaking of the Foundations*, 38-51. New York: Scribner's, 1948. First published in *The Protestant* (New York) 4/10 (February 1943): 43-48.

"The Formative Power of Protestantism." In *The Protestant Era*, 206-21. Chicago: University of Chicago Press, 1948. First published as "Das Religiöse als gestaltendes Prinzip: Protestantisches Gestaltung" in *Religiöse Verwirklichung*, 43-64. Berlin: Furche-Verag, 1930.

"Freedom and the Ultimate Concern." Lecture delivered at the Seminar on Religion and the Free Society, World Affairs Center, New York, sponsored by the Fund for the Republic. 9 May 1958. In *Religion in America: Original Essays on Religion in a Free Society*, ed. John Cogley, 272-86. Meridian Books, 1958.

"Freedom in the Period of Transformation." In *Freedom: Its Meaning*, ed. Ruth Nanda Anshen, 123-44. New York: Harcourt, Brace, 1940.

"The Freedom of Science." 1932. In *The Spiritual Situation in Our Technical Society*, ed. J. Mark Thomas, 61-64. Macon GA: Mercer University Press,

1988. First published as "Freiheit der Wissenschaft," in *Impressionen und Reflexionen: Ein Lebensbild in Aufsätzen, Reden und Stellungnahmen*, vol. 13 of *Gesammelte Werke*, ed. Renate Albrecht, 150-53. Stuttgart: Evangelisches Verlagswerk, 1972.

"Funeral Address at Pope John XXIII's Death." 1963. PTAH 415:011.

"The Future of Germany." Early 1940s. PTAH 404:007.

"Gegenwart und Religion." 1929. PTAH 206:025.

"Die gegenwärtige Krisis von Kultur und Religion." 1922. Lecture for the Kestner-Gesellschaft of Hannover. In *Religion, Kultur, Gesellschaft—Unveröffentlichte Texte aus der Deutschen Zeit (1908–1933), Erster Teil*, vol. 10 of *Ergänzungs- und Nachlassbände zu den Gesammelten Werken*, ed. Erdmann Sturm, 305-10. Berlin/New York: de Gruyter, 1999.

"Die gegenwärtige Lage des Protestantismus." Mid-1920s. PTAH 110:010.

"Die Geisteslage der Gegenwart: Ruckblick und Ausblick." 1930. In *Die Religiöse Deutung der Gegenwart: Schriften zur Zeitkritik*, vol. 10 of *Gesammelte Werke Band*, ed. Renate Albrecht, 108-20. Stuttgart: Evangelisches Verlagswerk, 1968.

"Die geistige Lage der Sozialismus." Fragments of a lecture outline. 1931. In *Religion, Kultur, Gesellschaft—Unveröffentlichte Texte aus der Deutschen Zeit (1908–1933), Zweiter Teil*, vol. 11 of *Ergänzungs- und Nachlassbände zu den Gesammelten Werken von Paul Tillich*, ed. Erdmann Sturm, 353-71. Berlin/New York: de Gruyter, 1999.

"Die Geistige Lage des Sozialismus." Late 1920s. PTAH 201:001.

"Germany Is Still Alive." *Protestant Digest* 1 (February 1939): 45-46.

"Gläubiger Realismus." Lecture delivered for the Älterentagung des Bundes deutscher Jugendvereine, Hannoversch-Münden. 9 July 1927. In *Philosophie und Schicksal: Schriften zur Erkenntnislehre und Existenzphilosphie*, vol. 4 of *Gesammelte Werke*, ed. Renate Albrecht, 77-87. Stuttgart: Evangelisches Verlagswerk, 1961. First published in *Theologen-rundbrief für den Bund deutscher Jugendvereibne e. V. Göttingen* 2 (November 1927).

"The God of History." *Christianity and Crisis* 4/7 (1 May 1944): 5-6. Also (in slightly edited form) in *The Shaking of the Foundations*, 29-33. New York: Scriber's, 1948.

"The Gospel and the State." *Crozer Quarterly* (Chester PA) 15/4 (October 1938): 251-61.

"Grounds for Moral Choice in a Pluralistic Society." 1963. PTAH 403B:030.

"Has Man's Conquest of Space Increased or Diminished His Stature?" In *The Spiritual Situation in Our Technical Society*, 185-95. Macon GA: Mercer University Press, 1988. First published in *The Great Ideas Today 1963*, ed. R. M. Hutchins & Mortimer J. Adler. Chicago: Encyclopedia Britannica, 1963.

"Historical and Nonhistorical Interpretations of History: A Comparison." Address delivered at the annual meeting of the American Theological Society, Eastern Branch. 14 April 1939. In *The Protestant Era*, 16-31. Chicago: University of Chicago Press, 1948.

"A Historical Diagnosis: Impressions of a European Trip." *Radical Religion* (New York) 1/1 (Winter 1936): 11-17.

"History as *the* Problem of Our Period." *Review of Religion* (New York) 3/3 (March 1939): 255-64.

"How Has Science in the Last Century Changed Man's View of Himself?" A Lecture for the Centennial Celebration of the Massachusetts Institute of Technology. 8 April 1961. In *The Spiritual Situation in Our Technical Society*, 77-82. Macon GA: Mercer University Press, 1988. First published in *The Current* 6/1-2 (1965).

"How Much Truth Is in Karl Marx?" *Christian Century* (Chicago) 65/36 (8 September 1948): 906-908.

"How My Mind Has Changed in the Past Decade." November 1960. PTAH 517:008.

"Human Fulfillment." In *Search for America*, ed. Huston Smith, 164-74. Englewood Cliffs NJ: Prentice-Hall, 1959.

"Humanität und Religion." Lecture given upon reception of the Hansiatic Goethe Prize, Hamburg. 1 July 1958. *Die Religiöse Substanz der Kultur: Schriften zur Theologie der Kultur*, vol. 9 of *Gesammelte Werke*, ed. *Renate Albrecht, 110-19. Stuttgart: Evangelisches Verlagswerk, 1967.*

"The Hydrogen Cobalt Bomb." Symposium. In *Theology of Peace*, ed. Ronald H. Stone, 158-59. Louisville: Westminster/John Knox Press, 1990. First published in *Pulpit Digest* (Great Neck NY) 34/194 (June 1954): 32, 34.

"I Am an American." *Protestant Digest* (New York) 3/12 (June-July 1941): 24-26.

"An Important Letter," *Bulletin of the Council for a Democratic Germany* 1/2 (25 October 1944): 1.

"Is a Science of Human Values Possible?" In *New Knowledge in Human Values*, ed. Abraham H. Maslow, 189-96. New York: Harper & Brothers, 1959.

"Ist der Kapitalismus an sich Sünde?" 1920s. PTAH 112:001.

"Jewish Influences on Contemporary Christian Theology." *Cross Currents* (New York) 2/3 (Spring 1952): 35-42.

"The Jewish Question: a Christian and a German Problem." Four lectures delivered at Der Deutschen Hochschule für Politik, Summer 1953. Trans. Marion Pauck, *North American Paul Tillich Society Bulletin* 30/3 (Summer 2004): 3-24. First published in *Schriftenreihe der Deutschen Hochschule für Politik*, Berlin, 1953. Subsequently published in *Das Religiöse Fundament des Moralischen Handelns: Schriften zur Ethik und zum Menschenbild*, vol. 3 of *Gesammelte Werke*, ed. *Renate Albrecht, 128-70. Stuttgart: Evangelisches Verlagswerk, 1965.*

"*Kairos.*" In *The Protestant Era*, 32-51. Chicago: University of Chicago Press, 1948. First published in *Die Tat* 14/5 (1922).

"Kairos." In *A Handbook of Christian Theology: Definition Essays on Concepts and Movements of Thought in Contemporary Protestantism*, ed. Marvin Halverson and Arthur A. Cohen, 193-97. New York: Meridian Books, 1958.

"Kairos and Utopia (Rauschenbusch Lectures)." 1959. PTAH 408:026.

"Kairos. Ideen zur Geisteslage der Gegwart." In *Der Widerstreit von Raum und Zeit: Schriften zur Geschichtsphilosophie*, vol. 6 of *Gesammelte Werke*, ed. Renate Albrecht, 29-41. Stuttgart: Evangelisches Verlagswerk, 1963. First published in In *Kairos. Zur Geisteslage und Geisteswendung*, ed. Paul Tillich, 1-12. Darmstadt: Reichl 1926.

"The Kingdom of God and History." Paper delivered at the 1937 Oxford Conference on Life and Work. In *Theology of Peace*, ed. Ronald H. Stone, 25-56. Louisville: Westminster/John Knox Press, 1990. First published in *The Kingdom of God and History*. London: George Allen & Unwin, 1938.

"Kirche und humanische Gesellschaft." Address before the Berneucher Group, 5 October 1930. In *Die Religiöse Substanz der Kultur: Schriften zur Theologie der Kultur*, vol. 9 of *Gesammelte Werke*, ed. *Renate Albrecht*, 47-62. *Stuttgart: Evangelisches Verlagswerk, 1967. First published in Neuwerk* (Kassel), 13/1 (April–May 1931): 4-18. A much-corrected English translation of this is found in PTAH 420:005 as "The Church and Humanistic Society." "Kirche und Kultur." Outline from 1919. In *Religion, Kultur, Gesellschaft—Unveröffentlichte Texte aus der Deutschen Zeit (1908–1933)*, Erster Teil, vol. 10 of *Ergänzungs- und Nachlassbände zu den Gesammelten Werken von Paul Tillich*, ed. Erdmann Sturm, 233-36. Berlin/ New York: de Gruyter, 1999.

"Klassenschichtung und Geisteslage." Outline from 1926. In *Religion, Kultur,Gesellschaft— Unveröffentlichte Texte aus der Deutschen Zeit (1908–1933), Zweiter Teil*, vol. 11 of *Ergänzungs- und Nachlassbände zu den Gesammelten Werken von Paul Tillich*, ed. Erdmann Sturm, 18-27. Berlin/New York: de Gruyter, 1999.

"Die Krisis von Kultur und Religion." Outline from 1920. In *Religion, Kultur,Gesellschaft— Unveröffentlichte Texte aus der Deutschen Zeit (1908–1933), Erster Teil*, vol. 10 of *Ergänzungs- und Nachlassbände zu den Gesammelten Werken von Paul Tillich*, ed. Erdmann Sturm, 293-302. Berlin/New York: de Gruyter, 1999.

"Läuterndes Feuer." Speech for the Goethe Day celebration. 18 May 1942. In *Impressionen und Reflexionen: Ein Lebensbild in Aufsätzen, Reden und Stellungnahmen*, vol. 13 of *Gesammelte Werke*, ed. Renate Albrecht, 275-78. Stuttgart: Evangelisches Verlagswerk, 1972. First published in *Aufbau/ Reconstruction* (New York) 8/22 (29 May 1942): 10.

"Lecture at Meadville." 1943. PTAH 421:001.

"Love, Power, and Justice." *The Listener* (London) 48/1231 (2 October 1952): 544-45.

Love, Power and Justice. New York: Oxford University Press, 1954.

"Man Against Mass Society." 1955. PTAH 409:001.

"Man and Society in Religious Socialism." *Christianity and Society* (New York) 8/4 (Fall 1943): 10-21.

"Marx and the Prophetic Tradition." *Radical Religion* (New York) 1/4 (Autumn 1935): 21-29.

"Marx's View of History: A Study in the History of the Philosophy of History." In *Culture in History: Essays in Honor of Paul Radin,* ed. Stanley Diamond, 631-41. New York: Columbia University Press, 1960.

"Marxism and Christian Socialism." Symposium with Eduard Heimann: "Marxism and Christianity." In *The Protestant Era,* 253-60. Chicago: University of Chicago Press, 1948. First published in *Christianity and Society* (New York) 7/2 (Spring 1942): 13-18.

Masse und Geist. Studien zur Philosophie der Masse: Masse und Persönlichkeit; Masse und Bildung; Masse und Religion. In *Christentum und Soziale Gestaltung: Frühe Schriften zum Religiöse Sozialismus,* vol. 2 of *Gesammelte Werke,* ed. Renate Albrecht, 35-90. Stuttgart: Evangelisches Verlagswerk, 1962. First published in *Volk und Geist* 1. Berlin/Frankfurt a.M.: Verlag der Arbeitsgemeinschaft, 1922.

"The Meaning of Anti-Semitism." *Radical Religion* (New York) 4/1 (Winter 1938): 34-36.

"Der Mensch im Christentum und im Marxismus." Lecture delivered at Robert-Schumann-Saal, Düsseldorf. 29 July 1952. In *Das Religiöse Fundament des Moralischen Handelns: Schriften zur Ethik und zum Menschenbild,* vol. 3 of *Gesammelte Werke,* ed. Renate Albrecht, 194-209. First published in *Schriftreihe des Evangelischen Arbeitsausschusses Düsseldorf* 5 (1953).

"Middle-Class Problems in Germany." Late 1930s. PTAH 404:006.

"Mind and Migration." *Social Research* (New York) 4/3 (September 1937): 295-305.

"Moralisms and Morality: Theonomous Ethics." In *Theology of Culture,* 133-45. New York: Oxford University Press, 1959. First published in *Ministry and Medicine in Human Relations,* ed. Iago Galdston. New York: International Universities Press, Inc., 1955.

Morality and Beyond. New York: Harper and Row, 1963. Repr.: Louisville: Westminster/John Knox Press, 1995.

"My Changing Thought on Zionism." 1959. PTAH 405A:004.

My Search for Absolutes. New York: Touchstone, 1967.

My Travel Diary: 1936—Between Two Worlds, ed. Jerald C. Brauer. New York: Harper & Row, 1970.

Mysticism and Guilt-Consciousness in Schelling's Philosophical Development. 1912. Trans. Victor Nuovo. Lewisburg PA: Bucknell University Press, 1974.

"The Nature and Significance of Existentialist Thought." *Journal of Philosophy* (New York) 53/23 (8 November 1956): 739-48.

"Die natürlich-schöpfungsmässige und geschichtlich-eschatologische Sinn der Technik." A very general outline. 1929/1930. In *Religion, Kultur, Gesellschaft—Unveröffentlichte Texte aus der Deutschen Zeit (1908–1933),* Zweiter Teil, vol. 11 of *Ergänzungs- und Nachlassbände zu den Gesammelten Werken von Paul Tillich,* ed. Erdmann Sturm: 250-51. Berlin/New York: de Gruyter, 1999.

The New Being. New York: Scribner's, 1955.

"Nicholas Berdyaev." *Religion in Life* (New York) 7/3 (Summer 1938): 407-15.

"Nichtkirchliche Religionen." In *Die Frage nach dem Unbedingten: Schriften zur Religionsphilosophie,* vol. 5 of *Gesammelte Werke,* ed. Renate Albrecht, 13-31. Stuttgart: Evangelisches Verlagswerk, 1964. First published in *Volk und Reich der Deutschen,* ed. Bernhard Harms. Berlin, 1929.

"Nietzsche and the Bourgeois Spirit." *Journal of the History of Ideas* (New York) 6/3 (June 1945): 307-309.

"Notes from a Book about Islam." Early 1960s. PTAH 545:001.

"Notes on Islam." Early 1960s. PTAH 422:018.

"Die ökonomische Geschichtesauffassung, ihre geistigen Zusammenhänge und ihre gegenwärtige Umbildung." Outline from 1923 or 1924. In *Religion, Kultur, Gesellschaft—Unveröffentlichte Texte aus der Deutschen Zeit (1908–1933),* Erster Teil, vol. 10 of *Ergänzungs- und Nachlassbände zu den Gesammelten Werken von Paul Tillich,* ed. Erdmann Sturm, 404-25. Berlin/New York: de Gruyter, 1999.

"On 'Peace on Earth.' " Paper delivered at the Center for the Study of Democratic Institutions, 18 February 1965. In *Theology of Peace,* ed. Ronald H. Stone, 174-81. Louisville: Westminster/John Knox Press, 1990. First published in *To Live as Men: An Anatomy of Peace,* 13-23. Santa Barbara CA, 1965.

On the Boundary. New York: Scribner's, 1936, 1964, 1966.

"On the Idea of a Theology of Culture." Address to the Berlin Kant Society. 1919. In *Visionary Science: "On the Idea of a Theology of Culture" with an Interpretive Essay,* trans. Victor Nuovo, 19-39. Detroit: Wayne State University Press, 1987.

"Open Letter to Emanuel Hirsch." October 1934. In *The Thought of Paul Tillich,* ed. Adams, Pauck, and Shinn, and trans. Victor Nuovo and Robert Scharlemann, 353-95. San Francisco: Harper & Row, 1985.

"Our Disintegrating World." *Anglican Theological Review* (Evanston) 23/2 (April 1941): 134-46.

"Our Protestant Principles." *The Protestant* (New York) 4/7 (August–September

1942): 8-14.

"Outlook for 1945." *Bulletin of the Council for a Democratic Germany* 1/3 (1 January 1945): 1.

"Past and Present Reflections on Christianity and Society." 1955. PTAH 409:005.

"Paul Tillich: Interview with Werner Rode." 1955. Andover-Harvard Library Microfilm 281, PTAH, bMS 621.

"The Permanent Significance of the Catholic Church for Protestantism." *Protestant Digest* (New York) 3/10 (February-March 1941): 23-31.

"The Person in a Technical Society." *Christian Faith and Social Action. A Symposium,* ed. John A. Hutchison, 137-53. New York/London: Scribner's, 1953.

Perspectives in Nineteenth and Twentieth Century Protestant Theology. New York: Harper & Row, 1967.

"Philosophie der Macht." Mid-1920s. PTAH 112:007.

"Philosophie der Macht." Outline from 1929. In *Religion, Kultur, Gesellschaft— Unveröffentlichte Texte aus der Deutschen Zeit (1908–1933), Zweiter Teil,* vol. 11 of *Ergänzungs- und Nachlassbände zu den Gesammelten Werken von Paul Tillich,* ed. Erdmann Sturm, 226-32. Berlin/New York: de Gruyter, 1999.

"Die Philosophie der Macht." Two lectures delivered to the Deutsche Hochschule für Politik, Berlin. 1956. *Die Religiöse Substanz der Kultur: Schriften zur Theologie der Kultur,* vol. 9 of *Gesammelte Werke,* ed. *Renate Albrecht, 205-232. Stuttgart: Evangelisches Verlagswerk, 1967.*

"Die philosophisch-geistige Lage und Protestantismus." Philosophische Vorträge und Diskussionen, ed. Georgi Schischkoff, 119-24. Wurzach/Württ.: Pan Verlag, 1948.

"The Political Meaning of Utopia." Four lectures delivered to the Deutsche Hochschule für Politik, Berlin. 1951. In *Political Expectation,* 125-80. New York: Harper & Row, 1971. Repr.: Macon GA: Mercer University Press, 1981.

"The Political Situation in Europe Since the Munich Conference." 1939. PTAH 406A:002.

"The Post-War Education of the German People." Early 1940s. PTAH 404:008.

"Power and Justice in the Postwar World." Speech from Summer 1944. In *Theology of Peace,* ed. Ronald H. Stone, 88-104. Louisville: Westminster/John Knox Press, 1990.

"The Present Theological Situation in Light of the Continental European Development." *Theology Today* (Princeton) 6/3 (October 1949): 299-310.

"The Present Social Structure and the Christian Church." 1958. PTAH 409:006.

"The Present World Situation and the Christian Message." 1945. PTAH 406A:014.

"Die prinzipiellen Grundlagen und die nächsten Aufgaben unserer Bewegung I." Outline from 1919. In *Religion, Kultur, Gesellschaft—Unveröffentlichte Texte aus der Deutschen Zeit (1908–1933), Erster Teil,* vol. 10 of *Ergänzungs- und*

Nachlassbände zu den Gesammelten Werken von Paul Tillich, ed. Erdmann Sturm, 237-49. Berlin/New York: de Gruyter, 1999.

"Die prinzipiellen Grundlagen und die nächsten Aufgaben unserer Bewegung II." Outline from 1919. In *Religion, Kultur, Gesellschaft—Unveröffentlichte Texte aus der Deutschen Zeit (1908–1933)*, Erster Teil, vol. 10 of *Ergänzungs- und Nachlassbände zu den Gesammelten Werken von Paul Tillich*, ed. Erdmann Sturm, 250-63. Berlin/New York: de Gruyter, 1999.

"The Problem of a Protestant Social Ethic." 1926. PTAH 209:033.

"The Problem of Power: Attempt at a Philosophical Interpretation." In *The Interpretation of History*, trans. Elsa L. Talmey, 179-202. New York: Scribner's, 1936. First published as "Das Problem der Macht, Versuch einer philosophischen Grundlegung." Neue Blätter für den Sozialismus 2/4 (1931).

"The Problem of Protestantism in a Collectivistic Age." Mid-1940s. PTAH 406B:037.

"The Problem of Theological Method." *Journal of Religion* (Chicago) 27/1 (Jan, 1947): 16-26.

"Problems of Christian Ethics: 4 Lectures." 1962. PTAH 403A:024.

"A Program for a Democratic Germany (A statement by the members of The Council for a Democratic Germany, Paul Tillich, chairman)." In *Theology of Peace*, ed. Ronald H. Stone, 105-10. Louisville: Westminster/John Knox Press, 1990. First published in *Christianity and Crisis* (New York) 4/8 (15 May 1944): 3-4.

"The Prophetic Element in the Christian Message and the Authoritarian Personality." *McCormick Quarterly* 17/1 (November 1963): 16-26.

"Protestant Approach to the Present World Situation: The Special Difficulties of the Protestant Approach." 1940s. PTAH 406B:033.

"The Protestant Message and the Man of Today." A lecture delivered to the Aarau Student Conference. March 1928. In *The Protestant Era*, 192-205. Chicago: University of Chicago Press, 1948. First published as "Das Religiöse als kritisches Prinzip: Die protestantische Verkündigung und der Mensch der Gegenwart." In *Religiöse Verwirklichung*, 25-42. Furche-Verag Berlin, 1930.

"The Protestant Principle and the Next Stage of History." Mid-1940s. PTAH 406B:036.

"The Protestant Principle and the Proletarian Situation." In *The Protestant Era*, 161-81. Chicago: University of Chicago Press, 1948. First published as the brochure, *Protestantisches Prinzip und proletarische Situation*. Bonn: Friedrich Cohen, 1931.

"Protestantische Vision. Katholische Substanz, Protestantisches Prinzip, Sozialistische Entscheidung." Vortrag, gehalten im Robert-Schumann-Saal zu Düsseldorf. 8 July 1951. *Schriftenreihe des Evangelischen Arbeitsausschusses (Düsseldorf)* 3 (1951). PTAH, BX4827, T 53, A1, #26.

"Protestantism and Anti-Semitism." Early 1940s. PTAH 416:010.
"Protestantism and Moral Anarchy." Early 1940s. PTAH 406A:026.
"Protestantism as a Critical and Creative Principle." In *Political Expectation*, trans. James Luther Adams and Victor Nuovo. 10-39. New York: Harper & Row, 1971. Repr.: Macon GA: Mercer University Press, 1981. First published in *Protestantismus als Kritik und Gestaltung, Zeites Buch des Kairos-Kreises*, ed. Paul Tillich, 3-37. Darmstadt: Otto Reichl Verlag, *1929*.
"The Purpose that Unites." 1944. PTAH 406A:008.
"Realism and Faith." In The Protestant Era, 66-82. Chicago: University of Chicago Press, 1948. This is Tillich's 1948 revision of his 1927 lecture, "Über gläubigen Realismus." "Gläubiger Realismus II," (found in GW IV, 88-106) is a retranslation (back into German) of "Realism and Faith."
"Refugees: The Consequence of a Half-Religious War Raging in Europe." Early 1940s. PTAH 404:003.
"The Relation of Religion to American Culture." Late 1930s. PTAH 409:007.
"The Relationship between Islam and Christianity." Early 1960s. PTAH 422:019.
"Religion and Political Ideologies." PTAH 408:020.
"Religion and Secular Culture." In *The Protestant Era*, 55-65. Chicago: University of Chicago Press, 1948. First published *Journal of Religion* 26/2 (1946).
"Religion and the Intellectuals." 1950. PTAH 515A:011.
"Religion as a Dimension in Man's Spiritual Life." In *Theology of Culture*, 3-9. New York: Oxford University Press, 1959. First published as "Religion (A broadcast talk, 28 November 1954: 'Religion as an Aspect of the Human Spirit')," in *Man's Right to Knowledge*, second series: "Present Knowledge and New Directions." New York: Herbert Muschel, Box 800, Grand Central, 1955. "Religion in Two Societies." Lecture in a Symposium on *The Contemporary Scene*, The Metropolitan Museum of Art, New York, 28-30 March 1952. In *Theology of Culture*, 177-87. New York: Oxford University Press, 1959. First published in *New York: Metropolitan Museum of Art*, 1954, 41-48.
"Religion und Großstadt." Outline from 1928. In *Religion, Kultur, Gesellschaft— Unveröffentlichte Texte aus der Deutschen Zeit (1908–1933), Zweiter Teil*, vol. 11 of *Ergänzungs- und Nachlassbände zu den Gesammelten Werken von Paul Tillich*, ed. Erdmann Sturm, 189-95. Berlin/New York: de Gruyter, 1999.
"Religion und Kultur." Outline from 1920. In *Religion, Kultur, Gesellschaft— Unveröffentlichte Texte aus der Deutschen Zeit (1908–1933), Erster Teil, vol. 10 of Ergänzungs- und Nachlassbände zu den Gesammelten Werken von Paul Tillich*, ed. Erdmann Sturm, 275-81. Berlin/New York: de Gruyter, 1999.
"Religion und Technik." Sparse Outline from 1929 or 1930. In *Religion, Kultur, Gesellschaft—Unveröffentlichte Texte aus der Deutschen Zeit (1908–1933), Zweiter Teil, vol. 11 of Ergänzungs- und Nachlassbände zu den Gesammelten Werken von Paul Tillich*, ed. Erdmann Sturm, 248-49. Berlin/New York: de

Gruyter, 1999.

"Religion und Weltpolitik." 1939. *Die Religiöse Substanz der Kultur: Schriften zur Theologie der Kultur*, vol. 9 of *Gesammelte Werke*, ed. Renate Albrecht, 139-204. Stuttgart: Evangelisches Verlagswerk, 1967. Albrecht places this fragment in 1938. The texts in the PTAH 205A:001 and 205A:002 have the year 1939 written on them in what appears to be Tillich's handwriting.

"Die religionsphilosophischen Grundlagen des 'religiösen Sozialismus.' " Lecture from 1924 or 1925. In *Religion, Kultur, Gesellschaft—Unveröffentlichte Texte aus der Deutschen Zeit (1908–1933)*, Erster Teil, *vol. 10 of Ergänzungs- und Nachlassbände zu den Gesammelten Werken von Paul Tillich*, ed. Erdmann Sturm, 454-66. Berlin/New York: de Gruyter, 1999.

"Die religiöse Erneuerung des Sozialismus." Lecture from 1922. In *Religion, Kultur, Gesellschaft—Unveröffentlichte Texte aus der Deutschen Zeit (1908–1933)*, Erster Teil, *vol. 10 of Ergänzungs- und Nachlassbände zu den Gesammelten Werken von Paul Tillich*, ed. Erdmann Sturm, 311-27. Berlin/New York: de Gruyter, 1999.

"Die religiöse Lage der Gegenwart." Outline from 1928. In *Religion, Kultur, Gesellschaft—Unveröffentlichte Texte aus der Deutschen Zeit (1908–1933)*, Zweiter Teil, vol. 11 of *Ergänzungs- und Nachlassbände zu den Gesammelten Werken von Paul Tillich*, ed. Erdmann Sturm, 214-25. Berlin/New York: de Gruyter, 1999.

"Die religiöse und philosophische Weiterbildung des Sozialismus." In *Christentum und Soziale Gestaltung: Frühe Schriften zum Religiöse Sozialismus*, vol. 2 of *Gesammelte Werke*, ed. Renate Albrecht, 121-32. Stuttgart: Evangelisches Verlagswerk, 1962. First published in *Blätter für Religiösen Sozialismus* (Berlin) 5/5-6 (1924): 26-30.

"Religiöser Sozialismus und Pazifismus." Outline from 1923 or 1924. In *Religion, Kultur, Gesellschaft—Unveröffentlichte Texte aus der Deutschen Zeit (1908–1933), Erster Teil, vol. 10 of Ergänzungs- und Nachlassbände zu den Gesammelten Werken von Paul Tillich*, ed. Erdmann Sturm, 371-74. Berlin/New York: de Gruyter, 1999.

"Religious and Secular Bases of Culture and Politics." 1953. PTAH 408:024.

"The Religious Relation Between Christianity and Judaism in the Future." Early 1940s. PTAH 416:011.*The Religious Situation*. 1925/1926. Tran. H. Richard Niebuhr. New York: Henry Holt & Co., 1932.

"The Religious Situation in Germany." 1939. PTAH 404:002.

"The Religious Situation in Germany Today." *Religion in Life* (New York) 3/2 (Spring 1934): 163-73.

"The Religious Situation in Post-War Era." 1962. PTAH 406A:007.

"Religious Socialism." In *Political Expectation*, trans. William B. Green, Victor Nuovo, and James Luther Adams, 40-57. New York: Harper & Row, 1971.

Repr.: Macon GA: Mercer University Press, 1981. First published as "Sozialismus: II. Religiöser Sozialismus" in *Die Religion in Geschichte und Gegenwart*, 637-48. Tübingen, 1930.

"The Religious Socialist Movement in Germany between the World Wars." 1939. PTAH 408:030.

"The Religious Struggle in Germany." 1939. PTAH 404:001.

"The Revolutionary Character of the Struggle Going on in the World Today." 1945. PTAH 406A:015.

"The Role of Judaism in Post-War World Reconstruction." Mid-1940s. PTAH 405A:001.

"Rundbrief, 1964." PTAH 802B:055.

"Schelling and the Beginnings of the Existentialist Protest." Translation of "Schelling und die Anfänge des existentialischen Protestes," Gedächtnisfeier zum 100.Todestag von Friedrich Wilhelm Joseph von Schelling am 26.September 1954. First published in *Zeitschrift für philosophische Forschung* [Meisenheim/Glan] 9/2 [1955], 197-208) PTAH, 203A:023.

"Seven Theses concerning the Nuclear Dilemma." In *The Spiritual Situation in Our Technical Society*, 197-98. Macon GA: Mercer University Press, 1988; and *Theology of Peace*, ed. Ronald H. Stone, 160-61. Louisville: Westminster/John Knox Press, 1990. First published as "Contribution to the "The Nuclear Dilemma—A Discussion." *Christianity and Crisis* 11/19 (1961): 203-204.

"Shadow and Substance: A Theory of Power." Lecture delivered at the Graduate School of the Department of Agriculture, Washington DC, 7 May 1965. In *Political Expectation*, 115-24. New York: Harper & Row, 1971. Repr.: Macon GA: Mercer University Press, 1981.

The Shaking of the Foundations. New York: Scribner's, 1948.

"The Social and Spiritual Forces in Germany Today." 1946. PTAH 404:005.

"The Social Functions of the Churches in Europe and America." *Social Research* (New York) 3/1 (February 1936): 90-104.

The Socialist Decision. 1933. New York: Harper and Row, 1977.

"Die soziale Zukunft in der Seele der Masse." 1920s. PTAH 110:003.

Der Sozialismus als Kirchenfrage. Leitsätze von Paul Tillich und Carl Richard Wegener. Berlin: Gracht, 1919. In *Christentum und Soziale Gestaltung: Frühe Schriften zum Religiöse Sozialismus*, vol. 2 of *Gesammelte Werke*, ed. Renate Albrecht, 13-20. Stuttgart: Evangelisches Verlagswerk, 1962.

"Sozialismus aus dem Glauben." 1928. PTAH 202B:004 and 209:038.

"Sozialismus und Christentum." 1919. In *Religion, Kultur, Gesellschaft—Unveröffentlichte Texte aus der Deutschen Zeit (1908–1933), Erster Teil, vol. 10 of Ergänzungs- und Nachlassbände zu den Gesammelten Werken von Paul Tillich*, ed. Erdmann Sturm, 231-32. Berlin/New York: de Gruyter, 1999.

"Der Sozialismus und die geistige Lage der Gegenwart." Neue *Blätter für den*

Sozialismus (Potsdam) 3/1 (January 1932): 14-16. (Discussion with Henrik de Man of a broadcast talk by Gustav Radbruch.) PTAH 206:017 and PTAH 421:022.

"Spiritual Problems of Past-War Reconstruction." 1942. In *The Protestant Era*, 261-69. Chicago: University of Chicago Press, 1948.

"The Spiritual World in the Year 1926." PTAH 420:004. Translation of "Die geistige Welt in Jahre 1926." In *Die Religiöse Deutung der Gegenwart: Schriften zur Zeitkritik*, vol. 10 of *Gesammelte Werke*, ed. Renate Albrecht, 94-99. Stuttgart: Evangelisches Verlagswerk, 1968. First published in *Reichls Bücherbuch* 17 Darmstadt (1926): 6-14.

"Die Staatslehre Augustins nach De civitate Dei." Vortrag vor der Marburger Studentschaft im Dezember 1924. In *Begegnungen: Paul Tillich über sich selbst und andere*, vol. 12 of *Gesammelte Werke*, ed. Renate Albrecht, 81-96. Stuttgart: Evangelisches Verlagswerk, 1971. First published in *Theol. Blätter* 4 (1925): 77-86.

"The State as Expectation and Demand." Trans. Victor Nuovo. In *Political Expectation*, 97-114. New York: Harper & Row, 1971. Repr.: Macon GA: Mercer University Press, 1981. First published as "Der Staat als Erwartung und Forderung," in *Religiöse Verwirklichung*, 212-32. Furche-Verag Berlin, 1930.

"A Statement," *Bulletin of the Council for a Democratic Germany* 1/1 (1 September 1944): 1, 4.

"Storms of Our Times." *Anglican Theological Review* 25/1 (January 1943): 15-32. Repr. (with minor changes), *The Protestant Era*, 237-52. Chicago: University of Chicago Press, 1948.

"Symposium on Philosophy of History." 1943. PTAH 206:034.

The System of the Sciences According to Objects and Methods. Trans. by Paul Wiebe. E. Brunswick NJ: Associated University Presses, 1981. First published as *Das System der Wissenschaften nach Gegenständen und Methoden*. Göttingen: Vandenhoeck & Ruprecht, 1923.

Systematic Theology, vols. 1, 2, and 3. Chicago: University of Chicago Press, 1951, 1957. 1963.

Systematische Theologie. 1913. Trans. Uwe Carsten Scharf. Berlin/New York: Walter de Gruyter, 1999.

"The Technical City as Symbol." In *The Spiritual Situation in Our Technical Society*, ed. J. Mark Thomas and trans. John C. Modshielder, 179-84. Macon GA: Mercer University Press, 1988. First published as "Die technische Stadt als Symbol." In *Dresdner Neueste Nachrichten* 115 (17 May 1928)."A Telegram." *Bulletin of the Council for a Democratic Germany* 1/3 (1 January 1945): 3.

"Theologians and the Moon." *Christianity Today* 3/1 (13 October 1958): 31.*Theology of Culture.* New York: Oxford University Press, 1959."Theses on

The Peace Treaty." Mid-1940s. PTAH 404:038.

"Tillich Challenges Protestantism." *The Protestant* 4/4 (February 1942): 4.

"The Totalitarian State and the Claims of the Church." *Social Research* (New York) 1/4 (November 1934): 405-33.

"Trends in Religious Thought That Affect Social Outlook." In *Religion and the World Order*, ed. F. E. Johnson, 17-28. New York: Harper, 1944.

Types of Man's Self-Interpretation in the Western World: 3 Lectures. (Lecture 2: "The Vertical Self-Interpretation of Man in the Late Ancient and the Medieval Period"; Lecture 3: "The Horizontal Self-Interpretation of Man in the Modern Period.") Early 1960s. PTAH 402:016.

"Über gläubigen Realismus." In *Main Works/Hauptwerke of Paul Tillich*, vol. 4: *Writings in the Philosophy of Religion*, 193-211 (Berlin/New York: de Gruyter, 1987). First published in *Theologische Blätter. Im Auftrage des Eisenacher Kartells Akademisch-Theologischer Vereine* (Leipzig) 7/5 (May 1928): 109-18.

"Um was es geht. Antwort an Emanuel Hirsch." *Theologische Blätter* (Leipzig) 14/5 (May 1935): 117-20.

"Die Umstellung der Debatte." Outline of a 1922 debate within the Kairos Circle. In *Religion, Kultur, Gesellschaft—Unveröffentlichte Texte aus der Deutschen Zeit (1908–1933), Erster Teil*, vol. 10 of *Ergänzungs- und Nachlassbände zu den Gesammelten Werken von Paul Tillich*, ed. Erdmann Sturm: 328-34. Berlin/New York: de Gruyter, 1999.

"Vertical and Horizontal Thinking." *American Scholar* (New York) 15/1 (Winter 1945–1946): 102-105.

"Victory in Defeat: The Meaning of History in Light of Christian Prophetism." *Interpretation* (Richmond) 6/1 (January 1952): 17-26.

"Visit to Germany." *Christianity and Crisis* (New York) 8/19 (15 November 1948): 147-49.

Voice of America Speeches. March 1942–May 1944. PTAH 602A, 602B, 603A, 603B, and 604.

"War Aims: Why War Aims?" *Protestant Digest* (New York) 3/12 (June-July 1941): 33-38.

"War Aims—II: What War Aims?" *Protestant Digest* (New York) 4/1 (August-September 1941): 13-18.

"War Aims—III: Whose War Aims?" *Protestant Digest* (New York) 4/2 (October-November 1941): 24-29.

"Was soll mit Deutschland geschehen? (a) Gegen Emil Ludwigs neueste Rede." In *Impressionen und Reflexionen: Ein Lebensbild in Aufsätzen, Reden und Stellungnahmen*, vol. 13 of *Gesammelte Werke*, ed. Renate Albrecht, 278-79. Stuttgart: Evangelisches Verlagswerk, 1972. First published in *Aufbau/Reconstruction* (New York) 8/29 (17 July 1942): 6.

"Was soll mit Deutschland geschehen? (b) Es geht um die Method—Antwort Paul

Tillichs an die Kritiker im ‚Aufbau'." In *Impressionen und Reflexionen: Ein Lebensbild in Aufsätzen, Reden und Stellungnahmen*, vol. 13 of *Gesammelte Werke*, ed. Renate Albrecht, 279-81. Stuttgart: Evangelisches Verlagswerk, 1972. First published in *Aufbau/Reconstruction* (New York) 8/32 (7 August 1942): 7-8.

"Die Weltgeschichtliche Zukunft Europas." Early 1940s. PTAH 201:015.

"What Has War Done to Us? Culturally!" 1945. PTAH 406A:010.

"What Is Wrong with Dialectical Theology?" *Journal of Religion* (Chicago) 15/2 (April 1935): 127-45.

"What Strategy Should the Church Adopt with Reference to Communism?" Early 1940s. PTAH 416:007.

"What Strategy Should the Church Adopt with Reference to Communism?" Early 1940s. PTAH 408:031.

"Wirtschaftspolitik unter kulturtheologischen Gesichtspunkt." In *Berliner Vorlesungen I (1919–1920)*, vol. 12 of *Ergänzungs-und Nachlassbände zu den Gesammelten Werken von Paul Tillich*, ed. Erdmann Sturm, 233-58. Berlin/New York: de Gruyter, 2001.

"The Word of Religion." In *The Protestant Era*, 185-91. Chicago: University of Chicago Press, 1948. First published as "The Word of Religion to the People of This Time." *The Protestant* 4/5 (1942).

"The World Situation." In *The Christian Answer*, ed. Henry P. Van Dusen, 1-44. New York: Scribner's, 1945.

"World War II and the Younger Churches." 1946. PTAH 514:022.

Secondary Sources

Abe, Masao. "A Buddhist View of 'The Significance of the History of Religions for the Systematic Theologian.'" *Meeting Papers: North American Paul Tillich Society* (November 1988): 1-8.

Adams, James Luther. *Paul Tillich's Philosophy of Culture, Science, and Religion.* New York: Harper & Row, 1965.

_____. "Tillich's Interpretation of History." In *The Theology of Paul Tillich*, ed. Charles W. Kegley and Robert W. Bretall, 294-309. New York: The Macmillan Co., 1952.

Akinwale, Anthony A. "Tillich's Method of Correlation and the Concerns of African Theologians." In *Paul Tillich: A New Catholic Assessment*, ed. Raymond F. Bulman and Frederick J. Parrella, 189-217. Collegeville MN: Liturgical Press, 1994.

Amelung, Eberhard. *Der Gestalt der Liebe: Paul Tillichs Theologie der Kultur.* Gerd Mohn: Gütersloher Verlagshaus, 1972.

_____. "Religious Socialism as an Ideology: A Study of the 'Kairos-Circle' in Germany Between 1919 and 1933." Th.D. thesis, Harvard University, 1962.

American Friends of German Freedom. *Germany Tomorrow*. New York: American Friends of German Freedom, undated, but between 6/1941 and 4/1945.

Arndt, William F. and F. Wilbur Gingrich. *A Greek-English Lexicon of the New Testament and Other Early Christian Literature*. Chicago: University of Chicago Press, 1979.

Arther, Donald. "Paul Tillich as a Military Chaplain." *North American Paul Tillich Society Newsletter* 26/3 (Summer 2000): 4-12.

Ashr, Jawad. "Paul Tillich and the Reconstruction of Sin and Salvation in Islamic Theological Anthropology." *Newsletter of the North American Paul Tillich Society* 29/1 (Winter 2003): 27-42.

Barzegar, Kayhan. "Socialist Republic of Gilan: The First Offensive of the October Revolution." *Discourse Quarterly Magazine* 3/4 (Spring 2002): 89-104.

Bense, Walter F. "Tillich's *Kairos* and Hitler's Seizure of Power: The Tillich-Hirsch Exchange of 1934-35." In *Tillich Studies: 1975*, ed. John J. Carey, 39-50. Tallahassee Fl.: North American Paul Tillich Society, 1975.

Bonino, José Míguez. "Rereading Tillich in Latin America: From Religious Socialism to the Exile." In *Religion in the New Millennium: Theology in the Spirit of Paul Tillich*, ed. Raymond F. Bulman and Frederick J. Parrella, 19-33. Macon GA: Mercer University Press, 2001.

Boss, Marc. "Religious Diversity: From Tillich to Lindbeck and Back." In *Religion in the New Millennium: Theology in the Spirit of Paul Tillich*, ed. Raymond F. Bulman and Frederick J. Parrella, 177-95. Macon GA: Mercer University Press, 2001.

Bowie, W. Russell. "Comment on the Report of 'The Commission on a Just and Durable Peace.'" *The Witness* 26/46 (15 April 1943): 5-6.

Brauer, Jerald. Endnotes to *My Travel Diary: 1936—Between Two Worlds*, by Paul Tillich, 185-92. New York: Harper & Row, 1970.

_____. Introduction to *My Travel Diary: 1936—Between Two Worlds*, by Paul Tillich, 9-26. New York: Harper & Row, 1970.

Buber, Martin. 'The Dialogue between Heaven and Earth.' In *On Judaism*, 214-25. New York: Schocken Books, 1967.

Bulman, Raymond F. *A Blueprint for Humanity*. Lewisburg: Bucknell University Press, 1981.

_____. "Theonomy and Technology: A Study in Tillich's Theology of Culture." In *Kairos and Logos: Studies in the Roots and Implications of Tillich's Theology*, ed. John J. Carey, 213-33. North American Paul Tillich Society, 1978. New Edition: Macon GA: Mercer University Press, 1984.

Burch, Sharon. "Women and Religion and the New Millennium." In *Religion in the New Millennium: Theology in the Spirit of Paul Tillich*, ed. Raymond F. Bulman and Frederick J. Parrella, 109-120. Macon GA: Mercer University Press, 2001.

Cali, Grace. *Paul Tillich First-Hand: A Memoir of the Harvard Years.* Chicago: Exploration Press, 1996.

Carey, John J. "Morality and Beyond: Tillich's Ethics in Life and Death." In *Tillich Studies: 1975*, ed. John J. Carey, 104-15. Chicago: The North American Paul Tillich Society, 1975.

_____. "Tillich, Marx, and the Interpretation of History." *Meeting Papers: North American Paul Tillich Society* (November 1989): 1-7.

_____. "Tillich, Marx and the Interpretation of History: A Prototype of a Marxist-Christian Dialogue." *The St. Luke's Journal of Theology.* 14/1 (January 1971): 3-15. Case, Adelaide. "Comment on the Report of 'The Commission on a Just and Durable Peace.'" *The Witness* 26/46 (15 April 1943): 5. Champion, James W. "Tillich and the Frankfurt School: Parallels and Differences in Prophetic Criticism." *Soundings* 69 (1986): 512-30. Cobb, Kelton. "Expanding the Stock of Sources in Tillich's Theology of Culture." *Meeting Papers: North American Paul Tillich Society* (November 1992): 13-23.

_____. "Reconsidering the Status of Popular Culture in Tillich's Theology of Culture." *Journal of the American Academy of Religion* 63/1 (Spring 1995): 53-85.

Council for a Democratic Germany. "Emergency Measures in Germany." *Bulletin of the Council for a Democratic Germany* 1/5 (May 1945): 5.

_____. "Germany's Collapse and the Hope for a Workable Peace." *Bulletin of the Council for a Democratic Germany* 1/5 (May 1945): 4.

Davies, Norman. *White Eagle, Red Star: the Polish-Soviet War, 1919-20.* United Kingdom: Pimlico, 2003.

Delling, Gerhard. , in *Theological Dictionary of the New Testament* 3 (Θ-K) ed. Gerhard Kittel, trans. and ed. Geoffrey W. Bromiley, 455-64. Grand Rapids MI: Eerdmans, 1965.

Donnelly, Brian. *The Socialist Emigre: Marxism and the Later Tillich* Macon GA: Mercer University Press, 2003).

Earley, Glenn David. "An 'Everlasting Conversation': Judaism in the Life and Thought of Paul Tillich." Ph.D. diss., Temple University, 1983.

_____. "Tillich and Judaism: An Analysis of the 'Jewish Question.'" In *Theonomy and Autonomy: Studies in Paul Tillich's Engagement with Modern Culture*, ed. John J. Carey, 267-80. Macon GA: Mercer University Press, 1984.

Eickoff, Jörg. "The New Being in Christ: Tillich's Universal Concept of Revelation as a Contribution to Inter-Religious Encounter in the Pluralistic Situation of Post-Modernity." *Newsletter of the North American Paul Tillich Society* 28/3 (Summer 2002): 18-23.

Enzmann, Marion. "Die politischen Ideen Paul Tillichs in der Weimarer Republik." *Tillich Journal: Interpretieren—Vergleichen—Kritisieren—Weiterentwickeln*

1 (1997): 68-71.

Ericksen, Robert P. *Theologians Under Hitler: Gerhard Kittel, Paul Althaus and Emmanuel Hirsch*. New Haven/London: Yale University Press, 1985.

Eschbach, Jean. *Au Coeur de la Resistance Alsacienne. Le Combat de Paul Dingler*. Fondateur De La 7eme Colonne D'Alsace, Chef Du Reseau Martial. Colmar : Do Bentzinger, 2003.

Falk, Richard A. *Martin Buber and Paul Tillich's Radical Politics and Religion*. New York: National Council of Protestant Episcopal Churches, 1961.

Fisher, James V. "The Politicizing of Paul Tillich: The First Phase." In *Tillich Studies: 1975*, ed. John J. Carey, 27-38. Tallahassee Fl.: North American Paul Tillich Society, 1975.

_____. "Review Essay: The Socialist Decision." *North American Paul Tillich Society Newsletter* 3/1 (December 1977): 21-27.

Fitch, Robert E. "The Social Philosophy of Paul Tillich." *Religion in Life* 27/2 (Spring 1958): 247-56.

Fletcher, Joseph F. "Comment on the Report of 'The Commission on a Just and Durable Peace.'" *The Witness* 26/45 (8 April 1943): 3.

_____. "Tillich and Ethics: The Negation of Law." *Pastoral Psychology*, 19 (February 1968): 33-40.

Forstman, Jack. *Christian Faith in Dark Times: Theological Conflicts in the Shadow of Hitler*. Louisville: Westminster/John Knox Press, 1992.

Friedlander, Albert H. "Tillich and Jewish Thought." In *The Thought of Paul Tillich*, ed. Adams/Pauck/Shinn, 175-96. San Francisco: Harper & Row, 1985.

Gablentz, O.H. "Paul Tillich in der Deutschen Hochschule für Politik." 1972. (PTAH, 901E:087)

Gass, John. "Comment on the Report of 'The Commission on a Just and Durable Peace.' " *The Witness* 26/45 (8 April 1943): 4.

Geffré, Claude. "Paul Tillich and the Future of Interreligious Ecumenism." In *Paul Tillich: A New Catholic Assessment*, ed. Raymond F. Bulman and Frederick J. Parrella, 268-88. Collegeville MN: Liturgical Press, 1994.

Gilkey, Langdon. "The Role of the Theologian in Contemporary Society," In *The Thought of Paul Tillich*, ed. James Luther Adams, Wilhelm Pauck, and Roger Lincoln Shinn, 330-50. San Francisco: Harper & Row, 1985.

_____. "Tillich and the Kyoto School." *Meeting Papers: North American Paul Tillich Society* (December 1987): 1-10.

_____. "Tillich's Early Political Writings." In *Gilkey on Tillich*, 3-22. New York: Crossroad, 1990. Glenn, C. Leslie. "Comment on the Report of 'The Commission on a Just and Durable Peace.' " *The Witness* 26/45 (8 April 1943): 4.

Glöckner, Konrad. "Personenhaftes Sein als Telos der Schöpfung. Eine Darstellung der Theologie Tillichs aus der Perspektive seiner Ethik." *Tillich Journal: Inter-*

pretieren—Vergleichen—Kritisieren—Weiterentwickeln 1 (1997): 74-79.

Graber, Glenn. "The Metaethics of Paul Tillich." In *Being and Doing: Paul Tillich as Ethicist*, ed. John J. Carey, 29-55. Macon GA: Mercer University Press, 1987.

Grant, Frederick C., Angus Dun, Joseph F. Fletcher, George F. Thomas, and Paul Tillich. "Panel Discussion of Tillich's "Storms of Our Times." *Anglican Theological Review* 25/1 (January 1943): 41-43.

Greene, Theodore M. "Paul Tillich and Our Secular Culture." In *The Theology of Paul Tillich*, ed. Charles W. Kegley and Robert W. Bretall, 50-66. New York: The Macmillan Co., 1952.

Gutteridge, Richard. *Open Thy Mouth for the Dumb! The German Evangelical Church and the Jews, 1879–1950*. Oxford UK: Basil Blackwell, 1976.

Haigis, Peter. "Erdmann Sturm (Hg): Ergänzung- und Nachlassbände zu den Gesammelten Werken Paul Tillichs, Bd. 7, Frühe Predigten (1909–1918)." *Tillich Journal: Interpretieren—Vergleichen—Kritisieren—Weiterentwickeln* 1 (1997): 17-19.

_____. "Erdmann Sturm (Hg): ‚Holy Love Claims Life and Limb. Paul Tillich's War Theology (1914–1918).' in *Zeitschrift für neuere Theologiegeschichte* (1994): 60-84." *Tillich Journal: Interpretieren—Vergleichen—Kritisieren—Weiterentwickeln* I (1997): 52-56.

_____. "Tillich's Early Writings in Social Philosophy and Social Ethics within the Context of His Theology of Culture." *North American Paul Tillich Society Newsletter* 26/1 (Winter 2000): 21-30.

Hammond, Guy B. "Does the Road of Providence Lead to Freedom? George Bush, Paul Tillich, and the Theology of History." Unpublished paper delivered before the "Tillich: Issues in Theology, Religion, and Culture Group" (A19-124), American Academy of Religion, Philadelphia (10 November 2005).

_____. "The Primacy of Ethics: Relationality in Buber, Tillich, and Levinas." *Bulletin of the North American Paul Tillich Society* 30/3 (Summer 2004): 24-30.

_____. "*Prophetic Realism: Beyond Militarism and Pacifism in an Age of Terror*, by Ronald H. Stone." *Bulletin of the North American Paul Tillich Society* 33/1 (Winter 2007): 5-6.

_____. "Review: A James Reimer, *Paul Tillich: Theologian of Nature, Culture, and Politics*." *Bulletin of the North American Paul Tillich Society* 33/4 (Fall 2007): 5-6.

_____. "Why Did Westerners Become Fascists? Fromm, Tillich, and Horkheimer on Character Types." *Meeting Papers: North American Paul Tillich Society* (November 1989): 8-12.

Hanaoka, Eiko. "Paul Tillich in Japan." Translated by Thomas F. O'Meara. *Bulletin of the North American Paul Tillich Society* 32/3 (Summer 2006): 6-9.

Heimann, Eduard. "Tillich's Doctrine of Religious Socialism." In *The Theology of Paul Tillich*, ed. Charles W. Kegley and Robert W. Bretall, 312-25. New York: Macmillan, 1952.

The Holy Bible. See New Revised Standard Version Bible. 1989/1990.

Hummel, Gert. "*Morality and Beyond*: Anthropology and New Ethics in Tomorrow's Information Society." In *Being and Doing: Paul Tillich as Ethicist*, ed. John J. Carey, 125-54. Macon GA: Mercer University Press, 1987.

Huntington, Samuel P. "The Clash of Civilizations?" *Foreign Affairs* 72/3 (Summer 1993): 22-49.

_____. *The Clash of Civilizations and the Remaking of World Order*. New York: Simon & Schuster, 1996.

_____. *Who Are We? The Challenges to America's National Identity*. New York: Simon & Schuster, 2004.

James, Robison B. *Tillich and World Religions: Encountering Other Faiths Today*. Macon GA: Mercer University Press, 2003.

Jutikkala, Eino and Kauko Pirinen. *A History of Finland*. New York: Dorset Press 1988.

Kirschbaum, Stanislav. *A History of Slovakia: The Struggle for Survival*. Griffin NY: St. Martin's, 1996.

Kitagawa, Joseph M. "Tillich, Kraemer, and the Encounter of Religions." In *The Thought of Paul Tillich*, ed. Adams/Pauck/Shinn, 197-217. San Francisco: Harper & Row, 1985.

Koshul, Basit. "The Divine, the Demonic, and the Ninety-Nine Names of Allah: Tillich's Idea of the 'Holy' and the Qur'anic Narrative." *Newsletter of the North American Paul Tillich Society* 29/1 (Winter 2003): 42-48.

Krell, Marc. "Constructing a Public Theology: Tillich's and Buber's Movement Beyond Protestant and Jewish Boundaries in Weimar Germany." Unpublished paper delivered before the "Tillich: Issues in Theology, Religion, and Culture Group" (A19-124), American Academy of Religion, Philadelphia (19 November 2005).

Kucheman, Clark A. "Professor Tillich: Justice and the Economic Order." *The Journal of Religion* 46/1, part 2 (January 1966): 165-83.

Laurie, Clayton D. *The Propaganda Warriors: America's Crusade Against Nazi Germany*. Lawrence: University of Kansas, 1996.

Lerner, Max. Introduction to *The Prince and the Discourses*, by Niccolo Machiavelli, xxv-xlvi. New York: Modern Library, 1950.

Lewy, Guenter. *The Catholic Church and Nazi Germany*. New York: McGraw-Hill, 1964.

Liebner, Petra. *Paul Tillich und der Council for a Democratic Germany (1933 bis 1945)*. Frankfurt am Main: Peter Lang—Europäischer Verlag der Wissenschaften, 2001.

Lindemann, Albert S. *A History of European Socialism* (New Haven: Yale University Press, 1983.

Lounibos, John B. "Paul Tillich's Structures of Liberation." In *Tillich Studies: 1975*, ed. John J. Carey, 63-74. Tallahassee FL: North American Paul Tillich Society, 1975.

Luther, Martin. *Commentary on Romans (1515)*. Trans. by J. Theodore Mueller. Grand Rapids MI: Kregel Publications, 1954.

_____. "Temporal Authority: To What Extent It Should Be Obeyed (1523)." Translated by J. J. Schindel. In Luther's Works 45: *The Christian in Society II*, ed. Walther I. Brandt, 81-129. Philadelphia: Muhlenberg Press, 1962–1971.

Machiavelli, Niccolo. *The Prince and the Discourses on the First Ten Books of Titus Livius*. New York: Modern Library, 1950.

MacLennan, Ronald B. "World War I and Paul Tillich: The Deconstruction and Reconstruction of Theology." Unpublished paper delivered before the "Nineteenth Century Theology Group" (A90), American Academy of Religion, San Francisco (November 23, 1997).

Manning, Russell. "Tillich's Theology of Culture after Postcolonialism." *North American Paul Tillich Society Newsletter* 28/2 (Spring 2002): 25-32.

Marx, Karl. "On the Jewish Question (1843)." In *The Marx-Engels Reader*, ed. Robert C. Tucker, 26-52. New York: W.W. Norton and Co., 1978.Martin, Bernard. *The Existentialist Theology of Paul Tillich*. New York: Bookman Associates, 1963.McCann, Dennis P. "Tillich's Religious Socialism: 'Creative Synthesis' or Personal Statement?" In *The Thought of Paul Tillich*, ed. Adams/Pauck/Shinn, 81-101. San Francisco: Harper & Row, 1985.Menczer, Bela. "Bela Kun and the Hungarian Revolution of 1919." *History Today* (London) 19/5 (May 1969): 299-309.Midgley, Louis C. "Politics and Ultimate Concern: The Normative Political Philosophy of Paul Tillich." Ph.D. thesis, Brown University, 1965. Minogue, K.R. Nationalism. New York: Basic Books, 1967. Mirejovsky, Lubomir. "Peace Issues in the Work of Paul Tillich." *North American Paul Tillich Society Newsletter* 14/2 (April 1988): 5-10. Moody, Linda A., "Paul Tillich and Feminist Theology: Echoes from the Boundary" *Meeting Papers: North American Paul Tillich Society* (November 1993): 18-24.

Murphy, John W. "Paul Tillich and Western Marxism." *American Journal of Theology and Philosophy* 5/1 (January 1984): 13-24.

Nair, Mira. "Bollywood Meets Hollywood," *The Arts, Creativity, and the Common Good* at the Westminster Town Hall Forum, broadcast over Minnesota Public Radio's "Midday with Gary Eichten," Thursday, 22 September 2005, hour 2, <http://news.minnesota.publicradio.org/programsmidday/listings/md20050919.shtml>.

New Revised Standard Version Bible (NRSV). 1989/1990.

Nicholls, A. J. *Weimar and the Rise of Hitler*.New York: St. Martin's Press, 1991.

Niebuhr, Reinhold. "Biblical Faith and Socialism: A Critical Appraisal." In *Religion and Culture: Essays in Honor of Paul Tillich*, ed. Walter Leibrecht, 44-57. New York: Harper & Row, 1959.

Nikkel, David H. "Polarities in Tillich's Thought on Revelation in the World Religions." *North American Paul Tillich Society Newsletter* 26/4 (Fall 2000): 2-6.

Novak, David. "Theonomous Ethics: A Defense and A Critique of Tillich." *Soundings* 69 (1986): 436-63.

_____. "Tillich and Buber." Meeting Papers of the North American Paul Tillich Society (November 1990): 9-16.

Nuovo, Victor. Translator's introduction to *The Construction of the History of Religion in Schelling's Positive Philosophy*, by Paul Tillich, 11-32. Lewisburg PA: Bucknell University Press, 1974.

_____. *Visionary Science: A Translation of Tillich's "On the Idea of a Theology of Culture" with an Interpretive Essay*. Detroit: Wayne State University, 1987.

O'Keeffe, Terence M. "Ethics and the Realm of Praxis." In *Being and Doing: Paul Tillich as Ethicist*, ed. John J. Carey, 87-105. Macon GA: Mercer University Press, 1987.

_____. "Ideology and the Protestant Principle." *Journal of the American Academy of Religion* 51/2 (June 1983): 283-305.

_____. "The Metaethics of Paul Tillich: Further Reflections." In *Being and Doing: Paul Tillich as Ethicist*, ed. John J. Carey, 57-67. Macon GA: Mercer University Press, 1987.

_____. "Tillich and the Frankfurt School." In *Theonomy and Autonomy: Studies in Paul Tillich's Engagement with Modern Culture*, ed. John J. Carey, 67-87. Macon GA: Mercer University Press, 1984.

Osgood, Phillips E. "Comment on the Report of 'The Commission on a Just and Durable Peace.'" *The Witness* 26/46 (15 April 1943): 5.

Palapathwala, Ruwan. "Beyond Christ and *System*: Paul Tillich and Spirituality in the Twenty-First Century." In *Religion in the New Millennium: Theology in the Spirit of Paul Tillich*, ed. Raymond F. Bulman and Frederick J. Parrella, 205-219. Macon GA: Mercer University Press, 2001.

Pauck, Wilhelm and Marion. *Paul Tillich: His Life and Thought*. San Francisco: Harper & Row, 1976.

Pedraja, Luis G. "Tillich's Theology of Culture and Hispanic Theology." *North American Paul Tillich Society Newsletter* 25/3 (Summer 1999): 2-10.

Peterson, Anna L. "Paul Tillich's Political Ethics: In Defense of Socialism." *Meeting Papers: North American Paul Tillich Society* (November 1992): 38-49.

Piediscalzi, Nicholas. "Paul Tillich and Erik H. Erikson on the Origin and Nature of Morality and Ethics." Ph.D. diss., Boston University, 1965.

Pipes, Richard. *Russia Under the Bolshevik Regime.* New York: Vintage, 1995.

Plaskow, Judith. *Sex, Sin and Grace: Women's Experience and the Theologies of Reinhold Niebuhr and Paul Tillich.* Lanham MD: University Press of America, 1980.

Price, Robert M. "Tillich on Christian Faith and the Plurality of World Religions." *Bulletin of the North American Paul Tillich Society* 30/4 (Fall 2004): 19-25.

Ramsey, Paul. *Nine Modern Moralists.* New York: Prentice-Hall, 1962.

Ratschow, Carl Heinz. *Paul Tillich.* Trans. Robert P. Scharlemann. Iowa City IA: North American Paul Tillich Society, 1980.

Reijnen, Anne Marie. "Paul Tillich and Capital Punishment: The Meaning of Power." *Bulletin of the North American Paul Tillich Society* 31/4 (Fall 2005): 6-10.

Reimer, A. James. *The Emanuel Hirsch and Paul Tillich Debate: A Study in the Political Ramifications of Theology.* Toronto Studies in Theology 42. Lewiston/Queenston/Lampeter: Edwin Mellen Press, 1989.

_____. *Paul Tillich: Theologian of Nature, Culture, and Politics.* Münster: Lit Verlag, 2004.

_____. "Tillich, Hirsch and the Confessing Church: On Issues Related to War and Peace." Unpublished paper delivered before the "Issues in the Thought of Paul Tillich Group" (A220), American Academy of Religion, San Francisco (24 November 1997).

Reisz, H. Frederick, Jr. "Liberation Theology of Culture: A Tillichian Perspective." In *Kairos and Logos: Studies in the Roots and Implications of Tillich's Theology,* ed. John J. Carey, 271-82. The North American Paul Tillich Society, 1978. New Edition: Macon GA: Mercer University Press, 1984.

Remick, Oscar E. "Value in the Thought of Paul Tillich." Ph.D. diss., Boston University, 1966.

Richard, Jean. "The Question of Nationalism." In *Religion in the New Millennium: Theology in the Spirit of Paul Tillich,* ed. Raymond F. Bulman and Frederick J. Parrella, 35-43. Macon GA: Mercer University Press, 2001.

_____. "The Socialist Tillich and Liberation Theology." In *Paul Tillich: A New Catholic Assessment,* ed. Raymond F. Bulman and Frederick J. Parrella, 148-73. Collegeville MN: Liturgical Press, 1994.

Ristiniemi, Jari. "Ethics as Expressionism: Things, Individuals, and Common Concerns," *Bulletin of the North American Paul Tillich Society* 33/3 (Summer 2007): 23-28.

_____. "Politics of Soul in a Changing Society: Tillich's Political Pathos of the 1920's in Light of Nietzsche's Moral Philosophy." *Bulletin of the North American Paul Tillich Society* 31/3 (Summer 2005): 9-15.

Rösler, Tabea. "Anthropological Perspectives in Tillich's Systematic Theology: A Constructive Framework in Dialogue with Feminist Process Theologies." *Bulletin of the North American Paul Tillich Society* 31/3 (Summer 2005): 33-41.

_____. " 'You Never See with the Eyes Only': Reconfiguring Paul Tillich's Concept of Personhood." *Bulletin of the North American Paul Tillich Society* 32/2 (Spring 2006): 27-33.

Rothchild, Jonathan. "Global Flows, Head Scarves, and Finite Freedom: Tillich on Globalization." *Bulletin of the North American Paul Tillich Society* 31/3 (Summer 2005): 16-21.

_____. "Review of Ronald H. Stone, *Prophetic Realism: Beyond Militarism and Pacifism in an Age of Terror.*" *Journal of Religion* 87/3 (July 2007): 459-61.

Runyon, Theodore. "Tillich's Understanding of Revolution." In *Theonomy and Autonomy: Studies in Paul Tillich's Engagement with Modern Culture*, ed. John J. Carey, 267-80. Macon GA: Mercer University Press, 1984.

Schäfer-Kretzler, Karin. "Einleitung." Paul Tillich's *An meine deutschen Freunde*, vol. 3 of *Ergänzungs- und Nachlass-bände zu den Gesammelten Werken von Paul Tillich*, 11-18. Stuttgart: Evangelisches Verlagswerk, 1973.

Seeberg, E. "Review of *Religise Verwicklichung*," *Deutsche Literaturzeitung* 1/17 (26 April 1930): 769-73.

Sherman, Franklin. "Tillich's Method of Correlation: Some Resonances in Jewish Thought." *Meeting Papers: North American Paul Tillich Society* (November 1990): 17-20.

_____. "Tillich's Social Thought: New Perspectives." *The Christian Century* 93/6 (25 February 1976): 168-72.

Shinn, Roger L. "Tension and Unity in the Ethics of Paul Tillich." In *Being and Doing: Paul Tillich as Ethicist*, ed. John J. Carey, 9-27. Macon GA: Mercer University Press, 1987.

_____. "Tillich as Interpreter and Disturber of Contemporary Civilization." In *The Thought of Paul Tillich*, ed. Adams/Pauck/Shinn, 44-62. San Francisco: Harper & Row, 1985.

Shulman, Holly Cowan. *The Voice of America: Propaganda and Democracy, 1941–1945*. Madison: University of Wisconsin Press, 1990.

Siegfried, Theodor. "The Significance of Paul Tillich's Theology for the German Situation." In *The Theology of Paul Tillich*, ed. Charles W. Kegley and Robert W. Bretall), 68-83. New York: Macmillan, 1952.

Slater, Peter. "The Relevance of Tillich's Concept of Creative Justice in the New Millennium." In *Religion in the New Millennium: Theology in the Spirit of Paul Tillich*, ed. Raymond F. Bulman and Frederick J. Parrella, 45-53. Macon GA: Mercer University Press, 2001.

Smith, Anthony D. *Theories of Nationalism*. New York: Harper & Row, 1971.

Smith, John E. "Paul Tillich." In *Thirteen for Christ*. Ed. Melville Harcourt: 67-82. New York: Sheed and Ward, 1963.

Soley, Lawrence C. *Radio Warfare: OSS and CIA Subversive Propaganda*. New York: Praeger Publishers, 1989.

Stenger, Mary Ann. "Paul Tillich and the Feminist Critique of Roman Catholic Theology." In *Paul Tillich: A New Catholic Assessment*, ed. Raymond F. Bulman and Frederick J. Parrella, 174-88. Collegeville MN: Liturgical Press, 1994.

Stenger, Mary Ann, and Ronald H. Stone. *Dialogues of Paul Tillich*. Macon GA: Mercer University Press, 2002.

Stinnette, Charles, Jr. "Fellowship Conference." *Christianity and Society* 5/4 (1940): 45-46.

Stone, Jerome Arthur. "A Tillichian Contribution to Contemporary Moral Philosophy: The Unconditional Element in the Content of the Moral Imperative." In *Being and Doing: Paul Tillich as Ethicist*, ed. John J. Carey, 69-85. Macon GA: Mercer University Press, 1987.

Stone, Ronald H. "Christian Ethics and the Socialist Vision of Paul Tillich." In *Tillich Studies: 1975*, ed. John J. Carey, 51-62. Tallahassee Fl.: North American Paul Tillich Society, 1975.

_____. "The Correlation of Politics and Culture in Paul Tillich's Thought." *Soundings* 69 (1986): 499-511.

_____. Introduction to *Theology of Peace*, by Paul Tillich, 9-24. Louisville: Westminster/John Knox Press, 1990.

_____. "Kairos Circle" Meeting Papers of the North American Paul Tillich Society (November 1989): 23-27.

_____. "Ontology of Power in Niebuhr, Morgenthau and Tillich." *Newsletter of the North American Paul Tillich Society* 28/2 (Spring 2002): 4-14.

_____. "Paul Tillich on Peace." *Meeting Papers: North American Paul Tillich Society* (November 1989): 17-22.

_____. "Paul Tillich: On the Boundary between Protestantism and Marxism." *Laval théologique et philosophique* 45/3 (October 1989): 393-404.

_____. *Paul Tillich's Radical Social Thought*. Lanham MD: University Press of America, 1986.

_____. "Paulus und Gustavo: Religious Socialism and Liberation Theology." *Meeting Papers: North American Paul Tillich Society* (December 1987): 17-26.

_____. *Prophetic Realism: Beyond Militarism and Pacifism in an Age of Terrorism*. New York: T.&T. Clark, 2005.

_____. "The Religious Situation and Resistance in 2001." In *Religion in the New Millennium: Theology in the Spirit of Paul Tillich*, ed. Raymond F.

Bulman and Frederick J. Parrella, 55-62. Macon GA: Mercer University Press, 2001.

_____. "Tillich and Niebuhr as Allied Public Theologians." *Bulletin of the North American Paul Tillich Society* 32/1 (Winter 2006): 3-7.

_____. "Tillich: Radical Political Theologian." *Religion in Life* 46 (Spring 1977): 44-53.

_____. "Tillich's Critical Use of Marx and Freud in the Social Context of the Frankfort School." *Union Seminary Quarterly Review* 33/1 (Fall 1977): 3-9.

_____. "Utopianism and International Relations." Unpublished paper delivered before the "Tillich: Issues in Theology, Religion and Culture Group" (A18-125), American Academy of Religion, San Diego CA (18 November 2007).

Stumme, John R. *Socialism in Theological Perspective: A Study of Paul Tillich, 1918–1933.* Missoula MT: Scholars Press, 1978.

Sturm Erdmann, "Between Apologetics and Pastoral Care: Paul Tillich's Early Sermons (1908–1918), *North American Paul Tillich Society Newsletter* 26/1 (Winter 2000): 7-20.

_____. "'Holy Love Claims Life and Limb': Paul Tillich's War Theology (1914–1918)." *Zeitschrift für neuere Theologiegeschichte* 2/1 (1995): 60-84.

_____. "Zwischen Apologetik und Seelsorge: Paul Tillichs frühe Predigten (1908–1918)." In *Spurensuche: Lebens- und Denkwege Paul Tillichs, Tillich-Studien, Band 5*, ed. Ilona Nord and Yorick Spiegel, 85-104. Münster: Lit Verlag, 2001.

Takeuchi, Yoshinori. "Buddhism and Existentialism: The Dialogue between Oriental and Occidental Thought." In *Religion and Culture: Essays in Honor of Paul Tillich*, ed. Walter Leibrecht, 291-318. New York: Harper & Row, 1959.

Tal, Uriel. *Christians and Jews in Germany: Religion, Politics, and Ideology in the Second Reich, 1870–1914.* Ithaca/London: Cornell University Press, 1975.

Taylor, A. K. P. "The Immediate Circumstances." In *The Nazi Revolution*, ed. John L. Snell, 3-15. Lexington MA: D.C. Heath and Co., 1973.

Taylor, Mark Kline. Introductory comment to "The Church and the Third Reich: Ten Theses," by Paul Tillich, 116. In *Paul Tillich: Theologian of the Boundaries*, ed. Mark Kline Taylor. London: Collins, 1987.

Taylor, Mark Lewis. "Prophetic Spirit and Political Romanticism in the U.S. Today." Unpublished paper delivered before the "Tillich: Issues in Theology, Religion and Culture Group" (A18-125), American Academy of Religion, San Diego CA (18 November 2007).

Thangaraj, M. Thomas. "Faith, Religion, and Culture: A Tripod for Interreligious Dialogue." *Meeting Papers North American Paul Tillich Society* (November 1991): 43-47.

Thayer, Joseph Henry, trans., rev. and enlarged by. *The New Thayer's Greek-*

English Lexicon of the New Testament. Indexes by Maurice A. Robinson (Lafayette IN: Book Publisher's Press, ©1981). Peabody MA: Hendrickson Publishers, 1981.

Thielicke, Helmut. "Christians and the Prevention of War in an Atomic Age." In *Religion and Culture: Essays in Honor of Paul Tillich*, ed. Walter Leibrecht, 335-40. New York: Harper & Row, 1959.

Thomas, J. Mark. "Theonomous Social Ethics: Paul Tillich's Neoclassical Interpretation of Justice." In *Being and Doing: Paul Tillich as Ethicist*, ed. John J. Carey, 109-23. Macon GA: Mercer University Press, 1987.

Thomas, Terence. "On Another Boundary: Tillich's Encounter with World Religions." In *Theonomy and Autonomy: Studies in Paul Tillich's Engagement with Modern Culture*, ed. John J. Carey, 193-211. Macon GA: Mercer University Press, 1984.

_____. *Paul Tillich and World Religions*. Cardiff: Cardiff Academic Press, 1999.

_____. "Response to Masao Abe's 'A Buddhist View of "The Significance of the History of Religions for the Systematic Theologian." ' " *Meeting Papers: North American Paul Tillich Society* (November 1988): 9-13.

Unno, Taitetsu. "Compassion in Buddhist Spirituality." In *Religion in the New Millennium: Theology in the Spirit of Paul Tillich*, ed. Raymond F. Bulman and Frederick J. Parrella, 165-176. Macon GA: Mercer University Press, 2001.

Vansittart, Robert G. *The Black Record of Germany—Past, Present and Future?* New York: New Avon, 1944.

Ward, Harry F. "Comment on the Report of 'The Commission on a Just and Durable Peace.'" *The Witness* 26/45 (8 April 1943): 4.

Watson, Melvin. "The Social Thought of Paul Tillich." *The Journal of Religious Thought* 10/1 (Autumn–Winter 1952-53): 5-17.

Weaver, Matthew Lon. "Paul Tillich and the Voice of America." *North American Paul Tillich Society Newsletter* 24/3 (Summer 1998): 19-29.

Weisskopf, Walter A. "Tillich and the Crisis of the West." In *The Thought of Paul Tillich*, ed. Adams/Pauck/Shinn, 63-80. San Francisco: Harper & Row, 1985.

West, Charles C. *Communism and the Theologians*. New York: Macmillan, 1958.

Wettstein, A. Arnold. "Re-Viewing Tillich in a Technological Culture." In *Theonomy and Autonomy: Studies in Paul Tillich's Engagement with Modern Culture*. ed. John J. Carey, 113-33. Macon GA: Mercer University Press, 1984.

Wiebe, Paul G. "The Significance of *The System of the Sciences* within Tillich's Thought." In *Tillich Studies: 1975*, ed. John J. Carey, 76-87. Chicago: North American Paul Tillich Society, 1975.

Williams, George H. "Priest, Prophet and Proletariat: A Study in the Theology of Paul Tillich." *The Journal of Liberal Religion* (Chicago) 1 (Winter, 1940): 25-37.

Wilson, John E. Comment to Matthew Lon Weaver. 13 March 2006.
Wise, Stephen S. and Nahum Goldmann. "World Jewish Congress." *Bulletin of the Council for a Democratic Germany* 1/5 (May 1945): 2. The Witness. "Six Pillars of Peace Issues by Church." *The Witness* 26/43 (25 March 1943): 4.
Wolbold, Matthias. "Against the Third Reich. Zur amerikanischen Erstveröffentlichungen der politischen Rundfunkreden Paul Tillichs." *Tillich Journal: Interpretieren—Vergleichen—Kritisieren—Weiterentwickeln*. 3 (1999) SS. 26-29.
_____." 'Meine Deutschen Freunde!' Die politischen Rundfunk-reden Tillichs während des Zweiten Weltkriegs." In *Spurensuche: Lebens- und Denkwege Paul Tillichs*, ed. Ilona Nord und Yorick Spiegel, 183-98. Münster/Hamburg/London: Lit Verlag, 2001.
_____. "Rundfunkarbeit deutscher Exilanten in den USA. Hintergründe und Wirkung." *Tillich Journal: Interpretieren—Vergleichen—Kritiseren—Weiter entwickeln* 4 (2000): 131-36.
_____. "Tillich als expressionistischer Propagandist? Eine Antwort auf die Vorwürfe Matthew Lon Weaver." *Tillich Journal: Interpretieren—Vergleichen—Kritisieren—Weiterentwickeln* 3 (1999): 84-87.

Index

105, 111, 114-16, 118, 123, 128-30,
194, 196, 201-202, 209, 211, 237,
240-41, 246, 249, 294-95, 296
See also Religious Socialism.
Socialism: Types, 66n8
Socialist Decision, The, 16, 27, 91, 95,
98-104, 118, 297
South African Truth and Reconcilia-
tion Commission, 25
Sovereignty of God Alone, 91, 202-
203, 214
Soviet Union. *See* U.S.S.R.
Space Exploration, 236, 256
Spanish Civil War, 176
State, The, 124-27, 138, 211
State, The Law Concept of, 124-27
State, The Power Concept of, 124-27
Stereotype, 162-67, 196, 199-200
Stirner, Max, 195
Stoicism, 125n107, 246
Sturm, Erdmann, 54-57, 60, 62, 69n21
Subjectivity and Objectivity, 135
System of the Sciences, The, 13
Systematic Theology, 28, 225

Taliban, The, 9
Technology, 13-14, 73, 82-83, 103,
114, 120, 122, 133-34, 135, 137,
141, 175, 181-82, 206, 240
Technology and World, 133-35, 141
Temple, Archbishop William, 180
Theocracy, 114, 131-32
Theology of Culture, 12-14, 19, 24,
27, 64-105, 286
Theonomy, 68, 72, 73-74, 76, 80-81,
87, 94, 255-56, 286-87
Theory, 135-36, 137, 141-42
Theory and World, 135-36, 141-42
Thomas of Aquinas, 71
*Thus Spake Zarathustra (Also Sprach
Zarathustra),* 62

Totalitarianism, 125-27, 137, 178,
207, 209
Tradition, 137
Tragic, The, 230
Transcendence(/Immanence), 39, 78,
79, 89, 120, 124, 133, 135, 139-40,
141-42, 285
Transmoral Conscience, 276
Trend and Chance, 249
Trinity, 32-35
Truth, 77, 156, 160-62, 181, 214
Truth, Practical, 181
Tyranny, 184-85, 233

Unhistorical Thinking, 246
U.S.S.R. (Union of Soviet Socialists
Republics), 124, 126, 177, 197,
222, 240-41
Union Theological Seminary, 10-11,
27
Unity, 33, 77-78, 108, 138-39, 182,
185-89, 219-23, 230, 233
Utopia, 29, 73, 77, 78, 101, 129n129,
130, 192, 194, 201, 202, 207-208,
240, 244-57, 267
Utopia, Spirit of, 248, 250, 253

Vacuum, 28-29, 115, 178, 197, 201,
208, 230, 231, 232-41, 256, 262
Vacuum, Akairotic, 208, 256, 292
Values, Philosophy of, 273n4
Vansittart, Lord Robert G., 162-63
Venturing Courage, 263-70
Versailles, Treaty of, 64
Vertical (vs. Horizontal) Thinking,
227-29, 254-55
Vocation, National, 91, 209, 244
Voice of America, 10, 19, 28, 144-90,
295

We-Self, 233